# THE
# TRANSFIGURATION
# OF POLITICS

# THE TRANSFIGURATION OF POLITICS

## Paul Lehmann

# SCM PRESS LTD

334 01679 7

First British edition 1975
by SCM Press Ltd
56 Bloomsbury Street, London

Typeset in the United States of America
and printed in Great Britain
by Fletcher & Son Ltd, Norwich

# ACKNOWLEDGMENTS

References to the Bible, unless otherwise indicated, are from *The New English Bible,* © The Delegates of the Oxford University Press and The Syndics of the Cambridge University Press 1961, 1970. Reprinted by permission. *The Jerusalem Bible* references are copyright © 1966 by Darton, Longman & Todd, Ltd. and Doubleday & Company, Inc. Used by permission of the publisher. Those from *The Revised Standard Version Bible* are copyright 1946 (renewed 1973), 1952 and © 1971 by the Division of Christian Education of the National Council of the Churches of Christ in the U.S.A. Used by permission.

Grateful acknowledgment is also made to the following for permission to reprint copyrighted material:

CHARING CROSS MUSIC, INC. for extracts from "The Sound of Silence" by Paul Simon, copyright © 1964 by Paul Simon. Used with permission of the publisher.

GRANADA PUBLISHING LTD for extracts from *Complete Poems 1913–1962* by E. E. Cummings; *The Wretched of the Earth* by Frantz Fanon, copyright © 1963 by Presence Africaine.

GROVE PRESS, INC. for extracts from *The Wretched of the Earth* by Frantz Fanon, copyright © 1963 by Presence Africaine; *The Autobiography of Malcolm X* by Malcolm X with the assistance of Alex Haley, copyright © 1964 by Alex Haley and Malcolm X. Reprinted by permission of Grove Press.

HARCOURT BRACE JOVANOVICH, INC. for extracts from *Complete Poems 1913–1962* by E. E. Cummings; *Ideology and Utopia* by Karl Mannheim.

HARPER & ROW, PUBLISHERS, INC. for extracts from "Romans Angry about the Inner World" from *The Light Around the Body* by Robert Bly, copyright © 1967 by Robert Bly. By permission of Harper & Row, Publishers, Inc.

HOLT, RINEHART, AND WINSTON for extracts from *My Life with Martin Luther King, Jr.* by Coretta King.

HUTCHINSON PUBLISHING GROUP LTD for extracts from *The Autobiography of Malcolm X* by Malcolm X with the assistance of Alex Haley, copyright © 1964 by Alex Haley and Malcolm X.

MACMILLAN PUBLISHING CO., INC. for extracts from "The Second Coming"
from *Collected Poems* by William Butler Yeats, copyright 1924 by Mac-
millan Publishing Co., Inc., renewed 1952 by Bertha Georgie Yeats.
THE M.I.T. PRESS for extracts from *Che: Selected Works of Ernesto Guevara*
edited by Rolando E. Bonachea and Nelson P. Valdes, copyright © 1970.
NEW DIRECTIONS PUBLISHING CORPORATION for extracts from *A Coney Island
of the Mind* by Lawrence Ferlinghetti, copyright © 1958 by Lawrence
Ferlinghetti.
OXFORD UNIVERSITY PRESS for extracts from *The Dark is Light Enough* by
Christopher Fry, copyright © 1954 by Christopher Fry.
PENGUIN BOOKS, INC. for extracts from *King: A Critical Biography* by
David L. Lewis (Baltimore, Md.: Penguin Books, Inc. 1970), copyright
© 1970 by David L. Lewis. Used by permission of Penguin Books, Inc.
RANDOM HOUSE, INC. for extracts from *City Without Walls and Other Poems*
by W. H. Auden, copyright © 1969 by W. H. Auden; *Collected Longer
Poems* by W. H. Auden, copyright © 1969 by W. H. Auden; *Revolutionary
Priest: The Complete Writings and Messages of Camilo Torres* edited by
John Gerassi, copyright © 1971.
ROUTLEDGE & KEGAN PAUL LTD for extracts from *Ideology and Utopia* by
Karl Mannheim.
VANDENHOECK & RUPRECHT for extracts from *Das Evangelium des Johannes*
by Rudolf Bultmann.
THE VIKING PRESS for extracts from *On Revolution* by Hannah Arendt, copy-
right © 1963 by Hannah Arendt. Reprinted by permission of The
Viking Press, Inc.
A. P. WATT & SON for extracts from "The Second Coming" from *Collected
Poems* by William Butler Yeats by permission of M. B. Yeats, Miss Anne
Yeats, Macmillian of London, and Basingstoke and Macmillan Co. of
Canada.
JOHN WILEY & SONS, INC. for extracts from *Exchange and Power* by Peter M.
Blau, copyright © 1964. Reprinted by permission of John Wiley & Sons,
Inc.

# CONTENTS

# PREFACE

It has been written that 1968 was "the year America's ulcer burst."
This epigrammatic assessment looks back upon the uprising of
students on many campuses across the United States—at Berkeley,
Michigan, and Wisconsin; at Stanford, Howard, and San Francisco
State—which seemed to culminate in the crisis at Columbia in
April-May of that explosive year. There had been "the long hot
summer" in Harlem (1964) and Watts (1965) and in Newark
and Detroit in 1967, which had not only inflamed long-pent-up
social frustrations and bitterness but city blocks as well. Of the
students and their campuses, the report leading up to this vivid
epigram declares: "They were graduates of an American nightmare in 1968 that stemmed mostly from the war they had now
come to fight—the year of riots and dissension, of assassinations
and Chicago, the year America's ulcer burst."[1]

An invitation had come from the President and Fellows of
Harvard College to deliver the Willian Belden Noble Lectures in
early December of that same year. It therefore seemed urgent, if
not unavoidable, somehow to address oneself to those events, especially since the Noble Lectures focused upon William Belden
Noble's "supreme desire to extend the influence of Jesus as the
Way, the Truth, and the Life." The obvious distance between Jesus

and the happenings of that ulcerous year seemed better designed for the keeping of silence. Yet "the scope of the Lectures" was wide, "as wide as the highest interests of humanity." Silence would have been tantamount to a declaration that Christianity had no significant relation to the revolutionary ferment beneath the surface of American society today; still less a liberating and a healing one. To break the silence meant there was only one way to go: straight into the center of the disjunction between Jesus and "the highest interests of humanity"; and to inquire *at the center* whether a direct confrontation between Jesus Christ and the revolutionary turmoil tormenting campuses and the country might turn up at least a minimal conjunction in terms of which a time without bearings might be borne.

Such a conjunction seemed ironically to be suggested by the time and place of the lectures themselves: Advent, and Memorial Church in the center of Harvard Yard. Advent signaled the time for remembering the messianic expectations of a "people who walked in darkness . . . dwellers in a land as dark as death" (Isa. 9:2); and for beginning all over again to live with the reality and the consequence of the happening that identified the conjunction of Christ expectations with Jesus of Nazareth. The place signaled rememberings pressing against the bitter confinements of death, of atonements deprived of healing because

> All the boots of trampling soldiers
> and the garments fouled with blood
> shall become a burning mass, fuel for fire.
>
> (Isa. 9:5)[2]

There is no one

> to bear the symbol of dominion on his shoulder;
>
> .   .   .   .   .   .   .   .   .   .   .   .   .
>
> to establish it and sustain it
> with justice and righteousness
> from now and forevermore.
>
> (Isa. 9:7)

The irony is that the Advent hope keeps on being hoped as though Advent were expendable.

"Center" used to function as a fairly tame and obvious mid-point, most stultifying perhaps in politics. But consider what has been happening to "center" since the university lost its coherence and cohesiveness as "the Republic of Letters." "Centers" have sprung up everywhere, sometimes with as little provocation as that provided by the fiscal charisma of some development officer. Though much of this proliferation often seems diffuse and aimless, it can scarcely be denied that the word "center" has come alive with the dynamic restlessness and expectation of a frontier. The critical intensity and depth of this frontier have been unforgettably identified by William Butler Yeats:

> Turning and turning in the widening gyre
> The falcon cannot hear the falconer;
> Things fall apart; the centre cannot hold;
> Mere anarchy is loosed upon the world,
> The blood-dimmed tide is loosed, and everywhere
> The ceremony of innocence is drowned;
> The best lack all conviction, while the worst
> Are full of passionate intensity.
>
> Surely some revelation is at hand;
> Surely the Second Coming is at hand.
> The Second Coming! Hardly are those words out
> When a vast image out of *Spiritus Mundi*
> Troubles my sight: . . .
> The darkness drops again; but now I know
> That twenty centuries of stony sleep
> Were vexed to nightmare by a rocking cradle,
> And what rough beast, its hour come round at last,
> Slouches towards Bethlehem to be born?[3]

It is, of course, the prospect of "the Second Coming" that gives to "the First Coming" its inaugural portent. The past does not cross over the present into the future. The future draws the present toward itself from the past. For Yeats, a deep and fateful disjunction had occurred between the center that holds and the center that cannot hold. Twenty centuries of hammering out what it takes to make and to keep human life human, released for celebration by a crib, have become "twenty centuries of stony sleep . . . vexed to nightmare by a rocking cradle." Wise men once came to Bethlehem, bringing treasures and following a star. Now, neither man nor rough beast, their hour come round at last, even "slouches toward Bethlehem to be born."

To be born is to die, not to live. The language of the logos has been swallowed up by the proliferation of languages without logos. "The ceremony of innocence is drowned," as the frenetic ritualization of scapegoats goes on. The best, who lack all conviction, and the worst, so full of passionate intensity, confront each other over the void of reciprocal anarchy and "the darkness drops again." Neo-Jacobinism always lurks in the wings as the desperate option of an empty center. "Jesus Christ," Pascal once remarked, "is the end of all things and the centre to which all tends. Whoever knows him knows the reason of everything."[4] Not knowing him, the university multiplies centers for multiplying reasons for everything—but without a liberating and compelling humanizing reason for anything.[5] Our culture, as Herbert Marcuse has shown, is far advanced—or is it regressed?—in one-dimensionality.[6]

Whether or not this question is the decisive question of the present century must be left open. However, the degree to which it is a formative question for our times—precisely as the question of the center—is indicated in an earlier Noble Lecture. At the turn of the century, Francis Greenwood Peabody took up the assignment to which these pages are addressed. He declared:

> The first thing . . . one should note is the obvious fact that Jesus Christ was not primarily a social reformer, or the deviser of a social programme, or the forerunner of social agitation or revolt. No description of his mission could be less accurate than to identify it with the social arrangements or readjustments or revolutions which are now so eagerly urged. . . . Now, instead of Christ the theologian, or Christ the ecclesiastic, we have offered to us a Christ who is an agitator, a revolutionist, a labor leader, or, as He has been lately called, "Jesus, the demagogue."[7]

Meanwhile, "the age of the social question," as Peabody called it, has become "the age of revolution." Consequently, Jesus, whom the earlier age found no way of acknowledging as a revolutionary lest he be despoiled as a "demagogue," we are called upon to reject as a "demagogue" lest he be despoiled as a revolutionary.

The pages that follow will seek to show *that the pertinence of Jesus Christ to an age of revolution is the power of his presence to shape the passion for humanization that generates revolution, and thus to preserve revolution from its own undoing. All revolutions aspire to give human shape to the freedom that being and staying human take; and all revolutions end by devouring their own children.*[8]

A corollary of this thesis is that in obedience to the gospel, the Christian church and the mentality of Christians must abandon their time-honored addiction to legitimacy; whereas revolutionaries could find in the gospel perspective and power for the fulfillment of their promises and the liberation from their fate. At stake is "the grandeur of man against the pettiness of the great," as Robespierre once remarked; or, as Hamilton expressed it, the vindication of "the honor of the human race."[9] *At the center—where the decisive action is—what is happening and what is required are nothing less than the transfiguration of politics.*

To the President and Fellows of Harvard College I hope to be able to express, through this expanded form of the lectures, some measure of appropriate gratitude for the privilege of their appointment as the William Belden Noble Lecturer for 1968–69. To the then President Nathan Pusey, as also to the Reverend Dr. Charles P. Price, then Preacher to the University, my warm thanks are due. In addition to the Ministers' Conference at Union Theological Seminary, New York, during the summer of 1969, and a variety of campus occasions, two lectureships in particular have provided welcome opportunity both to clarify the argument and to keep its pertinence to the tumult and struggle of a more human future in the making in the foreground of attention.

The biblical material was especially rethought and revised for presentation as the seventieth annual E. T. Earl Lectures at the Pacific School of Religion in Berkeley, California, in February 1971. And in October of that same year, the exploration of some of the implications of the paradigm of the Transfiguration of Jesus for a typology of current revolutions was greatly furthered by the invitation of the Dean and Faculty of the Divinity School at Duke University to deliver the James A. Gray Lectures. To President Stuart Leroy Anderson, and to his successor, President Davie Napier, and their colleagues in the faculty of the Pacific School of Religion; as to Dean Robert Cushman, and to his successor, Dean Thomas Langford, and their colleagues in the Divinity School at Duke University, I wish to express my considerable gratitude for the enrichment and cordiality of these occasions.

Since President Emeritus John C. Bennett, nearer colleagues, and fellow students at Union Theological Seminary can never know how much their encouragement and forbearance have assisted the expansion and completion of the inquiry upon which the original lectures were embarked, I wish in this place to tell them so. In particular, however, I wish to thank my colleague, James H. Cone, who, in addition to numerous friendly reminders that in the making of books, as in other human tasks and hopes, perfectionism is a sin, gave instructive attention to the discussion of the Black Revolution. And in very special ways, three colleagues have sustained the persistence required to overtake the doubts and diversions of too many months under the weight of what had been begun and of the unwisdom of leaving it unfinished. Except for their careful and substantive reading of the entire manuscript and the favor of their invaluable suggestions for the improvement of the argument both in content and in style, I should scarcely have managed the confidence and determination to see it through. I hope that J. Louis Martyn and Christopher Morse of Union Theological Seminary, New York, and Charles Dickinson of Union Theological Seminary, Richmond, Virginia, will be able to find in this acknowledgment some indication of my deep gratitude to them.

At an early stage of the manuscript, and again as it neared completion, the Reverend Wallace M. Alston, Jr., of Princeton, New Jersey, generously placed time and conversation and criticism at my disposal. And throughout, access to the remarkable resources of the Library of Union Theological Seminary, New York, and of the Missionary Research Library there, has not only been indispensable as these pages were taking shape, but has been greatly facilitated by the unfailing consideration and help of the Librarian, Robert F.

*Preface* XV

Beach, and his Assistants, William M. Robarts and Ansom Huang, and of the Reference Librarians, Barbara M. Griffis, Richard D. Spoor, and Seth Kasten. Last, but by no means least, I am enormously grateful to Linda Ginsburg who has given generously of her skill, learning, and friendship in the preparation of the typescript.

The preparation of the manuscript for printing has been greatly assisted by the confidence, competence, and dedicated effort of the editorial staff of the Religious Books Department of Harper & Row, and I wish cordially to thank Clayton E. Carlson, Richard Lucas, and Eleanor Jordan.

PAUL LEHMANN

*Union Theological Seminary, New York*
*Epiphany 1974*

# PART ONE

# REVOLUTION, HUMANIZATION, AND STORY

CHAPTER 1

# REVOLUTION AND HUMANIZATION

In her remarkable book *On Revolution,* Hannah Arendt makes the arresting point that revolution is born of the passion for humanization; but the passion for humanization is unable to give sustaining shape to revolution.[1] Whether Arendt is also correct in regarding the American Revolution as the only successful revolution, and thus as the exception to the generalization that all revolutions devour their own children, may be debatable. As of now, at any rate, the question must be regarded as still open. A social phenomenon whose passion, diversity, and subtlety almost defy specificity makes any assessment of positive results problematical enough. But in these days, the political alternation of youth between alienation and conformity (which is a kind of subliminal alienation), the scarcely tempered resentment of black people, of those condemned to live in urban ghettos, and of the poor against existing holders and institutions of power, threaten to make the American "exception" the most poignant instance of the tragic rule. The line from Watts to Watergate may not be straight; but it is certainly tortuous —and ominous.

Almost more ominous is the national self-congratulation with which the *New York Times,* looking back upon the results of 5 November 1968, allowed itself to indulge editorially. The *Times'*

"Postscript to an Election" concluded with the comfortable assurance that "the radical extremists from both ends of the spectrum—the Birchites and Wallace-ites as well as the black 'militants' and white radicals—still possess the power to provoke confrontations and rouse hysteria. But this is their only power in a nation which once again has voted for moderate alternatives and affirmed orderly electoral processes."[2] This is the self-righteousness that blindly mistakes a historical reprieve for historical wisdom. Alike indifferent to the fact that the party system has obstructed Jeffersonian hopes for a democratic society by preventing "a body politic which guarantees space where freedom can appear" and to the warnings of Israel's prophets that self-righteousness feeds upon injustice, the *Times,* in olympian detachment, has ignored the experience of righteousness in history, which is that those "who sow the wind shall reap the whirlwind" (Hos. 8:7).[3] It is all so like the tragicomedy that provided the occasion for the first use of the word *revolution* in a political sense. During the night of 14 July 1789, when Louis XVI heard from the Duc de la Rochefoucauld-Liancourt of the fall of the Bastille, of the liberation of a few prisoners, and of the defection of the royal troops before a popular attack, the king exclaimed, "C'est une révolte." "Non, Sire," replied Liancourt, "c'est une révolution."[4]

In Europe and America at least, we owe to the French Revolution, and to Hegel's response to it, the possibility of bringing to the semantic and historical diversity of revolutionary happenings a focus and prospect of meaningful interpretation. Although one may well regard Machiavelli as "the spiritual father of revolution," Hegel is the father of "the mentality of revolution."[5] It is Hegel's response to the French Revolution that shapes the way in which we must also begin to understand what is happening to us, no matter how firmly Marx prevents us from ending as and where we began. Arendt's wistful confidence in Jefferson's proposal of "elementary republics of the wards" and Marcuse's wistful confidence in the language and politics of "the Great Refusal" seem to meet in a revolutionary stalemate of unfreedom, evident in large measure in "the sinister confidence in the power and language of facts" and in "the totalitarian tendencies of the one-dimensional society."[6] The bond between revolution and humanization is freedom. And freedom functions as this bond because freedom is at once the root and the fruit, the sign and the seal of revolution, at the level both of happening and of mentality.

In our world the nature of things and the nature of human things so engage experience and thought as to assign to nature temporal precedence over humanity and to humanity *primacy* in and over nature. In such a world *revolution is the lifestyle of truth*. This is the more the case, since the dynamics of human reality as originally designed have been profoundly challenged by a counterthrust of power that confuses freedom with enslavement and counterfeits enslavement as freedom. Thus, in the language of the Fourth Gospel, to live and think in a revolutionary way is "doing the truth" (3:21) and being in truth. Contrariwise, the mentality and practice of the status quo are living in illusion and falsehood: in *illusion,* because the dynamics of reality are such as to bring to naught the things that are, by the things that are not;[7] in *falsehood,* because to fail to come to terms with reality is to practice its denial. This is why *hypocrisy,* not crime, is the mortal sin of revolution; and why the facile and noisy talk about "law and order" as the precondition of freedom is hypocrisy. Writes Arendt, in words about the French Revolution:

> What made the hypocrite so odious was that he claimed not only sincerity but naturalness, and what made him so dangerous outside the social realm whose corruption he represented and, as it were, enacted, was that he instinctively could help himself to every "mask" in the political theater, that he could assume every role among its *dramatis personae,* but that he would not use the mask, as the rules of the political game demand, as a sounding board for truth but, on the contrary, as a contraption for deception.[8]

At least since the First Epistle of John, the coinherence of "walking in darkness" and of being "a liar and a stranger to the truth" has been a matter of record.[9] Indeed, the revolutionary ferment of our times exhibits its authentic kinship with the revolutionary tradition of modern times not only in its sensitivity to, and rage against, hypocrisy. There is the more ominous, and perhaps ultimately tragic war within itself, between a passionate espousal of revolutionary promises and an impatience, sometimes furious impatience, with the faltering, and even failing realization of those promises.

It is a tortuous but, as history goes, terrifyingly short way from Madison's grim estimate that democracies "have in general been as short in their lives as violent in their deaths" to Marcuse's dour Marxian conclusion that "liberation of inherent possibilities no longer adequately expresses the historical alternative."[10] Yet Marcuse has risked an alternative that makes everybody nervous except those who have become "outsiders" in their sense of having been deprived of options. He writes:

> The advancing one-dimensional society alters the relation between the rational and the irrational. . . . The realm of the irrational becomes the home of the really rational—of the ideas which may "promote the art of life." . . . The aesthetic dimension still retains a freedom of expression which enables the writer and artist to call men and things by their name—to name the otherwise unnameable.[11]

Before yielding to the temptation to dismiss Marcuse out of hand, one is well advised to look fearlessly and sharply into the widening chasm that, from Robespierre to Madison and Hamilton, and from Madison and Hamilton to Marx and Marcuse, threatens to sever revolutionary possibilities from revolutionary achievements. This is the chasm between people who had, slowly and with much suffering, become citizens and citizens who had discarded their birthright and become people (*le monde*); between civil rights and natural rights; between political radicalization and social radicalization; between revolution and anarchy;—in short, between the Revolution and the Reign of Terror. In Arendt's sobering and moving words:

> Since the days of the French Revolution, it has been the boundlessness of their sentiments that made revolutionaries so curiously insensitive to reality in general, and to the reality of persons in particular, whom they felt no compunctions in sacrificing to their "principles," or to the course of history, or to the cause of revolution as such.[12]

Turning now from the dynamics and the denouement of the reciprocity between revolution and humanization, it must be noted more precisely what it is that joins revolution and humanization and what it is that differentiates them. Common to revolution and humanization are the passion, process, and promise through which happenings in history make room for what is human in people and in society and for what it takes to make and to keep human life human. What differentiates revolution from humanization is the story by which revolutions are saved, that is, preserved from the fate of devouring their own children and liberated for the realization of their humanizing promises. Indeed, revolutions are happenings in human affairs of sufficient depth, intensity, and consequence as to require a story to hold these happenings together.

The word *story,* in this context, refers to the way in which one generation tells another how the future shapes the present out of the past; how destiny draws heritage into the human reality and meaning of experience, which is always a compound of happenings, hope, and remembrance; how promise and disillusionment, celebration and suffering, joy and pain, forgiveness and guilt, renewal and failure, transfigure the human condition and are transfigured in it. In this way "the wonderful works of God" are made known both to those who believe in him and to those who no longer believe in him; both to those who are afar off and to those who are nigh.[13] The political dimensions of human affairs and the human dimensions of politics are in running confrontation and differentiation; distinguishable yet inseparable.

By a curious—or is it a providential?—coincidence astronomy has joined both philosophy and politics in the revolutionary enterprise. The world of orderly meanings and the world of meaningful order converge under the insistent pressure of freedom to make as many new beginnings in history as being and staying human require. It will be recalled that when Plato refined the search of Socrates for a secure foundation for the body politic, he took his cue from the regularity and harmony of the planetary motions. The wonder of the stars in their courses suggested to Plato a human counterpart in the wonder, the harmony and the primacy of the human soul.[14] Thus the political dimensions of human affairs and the human dimensions of politics were forever joined in the Western cultural story. Haunting the union was the question whether the stars were the friendly guardians of the freedom required by the commonwealth or whether they signaled an ineluctable necessity according to which happenings destroyed heroes, hope became *hybris,* and the center of nobility became the seat of a tragic flaw. As Charles Cochrane has brilliantly explained: classical culture declined because it had no doctrine of providence. It lacked a liberating story in the power of which the involvement of character with circumstance could achieve the "creative politics" indispensable to "making the world safe for civilization."[15] So fatefully do the world of orderly meanings and the world of meaningful order intersect.

As things turned out, this platonic disposition of the semantics of revolution reached its apex in the natural sciences through Copernicus' *De revolutionibus orbium coelestium.*[16] By virtue of these astronomical associations, the word *revolution* initially meant *recurrence,* or *restoration,* since governments, like the stars, were under a preordained cycle of return owing to the same irresistible force. In this sense the word was applied to "the Glorious Revolution" that brought William and Mary to the throne of England in 1688. At the level of language as at the level of life, it remained for the French Revolution to alter the meaning of the word and to shape its modern sense. Although "the men of the revolutions" in France and in colonial America "were firmly convinced that they would do no more than restore an old order of things that had been disturbed and violated by the despotism of absolute monarchy or the abuses of colonial government,"[17] they were actually resolving the paradox of restoration and novelty in favor of novelty.

Novelty had already informed the claims of Galileo, Hobbes, and Descartes in science, political theory, and philosophy. It captured the revolutionary spirit when the old astronomical association of irresistibility was combined with the social question in a fresh passion for freedom. When "men began to doubt that poverty is inherent in the human condition,"[18] the days of the established authorities began to be numbered. Confrontation was beginning to overtake restoration as the political order of the day. What the Duc de la Rochefoucauld-Liancourt saw on the night of his startling remark to Louis XVI was

> the uprising of the people for freedom, . . . the poor and the downtrodden, whom every century before had hidden in darkness and shame. What from then on has been irrevocable . . . was that the public realm—reserved, as far as memory could reach, to those who *were* free, namely carefree of all the worries that are connected with life's necessity, with bodily needs—should offer its space and its light to the immense majority who are not free because they are driven by daily needs.[19]

If the American counterpart of the goings on in Paris lacked the specter of poverty, it did not lack sense and situation for new beginnings, or the passion for freedom, or the conviction of irresistibility in the guise of a providential gift of a future and an opportunity. Thus the story of the semantics of revolution exhibits a radicalization in the repackaging of freedom, irresistibility, novelty, and poverty *and* in the risk of violent overthrow required by an enlarging human participation in the struggle for freedom and for a new order in human affairs.

## CHAPTER 2

# REVOLUTION, HUMANIZATION,
# AND THE MESSIANIC STORY

So much for the world of orderly meanings. The world of meaningful order evokes another, and even more insistent story. Wittgenstein has remarked that "the speaking of language is part of an activity, or of a form of life."[20] Just so, story is the narration in the power of language and of social cohesion of what it takes to be and to stay human in the world. Consequently, at the center—where the action is—story is the mode of the experience of a presence in the present whose power liberates as it binds and binds as it liberates. The semantics of revolution exhibit the bond between revolution and humanization through the radicalization of the relation between restoration and novelty, between order and the freedom for a new beginning in human affairs. The practice of revolution exhibits the bond between revolution and humanization through the radicalization in the power of presence (truth!) of the relation between the new beginning and the realization of its promises. If the dynamics by which all revolutions devour their own children are to be transfigured so as to become the dynamics by which revolutions serve the promises that call them into being, the story makes all the human difference in the world.

Arendt has called attention to the political significance of four such stories, rejecting three and underlining the fourth as the sustaining way ahead. The promising one has to do with the act of new beginning itself, with the *founding* of a city or commonwealth rather more than with the Founder or Founders. The Founders whom Arendt rejects are Cain, Romulus-Aeneas, and Christ. The accepted act of founding is the bringing forth on this continent "a new nation," as Lincoln was later to echo Jefferson's hopes and concerns, "conceived in liberty and dedicated to the proposition that all men are created equal."[21] For our present purpose, the stories may be identified as Primal (Cain), Ancestral (Romulus-Aeneas), Messianic or Christ (Jesus), and Heroic (the act of founding by founding fathers).

Tempting as it is to embark here upon a recital, the telling of the stories must be forborne. Our immediate concern is with the light shed by these stories upon the bond between revolution and humanization, and upon the question of the power of the story to keep revolutionary promise, passion, and achievement fulfillingly together. Cain, it will be recalled, murdered Abel; and Romulus slew Remus. Romulus belongs functionally with Cain, but narratively with Aeneas. These associations tell us that both biblical and classical antiquity connect political beginnings with violence and offer a primal sign of what revolutions can do neither with nor without. The astonishing tenacity of the tale of violence is almost frighteningly measured by the current revival of Hermann Hesse. Almost a century earlier, another Herman began his human pilgrimage only to leave behind at death a manuscript that expressed his own perception of the depth and range of the Cain story.

Melville's *Billy Budd* ponders indirectly the implications of a reversal of the Cain story. Suppose Abel had killed Cain! "Don't you see," Melville seems to be saying, "that from this deed of violence the same chain of wrongdoing will follow, only that now mankind will not even have the consolation that the violence it must call crime is indeed characteristic of evil men only?"[22] Good men do violence too! By 1917, however, the story has undergone another and more intense reversal. Now it is not Abel who kills Cain. The fratricide remains as the story has always told it. The reversal is that Cain is not evil but gifted and creative, the bearer of his own guilt and the transformer of his suffering through the vicarious exhibition in his own body and spirit of the excellence to which all human beings aspire but few attain.

> So they did not interpret the sign for what it was—a mark of distinction—but its opposite. People with courage and character always seem sinister to the rest. . . . In short, I mean Cain was a fine fellow and this story was pinned on him only because people were afraid. . . . Ultimately all men are brothers. So, a strong man slew a weaker one: perhaps it was truly a valiant act, perhaps it wasn't.[23]

What in Melville approaches the boundary of despair, in Hesse approaches the boundary of titanism. Or is it that Melville's agony exhibits the scars of a humanity reaching for transfiguration; whereas Hesse's agony exhibits the scars of a humanity reaching for its own identity? Since the primal crime, the human search for identity is correlative with the reaching for transfiguration! "Cain said to the Lord, 'My punishment is heavier than I can bear. Thou hast driven me today from the ground, and I must hide myself from thy presence. I shall be a vagrant and wanderer on earth, and anyone who wants me can kill me" (Gen. 4:13–14).

The primal story is indeed too great to be borne. It undergoes ancestral modification. The conjunction of violence with new beginnings acquires an altered accent with the founding of a city, the person-made space where there is room for the freedom to be human in the world.[24] The primal story was not, of course, displaced. It lingered in the minds and memories of people and hovered over their deeds as a sign of the curse upon the human race as a whole. Meanwhile, the revolution makers drew upon the two foundation legends familiar to them from the Bible and from Virgil. Virgil's "Then he founded a city!" gathers into words of percussive vibrancy what the liberation from slavery and from annihilating conflict had really come to, really had been all about.[25] It was a new beginning that signaled not only tthe transition from bondage to freedom but the happenings of such a transition in the fullness of time, and by the appearance of great leaders. If America's Founding Fathers did not adopt a revolutionary calendar, as did the French, and after them the Marxists, the reason is due to no lack of conviction about the *ex nihilo* character of beginning. It may rather have been due to the immediacy and similarity of an environment that suggested, as Daniel Boorstin has pointed out, that "the basic reality in their life was the analogy with the children of Israel. They conceived that by going out into the wilderness, they were reliving the story of the Exodus."[26]

In doing so, it would not have escaped them that the Exodus meant, above all, carrying no gods along but following instead a God who waits and acts to bestow a land of promise. Such a context made a new calendar superfluous. Aeneas, however, "origin of the Roman stock," had come "carrying Ilium and her conquered household gods into Italy," so that a new city required a new calendar.[27] The Exodus was an eschatological event; the founding of Rome was a temporal event with a claim upon eternity. A revolutionary calendar means that time is not so much fulfilled as being-filled-up. Eschatology sets beginnings under a promise that has ruptured the chain of cause and effect and broken open a future that has liberated freedom from the paralysis of the past. A claim upon eternity begins under the shadow of past glory, looking backward for the clue to the way ahead and forward to a guaranteed permanence of what is past. But revolution always walks a tightrope "between a no-longer and a not-yet."[28] The primal crime is not so much assuaged as sublimated by the bearer of the promise, and the movement is on toward the celebration of the act of founding rather than of the Founder. At the beginning of the beginning, Moses and Aeneas were at the center of the experience of freedom. As "the new" became the hallmark of the heritage of what it takes to be human in the world, the Exodus and the Eternal City surpassed even the greatness of the heroes in the story of what human beings can do in the fullness of time, or in making time full. The ancestral story touches the edge of the heroic.

The heroic story is the notable appropriation of the American Revolution. It contains at once the secret of the humanization of the hero and of whatever success may be claimed for the Revolution itself. The hero of classical antiquity was either a dramatic or a legendary figure. In the first case, the hero, possessed of no power over circumstances, nobly bows to them. In the second case, the hero, divinely empowered to make a new beginning, is not equally empowered to eradicate the "tragic flaw," by which power must absolutize itself in order to maintain itself and thereby undoes itself.[29]

The hero of the American Revolution, however, was a very human inaugurator of a new beginning in a new sense, the sense of a fresh historical moment, the promise of which overtook its ambiguities. Says Arendt:

> When the Americans decided to vary Virgil's line from *magnus ordo saeclorum* to *novus ordo saeclorum*, they admitted that it was no longer a matter of founding "Rome anew" but of founding a "new Rome," that the thread of continuity which bound Occidental politics back to the foundation of the eternal city ... was broken and could not be renewed.[30]

Nor was this new sense of "the new" simply an extension of the passion and promise of the major European revolutions directed against the absolutist pretensions of the monarchy, and toward a substitute form of government.[31] This new sense of "the new"

> came to dominate political discussion everywhere, to divide discussants into radicals who recognized the fact of revolution without understanding its problems, and conservatives who clung to tradition and the past as to fetishes with which to ward off the future, without understanding that the very emergence of revolution on the political scene as event or as threat had demonstrated in actual fact that this tradition had lost its anchorage, its beginning and principle, and was cut adrift.[32]

This new sense of "the new" was and is still new in "the year America's ulcer burst" and in its aftermath: "a generation of peace."

As regards the heroic story, this new sense of "the new" focused upon the conjunction of the new American experience and a new concept of power. Power came to be understood and practiced as the implementation of promise and as distinct both from law and from sovereignty. As the implementation of promise, power is the enabling action of a freely convenanted "civil Body Politick" that, "held together solely by the strength of mutual promise 'in the

Presence of God and one another,' supposedly was powerful enough to 'enact, constitute, and frame' all necessary laws and instruments of government."[33] Thus the revolutionary promise of a new beginning resolves the problem of its preservation through the visibility of the point upon which power, law, and sovereignty, in their separateness and inseparability, converge. *This point is an authority that binds as it liberates and liberates as it binds.*

The etymological root of *auctoritas* is *augere,* and its political usage points to what it takes to enlarge or increase what has been started. What it takes is a creative relation—that is, one which reciprocally liberates and binds as it continues—between *beginning* and *basis,* between *origin* and *ongoing,* between the *loosening* of ties that bind and the *binding* of the ties that keep what has been loosed from falling apart. The perennial crisis of authority is the tension between the new and the established, i.e., the new on the way to becoming old and the old resisting the new as a threat. On the record, this tension lacks—*at the center*—the sustaining power of a presence through which it may transcend its dissolution. The revolution ends in a Reign of Terror; the *Princeps* becomes *Imperator*; the divine right of power becomes power by divine right; the *vox populi* becomes the *vox dei*. And in its most recent guise, this crisis of authority takes the form of the displacement of *executive privilege* by the *privilege of the executive*. As with Napoleon, for whom the distinction between *constituted* power (*pouvoir constitué*) and constituting power (*pouvoir constituant*) came increasingly to be a distinction without a difference, the 37th President of the United States repeatedly announces: *"Je suis le pouvoir constituant!"*

In a letter to the Marquis de Mirabeau, of 26 July 1767, Rousseau remarked: "The great problem in politics, which I compare to the problem of squaring the circle in geometry . . . (is): How to find a form of government which puts the law above man." The trouble was, as he went on to say, that to put "the law above man and thus to establish the validity of man-made laws, *il faudrait des dieux!*"[34] Robespierre needed more than a Supreme Being. He needed, as he said, an "Immortal Legislator," or, in a different context, a "continuous appeal to Justice." This meant the need for "an ever-present trancendent source of authority that could not be identified with the general will of either the nation or the Revolution itself" but which "might function as the fountainhead of justice from which the laws of the new body politic could derive their legitimacy."[35] Thus could the new beginning be assured of an appropriate and stabilizing continuity. The failure to discern such a transcendent source of authority, and to act accordingly, would mean sooner or later that revolutionary passion and promise had arrived at an inescapable "moment of truth." As Robespierre himself prophetically put it, in his last speech, "we shall perish because, in the history of mankind, we missed the moment to found freedom."[36]

In America, however, the perennial crisis of authority' was brought to a unique resolution. Here revolutionary promise and experience ushered in a "new birth of freedom." "Its story," says Arendt, "as an independent entity begins only with the Revolution and the foundation of the republic."[37] The story provided the perspective and the rationale for the legitimization of power in and by the act of founding itself. As Hamilton put it, in the opening paragraph of *The Federalist 1*:

> It has frequently been remarked that it seems to have been reserved to the people of this country, by their conduct and example to decide the important question, whether societies of men really are capable or not of establishing good government from reflection and choice, or whether they are forever destined to depend for their political constitutions on accident and force.[38]

There is yet another story in the relations between revolution and humanization. This story is crucial to the present discussion because it forcefully raises the question of a third option. We are confronted by the messianic story, the story of Jesus as Christ. On the revolutionary record, it must be admitted that Jesus Christ has been left behind by the ongoing dynamics of "the highest interests of humanity." On this record, the City of God has collapsed into the Secular City more completely than even the most negative reading of Harvey Cox has ventured to claim. Like "Resurrection City," the road from "Exodus to Easter" has become a shambled detour of inhumanity on the road from "the Great Society" to the "Society of Togetherness"; and the poetic politics of "the Great Refusal" are exposed as a psychedelic fantasy on the nearer edge of madness. There is still no peace in Vietnam and Watergate is still close enough to Kent State and Jackson and "the Crisis at Columbia" to lend a poignant persistence to the Hamiltonian option. In short, there is no third option between the power to establish "good government from reason and choice" and the unending dependence of societies "for their political constitutions on accident and force."

What, then, does the Christ story point to and what is its bearing upon the Hamiltonian option and upon the problems that seem at the moment to be confirming it?

We come here upon a major difficulty with Arendt's reading of the Christ story in relation to the revolutionary record. Arendt thinks that the fact "that no revolution was ever made in the name of Christianity prior to the modern age" argues against the view "that Christian teachings are revolutionary in themselves." The claim that "it needed modernity to liberate the revolutionary germ of the Christian faith, . . . obviously is begging the question."[39] Surely, one may reply, "no more obviously than the claim that it needed modernity to liberate the revolutionary germ of revolution itself, by shifting the referentiality of the experience of revolution from astronomy to politics." One *can* read Augustine's messianic view of history as remaining "bound within the cycles of antiquity."[40] But why should one deny to Augustine what one is prepared to allow to Virgil? If the Fourth Eclogue was so attractive to the Romans because of its celebration of the intrinsic link between the birth of a child and the promise of a new beginning, yet did not break the hold of historical recurrence upon their minds, Augustine's powerful assessment of the power of the presence of Christ as the center of history need not be dismissed as transmundane and ineffective because it did not destroy cyclism.[41]

More problematic, however, is Arendt's reading of the new understanding of power derived from the covenantal tradition. Acknowledging that she does not wish to enter upon a discussion of "the relationship between Puritanism and American political insti-

tutions," she rests content with a belief "in the validity of Clinton
Rossiter's distinction between Puritans and Puritanism, between
the magnificent autocrats of Boston and Salem and their inherently
revolutionary way of life and thought."[42] From this confession of
faith, the conclusion is reached that a theocratic and a covenantal
view of ultimate political authority "are somehow incompatible."

It may be that "the notion of covenant presupposes no-
sovereignty and no-rulership."[43] If so, this would be the secular
version of covenantal authority, the social contract, about the
prospects of which Rousseau and Hobbes were seriously at odds;
and in relation to which Professor John Rawls has recently undertaken an impressive formulation of a transcendent *sine qua non*
called "the original position."[44] Moreover, such an enlightened re-
ductionist view of the matter is puzzlingly indifferent to the fact
that a major issue of *The Federalist* is precisely the question whether
humanistic or theocratic presuppositions are inherent in the covenantal doctrine of power. The forebear of these "magnificent autocrats of Boston and Salem and their inherently revolutionary way
of life and thought," John Calvin, would have found in God's
refusal to delegate his sovereignty to any earthly power the best
guarantee of the responsible exercise of political power. It has,
moreover, been brilliantly shown that far from having "no influence
whatever on what the men of the Revolution did or thought," "these
strictly religious influences and movements" nurtured the very
phrases that found their way into the revolutionary struggle and
into the founding documents.[45]

Nevertheless, like Yeats' falcon, Arendt keeps "turning in the
widening gyre," reporting the while from afar and *contra* Yeats,
"the centre (that) cannot hold," as she keeps on insisting that it
has. Her discerning eye has caught a glimpse of the crucial revolutionary insistence and of the pertinence of the Christ story to it.
"The revolutions," she notes, "still occurred within a tradition
which was partly founded on an event in which the 'word had
become flesh,' that is, on an absolute that had appeared in historical
time as a mundane reality."[46] This absolute had been the monarchy
by divine right under the tutelage of the church. The revolutions
had been prepared by secularization for an "enlightened" repudia-

tion of this authority. They had scarcely been prepared, however, for the emergency "which drove the very 'enlightened' men of the eighteenth century to plead for some religious sanction at the very moment when they were about to emancipate the secular realm fully from the influences of the churches and to separate politics and religion once and for all."[47]

The promises of the revolutions had been forced by the dynamics of their passions into a collision course with the stubborn radicality of good and evil in human affairs. Rousseau and Robespierre alike oversimplified the evil against which their revolutionary passions were directed and oversimplified the good for which their revolutionary promises held out the prospect of realization. The Hamiltonian option shows that their counterparts in the colonies had a livelier awareness of the enormous uncertainty of the confrontation of goodness and power. As far as Arendt can see, "the only completely valid, completely convincing experience Western mankind ever had with active love of goodness as the inspiring principle of all action (was the) consideration of the person of Jesus of Nazareth."[48] But then, as far as she can see, we must turn this experience over to the poets, from whom we can learn "that absolute goodness is hardly any less dangerous than absolute evil" and that there is a "goodness beyond virtue" and a "wickedness beyond vice."[49]

The immediate revolutionary experience to which the poets tried to relate Jesus was the French experience. In order to do this, they "dared to undo the haloed transformation of Jesus of Nazareth into Christ, to make him return to the world of men."[50] Apart from the question whether Melville and Dostoevski understood the effective presence of Christ in the midst of the predicament of power in this way, the crucial question is whether the messianic story is *exhausted by this possibility*. Jesus' own self-identification with the messianic tradition of Israel's prophets and the accounts in the gospels of his teaching concerning the kingdom of God and of his own involvements with power, certainly support every effort to "undo the haloed transformation of Jesus of Nazareth into Christ, to make him return to the world of men." But when we face up to this messianic story in its original and originating context, it exhibits another point and purpose altogether. They are, to invert and sharpen the thrust of Arendt's phrase, *the hallowed transfiguration of the world of men by the continuing presence and power in and over human affairs of Jesus of Nazareth as the Christ.*

It is not enough to pursue the problem of power in disregard of the problem of presence. The passion and promise of the pursuit, undertaken in this way, keep doing haloed transformations that have to be undone. But to pursue the problem of power inseparably from the problem of presence is to begin to discern a third possibility exactly where Hamilton posed the problem. When the problem of power is discerned as itself the sign of the problem of presence, then, we can begin to push beyond the tenuous option between reflection and choice or accident and force in the attempt to establish good government among men. The Christ story is the story of the presence and power of Jesus of Nazareth in and over the ambiguity of power in human affairs. It tells in word and deed of the liberating limits and the renewing possibilities within which revolutionary promises and passions make room for the freedom to be and to stay human in the world. As the inaugurator of a "new age," the "age to come" in the midst of the "old age" the "age that is passing away," Jesus is a revolutionary, as surely as revolution and humanization, history and fulfillment, are inseparable from one another. The divisive, healing, transfigured, and transfiguring Christ is not to be despoiled as the model of a new humanity because of what has been made of him—pantocratic ruler, spiritual teacher and leader, demagogue, or social ideologist. As the model of a new humanity, he involves us in the struggle for a new and human future. The way leads from a politics of confrontation to a politics of transfiguration and the transfiguration of politics.

PART TWO

# A POLITICS OF CONFRONTATION

CHAPTER 3

# THE DARKNESS OF THE GOSPEL

Revolution and humanization have to do with the passion, process, and promise through which happenings in history make room for freedom, i.e., for what is human in man and in society, and for what it takes to make and to keep human life human in the world. Revolutions happen when the burden of unfreedom becomes unbearable and explodes into a new beginning, with a story all its own. The catalyst is the social question, identified as the question of the poor, which Marx was the first to lift from the level of human misery to the level of trenchant political, economic, and philosophical analysis. With Marx "the poverty of philosophy" became "a philosophy of poverty," the "Holy Family" became the "human family," and the altered role of the poor in giving shape to the specifically modern and authentic sense of the word *revolution* acquired a concrete and unavoidable intelligibility.[1] We are all caught up in a Marxian world.

Revolutions, however, intensify the ambiguity of power and end in a crisis of authority. The ambiguity of power is its drive to absolutize itself because it cannot validate itself. The crisis of authority is the unstabilizing tension between the promise of a new beginning and the prospect of its realization, between *principium* and *principle*. The point of intersection between the power to begin anew and the power to increase what has been begun, exposes a power vacuum instead of a power that binds as it liberates and liberates as it binds. "To find a form of government," as Rousseau discovered and reported, "which puts the law above man and thus to establish the validity of man-made laws" requires the gods. *Il faudrait des dieux*![2] But revolutions either exile the gods or deify the passports by which they admit them.

Haunted by this dilemma, revolutions are nourished by story. Story, we were suggesting, is the verbal form of freedom—i.e., what it takes to be and to stay human in the world—and that which shapes the content of freedom. Story is a sign that experience has changed a way of thinking, and that a way of thinking has changed experience. As Hegel carefully and rightly saw, revolution exhibits the coincidence of mentality and happening. Hence, we ventured a Hegelianism of our own by saying that "revolution is the lifestyle of truth."[3] The role of the Christ story in the nourishment of the revolutionary tradition in the West is a matter of record. Biblical and classical memories and hopes focus upon liberation from slavery and upon the wonder whereby the promise of new beginnings takes form in the power of a renewing birth. Hegel's early preoccupation with theology, which "interpreted Christianity as having a basic function in world history, that of giving a new 'absolute center to man and a final goal to life,' "[4] indicates not only how closely the messianic theme was part of his own response to the French Revolution, but also one of the primary roots along which Messianism found its way into Marxism.

Thus the record raises the question of the lifestyle of truth but leaves open the question of the truth that shapes the life so styled. Hegel concluded, as revolutionaries and nonrevolutionaries alike have increasingly concluded, that "the revealed truth of the Gospel could not fit in with the expanding social and political realities of the world. . . ."[5] But the political version of squaring the circle remains to trouble our time of revolutionary troubles.

The passion for freedom that ends in a crisis of authority perennially imperils revolutionary promises by revolutionary fate. Hence, the story by which revolutions are nourished makes all the difference in the world. "At the still point of the turning world," to borrow T. S. Eliot's arresting phrase, there is also the point of no return.[6] It is the point at which the ambiguity of power and the crisis of authority encounter and involve the story of a presence. At the center, the problem of power and the problem of presence are—either fatefully or freeingly—joined.

At this critical juncture the messianic story scarcely floods us with light. It overshadows us instead with darkness. Indeed, one is wont to say "deep darkness." The darkness of the gospel is its obvious unfitness in dealing with the reality of power, with the centrality and ambiguity of power in human affairs. Hegel's early estimate seems so right as to be irrefutable. It simply gathers a mounting consensus into words. But then, to make matters worse, there are the radicalization of the crisis of authority in Marxism-Leninism and, worst of all, the devastating sense that, where power is concerned, Jesus simply lets us down. He does this at least at three levels. To the weakness of power, Jesus juxtaposes the power of weakness. To the exercise of power, he juxtaposes the refusal of power. To the pervasiveness of power, he juxtaposes the transfiguration of power.

These paradoxes permeate—and for the most part have paralyzed—the dynamics of the gospel in confrontation both with established power and with revolutionary challenges to the Establishment. The possibility that there may be "no exit" from the power paralysis of the gospel haunts every attempt to explore alternatives. Yet the presence and power attested by the messianic story exert a continuing pressure upon the course of human events that makes unavoidable a confrontation with the revolutionary age in which we live. Indeed, the paradoxes of power, which Jesus of Nazareth recognized and practiced, express his own version of a politics of confrontation. Jesus' juxtaposition of the power of weakness to the weakness of power acquires revolutionary pertinence through a confrontation between Jesus, on the one hand, and Marx and the Establishment, on the other. His juxtaposition of the refusal of power to the exercise of power acquires revolutionary pertinence through two paradigmatic New Testament interpretations of Jesus' politics of confrontation. Jesus' juxtaposition of the transfiguration of power to the pervasiveness of power exposes the darkness of the gospel as the threshold of light and opens the way toward a revolutionary politics for Christians as a politics of transfiguration.

We shall consider Jesus' politics of transfiguration in the following parts of this discussion. Meanwhile, there is a preparatory movement toward the threshold of transfiguration that must be explored. It is provided by Jesus' politics of confrontation that sets out from the juxtaposition of the power of weakness to the weakness of power.

# CHAPTER 4

# JESUS, MARX,
# AND THE ESTABLISHMENT:
# THE POWER OF WEAKNESS
# AND THE WEAKNESS OF POWER

In our revolutionary world, the strength that shows itself as weakness meets the weakness that shows itself as strength in the confrontation between the Marxist-Leninist view of the focus of revolutionary power and passion and Jesus' view of the power of revolutionary passion and promise.[7]

In *Die Deutsche Ideologie* ("The German Ideology") Marx had declared: "Not criticism, but revolution, is the motive force of history."[8] This, together with the famous metaphor of revolution as "a midwife," underlines Marx's concern to alter the understanding of the role of force in history. This is a *revolutionary*, not a diabolical role. Revolutionary force, Marx had explained, "is the midwife of every old society that is pregnant with the new; . . . it is the instrument by the aid of which social movement forces its way through and shatters the dead, fossilized, political forms . . ."[9] Of these *obiter dicta* of revolution in our still Marxian world we remind ourselves because of Lenin's identification of the issue to which these *dicta* point. Indeed, particularly in view of the fact that "no revolution has ever solved the 'social question' and liberated men from the predicament of want, but all revolutions . . . have . . . used and misused the mighty forces of misery and destitution in their struggle against tyranny or oppression," and especially in view of the dark-

27

ness of the gospel as regards the relations between the poor and the problem of power, Lenin's account of what the focus of revolution really is, goes straight to the heart of the matter. He writes:

> What is at issue is neither opposition nor political struggle in general, but *revolution*. Revolution consists in the proletariat *destroying* the "administrative apparatus" and the *entire* state machine, replacing it with a new one, consisting of the armed workers. . . . The point is whether the old state machine (bound by thousands of threads to the bourgeoisie and permeated through and through with routine and inertia) shall remain, or be *destroyed* and replaced by a *new* one. Revolution consists in the new class *smashing* this machine and commanding, governing with the aid of a *new* machine.[10]

Memories are notoriously short. But forgotten happenings have a way of casting a long shadow over times to come. Thus, the last two weeks of August 1968, as the Democratic Party met in National Convention in Chicago, and Mayor Daley's police brutally attacked a motley crowd of demonstrators for peace and freedom assembled in Grant Park; not to mention that dismaying night of 21 October 1967, as thousands marched around an armed and barricaded Pentagon in passionate protest against an unconscionable American military involvement in Southeast Asia, may now be only dimly recalled. But these grim doings do not on that account make Lenin's grim assessment of the confrontation of the force of revolution with the power of the state less remote than we had allowed ourselves to think it was. That assessment has not yet been safely overtaken by events. We may be living in a "post-Christian" world, but we are not yet living in a post-Marxian one. Marxism-Leninism is still the bearer of the revolutionary ferment of our time. Despite the stresses and strain of power, of heresy and schism within the communist movement, and despite the technological alterations in the power struggle, the Marxist-Leninist account of the impact of power upon revolutionary promise and passion is still the point from which to take our bearings in the revolutionary situation in which we live.

According to this account, the state is the machinery of government, and government is the control center of the state. Taken together, state and government are the foci of effective power in human society. Obviously the forms of government vary, as do also the operational styles of control of the state machinery. But there can be no effective social change apart from a change at the control center of power; and conversely, the dynamics of social change are such that when existing power fails to make room for the freedom to be human for men in society, the moment has arrived for an attempt by *force majeure* to "shatter the dead, fossilized political forms." This is, of course, the moment of violence. Violence is the sign of an emerging impasse between the dynamics of social development and the existing organization of social and administrative power operative through the machinery of the state. As Marx and Lenin understood violence, it was the application to the power of the state of the revolutionary *force majeure*. Meanwhile, however, violence, too, has become radicalized. It functions now in reverse, as the application of the power of the state to the revolutionary *force majeure*. The reason for this is, in Marcuse's phrase, that "technological rationality has become political rationality."[11] In his Preface to Marx's analysis of *The Civil War in France* (1871), Engels had distinguished between the philosophical conception of the state and the state as a power reality. According to the former, "the state is 'the realization of the idea,' or the Kingdom of God on earth, . . . the sphere in which eternal truth and justice is or should be realized." According to the latter, Engels wrote: "In reality, . . . the state is nothing but a machine for the oppression of one class by another, in the democratic republic no less than in the monarchy."[12]

Engels of course, had Hegel and Bismarck's Germany in mind. But the dynamics of social change, at an accelerating tempo, enlarged the scope and confirmed the focus of Engels' analysis. Indeed, we can understand Arendt's estimate of the success of the American Revolution when we recall that Marx and Engels had excluded England from their conclusions about the Continent, on the ground that there a minimal bureaucracy and the absence of a militarist clique seemed to make room for the possibility even of a people's revolution. If a fiercely probing social analyst like Lenin could seriously propose the German postal system of the 1870s as a model of the revolutionary alternative to "the bureaucratic machine of the modern state,"[13] Arendt is surely entitled to an oversimplification in proposing Jefferson's "elementary republics of the wards" as an institution appropriate to the spirit of revolution.[14] Lenin, however, had moderated the incongruity of his proposal (and we wonder why Arendt had not) by a sober estimate of what World War I had done to England's revolutionary prospects. By 1917, Lenin could write:

> Today . . . this restriction made by Marx is no longer valid. Both England and America, the biggest and last representatives —in the whole world—of Anglo-Saxon "liberty," in the sense that they had no militarist cliques and bureaucracy, have completely sunk into . . . the bloody morass of bureaucratic-military institutions which subordinate everything to themselves. . . . Today, both in England and in America, "the preliminary condition for every real people's revolution" is the *smashing*, the *destruction* of the "ready-made state machinery" brought in those countries to "European," general imperialist, perfection in the years 1914–1917.[15]

When a former President of the United States and Marx, Engels, and Lenin worry, in almost the same language, about power, government, and social change, the coincidence is a sobering sign of an omnious shadow over the shape of things to come. President Eisenhower wondered aloud about the human future of American society under the aegis of what he called "the industrial-military complex." Almost a century earlier, Marx had firmly declared "that the next attempt of the French Revolution will be no longer, as before, to transfer the bureaucratic-military machine from one hand to another, but to *smash* it, and this is essential for every real people's revolution on the Continent. . . ."[16] Lenin then takes up this declaration and writes that it briefly expresses "the principal lesson of Marxism regarding the task of the proletariat in relation to the state."[17] Between Marx and Lenin, on the one hand, and between Lenin and Eisenhower, on the other, the "ready-made state machinery" has been brought, not only in England and America, but in Lenin's own revolutionary society, the Soviet Union, "to 'European,' general imperialist perfection," not only "in the years 1914–

17," but in the years 1939-45 and after; and to unanticipated, though internally necessary, technological perfection. As Marcuse explains:

> Technical progress, extended to a whole system of domination and co-ordination, creates forms of life (and of power) which appear to reconcile the forces opposing the system and to defeat or refute all protest in the name of historical prospects of freedom from toil and domination. *Contemporary society seems to be capable of containing social change*—qualitative change which would establish essentially different institutions, a new direction of the productive process, new modes of human existence. . . . As a technological universe, advanced industrial society is a *political* universe.[18]

In such a society, the room to be human that freedom takes has become a pale shadow of its revolutionary self. The passion and promise of a new beginning have been reduced to "repressive tolerance."[19]

This reduction is only the latest in the line of operational setbacks to the Marxist-Leninist analysis of power. Barrington Moore has shown that almost all of Lenin's hopes were disappointed. In industry, a centralized system of control by the workers did not lead to the eventual achievement of full equality. In agriculture, large-scale cooperative farming has not replaced the small peasant proprietors. Internationally, a successful revolution in Russia has not only not established socialism in Europe but has entered instead into the fury of doctrinal schism. The *dilemma of power*, as Moore calls it, is that the goals of the new society cannot wait upon methods that achieve them without compromise and, in turn, the means required by immediate political decisions obstruct the goals to such a degree as to require the indefinite extension of the time of achievement as the price of adhering to the goals.[20] Disappointment and a dilemma, however, do not invalidate the Marxist-Leninist radicalization of the ambiguity of power and the crisis of authority accompanying it. The state is the crux of revolutionary success or revolutionary failure because the state is both *locus* and *focus* of the problem of power, since in the state the ideological and the operational levels of power meet.[21]

When the messianic story confronts the dynamics of revolution, the power of a presence that liberates as it binds and binds as it liberates meets the dilemma of the state and revolution. It is not too much to say that, in the revolutionary context of our present time of troubles, the issue of power is drawn between Jesus and Marx. Ernest Renan was right for the wrong reasons and Karl Marx was wrong for the right reasons, and the dynamics and the focus of the question of revolution provide the confrontation with which they struggled with an ultimate urgency. Renan rightly saw that Jesus was at the center of the reciprocity between revolution and humanization, loosed by the French Revolution and intensified by the altered role of the poor. Renan wrongly disregarded the boundary on which the strength that shows itself as weakness meets the weakness that shows itself as strength. So Jesus became a demagogue, bearing a revolutionary program, instead of Messiah, bearing a revolutionary presence. Marx wrongly judged that the messianic presence of Jesus had run its historical course and required a historical displacement by the destiny of a revolutionary people. But Marx rightly recognized the saving significance of the passion and promise of a revolutionary force in history, for all those in history whose freedom to be human had been denied by oppression, exploitation, and the sheer brutality of power. With Marx (and of course Lenin) we come in a fundamental and frightening sense to the end of the road as regards the ambiguity of power and the crisis of authority.

The default of the state upon the revolution—whether through its inability to serve as the instrument of revolutionary promise and policy, as in Marxist governments, or through the widening gulf between the administrative machinery of the state and revolutionary passion and promise, as in the West—means that power cannot provide itself with the authority required by its revolutionary role. The weakness of power is that of itself it cannot make room for the freedom that being and staying human in the world take. This function of power takes a rebirth of wonder; or, as Augustine put it, an elemental piety. Such piety begins as a response to a presence, a presence that confronts the weakness of power with the power of weakness. The power of weakness, when borne by a messianic presence, is the disclosure in weakness of a strength that turns, as it were, the flank of the strength that has been unmasked as weakness. According to the messianic story that is the Gospel: Jesus is the Christ, whose very human presence at the center where being and staying human in the world make all the difference in the world, sets power free in binding power to his new beginning "for the whole human running race,"[22] and in that bondage liberates power from the futility of its self-absolutization.

## CHAPTER 5

# THE EXERCISE OF POWER
# AND THE REFUSAL OF POWER

When Jesus Christ functions as the power of messianic presence at the center of the revolutionary struggle for humanization, power acquires a freedom in bondage. But this freedom in bondage does not immediately or easily dispel the darkness of the gospel. Christians, at least, should learn from Marxists that the state, like the proverbial leopard, does not easily change its spots. And they should learn from Jesus that one does not start to build a tower without first counting the cost (Luke 14:28), and that a premature celebration of the messianic presence is vulnerable to demonic distortion, as well as open to divine enablement (Mark 8:32–33). Indeed, the darkness of the gospel thickens before a break in it really signals the dawn. What good is the promise of freedom from the crisis of authority that haunts the dilemma and the ambiguity of power, when Jesus confronts the exercise of power with the refusal of power? There are, indeed, two paradigms of this refusal in the earliest attempts to live by the power of the messianic presence in the world of human affairs. These paradigms have so insistently been understood as supportive of the state and in no sense supportive of revolution, as markedly to abort, if not to cancel, the freedom promised by the power of weakness in its refusal to exercise the power of strength. It may be that an allowable alternative to an insistent tradition connot be persuasively put forward. But if Jesus is not to be regarded as running out on Marx, and, in so doing, altogether on the question of revolution, the time for a try at such an alternative is long overdue.

The paradigms are provided by the way in which Paul of Tarsus understood the implications of Jesus' messianic presence for the state and revolution, and by Jesus' own behavior, as reported in another unforgettable nocturnal conversation by the author of the Fourth Gospel. The former comes to us in the Letter to the Romans, at chapter thirteen (vv. 1–10); the latter comes to us at the close of the eighteenth and the opening of the nineteenth chapters of the Gospel according to John (18:33–40; 19:1–16). We shall consider them in the chronological order of the documents, which happens also to be the order of deepening darkness, as regards Jesus Christ and the question of revolution.

A. EXPOSING THE DISESTABLISHMENT OF THE ESTABLISHMENT:
   SUBMISSION—ROMANS 13:1–10

We begin with the Letter to the Romans as a paradigm of a *politics of confrontation*. The text of the passage reads:

> Every person must submit to the supreme authorities. There is no authority but by act of God, and the existing authorities are instituted by him; consequently anyone who rebels against authority is resisting a divine institution, and those who so resist have themselves to thank for the punishment they will receive. For government, a terror to crime, has no terrors for good behavior. You wish to have no fear of the authorities? Then continue to do right and you will have their approval, for they are God's agents working for your good. But if you are doing wrong, then you will have cause to fear them; it is not for nothing that they hold the power of the sword, for they are God's agents of punishment, for retribution on the offender. That is why you are obliged to submit. It is an obligation imposed not merely by fear of retribution but by conscience. That is also why you pay taxes. The authorities are in God's service and to these duties they devote their energies.
>   Discharge your obligations to all men; pay tax and toll, rever-

ence and respect, to those to whom they are due. Leave no claim
outstanding against you, except that of mutual love. He who loves
his neighbor has satisfied every claim of the law.

On the face of it, this passage seems to interpose an insuperable
barrier between Jesus Christ and the question of revolution. How
else is one to understand the obvious meaning of the words than
as a Gospel mandate to submit to existing authorities? This is to be
done, moreover, not merely from fear of retribution but in conscience. The deepest springs of human motivation and the stabilizing structures of life in this world are joined in an obedience to
existing authorities, not only without mental reservation but out
of the specific knowledge of what God expects of humanity and
of what humanity owes to God, which the conscience provides. As
though to make the point doubly emphatic, those whose acts are
right need have no fear of the existing authorities, for they will
receive their approval. Fear of these authorities is already a sign of
some rebellious disobedience under way, for which punishment is
proper and should occasion no surprise. The symbol of this punishment is the sword, and the instrument of this exercise of power is
government. Even the apparent exception to this law of obedience,
mutual love, turns out to be the satisfaction of every claim of the
law. Conclusion: A Christian is obliged to submit to the government under which he or she lives! Where Jesus Christ is involved in
human affairs, revolution hasn't a chance! Thus, our concerns to
this point have collapsed under the impact of a single straight look
at a New Testament text.

What a relief it would be if one could report that the "Constitution of the Canon of Sacred Scriptures" had been carelessly read
by the committee preparing it, so that certain untoward passages
had not been adequately screened; or that Paul of Tarsus had a
publisher's deadline to meet, which resulted in the unhappy coincidence of a bad night before the day on which the question of
the state and revolution arrived at the top of his writing agenda!
The consensus of commentators is that the question certainly was
at the top of the writing agenda, though not a top-drawer issue
as regards the Letter to the Romans as a whole. The role of

Christians in the state, and the attitude of Christians toward the state, presuppose a radical revision of perspective upon life in this world in relation to which the question of the state finds its due place. This helps a little to soften the bald antithesis between Jesus Christ and the question of revolution, but the net result has been little discernible difference either in theory or in practice. At this point, the darkness of the gospel gets very dark indeed.

Nevertheless, we must set out from this radical revision of perspective upon life in this world if we are to move through this darkness to some understanding of what the Christian really means by being "obliged to submit." The perspective is derived from the messianic function of Jesus as the inaugurator of a "new age" in the midst of the "old age." This means, as Luther thought of it, that, "just as Christ does," the Christian "bears two forms in himself, for he is a dual being (*Gémellus*, twin-born)."[23] As body and spirit, " a believer is exalted once for all above all things and yet is subject to all things."[24] Or it means, as Bishop Nygren has pointed out, that Paul was concerned about tendencies among Christians of his time to rush into the freedom that life in the "new aeon" promised, in anarchic indifference to the order of life in the "old aeon," which plainly had not disappeared. "Here Paul takes a most emphatic position against the fanatical view which makes the gospel into a law for society. . . . The two aeons do interpenetrate, but that does not mean that they may be arbitrarily confused."[25]

A suggestion of a different kind stresses not so much the contrast between the two ages as that between the law of love and the Torah. Common to Paul and some accents in the Jewish theology that shaped Paul's pre-Christian experience was a search for the inner meaning of the Law. Paul and some rabbis could agree that the core of the Law is love of one's neighbor. Thus the influence of Jesus was not the abrogation but the fulfillment of the Law, fulfillment in the sense of universalizing the scope of the Law and admitting of no exceptions. On this view, the "you are to submit" of verse 5 is to be carefully qualified by its relation to verse 8: "leave no claim against you, except that of mutual love." *Opheilete* (in the phrase "owe no man anything") has a double meaning. The

Greek verb *opheilein* may mean "owe" in the sense of "being in debt," or "owe" in the sense of "being obligated." Applied to the state, it is suggested, Paul uses the first sense; applied to the neighbor, the second sense. Thus the Christian is not to be indebted to the state in any way, for the state belongs to the creation, to the age that is passing away. But the Christian is *obligated to* the neighbor, to unrestricted love. "The state forms only a limited area of human relationship (in terms of God's created order). A Christian's relationship to his fellowman is broader more radical and refers to the depth of God's law."[26]

On this reading, the tension under which the Christian lives is not so much the tension between submission to the state under the authority of God and freedom in the spirit of which Christ's authority under God is already a foretaste. The critical tension is between the state and the neighbor. Submission to the state, then, takes the form of negative obedience amounting to indifference. Making sure that the state has no claim against you, paying "tax and toll, reverence and respect, to those to whom they are due" (v. 7), is simply a realistic attempt at being as wise in one's own generation as are "the children of this world" (Luke 16:8 AV). The obligation to the neighbor, however, is a positive obedience, which admits of no exceptions, including the exception of the state. The state and the neighbor are thus joined in a single obedience to the "higher law" of love. Submission and responsibility both express the revolutionary perspective upon life in the world introduced by the presence of Jesus Messiah and implemented by the practice of love. Consequently, the oft-cited "we must obey God rather than men" (Acts 5:29) loses its force and function as an exception to the rule of submission, and becomes the effective rule of obedience to love in action. The Christian is now free from the embarrassment of an *in extremis* disobedience to a state toward which submissive obedience has suddenly become too much. The responsibility that now binds the Christian under this freedom is the unexceptional responsibility of love. As verse 10 puts it: "Love cannot wrong a neighbor; therefore the whole law is summed up in love." Paul rightly saw that the state raises in a very concrete way the crucial question of the difference that the presence of Jesus Messiah makes to the power through which men struggle to make room for the freedom to be and to stay human in the world. The issue is drawn, not between submission and resistance, but between the thrust and direction of the power of love in a world where "there is no authority but by act of God" (v. 1) and the thrust and direction of rebellion against authority, against government, which is a terror to crime but has no terrors for good behavior (vv. 2–3).

Drawn in this way, Paul and Marx agree that the question of the state and revolution is the critical instance of the passion and promise by which revolution and humanization are joined in the world. They agree, too, that the state is the instrument, not the source, of authentic sovereignty, and that the state and revolution are on a collision course, so long as the state obstructs and does not serve authentic sovereignty. As Paul interprets Jesus, however, it would appear that Jesus sees more clearly than does Marx (and with him the makers of revolution and the shapers of modern revolutionary experience) that revolutions imperil the love that they so passionately practice by devouring their own children either through the self-justification of their own authority or through dissipation as rebellion against authority. A politics of confrontation in Jesus' sense is neither submission to, nor legitimation of, existing governments. *It is a much more subtle practice of the love of neighbor that recognizes in existing authorities the great divide between a self-justifying legitimacy that ends in the tyranny of order and a self-justifying rebellion that ends in the tyranny of anarchy.* Love knows that the fear of retribution amplified by conscience is a more faithful service to revolutionary passion and promise than a revolution that aborts itself in a rebellion that brings down upon itself the power of the sword of retribution. But love also knows that existing authorities, as God's agents of punishment, are not exempt from love's claim upon the law. In exercising retribution upon the offender, these authorities work both for the offender's good and for their own undoing. Thus the practice of love is at once the fulfillment of revolution and the fulfillment of the law.

Admittedly, this attempt to interpret the power of the presence of Jesus in and over the ambiguity of power and the crisis of authority to which this ambiguity leads, seems like an attempt to shore up an authority figure who has in fact been overtaken by events. It is not accidental that Luther and those who stand in his ecclesiastical succession have been drawn upon to tell us where Paul thought that Jesus came out on the question of the state and revolution. Lutherans have not been conspicuously in the foreground of revolutionary endeavor. Yet, when it comes to "a politics of confrontation," Calvin and those who stand in *his* ecclesiastical succession have scarcely taken a different tack. They have, it is true, exhibited a livelier sense for the fact that the ambiguity of power requires a corresponding flexibility in the responsibility of those who exercise power, and a more active exercise of the priority of obedience to God over obedience to human authorities in human affairs. The root of this liveliness is a positive, as against a merely negative, view of government, and a shift of focus from monarchy to magistracy. Commenting on the Pauline phrase "for there is no power but of God," Calvin remarks, "that powers are from God, not as pestilence, and famine, and wars and other visitations for sin are said to be from him, but because he has appointed them for the legitimate and just government of the world."[27]

The discussion of civil government in the *Institutes* begins, very much in the manner of Luther, with the distinction between soul and body. Calvin is at pains to make it clear that "this distinction does not lead us to consider the whole nature of government as a thing polluted, which has nothing to do with Christian men."[28] He then goes on to enumerate the positive offices of government, which are: "to cherish and protect the outward worship of God; to defend sound doctrine of piety and the position of the church; to adjust our life to the society of men, to form our social behavior to civil righteousness, to reconcile us with one another, and to promote general peace and tranquility."[29] Nevertheless, Calvin is acutely aware both of the weaknesses of kings and of the limitations of the people as regards political power. Hence he searches for a viable instrument of meaningful obedience to existing authorities. "It is very rare," Calvin declares, "for kings so to control themselves that their will never disagrees with what is just and right; or for them to have been endowed with such great keenness and prudence, that each knows how much is enough."[30]

In Geneva, Calvin induced the Little Council to hold meetings, monthly or quarterly, for the purpose of mutual criticism, under pledge of secrecy.[31] Calvin's governmental preference for "a system compounded of aristrocracy and democracy,"[32] while mainly due to his realism about the corruptions of power when exercised, is also due to his struggle to find an option between tyranny and anarchy. He thought of the magistracy, under pressure of the people, as the functional instrument for obeying God rather than men in human affairs. "*Audeant principes, et terreantur*" ("Let the princes hear, and be afraid"), he declares! And while McNeill rightly notes that this "startling and powerful phrase . . . does not threaten revolution, since it is God that princes are to fear,"[33] nevertheless, when we consider it in relation both to the *Commentary on Romans* and to the last chapter of the *Institutes*, especially its closing peroration, we get some confirmation of a reassuring direction Calvin's mind was taking in the matter of the state and revolution. The *Commentary* (1540) preceded the fully expanded statement of Christian faith (1559) by nearly two decades. But the circumstance that since the first edition of the *Institutes* (1536) the discussion of civil government remains consistent in its concerns and constant in its place at the end of the work, suggests the seriousness with which Calvin took political affairs. In the *Commentary*, the sentence already quoted, concerning the positive view of government, is followed by another through which Calvin's unease shows. "For though tyrannies and unjust exercise of power, as they are full of disorder are not an ordained government," it reads, "yet the right of government is ordained by God for the well-being of mankind."[34] And the *Institutes* ends by declaring that

in that obedience which we have shown to be due the authority of rulers, we are always to make this exception, indeed, to observe it as primary, that such obedience is never to lead us away from obedience to Him to whose will the desires of all kings should be subject, to whose decrees all their commands ought to yield, to whose majesty their scepters ought to be submitted. And how absurd it would be that in satisfying men you should incur the displeasure of Him for whose sake you obey men themselves! . . . If they command anything against Him, let it go unesteemed.

And here let us not be concerned about all that dignity which the magistrates possess; for no harm is done to it when it is humbled before that singular and truly supreme power of God.[35]

For Calvin himself, however, and for his time, this remained a direction along which he was trying to resolve the problem of power. It was not a firmly fixed position. Nevertheless, the direction hints of liberating possibilities. These possibilities were not altogether lost upon later times; and they remain for us also to consider again. Meanwhile, the status-quo reading of Romans 13 claims also Calvin's support. "Rulers," he declares in the *Commentary*, "never abuse their own power by harassing the good and the innocent without retaining in their despotic rule some semblance of just government. No tyranny, therefore, can exist which does not in some respect assist in protecting human society. . . . To introduce anarchy, therefore, is to violate charity, for the immediate consequence of anarchy is the disturbance of the whole state."[36] The *Institutes* echoes the same conviction in recalling a saying widespread during the reign of Nerva: "It is indeed bad to live under a bad prince with whom nothing is permitted; but much worse under one by whom everything is allowed."[37]

It would be easy to dismiss this bald "either-or" as fallacious in logic and false in fact. An excluded middle and an oversimplification of the gray areas of any given status quo can scarcely resolve the problem of power caught in a deep crisis of authority. Fundamentally, however, the collision course on which the state and revolution are set ignores logic and brings the complexity of social change under a decisive limit. We who live under the pervasive subtlety of "repressive tolerance" and the irritating unpredictability of the "politics of the Great Refusal" should begin to recognize that the passion and promise of revolution have come full circle and that the shoe is now on Calvin's other foot. "It is indeed bad to live under a prince with whom everything is allowed but much worse under one with whom nothing is permitted."

By an odd coincidence of history—or is it providential?—the third possibility for which Hamilton's option calls presupposes the third possibility for which Calvin's polarization calls. This polarization is identical with that through which the mind of Jesus Christ by way of Paul of Tarsus has informed—or is it infected?—the mind of the Christian ever since. "Whether societies of men really are capable or not of establishing good government from reflection and choice, or whether they are forever destined to depend for their political constitutions on accident and force" (Hamilton),[38] depends upon whether there is a presence in and over the struggle of men for the freedom to be and to stay human in the world whose power breaks the stranglehold of the fateful rhythm between tyranny and anarchy over the passion and promise of revolution in human affairs. It could be that Paul's attempt in Romans 13 to probe the mind of Jesus has exposed the nerve of a politics of confrontation quite other than that of submission to existing authorities, whether as a check upon the political irresponsibility of those who prematurely celebrate the freedom of the "new age," or as a reluctant obedience "to God's agents working for . . . good" because the ultimate alternative is worse.

What would such an exposure look like? By another odd coincidence—or is it providential?—it looks very much like that Lutheran suggestion according to which the context of Paul's discussion of the state and revolution is the relation between the Torah and the law of love.[39] Its focus is not so much upon two poles of the inner meaning of the Law, e.g., the state and the neighbor, an order of creation and an order of the new age inaugurated by Jesus, as upon law and love as twin responses to the crisis of authority posed in human affairs by the ambiguity of power. By another odd coincidence—or is it providential?—Karl Barth has anticipated Herbert Marcuse. The clue to such a possibility lies buried in the now very largely forgotten commentary of Karl Barth's on the Letter to the Romans. We had not read it in many a year. But under the pressure both of Hamilton's and Calvin's third option, we ventured to check out what had somehow haunted us since the very first reading. This was Barth's juxtaposition between submission and love. Barth confronts "the great negative possibility of revolution" with "the great positive possibility of love," that is, of an altered mentality, a radically changed lifestyle, expressed in a direct and unaffected response to a new order in the making, breaking in upon the order that is passing away. Says Barth:

> We define love, not as a human act of thought and will, which is only the psychological presupposition, but as that absolute matter-of-factness toward the problematical character of existence . . . , a matter-of-factness in the strength of which man acknowledges God, lays hold of him, hangs upon him . . . as upon the ultimate affirmation in the ultimate negation of the total givenness of life. Love is man's existential standing before God: man's being touched by the freedom of God and in this confrontation being established as a Person.[40]

Barth, like Calvin, is wrestling with Paul's attempt to come to terms with a lifestyle of freedom without the anarchy of license; to leave behind the letter of the law that kills, while remembering also that love is the fulfillment of the law. In a passage decisive for a politics of confrontation, Barth writes:

> The protest against the course of this world should be *made* through "mutual love" and not be abandoned. Indeed, we are reminded in chapter 12:2 that an act is ethically positive which does *not* adapt itself "to the pattern of this present world," that testifies within these boundaries, in a completely hidden way, of the strangeness of God. The "*great* positive possibility" we call love on the same basis that we have called "submit" the "great negative possibility": once again, not because of individual acts, but because of the totality (*Zusammenhang*) of all "positive" (protesting!) acts which can be called ethical. Or again, we are concerned here with the meaning of an ethical lifestyle (*Gesamthaltung*). We call "love" the "great *positive* possibility," precisely because in the act of love the revolutionary meaning of all ethos is exposed, because love actually has to do with the negation and the breaking down of that which exists. It is love that also ultimately declares the reactionary man to be in the wrong, in spite of the wrong that the revolutionary does. For insofar as we love one another, we *cannot* wish to maintain the status quo. Instead, we do in love the new thing that casts down what has become old. Thus what we are talking about is the breach in the wall of incomprehensible inaction, which is the still more incomprehensible action of love."[41]

The remarkable timeliness of Barth's account of revolution is due, however, not only to the context of a lifestyle of freedom from within which he deals with the social and political negation of freedom. More crucial is his assessment of the relation between the great negative possibility that limits revolution and the possibility of a functional politics. Barth is persuaded that all those who have understood Romans 13 as a legitimization of legitimacy have completely misunderstood what was on Paul's mind. Paul is concerned with the power of the presence of Jesus to make all things new. And in chapter 13 he comes to the problem of the power by which the existing order exists and is changed. On this reckoning, the Establishment is not the problem, because the Establishment is already condemned. It is God's agent and has certain services and duties to which its energies are devoted. But the dialectic of legitimacy is that in confusing itself with the order of God it begets its own downfall (467).

Parenthetically, yet pointedly, Barth declares that "the law-and-order people (*Ordnungsmaenner*), who would like to strengthen their established position through existing institutional arrangements, are reminded that revolution is 'instituted' as the evil that is to direct them toward that which is good, so that without romanticism or self-justification, they might turn about and be law-and-order people no longer" (469). The dialectic of revolution, on the other hand, is that the revolutionary is always nearer to what God is doing in the world to make human life human but is imperiled by the temptation to mistake his own "no" to the existing order for the new order. The revolutionary is more vulnerable than the conservative to being overcome of evil, because with his negation he comes so very near to God (463–64). Evil is no answer to evil (464). For this reason, that is for the sake of the right in revolution, Barth follows Paul in drawing such a tight rein upon it.

Submission to the supreme authorities is as far removed from the divine justification of revolution in its usual political sense, as it is from the divine justification of existing authority in its usual political sense. Both Establishment and anti-Establishment confuse the order that the one seeks to preserve, the other to overthrow, with the new order of freedom to be human in the world that God has already inaugurated with the presence of Jesus Christ in the world. But—and here we come upon Barth's extension of the direction toward which Calvin's mind was moving—just because revolution is the lifestyle of truth, that is, nearer to what God is doing in the world, revolution is protected through submission against its own undoing and preserved for participation in the tentativeness that is the true stuff of politics. Says Barth:

> The constrictions (*Krampf*) of the revolutionary may then give away to quiet misgivings about what is "just" and "unjust," quiet, because *ultimate* affirmations and accusations are no longer pertinent, quiet, because a wise reckoning with "reality" (will have happened), a reckoning that has left the *hybris* (pride) of the war of the good against the evil behind, that (exhibits) an honest humanity and worldliness that know that wherever men risk their experiments, play their strange chess games, of uniting with or opposing other men, in state or church or society, they are not (enlisted) in the battle (*Gegensatz*) of the kingdom of God with Antichrist. Politics . . . become possible the moment the essentially gamelike character of these struggles (*Sache*) is exposed to the clear light of day in which it becomes obvious that there can be no talk about objective rightness, . . . in which the ring of absoluteness disappears from the claims and counterclaims, in order to make room for a perhaps relatively measured, perhaps relatively radical, disregard of all human possibilities.[42]

Thus the truth of revolution issues in the practice of love. On the boundary of submission to existing authorities, the power of the presence of Jesus Christ resolves the crisis of authority by liberating the exercise of power from the ambiguity of its own dominion. His presence on that boundary means that the confrontation between the revolutionary and the existing authorities will have exposed *their* point of no return, the fact that their day is done. Every show and use of the sword is the exercise of their appointed ministry brings them nearer to the dawn of their dispatch. For the revolutionary, meanwhile, the confrontation will have identified the point of the next advance, of the break-through of the shape of things to come. This is the point at which love effects the transfiguration of submission into the freedom to be and to stay human in the world. Love exalts the humanity of the neighbor above the cause that proclaims its advent, and transfigures the passion of revolution so that its promises may in truth be born. Love frees the revolution for the practice of the truth in its cause. Tom Wicker has put it this way, in what must surely be one of the major political understatements of the century. Writing about what he called "The Nightmare in Chicago," he noted certain "lessons for the future." "One of these lessons," he said, "is that a 'get-tough' policy is seldom sensible when great human issues are at the root of human unrest."[43] That such sensibility should elude existing authorities should occasion no surprise. They have their appointed end, and in the pursuit of their own undoing they meanwhile are God's agents for the good of the revolutionary. That such sensibility is always too little for the revolutionary is also not surprising. But it *is* regrettable. It is regrettable because it means that the revolutionary has hurried beyond the point of waiting for a rebirth of wonder toward the intensification of his own anxieties. It means that *Realpolitik* has hidden from him the reality of politics. In bypassing the presence in the confrontation the revolutionary has in Robespierre's phrase "missed the moment to found freedom."[44]

Thus *submission* to existing authorities is *not* the confusion of obedience to God with the acceptance of the status quo. It is the confrontation of the weakness of power with the power of weakness. In this confrontation, the fear of retribution has been overruled by conscience, that is, by the discernment that obedience to God and the practice of love for the neighbor are the twin safeguards against the fury by which revolution in the exercise of power begins to devour itself. With the weakness that shows itself as strength, revolution exhibits the fact that the humanizing purposes of God have already outrun the duties to which existing authorities, in God's service, devote their energies. In the power of this weakness, submission becomes the moment—not of obedient surrender but of obedient waiting.[45] In that waiting, the revolution manifests its sure and certain hope in its high calling to the freedom that being and staying human in the world takes. In that waiting, *submission* becomes the companion of *silence* in a politics of confrontation by which revolutionary anxieties disappear in a rebirth of wonder.

> I am waiting . . . [wrote Lawrence Ferlinghetti],/I am waiting for a re-birth of wonder./I am waiting for the age of anxiety to drop dead.[46]
> My Kingdom does not belong to this world [said Jesus of Nazareth]. If it did, my followers would be fighting to save me from arrest. . . . My kingly authority comes from elsewhere. . . . My task is to bear witness to the truth. For this was I born; for this I came into the world, and all who are not deaf to truth listen to my voice.[47]

B. UNMASKING POWER BY TRUTH: SILENCE—JOHN 18:33–40; 19:1–16

According to Paul of Tarsus, the implications of Jesus' messianic presence for the state and revolution are the exposure of the human reality of politics through a confrontation whose code word is: *submission*. We turn now to the author of the Fourth Gospel, who takes a further step in the exposure of the human reality of politics through a confrontation whose code word is: *silence*. The deepening darkness of the gospel before the fact and the problem of power in the world is dramatically heightened by the account of another nocturnal and fateful conversation in the story of revolution. The scene has shifted from Paris to Jerusalem. The conversation takes place, not between a king and his principal courtier, but between a Roman governor of a difficult and dissident province of an Empire and a prisoner whose condemnation to death by crucifixion the governor is anxious to avoid. In the story of revolution, the role of Louis XVI and the Duc de la Rochefoucauld-Liancourt has been anticipated by Pontius Pilate and Jesus of Nazareth. Once again, we face the juxtaposition that Jesus makes when dealing with power. It is the juxtaposition of the exercise of power and the refusal of power. The paradigm has been recorded in the Fourth Gospel, at chapter 18:33–40; and chapter 19:1–16. It reads as follows:

> Pilate then went back into his headquarters and summoned Jesus. "Are you the king of the Jews?" he asked. Jesus said, "Is that

your own idea, or have others suggested it to you?" "What! am I a Jew?" said Pilate. "Your own nation and their chief priests have brought you before me. What have you done?" Jesus replied, "My kingdom does not belong to this world. If it did, my followers would be fighting to save me from arrest by the Jews. My kingly authority comes from elsewhere." "You are a king, then?" said Pilate. Jesus answered, " 'King' is your word. My task is to bear witness to the truth. For this was I born; for this I came into the world, and all who are not deaf to truth listen to my voice." Pilate said, "What is truth?", and with those words went out again to the Jews. "For my part," he said, "I find no case against him. But you have a custom that I release one prisoner for you at Passover. Would you like me to release the king of the Jews?" Again the clamour rose: "Not him; we want Barabbas!" (Barabbas was a bandit.)

Pilate now took Jesus and had him flogged; and the soldiers plaited a crown of thorns and placed it on his head, and robed him in a purple cloak. Then time after time they came up to him, crying, "Hail King of the Jews!" and struck him on the face.

Once more Pilate came out and said to the Jews, "Here he is; I am bringing him out to let you know that I find no case against him"; and Jesus came out, wearing the crown of thorns and the purple cloak. "Behold the Man!" said Pilate. The chief priests and their henchmen saw him and shouted, "Crucify! crucify!" "Take him and crucify him yourselves," said Pilate; "for my part I find no case against him." The Jews answered, "We have a law; and by that law he ought to die, because he has claimed to be the Son of God."

When Pilate heard that, he was more afraid than ever, and going back into his headquarters he asked Jesus, "Where have you come from?" But Jesus gave him no answer. "Do you refuse to speak to me?" said Pilate. "Surely you know that I have authority to release you, and I have authority to crucify you?" "You would have no authority at all over me," Jesus replied, "if it had not been granted you from above; and therefore the deeper guilt lies with the man who handed me over to you."

From that moment Pilate tried hard to release him; but the Jews kept shouting, "If you let this man go, you are no friend to Caesar; any man who claims to be a king is defying Caesar." When

Pilate heard what they were saying, he brought Jesus out and took his seat on the tribunal at the place known as "The Pavement" ("Gabbatha" in the language of the Jews). It was the eve of Passover, about noon. Pilate said to the Jews, "Here is your king." They shouted, "Away with him! Away with him! Crucify him!" "Crucify your king?" said Pilate. "We have no king but Caesar," the Jews replied. Then at last, to satisfy them, he handed Jesus over to be crucified.

As we try to probe this paradigm for its bearing upon a politics of confrontation, we shall venture to draw upon the exegetical learning, care, and imagination of two of the most widely recognized New Testament scholars. In the light of what Adolf Schlatter and Rudolf Bultmann have written it may be noted that there are four aspects of power in operation that are underlined by the encounter between Pilate and Jesus.[48] The first of these aspects concerns the authority of power exposed by the question of the kingship of Jesus. A second concerns the relation between power and truth. A third aspect of the conversation underlines the radicality of the power confrontation. And the fourth focuses upon the enormous power of silence. Let us consider, in turn, each of these aspects of power in operation.

### 1. The Authority of Power and the Question of the Kingship of Jesus

The opening gambit of this paradigm of a politics of confrontation is Pilate's allusion to the kingship of Jesus. "Are you the king of the Jews?" he asks. In Bultmann's view, the question was unmotivated; i.e., it was not a ploy but a simple procedural inquiry that Pilate's office required of him.[49] Yet Pilate did put an official question. As such, the very matter-of-factness of his inquiry was operationally pivotal, not pointless. It carried the burden of the issue of the confrontation. Jesus had been brought up on a problematical view of kingship. The question whether kingship is instrumental to power whose authority lies elsewhere, or whether the authority of power is intrinsic to kingship, was exactly the ambiguity of kingship that Old Testament experience and memory had carried as far as the purposes of God himself. "In those days there was no king in Israel, and every man did as he pleased." So the book of Judges concludes (21:25 JB).[50] And when the monarchy was institutionally launched, the tension between the will of the people and the will of God is unmistakable. "When that day comes," Samuel warns at the instruction of Yahweh, "you will cry out on account of the king you have chosen for yourselves, but on that day God will not answer you. . . . Obey their voice and give them a king" (I Sam. 8:18, 22 JB).[51] Professor von Rad has remarked that "for Israel, the kingship was thus on the whole a new-comer, indeed, a latecomer. Accordingly, an almost immediate tension with fundamental traditions of faith, a tension which it (the kingship) never surmounted, could scarcely be avoided."[52] As for Pilate, the *pax Augusta* was scarcely a generation on its short-lived way toward its end, so that for him the kingship was axiomatically the bearer of the authority of power.[53] The kingship as an operational embodiment of a distinction between the exercise of power and the authority of power involved subtleties beyond his experience, and perhaps also beyond his grasp. Pilate's unwitting entanglement in these subtleties lends a tragic irony to the Johannine passage that can scarcely fall outside the author's literary intention.

The state best exhibits its disregard of the ambiguity of authority in the operation of power by regarding the self-evidence of kingship as the justification of kingship. Indeed, the dynamics are such that, the more self-evident the instrumentality of the state in the exercise of power is, the more self-evident is its authority. As Bultmann puts it: "The state knows kingship in a political sense only."[54] Nor is there—except for the "only"—any quarrel between Jesus and Pilate over the state and its operation. To venture an anachronism, Jesus is blameless, not least because he has carried out the injunction and the logic of Romans 13. He does not owe the state a thing! On the other hand, whether Bultmann is entirely right in declaring that the kingship of Jesus has *no* political character may be wondered about precisely because of that "only" to which his interpretation of our passage has already referred.

Indeed, this "only" exposes the paradigmatic significance of the presence of Jesus before Pilate. The politics of confrontation here exhibited concerns the relation between the exercise of power and the reality of power. The question is whether or not the reality of power points beyond itself to a source of power whose purposes shape the exercise of power. A politics of confrontation is defined by the eruption of the question: *By what or by whose authority power is power?* The dynamics of power are such that whenever the exercise of power becomes detached from the authentic purposes of power, a crisis of self-evidence arises. When this crisis of self-evidence reaches its moment of truth, a revolution happens. Revolutions mark those turning points in human affairs at which the gap between the validation of power by self-evident purposes and the exercise of power through self-justifying authorities and structures of power has passed beyond the point of no return. The point of no return is the moment of truth in disregard of which the exercise of power and the structures of power continue to function in falsehood. They do not correspond with reality: neither with the reality of the world in which power is a fact, nor with the reality of the purposes by which and for which both the world and power have been shaped.

Thus if the state knows kingship in a political sense *only*, its exercise of power is to be judged by the limits of its own understanding of power. This criterion means that the state validates power, and always in such a way as to justify itself in the use of its power. Clearly, power in a political sense *only* has transformed the meaning and function of politics from a human sense to a power sense *only*. In short, politics is, by definition, power politics. The meaning and point of the kingship of Jesus, however, is that politics involve ultimate purposes as well as penultimate authority. Consequently, the self-justification of power in and by the state is broken through by the power of a Presence who calls all power into question. In language suggested by the New Testament, the kingship of Jesus is an *eschatological* power reality. Its origin is elsewhere; and in the exercise of this power, Jesus exhibits a different power style.

## 2. The Relation Between Power and Truth

The rupture of the self-justification of power by the calling into question of all power, forces the use and validation of power back upon the question of the ultimate point and purpose of power. This is the question of truth. Thus the nocturnal conversation between Jesus and Pilate turns into a confrontation. In this confrontation, the ambiguity of power and the ambiguity of Presence are juxtaposed. The ambiguity of power is that power cannot of itself fulfill or justify itself. The ambiguity of Presence is that it is at once concretely *there* in the world of time and space and things and an invasion of that world from another world, the world of origin and destiny, of an originating purpose and a purposed fulfillment. With discrimination, at once subtle and deliberate, the author of the Fourth Gospel has conjoined in a double "for this," the unmistakable human presence of Jesus with a mythological (Bultmann) indication of the point and purpose of his presence. "*For this* was I born," says Jesus, "*for this* I came into the world . . ." (John 18:37; italics mine).[55] The point and purpose of the presence of Jesus *in the world*, and now before Pilate, are to bear witness to the truth, that is, "to make effective room for the reality of God over against the world in the great trial between God and the world."[56]

In order rightly to assess what is going on in this confrontation between Jesus and Pilate, we must keep in mind the particular sense of the word *truth, aletheia*, which the author of the Fourth Gospel had on his mind. It is not too much to say that *truth*, in the Fourth Gospel generally, and focally in the passage before us, is a word used in a *political* sense, not in a *theoretical* sense. It is a *participatory*, not a *speculative* word. It expresses a movement and a relation in which men are caught up and involved. It does not refer to a fundamental seeing into the being and reason underlying and shadowed in all that exists and is experienced. The range, depth, and import of this distinction are marked by the way in which the Gospel of John associates *truth* with *life* and with *faith*. Truth refers to the fundamental relation between God and the world, according to which God is distinct from the world, yet involved in it in a personal way. He brings the world to pass and to pass away. He sustains, renews, and fulfills the world in its coming to pass and in its passing away. He is the Giver of life and the shaper of purposes that guarantee to *life* an ultimacy that death cannot claim; to *hope* a certainty that what is coming to be is a surer sign of life's meaning than what is; and to *faith* the assurance that it makes sense to trust what faith knows in this life about this life and about the life of the world to come. So the word *God* properly refers to the Father of Jesus Christ, and with him and through him of all "who in his great mercy (have been given) new birth into a living hope by the resurrection of Jesus Christ from the dead" (I Pet. 1:3).[57] "In him all fatherhood in heaven and in earth is named" (Eph. 3:14 RSV), and he has made men "fit to share the heritage of God's people in the realm of light" (Col. 1:12).

The Fourth Gospel shares in this chorus of God's reality and Fatherhood; and of humanity's filial and human, human and filial (the reciprocity is fundamental and ultimately inescapable) participation in it. But in the Fourth Gospel the accents are sharp and they converge upon the moment of truth. "God's *aletheia* (truth) is thus God's reality which alone is reality because this reality is life and gives life. The seeming reality of the world is *pseudos* (pseudo) because it is pretentious (*angemasste*) reality in opposition to God and as such is really nothing (*nichtig*) and brings death. The promise of the knowledge of the truth (*aletheia*) is thus substantively identical with the promise of life (*zoe*)."[58] The moment of truth (and life) is the presence of Jesus of Nazareth in the human story, and the power launched by his presence to discern the difference between reality and pseudo-reality, between truth and falsehood, between life and death.

Congruent with God's gift of truth and life to man in the world is his gift of faith and knowledge. The participatory character of man's involvement through Jesus in the truth-life syndrome is forcefully underlined by the use of the participial forms of believing and knowing by the author of the Fourth Gospel. Believing in Jesus is no blind acceptance of a dogma. Instead it is the illumination of human existence in genuine self-understanding that follows from acknowledgment of God as creator, Father, and life-giver. Conversely, this self-understanding is truth-oriented life because, in and through this understanding, man is set free from his perennial care about his life and free for the actual living of it. As Bultmann puts it: "The precise characterization of believing (*Glauben, pisteuein*) shows itself as a *life-style* (*Haltung*) that abandons the previous self-understanding of man, and knowing (*ginoskei*) shows itself as nothing other than as a structural moment of believing (*Glauben, pisteuein*) itself, insofar as believing understands itself."[59]

The political thrust of this participial "lifestyle" is exposed in the confrontation between Jesus and Pilate. The question of the Establishment is up; the question whose world this is, and by what or whose authority. It is understandable that Pilate should have asked Jesus, "Where have you come from?" When Jesus refuses to answer, Pilate moves to a more pointed cross-examination. "Do you refuse to speak to me? Surely you know that I have authority to release you and I have authority to crucify you." On the identity question, Jesus is silent. To the authority question, he makes a matter-of-fact reply. "You would have no authority at all over me if it had not been granted you from above. Therefore the deeper guilt lies with the man who handed me over to you" (John 19:11).[60] Both questions presuppose the gulf between Jesus and Pilate over the question of truth. Pilate's honest perplexity about truth was revealed in his puzzlement that power should require truth if it sought to command authority.

Pilate was a realist whose chain-of-command conception of power made it impossible for him to understand the lifestyle of Jesus. Confronted by the lifestyle of Jesus, however, the worldly realism of Pilate is exposed as pseudo-realism. Pilate is unable, either by conviction or by role, to exhibit the unity of truth and power and authority. When power is divorced from truth, authority loses its integrity. When truth is divorced from power, the exercise of power is doomed to self-defeat because power can function only under the spurious authority of self-justification and falsehood.

Jesus, on the other hand, affirms, both by conviction and by role, that the only authority power has is the authority of truth.

He exposes the issues of life and death, where truth comes to light. In so doing, he sets the initiatives straight. Jesus could have avoided the confrontation with Pilate by not going to Jerusalem at all. But he went because the moment of truth had arrived. As the writer of the Fourth Gospel puts it: "Jesus knew that his hour had come . . ." (John 13:1). In that moment of truth, "the Prince of this world" takes over; and as Jesus goes to his crucifixion, the "Prince of this world" stands condemned (John 14:30 av).

Exactly in line with Romans 13, the Establishment goes on "doing its thing." As God's agent working for good, the Establishment both checkmates the devil and is on its way out. In that moment of truth, it becomes clear that it is not he who challenges the Establishment who has provoked the confrontation but the Establishment itself. "Therefore the deeper guilt lies with the man who handed me over to you," said Jesus, (John 19:11). This is why a revolutionary lifestyle is always more apt to have truth on its side than are established patterns of thought and ways of doing things when they come under the challenge of a revolutionary lifestyle. Yet if the Establishment is exposed to the self-deception of supposing that the revolutionary has provoked the confrontation, the revolutionary is exposed to the self-deception of supposing that crucifixion is a program rather than a price to be paid for making time and space make room for being human in the world.

Nevertheless, the kinship between Jesus and the revolutionary is rooted in their common sensitivity to the boundary between the realism of a politics of the power of truth and the pseudo-realism of a politics whose power has lost its claim to truth. The confrontation between Jesus and Pilate underscores the great gulf between *political realism* and *Realpolitik*. *Realpolitik* is politics with the accent upon the primacy of power over truth. *Political realism* is politics with the accent upon the primacy of truth over power. *Realpolitik* increasingly succumbs to the temptation of confusing immediate goals and gains with ultimate outcomes and options and seeks validation by increasingly dubious authority. *Political realism,* on the other hand, involves an increasing struggle against the temptation to overcome irrelevance through premature ventures to close the gap between the ultimate and the immediate, thus overdrawing on the truth in its power. Ever and again, the successors of Jesus have sought to convert the moment of truth exposed by his presence into a blend of political realism and power politics (Caesaro-papism, theocracy, sectarian withdrawal) that seeks to effect the triumph of Jesus over the "Prince of this world" in this world. Meanwhile, the successors of Pilate follow him in opting for the view that the state can have no interest in truth, i.e., in radical reality. In so doing, they convert the moment of truth exposed by the presence of Jesus into a politics of power that disregards the real and exalts the possible as necessary.

In the course of human events, the darkness of the gospel gets very dark indeed. For the truth is that Jesus is the truth! He is the truth primally and primarily in a political sense; consequently and correlatively in a theoretical or philosophical sense. But this truth can be exposed only by confrontation and practiced by appropriation. It cannot be imposed by concordats of conformity that make orthodoxy the test of loyalty or policy, and heresy interchangeable with treason. Disciples are the true citizens; but discipleship is no criterion of citizenship. This, in addition to the particular circumstances amidst which he wrote, is why Dietrich Bonhoeffer could conclude: "Treason had become true patriotism and the normal love of country had become treason."[61] How dark can the light get, when truth can only inform policy, never make it; when truth can function conformatively only, never transformatively?[62] Truth of this order plainly lies so deeply beneath the general will as to be unable either to surface as the consent of the governed or to forge a social contract. Truth of this order is plainly irrelevant to politics. Pilate's skepticism is sustained by the power realities of political life. "What is truth?"[63]

But if, in Christopher Fry's phrase, "the dark is light enough," it is because "the light shines on in the dark, and the darkness has never mastered it."[64] Pilate could neither ignore Jesus nor do away with him. He could neither ignore the ultimate questions nor answer them. So he put all the right questions: "Where have you come from?" "What is truth?" "Surely you know that I have authority . . . ?" "Then, at last, to satisfy them, he handed Jesus over to be crucified" (19:16). The confrontation between Jesus

and Pilate has come full circle. We are back at the point of no
return at which the moment of truth is being overtaken by events.
The moment had arrived to be taken up. Instead, it was passed
up. The question of truth that initially erupted from perplexity
submerged again in a cynical evasion that left the decisive responsibility to others. In a world defined by God's reality, Pilate's action
involved in effect a commitment to falsehood. And Jesus and the
revolutionaries are together again. Their kinship on the boundary
between *political realism* and *Realpolitik* is nourished by the shared
convictions that all politics involve hidden or open commitments,
and that there is one commitment, above all others, that is the
decisive response to reality.

The concern of the revolutionary with making time and space
make room for freedom is the authentic sign of the human reality
of politics. The sign is authentic because the revolutionary, although
he is no freer of the temptation to self-justifying power than are
"the existing authorities," as we have seen, is nevertheless nearer
to the center and direction of God's purposes for human life in
and for the world. That the making and keeping of human life
human is what God is mainly up to in the world are the point and
the meaning of the presence of Jesus of Nazareth in the world.
When Jesus tells Pilate that his "kingdom does not belong to this
world," and that his "task is to bear witness to the truth"
(18:36–37), he does not wish to be understood as leaving the
world to its own devices while pursuing totally otherworldly expectations. Instead, as Adolf Schlatter has finely noted, "Jesus
describes himself as sovereign lord, and the territory over which
he exercises his sovereign power is humanity without exception
. . . That the truth has a witness who stands up for the truth with
word and deed, in life and death, is the vocation given to Jesus
by his birth and his entrance into humanity, and from this his royal
power is derived."[65] So Jesus, to borrow a current idiom, "tells it
like it is" because he knows "where it's at"! He "puts his body
on the line and his mouth where the action is!" So, too, everyone
who knows "where it's at," "tells it like it is." "All who are not
deaf to truth listen to my voice" (18:38)! They do not need to
fight to save the truth and its bearer from arrest. They are simply

called to be where the action is. They know "what the score is." "The score" is that at the moment of truth the power that shows itself as strength is overcome by the power that shows itself as weakness. The weakness of power is that when power is confronted by the authority of truth, it is no match for the power of weakness that bears the mark of truth.

## 3. The Radicality of the Power Confrontation

The Johannine paradigm now reaches its climax. The probing irony is tense with the imminence of an ultimate judgment. It is as though the world had been brought, by the fury of humanity, to the brink of an explosion either into light and life or into deep and destructive darkness from which there is no escape. The confrontation between a calm and confident Jesus, with the inexorable momentum of reality on his side, and an uneasy and tormented Pilate, ineluctably entrapped in pseudo-reality, is joined head-on. With consummate, dramatic artistry, the Fourth Evangelist has drawn "the whole human running race"[66] into the orbit of his proleptic version of A.D. 1984 and 2001 combined. The lines are drawn between the truth that sets men free in the power to be human in the world, and the power that subverts its divine appointment for the ordering of righteousness into the disorderly erosion of the humanity of humankind through the maintenance of law and order.

> Once more Pilate came out and said to the Jews, "Here he is; I am bringing him out to let you know that I find no case against him"; and Jesus came out, wearing the crown of thorns and the purple cloak. . . . The Jews answered, "We have a law; and by that law he ought to die, because he has claimed to be the Son of God." . . . "If you let this man go, you are no friend to Caesar; any man who claims to be a king is defying Caesar." . . . Then at last, to satisfy them, he handed Jesus over to be crucified. (19:4, 5, 7, 12, 16)

Bultmann has noted the parallelism in the text of this paradigm between the "truth-power passage (18:33–37) and the "state-power" passage just cited. He then goes on to say:

> The content of Jesus' conversation with Pilate (i.e., in 18:33–

37) concerns the relation between the power of the state and the power of God. The aim is to make clear that the authority of the state, as grounded in God, stands over against the world; that the authority of the state does not belong to the world and thus the state can and should act independently of the world; and consequently, that the implementation of policy by the state (*der Vollzug des staatlichen Handelns*) confronts an either/or: God or World? The responsible representative of the state can be open for God as readily as to the world. Openness for God—this would mean for the state as such nothing other than a simple sobriety (*schlichte Sachlichkeit*) about the responsibility for justice (*Recht*). Pilate chose to be neutral as regards the claim of Jesus, and he could do this from the perspective of the state because the state as such cannot be required to acknowledge revelation. Pilate's neutrality would have been instrumental to justice (*waere im Recht*), if it were no more than the implementation of the impersonal nature (*Sachlichkeit*) of the office. It was obvious, however, that such a sober adherence to the nature of the office would mean a decision against the world. Thus, it was no less obvious that this adherence would have required openness for God. *An unchristian state is basically possible; but not an atheistic one.* The question whether Pilate would have the strength for a decision against the world, should he refuse to acknowledge the Revealer, thus repeats itself in the form of the question whether he would be open to the claim of God given in his office, if he personally refuses the claim of Jesus? . . .

Pilate understands Jesus' word. The hint at the divine origin of his *exousia* (authority) through the mouth of a Jesus surrounded by an atmosphere of the uncanny (*des Unheimlichen*) can only increase the anxiety before the presence of this mysterious presence (*dieser raetselhaften Gestalt*). Pilate wanted to release Jesus. But his "lifestyle" (*Haltung*) . . . was ambivalent. The fear of the world and the fear of the mysterious (*dem Unheimlichen*) are in conflict. Which will be victorious?[67]

The victory belongs to him who knows the reality and the secret of the royal power of humanity. Truth, power, authority, justice, converge upon the presence of Jesus, in whom the priority of God and the humanity of man are met. To paraphrase Robespierre: "At stake is the grandeur of man against the pseudonomy of the great."[68] What power does with, for, and to the humanity of man is the sign of whether God and the world are on a collision course or whether they are conjoined in the reconciling, liberating, and fulfilling enterprise of humanization in this world and in the next. The presence and power of Jesus of Nazareth in our history have made and continue to make the humanity of man the criterion of power and authority. The humanity of man is the operational sign of the truth at work in the world, making time and space make room for freedom.

*"Idou ho anthropos!" "Ide ho basileus hymōn!"* ("Here is the man!" "Here is your king!" (John 19:5, 14).[69] Or as Luther, with his uncanny literary sensitivity to the idiomatic, on the way to the colloquial without becoming trivial, has put it: "Look! What a *man*! . . . Look! This is your *king*!"[70] The royal trappings worn by Jesus, viz., the crown of thorns and the purple cloak (but not insignificantly perhaps minus the mock-scepter cane), are patently a mockery of Jesus' royal pretensions and a ridicule of his weakness masquerading as strength.[71] How undangerous can any human being get! "In fact, it is just such a man who claims to be the king of truth! The *ho logos sarx egeneto* has become visible in its most extreme consequences."[72] Jesus, on the other hand, at the apex of defenselessness, and all but at the nadir of helplessness, dramatically reverses the field. His silent presence turns the unmasking devised by his accusers and his judge against itself. It is *they* who stand before the world unmasked. God's "man of the ages" is on location as the "man for others" whose being "here" is the release into the world, from its Creator and Life-giver, of the reality and the power of authentic humanity.[73] " 'Here he is; I am bringing him out to let you know that I find no case against him'; and Jesus came out, wearing the crown of thorns and the purple cloak" (19:4, 5). "Here is your king!" (19:14).

The record notes that Pilate's first indication of "who's who and what's what" was uttered outside, across the threshold of his headquarters. "Here he is! . . . Here is the man!" The second indication of identity and reality, however, is more specific. Place and time are given. Pilate "took his seat on the tribunal at the place known as 'the Pavement'. . . ." "It was the eve of the Passover, about noon" (19:14). Pilate mounts the tribunal. The decision can no longer be postponed. Normally, he would have been seated on the tribunal throughout the whole trial. But this was a different case. Different indeed! Temporizing with a decision that he could not ultimately avoid, Pilate is caught up in the intensifying pressure of reality upon identity, and, in a sense both literal and ultimate, *finally* takes his seat upon the tribunal and lets the verdict fall. Caught between Jesus and Caesar, he plays both ends against the middle, and writes the state's own epitaph—and his. " 'Here is your king!' . . . Then, at last, he handed Jesus over to be crucified" (19:14–16). The ironical exposure of "who's who and what's what" means that the king handed over to be crucified heralds the appointed end of the state on its appointed way.

The clamor for law and order proved to be no formula for preventing crime in the streets. It managed to give Caesar a victory over Christ. But it was a pyrrhic victory. The Establishment would, of course, go on for several centuries; and after its collapse there would be other Establishments to grasp its pseudo-scepter. In the succession of Caesar, however, there was "no exit" from a fatal flaw. Missing was a "logos of power" adequate for "creative politics."[74] The breakthrough of authentic humanity as the criterion of power effected by the presence of Jesus could no more be turned back than the darkness could put out the light. "It was the eve of the Passover, about noon." The Jewish festival of deliverance was about to begin. The "road from Exodus to Easter"[75] was on the nearer edge of its symbolic culmination.

This time a world-shaking and a world-making happening was underway. "As the festival commemorating Israel's historical liberation through an act of God begins, the guilt of the people condemns exactly him to death in whom God is bringing to pass the eschatological liberation of the world."[76] Perhaps the most awesome thing about the imminent crucifixion was—and is—the ambiguity hidden in its inevitability. Jesus, like Pilate, was on his way to his appointed end. But whereas Pilate's exercise of power was caught in the vise of inevitability and the will-to-power, Jesus' refusal of power was caught in the vise of inevitability and the will-to-death of the people of destiny. Pilate's reluctant acceptance of the unavoidable is the final irony of the exercise of power, the strength of which is weakness. The people's passionate pressure to make the unavoidable *happen* is the ultimate pathos in a refusal of power, the weakness of which is its strength. Like Nietzsche's tightrope walker,[77] Jesus goes down before established power, which he must oppose, *and* the fury of the people of destiny whose destiny he has come to affirm and whose fury he has come to abate.

In willing the death of their deliverer, the death-wish of the people of destiny embraces the whole of humankind in the immolation of the power to be fulfilled. This power of the presence of the deliverer is always at once beyond their reach and within their grasp. The Establishment is always arrayed against the people of destiny because its responsibility for law and order is always corrupted by its will-to-power. The Establishment yields reluctantly to change because it lacks the passion for deliverance. It looks for no deliverance beyond itself. The revolutionary, on the other hand, is always joined with the people of destiny both in their passion for deliverance and in their rejection of the deliverance that is already in their midst. The revolutionary hurries past the moment of freedom because he fails to discern the patience for freedom required by the fury of his own impatience. So the immolation continues.

Jesus is victimized both by self-justifying self-righteousness and by self-justifying fanaticism. His presence is *there*, the talisman of freedom both from witch-hunts and from scapegoats, from the evasion both of responsibility and of guilt. But instead of taking up this freedom, the Establishment succumbs to the "Jezebel-syndrome," which immolates the future in the name of the past; and the revolutionary succumbs to the "Samson syndrome," which immolates the past in the name of the future.[78] So Jesus is handed over to be crucified; and "in his body on the tree" he bears the scars of the Messiah and of Azazel, of the "Anointed of Yahweh" who is the "Son of Man" and of the guilt-ridden animal that the people have driven from their midst.[79] "Look! What a man! . . . Look! This is your king!" "*Philanthropia* (love, as respect for man as man) was a mark of Roman politics. For those opposed to Jesus, however, humane consideration carried no weight. They

were fighting for the honor of God that has been violated by anyone who calls himself the Son of God. There is no safeguard
(*Schonung*) for man when God's justice (*Recht*) has been disregarded. This safety Jesus did not even seek."[80]

## 4. The Power of Silence

Unlike Socrates, who had to be reminded by his jailor to stop
talking so that the hemlock might take its unimpeded course, Jesus
does not say a word.[81] The recognition of the Presence, whose
power liberates as it binds and binds as it liberates, cannot be
assisted by speaking. The Fourth Gospel recounts an earlier question concerning Jesus' identity, which suggests that those who have
not caught on to what is going on from his words and deeds will
not be persuaded by a clearly expressed self-identification. Another
festival was in progress. Walking on a winter's day, in Solomon's
Portico in Jerusalem, those among his own people who sought a
case against him "gathered round him and asked: 'How long must
you keep us in suspense? If you are the Messiah say so plainly.'
'I have told you,' said Jesus, 'but you do not believe. My deeds
done in my Father's name are my credentials, but because you
are not sheep of my flock you do not believe. My own sheep listen
to my voice; I know them and they follow me. . . .' " (John
10:22–27). Much, much later in the human story, the line between
self-identification and self-incrimination was to be drawn in constitutional law. But this development, valuable as it is in setting
limits to the malice in man's inhumanity to man, is fundamentally
significant as a measure of the widening gap between self-identification and self-incrimination, and of the enormous power of silence
in making room for the "shock of recognition."

On trial for narrowing the gap between his identity and his words
and deeds—between "who's who and what's what"—Jesus demon-
strates that neither proclamation nor declamation, but only silence
can redeem the time so that participation in the power of his Presence marks the beginning of participation in the truth that sets
men free. The freedom of and in this truth is the power to be who
you are where you are. The corollary, of course, is that the power
of falsehood, of the lie, can neither be persuaded nor convinced.[82]

The truth in confrontation with the lie!—this is fundamentally why, as already noted, hypocrisy, not crime, is the mortal sin for revolutionaries.[83] When hypocrisy is practiced as a social ploy or a social policy,[84] the crucifixion of truth by power has begun to happen and the hatred of the world for the presence and power of Jesus is headed for the countdown. The humiliation of the truth is the ultimate sign of the contempt of the world for what it takes to make and to keep human life human. "In its hatred against revelation, the world is on the way to surrendering its hope which, despite its enmity against God, informs its innermost depths. The indication of these depths is the perhaps unavowed yet ineradicable awareness (*in dem vielleicht uneingestandenen, aber doch nicht vertilgbaren Wissen*) of its insufficiency, its impermanence, its lack. of fulfillment. When the world suffocates this awareness and deliberately cuts off its hope, the world makes of itself an inferno."[85]

The prospects and the power for authentic humanity thus presuppose an ultimate commitment. The commitment is an affirmation of, and involvement in, the messianic reality, dynamics, and direction of the truth. The confrontation between Jesus and Pilate culminates in silence because, as Schlatter has remarked, "when man sets out to investigate the participation of Jesus in God (*den Anteil Jesu an Gott*) and to subordinate this participation to man's evaluation of it, the witness to the truth can only keep silent."[86] This silence means that the decision between life and death, good and evil, between a future of human fulfillment as against a future of human disintegration and destruction, can no longer be postponed. Hesitation is already a rejection of messianic reality and its humanizing lifestyle.

> No proclamation of God's activity and sovereignty, however powerful; no declaration concerning the mission of Jesus, however meaningful (*inhaltsreich*), could take the place of the meaning that the phrase "the Anointed One" had for the Jews. With this designation, the prophetic promise became for the first time unambiguously and concretely present (*unzweideutig in die Gegenwart hineingestellt*). This is why the messianic Name was so decisive. Had Jesus articulated that Name, he would have confronted the Jewish people and all mankind with the claim

(*Forderung*) for unlimited obedience through which everything would have been given into his hands.[87]

When the confrontation between Jesus and Pilate reached its moment of truth, its maximum radicalization, the Name had been hidden in the Presence; the Word had been wrapped in silence. But the inexorability of an unconditional commitment remained. Hidden in that unobtrusive claim was the discovery that obedience is the highway of freedom.

So the code word uncovered by this paradigm of a politics of confrontation is: *Silence!* The silence of Jesus is the sign that the end is the beginning of a new and humanizing order of human affairs (*novus ordo saeculorum*). The boundary between confrontation and crucifixion, between the acceptance and the rejection of an unconditional commitment to Jesus' messianic lifestyle, comes into view whenever and wherever the passion for freedom and a new beginning and a new order of human affairs has been paralyzed by a dehumanizing conflict between power and truth. When power crucifies truth, it signals to all the world that it has come to its effective end. When truth confronts the power to crucify with the power of silence, it passes beyond the rhetoric of liberation and signals to all the world the appointed rightness in a revolutionary lifestyle that only silence can express. It is almost as though Paul Simon had sent "The Sound of Silence" straight into our present from Pilate's own headquarters on that night when confrontation turned out to be the prelude to crucifixion.

> "Fools!" said I, "You do not know
> Silence like a cancer grows.
> Hear my words that I might teach you,
> Take my arms that I might reach you."
>
> But my words like silent raindrops fell
> And echoed in the wells of silence.
>
> And the people bowed and prayed
> To the neon gods they made;
> And the sign flashed out its warning
> In the words that it was forming
> And the sign said, "The words of the Prophets are

> written on the subway walls and tenement halls
> And whispered in the sounds of silence."[88]

Mighty Babylon's Nebuchadnezzar could not read the graffiti either, but Daniel could.[89] Daniel was not consumed by the fire, but dissolution reduced to "a pitiful helpless giant,"[90] the mightiest power in the world, whose king and whose armies could not face the humiliation of defeat in the power of the truth that alone makes men free and human life human in the world.

The prophets and the poets and the graffiti writers are on the move.[91] Talk about football and surfing will not do.[92] The young have seen visions while the old dream no dream because they cannot sleep at night. Sometimes the graffiti could be read on a G.I.'s helmet as he jumped from a helicopter under enemy fire in Cambodia: "We are the unwilling, led by the unqualified, doing the unnecessary, for the ungrateful."[93] Sometimes the graffiti can be read in the agony and shame and humiliation of people reclaiming their humanity along a hot and dusty road going from Augusta to Atlanta. "Our actions," they say, "will determine whether America lives as a democracy or whether Rapp Brown is right—that you must burn it down and hope to build a new nation. America needs only to be true to what you've got on paper."[94] Sometimes the graffiti can be read in the blood on a college campus where sullen and armed law and order rifles the silence of incredulous and bewildered standers-by.

> "I wasn't particularly interested in throwing rocks or anything like that," Lucia said. "But I was very much against what he did in Cambodia, and I was hoping the rally would produce something, you know, really true. . . . I saw the men firing, and I saw the kids fall, and they looked out over the crowd and there were people carrying, you know, people with blood all over them, downhill and I just couldn't believe it. . . . There's no way to describe the pain that I saw in people's faces or in their voices.[95]

Verily, it seems that, as Auden has lately put it:

> In states unable
> To alleviate Distress
> Discontent is hanged.[96]

Pilate may have been the first to run headlong into the impregnable conjunction of revolution with truth, for which Jesus lived and died, and rose again, but he has not been the last to discover it. Robert Bly has tellingly brought us back into Pilate's world and face to face with his predicament, with his inability to make the ultimate commitment and consequent missing of the moment to found freedom. "Romans Angry About the Inner World" is Bly's way of putting Pilate's world and our world together, and of "telling it like it is":

> What shall the world do with its children?
> There are lives the executives
> Know nothing of.
>
> .   .   .   .   .   .   .   .   .   .   .   .   .
>
> The other world is like a thorn
> In the ear of a tiny beast!
> The fingers of the executives are too thick
> To pull it out!
> It is like a jagged stone
> Flying toward them out of the darkness.[97]

*Silence* thus joins with *submission* as the *ultima ratio* of a Christian involvement in the dynamics, the aim, and the strategy of revolutionary happenings. Silence and submission are the twin signs of a politics of confrontation that have arrived at the moment of truth and life. For the revolutionary, this means encounter with a Presence whose power sets the revolution free for the providential, prophetic, and human rightness of its occasion and purpose and free from the self-justifying self-vindication that obstructs what God is doing in the world to make time and space make room for freedom. For the revolutionary, this means the surrender of fanaticism to reconciliation in the discerning confidence that his hopes have already begun to take human shape in his time and place, and that no Establishment can put his hopes to shame.

For existing authorities, this means the acceptance of the judgment that has come upon them through the revolutionary in the discerning confidence that their time has come, and that the measure of faithfulness is their being reconciled to being the Establishment no longer. ". . . To shame the wise, God has chosen what the world counts folly, and to shame what is strong, God has chosen what the world counts weakness. He has chosen things low and contemptible, mere nothings, to overthrow the existing order. And so there is no place for human pride in the presence of God" (I Cor. 1:27–30). The *ultima ratio* of submission and silence is their power to expose the weakness of power before the power of weakness. Such an exercise of power in the refusal of power turns, as it were, the flank of established power in the power of a Presence who binds as he liberates and liberates as he binds. There *are* lives the executives know nothing of. The other world is like a jagged stone flying toward them out of the darkness.

By a kind of *descensus ad inferos*,[98] we have been probing the darkness of the gospel in face of the dynamics and use of power in the world. From the bottom of that descent into the pit, Joseph was once destined to ascend from darkness into light and to turn the flank of power.[99] At the center, falling apart as the "ceremony of innocence" was being drowned, Jesus once wrestled all night and sweat great drops of blood, only to rise to face his crucifixion with the power of forgiveness on his lips and the imminent finish of the drama of humanization on its way (Luke 22:39–46). If, in Christopher Fry's phrase, "the dark is light enough," it may be added, from the bottom of that darkness, it is what you see that makes the difference. At the bottom of that darkness, confrontation is discernible as the threshold of transfiguration. Here the obvious unfitness of the Gospel for dealing with the centrality and ambiguity of power in human affairs shows itself as the hidden fitness of the Gospel for dealing with the reality of power. The power of the Gospel is its indication of a Presence who sets power free from its own crisis of authority and free for a Center that begins to hold.

The Gospel is no more for Christians *only* than only Christians are revolutionaries. Perhaps, however, Christians are the ultimately real revolutionaries because their ultimate commitment commits them to keeping revolution and truth and life effectively together. Christians have glimpsed in the darkness of the Gospel the illuminating confidence that "freedom *for* revolutionary action can be bound up in faith with freedom *from* the coercion of revolutionary action. . . . Perhaps they are something like the fools of revolution.

... (But) where this spirit of freedom reigns, ... there the revolution within the revolution can take place, the deliverance of revolution from the alienating forms which it assumes in the struggle."[100] If Che Guevara is right that "the vocation of every lover is to bring about revolution," the Christian is he who has discerned that "the vocation of every revolution is to bring about love."[101]

# PART THREE

# A POLITICS OF TRANSFIGURATION

## CHAPTER 6

# TRANSFIGURATION AND POLITICS

The vocational conjunction of revolution and love involves an ultimate perspective and direction for the operation of power in human affairs. The phrase "a politics of transfiguration" is designed as a rubric under which some attempt to identify and to describe this perspective and direction may be undertaken. Sooner or later, the revolutionary dynamics of humanization reach a crucial divide between the futility and the freedom of power in the achievement of revolutionary promises and purposes. At this point, the fate of revolution threatens inexorably to deprive it of a future; and the future of revolution requires a power through which the fate of revolution may be broken and revolutionary promises and purposes be liberated for a politics of humanization.

Admittedly, the attempt to link the word *transfiguration* with the word *politics* requires some explanation. The association is neither familiar nor obvious. If there is a common referent to which these words point, it seems difficult to come by, and more likely to be either trivial or contrived. If what is at stake is some power move beyond the fate of revolution, and toward a future for revolution, why not speak of a "transformation" of power; or, as Reinhold Niebuhr taught many of us to say, of a "transvaluation" of power?[1] A change in the form of power (transformation) expresses

a marked shift from the "old" to the "new," from the "familiar" to
the "different," in the kind of power used and in the uses to which
a different kind of power is put. *A transvaluation of power* expresses a shift in the kind and use of power at once more urgent
and more dialectical than is suggested by the phrase *transformation
of power*. Options are no longer as simply or as pragmatically
determinable as a change from one kind of power to another, from
one use of power to another, implies. There is an immediacy and
decisiveness, as well as an inescapable concreteness about the experience of power: its application, its consequences and possibilities, which require a markedly altered perspective and purpose in
the assessment and the use of power.

Transvaluation means the turning of an accepted value inside
out, so that its ordinary sense undergoes a fundamental inversion,
owing to a thrust and claim at the very center of a human relation.
Applied to power, for example, when the solution to a conflict
between nations is sought by negotiation instead of by military
might, a transformation of power has occurred. Similiarly, when,
in industrial relations, arbitration displaces a lockout or a strike, a
transformation of power has occurred. On the other hand, when
the hatred of an enemy is displaced by the practice of love toward
him, an inversion or transvaluation of values has occurred. Similarly, when, as in the case of the Catonsville Nine,[2] the records of
a draft board are stolen and burned, the inviolability of property
in human relations is turned inside out and undergoes a fundamental inversion, owing to the inviolability of the human claim upon
it. The inviolability of this claim is anchored in a way of looking
at life and of living it according to which the involability of property
inheres not in itself but adheres to its human function.

The human function of property, in turn, is validated by a different order of valuation. This is an order according to which the
ultimate destiny and purposefulness of the world require the making over and making new of whatever retards or prevents the
humanization of human life. Such an inversion sharply raises the
question whose world this is, and by whose authority. It makes
irrelevant the concern that property thus violated will be denied
its proper due and safeguard. On the contrary, such an inversion

has crossed the line between morality and religion through what Kierkegaard called "a teleological suspension of the ethical."[3] An action has become a happening—not generalizable but testimonial; not pragmatic but symbolic. A transvaluation of values has occurred.

When, however, as in the case of the 20 July 1943 assassination attempt against the life and power of Adolf Hitler, a conspiracy involving killing goes into action, a transfiguration of power has occurred. The assassination attempt, whether it fails, as in this case, or whether it succeeds, exposes a turning point in the course of human events. On the farther side of such a turning point, actions once ordered and valued in one way acquire a different perspective, purpose, and significance even though the principal factors in the action are similar and familiar. Thus, in like manner, the disorderly behavior in Judge Julius Hoffman's courtroom, during the trial of the Chicago Eight, culminating in the gagging of the Black Panther leader Bobby Seale, exposes a transfiguration of the relations between injustice and justice, in, with, and under the familiar canons of judicial procedure.[4] It is scarcely likely that Chief Justice Warren Burger's appeal for civility in the courts, in the course of an address nearly two years later, had no relation to this celebrated trial.[5] Whether merely coincidental or merely implied, the Chief Justice's admonitions on civility document a transfiguration under way in the human meaning, function, responsibility, and practice of law.

Patently, the Chief Justice thought that breaches of civility had been committed by the attorneys for the defense. Contrariwise, the attorneys for the defense and their clients thought that civility had already taken flight from justice in the enactment of the law under which they were being called to show cause why punishment should not be meted out. These differences of judgment are variables in a highly controversial situation. But they are only indirectly related to the question of the fundamental relation, if any, between civility and justice and the proceedings in Judge Hoffman's courtroom on the one hand, and transfiguration on the other. We venture to suggest that there was indeed such a relation.

The basic issue being fought over and fought out in that courtroom was the human reality and meaning of justice in relation to law. The Chief Justice's solemn soliloquy on civility rightly noted the rising incidence of incivility in courtroom decorum. But instead of bringing the magisterial wisdom and responsibility intrinsic to the Presidency of the Supreme Tribunal of this Republic to bear upon the fundamental human reality to which the question of civility points, the Chief Justice chose to take moral flight above the pain and passion of mounting courtroom disorders, and to lecture his professional colleagues upon courtroom manners. In this context, the preservation of civility means the preservation of an order of urbanity in judicial process. But the human reality of this same judicial process exhibits a deepening tension between the *urbane* and the *urban* and an intensifying struggle to achieve an authentic relation between justice and law, and thus a genuinely civil order.

In a genuinely civil order, civility means the pursuit of justice under law through the practice of law under justice. A transfiguration has occurred. In this quite specific case and trial, and in the Chief Justice's failure of insight, fundamental human issues of life and death, justice and injustice, truth and falsehood, liberation and oppression, were, and are, decisively at stake. A breaking out of old and dehumanizing confinements in the direction of liberating possibilities for a civility struggling to take humanizing shape is going on. A reversal of priorities in the judicial ordering of human affairs has reached its moment of truth and its point of no return. Transfiguration means the ingression of "things that are not" into the "things that are,"[6] so that man may come abreast of God's next move in giving human shape to human life. "God is the beyond in the midst of our life."[7] And justice is being transfigured in the courts. No longer is justice to be understood or sought for as a function of law. Instead, law has become a function of justice.

Transfiguration connotes a radicalization of transvaluation as transvaluation connotes a radicalization of transformation. The common referent of all three words and happenings is in the kind of power used and the purposes to which such uses are put. The change in the kind of power used may be as marked as the difference between a bullet and a ballot, a strike and a fast. The change in the uses of power may be as marked as the difference between victory and accommodation, tactics and balance, challenge and surrender, in a conflict of power. The purposes toward which the uses of power are put may differ as markedly as the differences between "a continuation of policy by other means"[8] and a dramatic confrontation of oppression at long last become humanly intolerable; between the prevention of a loss of power and the taking over of power long overdue. The dynamics of power are such that the rate and range of social change ever and again reach a point of intensity that breaches the limits of tolerance[9] and erupts in a sharp juxtaposition of systemic and revolutionary power, of an established order as against a new order in human affairs (a *novus ordo saeculorum*).[10] The line is drawn between a self-justifying perpetuation of power at the service of the established order of things and a revolutionary use of power for the liberation of man for human fulfillment.

The radicalization of power signaled by its movement from transformation to transvaluation to transfiguration is the sign that the operation of power has arrived at its moment of truth. At such a moment the dynamics of power and the human reality and purpose of power correspond. This correspondence is the threshold of transfiguration on which the presence of Jesus of Nazareth in the human story floods the darkness of the gospel and the fateful futility of power with "the light of revelation—the revelation of the glory of God . . . ,"[11] that is with the panorama and the promise of what God in his God-ness is up to with and for man in the world. To return to the Corinthian letter,

> it may be that we are beside ourselves, but it is for God; if we are in our right mind, it is for you. For the love of Christ leaves us no choice, when once we have concluded that one man died for all and therefore all mankind has died. His purpose in dying for all was that men, while still in life, should cease to live for themselves, and should live for him who for their sake died and was raised to life. With us therefore worldly standards have ceased to count in our estimate of any man; even if once they counted in our understanding of Christ, they do so now no longer. When anyone is united to Christ, there is a new world; the old order has gone, and a new order has already begun. (II Cor. 5:13–17)

There is, in short, a politics of transfiguration. Sooner or later, the dynamics of power drive politics across the crucial divide between the futility and the freedom of power where a revolutionary radicalization of power signals a transfiguration under way. The transfiguration under way is the confrontation of politics in a more or less familiar sense with the possibility and power of making room for freedom in so unfamiliar a sense as to take nothing less than a *metabasis eis allo genos* (a totally other foundation for things), to begin to move from rhetoric to action, from the possession of power to the practice of love "where the action is." Transfiguration means that Rousseau's circle has been squared.[12]

CHAPTER 7

# THE TRANSFIGURATION OF JESUS AS A
# POLITICAL PARADIGM: MATTHEW 17:1–8

The perspective and direction for the operation of power identified by the word *transfiguration* presuppose as well as implement the gospel. The fact is that the present venture upon a "politics of transfiguration" was suggested to us by another New Testament paradigm of hitherto unsuspected pertinence to the significance of Jesus Christ for the question of revolution. The text is given in the first eight verses of the seventeenth chapter of the Gospel according to Matthew. It reads as follows:

> Six days later Jesus took Peter, James, and John the brother of James, and led them up a high mountain where they were alone; and in their presence he was transfigured; his face shone like the sun, and his clothes became white as the light. And they saw Moses and Elijah appear, conversing with him Then Peter spoke: "Lord," he said, "how good it is that we are here! If you wish it, I will make three shelters here, one for you, one for Moses, and one for Elijah." While he was still speaking, a bright cloud suddenly overshadowed them, and a voice called from the cloud: "This is my Son, my Beloved, on whom my favor rests; listen to him." At the sound of the voice the disciples fell on their faces in terror. Jesus then came up to them, touched them,

and said, "Stand up; do not be afraid." And when they raised
their eyes they saw no one, but only Jesus.[13]

## A. JESUS TRANSFIGURED: BREAKING IN AND BREAKING UP
## THE ESTABLISHMENT

"And in their presence he was transfigured" (v. 2). The Greek
text says: "*kai metamorphōthe emprosthen autōn.*" We are confronted here with a breakthrough happening with the seal of reality
upon it. It is adumbrated already at the frontier of language. In
Hellenistic usage, the word *metamorphousthai* ("to be changed";
and variants) often referred to the fundamental transformation of
a body that came about owing to its release from confinement to
matter. More specifically, the word not infrequently denoted a rebirth of body and soul, i.e., of a person on the way to deification.[14]
In New Testament usage, however, *metamorphousthai,* in a strong
phrase of Johannes Behm's, "has nothing to do with Hellenism."[15]
The force of the word is apocalyptic. It denotes the radical changes
imminent in the world owing to a sudden foretaste of the long-
promised and long-expected new world to come. Jesus—"was
transfigured (changed)." And "in their presence"! The force of
the phrase "in their presence" (*emprosthen autōn*), both in Matthew and Mark, as well as the use of the words *to horama* (v. 9) in
Matthew and *eidon* in Mark (9:8), and *ophthe* in both (v. 3; Mark
9:4), underline the intention of the Evangelists to stress the objectivity of what was going on.[16] Here was no merely subjective experience, an interior vision, devoid of external focus. On the
contrary, here was a happening, pulling past, present, and future
together, conjoining history and hope, decisions-in-the-making and
the making of decisions, in the immediate confrontation of a commanding Presence with an inescapable present. What is going on
is the pressure of the end-time upon times rapidly coming to an end.
The messianic dynamics of reality, concretely human and humanly
concrete in an experienced story of covenant, exodus, advent,
crucifixion, and parousia, is on the nearer edge of the exposure of
its "messianic secret." At stake are the revolutionary character of
reality and the reality of the revolutionary response to this reality,

in a world once lived and died in by Jesus of Nazareth, the Christ, and over which he still presides.

It could be argued against this paradigmatic reading of the Transfiguration pericope that its significance has been vastly over-stated in view of the conspicuous inattention to it for most of the church's history. In the Eastern Church, the Transfiguration takes its place as an annual Feast Day,[17] and there are occasional comments on the text in Tertullian, Origen and Chrysostom.[18] But in the literature of the Apostolic Fathers and of the second-century Apologists, the Transfiguration seems to be altogether ignored. Indeed, not until the nineteenth century was serious interpretive attention given to the Transfiguration; and then the accent fell upon the plausibility of the happening in the light of current canons of philosophical and literary interpretation. If the early Church found it possible to subordinate the Transfiguration to its preoccupation with the Baptism, Passion, and Resurrection of Jesus, the nine-teenth-century interpreters found it possible to subordinate the Transfiguration to physical, e.g., atmospheric, psychological, and literary perspectives and findings. This line of interpretation still persists; and in our own day, no less an authority than Rudolf Bultmann disposes of the pericope of the Transfiguration as a legend, compounded of a resurrection story, of Exodus 24, and of heavenly figures, later named Moses and Elijah "possibly to certify the Messiahship of Jesus."[19]

Nevertheless, we venture to underline the importance of the account of the Transfiguration in the gospels for the understanding both of the significance of the presence of Jesus Christ in the human story, as the Evangelists stress it, and of the significance of that presence for the question of revolution. In doing so, we set out from a point common to the preoccupation of the early Church with Jesus' Baptism, Passion, and Resurrection and to the critical residue of scholarly biblical interpretation since the nineteenth century. The common point concerns the human and historical reality of Jesus' Messiahship. Here—in the crucible of messianic identity, function, and destiny—Jesus' relations to God and to man, to Israel and to the church, to principalities and powers and to new and fulfilling times and seasons of creativity and consummation,

converge. The Transfiguration unlocks the messianic secret and un-
covers a strategy of discipleship, e.g., of commitment, involvement,
and expectation, in a world whose time has come, and in the midst
of which a new and human God-man world is on its way.

There is a very considerable agreement among the Synoptic
authors in their accounts of the Transfiguration. The sequence runs
as follows: (1) a specific time reference; (2) the choice of three
disciples: Peter, James, and John; (3) the ascent of the mountain;
(4) the Transfiguration of Jesus; (5) the appearance of Moses
and Elijah; (6) Peter's suggestion that three shelters (tabernacles
or booths) be set up; (7) the overshadowing cloud; (8) the voice
from the cloud; (9) Jesus is seen alone.[20] Of no little further importance to the understanding of what is going on is the agreement
among the Evangelists about the setting of the account. Mark and
Matthew place it between the confession of Messiahship at Caesarea
Philippi and the Passover confrontation in Jerusalem. En route,
Jesus converses with his disciples, mainly about sufferings that are
to come for him, and by implication also for them. Although Luke
makes no mention of Caesarea Philippi as the locale of the confession, he does note the discussion about Jesus' messiahship, and
amplifies the discussion about suffering to come with Kingdom and
conflict parables, and with an account of the "mission of the
seventy." *The New English Bible* correctly and strikingly groups
this material under the heading: "Journeys and encounters" (Luke
9–18:30); "Growing tension" (Mark 7–10:31). Thus the Transfiguration occurs in the Synoptic accounts as a kind of dramatic
mid-point between the imminent exposure—one might almost say,
explosion—of the messianic secret and the imminence of a messianic exodus. It is as though the whole history of Israel had gone
into a sudden inversion. The protracted journey from Exodus to
Advent had suddenly come full circle in a prodromal crisis of Advent and Exodus.[21]

Only the most casual and exterior reading of the gospel accounts
of the Transfiguration and its setting could fail of being drawn into
the mounting tension of time running out as the narrative moves
from Jesus' scarcely veiled self-identification, elicited from his
disciples in a confession of messiahship, through conflict, challenge,

confrontation, to crucifixion. The time is indeed at hand! The question of the Establishment is up for overturn in a radical shift of perspective and direction, and a consequent revision of priorities about "who's who and what's what." The question Whose world is this and by whose and what authority? is heading for the countdown and a liftoff in a blinding light of shattering presence and power after which the world never can and never will be the same again. A transfiguration—in this case, *the* Transfiguration—has happened! And neither history nor nature, society nor culture, nor man himself will be experienced as before, for they will not *be* as before. In the Transfiguration of Jesus of Nazareth, the Christ, the politics of God has transfigured the politics of man. "And in their presence he was transfigured; his face shone like the sun, and his clothes became white as the light" (v. 2). Or as Mark with characteristic concreteness observes: "with a whiteness no bleacher on earth could equal" (Mark 9:3).[22]

In that light, the mystery and meaning of the ultimate presence and power by which reality *is*, and is defined and directed, are unveiled and concealed in the hiddenness and openness of a human person whose presence and power set the whole off-course world and human story on course again. An interpenetration of presence and power has occurred. The Maker, Sustainer, Reconciler, Redeemer, and Fulfiller of heaven and earth, and of all things visible and invisible, has come awesomely and transformingly near the turmoil and travail of the human story: its sin and suffering, its exploitation and enmity, its promise and possiblity, its forgiveness and fulfillment. And in the imminence of this divine presence and participation, a human presence and pioneer are released, with the power of a liberating and fulfilling lifestyle for "the whole human running race." Thus Luther, with his notable genius for identifying what the dynamics of a world that is God's, since God's in the world, add up to, declares:

> All this is aimed at proclaiming this man Jesus and at believing him throughout the whole world, that he is true God and man, true son of God and man, true son of God and son of Man, true Christ and King, Priest and Lord, promised from the Father in

the Holy Spirit through the law (Moses) and the prophets (Elijah), that healing (*Heil*) and life should be in him only and alone, and that all things should be in his hands because he is the son and heir. . . . *The whole Trinity (Dreieinigkeit) is here manifest for the strengthening of all the faithful:* Christ, the Son in his glory, the Father in the voice which declares the Son to be Lord and heir, the Holy Spirit in the shining cloud or in the generating (*Einfloessen*) of faith.[23]

## B. MOSES AND ELIJAH: TRANSFIGURATION MOTIFS

"And they saw Moses and Elijah appear, conversing with him." (v. 3). Upon Moses and Elijah converge what we may now describe as the two formative motifs of the Transfiguration paradigm. One of these motifs is the heaven-earth-glory theme; the other is the messiah-suffering-vindication theme. The first is the reality theme; the second is the redemption theme. The first is the presence (or truth) theme; the second is the power (or life) theme. The convergence of these two motifs and their variants upon Moses and Elijah and their conversation with Jesus on the mountain underlines the revolutionary political thrust at the core of the accounts of the Transfiguration. When Jesus Christ runs headlong into the question of revolution and the question of revolution runs headlong into Jesus Christ, both faith and politics undergo a transfiguration that makes faith inseparable from politics and politics inseparable from faith. Religious faith, then, becomes a stance more central and sobering than creedal assent, liturgical repetition, or private belief or personal trust. It becomes involvement, with heart and mind and soul and strength, in and with a formative way of looking at life and of living it. This is what Dietrich Bonhoeffer's well-known, but perhaps less than well-understood, aphorism *really* is getting at: "Only he who believes is obedient, and only he who is obedient believes."[24] Politics too undergo a transfiguration. They become more than "the art of . . . directing rationally the irrationalities of men," as Reinhold Niebuhr once succinctly declared.[25]

Politics are still, as Niebuhr declared in an early work, "an area where conscience and power meet, where the ethical and coercive factors of human life will interpenetrate and work out their tentative and uneasy compromises."[26] They are still "the study of the form of the political community that is the best of all forms for a people able to pursue the most ideal mode of life" (Aristotle). Politics are still the "science of the polis" of what it takes to make time and space make room for freedom.[27] But when the "things that are" undergo the ingression of "the things that are not," politics are transfigured.[28] They are a response of analysis and action to the pressure of reality upon human power arrangements making room for God's freedom for man to be human in this world and the next.

On that "high mountain" where Jesus was transfigured, Moses and Elijah are the bearers of this ingression. Only Luke tells us what the conversation was about. It concerned the imminent exodus and vindication of Jesus. They "spoke of this departure, the destiny he was to fulfill in Jerusalem" (9:31). This accords with Mark's assignment of priority to Elijah over Moses in the dynamics of what was going on, as well as with his concern to underline the difference between Jesus' interlocutors and Jesus himself. When Mark tells us that "they saw Elijah appear, and Moses with him . . ." (9:4) and that, on the way down from the mountain, Jesus implicitly identifies Elijah with the murdered John the Baptist,[29] he all but lets the messianic secret out in a marked break with Jewish Elijah-belief and in a sharply drawn power line between Jesus and the Establishment. What *they* did to John, *they* are already conspiring to do to Jesus. And *they* will do it.

> The stress on Elijah's presence at the transfiguration shows that the fulfillment of "all things" (9:12) is no longer merely imminent but has arrived. The transfiguration is, as it were, the vestibule of the passion, and Elijah is present to testify to the final importance of impending events. And with him is Moses, the representative of the old covenant and the promises, now shortly to be fulfilled in the death of Jesus.[30]

So Elijah is John the Baptist and Jesus is Elijah.

Correlative with this messianic line into the exodus sequence is the other side of the coin. Mark also takes account of the heaven-earth-glory theme, the reality theme adumbrated in that conversation on the mountain. Jesus is not only *like* Elijah and Moses; he is also *different* from them. Jesus not only joins them in the accelerating tempo of the wrap-up of the old age and the unwrapping of the new age; but, unlike them, he is already in control of the new order of things and at the work of clearing the old order out of the way and getting the new order under way. It has been noticed that there is a certain parallelism between Mark's account of the Resurrection and his account of the Transfiguration.[31] Indeed, Mark seems deliberately to associate the transfigured and the risen Christ. The glory with which the Transfiguration exalts Jesus is the form he was believed to possess from the moment of the Resurrection, and in which he was thought to have revealed himself to his disciples. Thus, for Mark, "the Transfiguration (is) the prefigurement of the Resurrection."[32]

In this context, a significant difference between Jesus, on the one hand, and Elijah and Moses, on the other, comes into view. Whereas Elijah and, according to a variant Jewish tradition, also Moses, did not die but were translated to heaven, Jesus did die and was raised from the dead. He is thus a greater figure than either Elijah or Moses.[33] "In Mark's hands, the Elijah expectation is radicalized and transformed even while the old framework is preserved."[34] Calvin finds a hint of this radicalization also in Matthew, although Matthew did not pause over the distinction between translation and resurrection. Calvin says:

> Moses and Elijah did not then rise on their own account, but in order to wait upon Christ. . . . I have no doubt whatever that Christ intended to show that he was not dragged unwillingly to death, but that he came forward of his own accord, to offer to the Father the sacrifice of obedience. The disciples were not made aware of this till Christ rose; nor was it even necessary that, at the very moment of his death, they should perceive the divine power of Christ, so as to acknowledge it to be victorious on the Cross; but the instruction which they now received was intended to be useful at a future period both to themselves and to us, that no man might take offense at the weakness of Christ, as if it were by force and necessity that he suffered.[35]

Although Mark reverses Matthew's order by introducing Elijah before Moses into the conversation with Jesus on the mountain, he reverts to the usual order in the report of Peter's estimate of what was going on. Matthew's point is that Moses and Elijah are there as bearers of the Law and the Prophets toward the fulfillment about to break in with Jesus' challenge to the Establishment, and in his inauguration of a new and human order of things. The point lies in its attribution of roles, not in its central thrust, if one also takes due account of the possibility that the Law and the Prophets are both focused upon Moses, whereas Elijah is mentioned as the eschato-logical restorer of all things.[36] Here the redemption (messianic) theme and the ressurrection (reality) theme intersect. In either case, the Law and the Prophets, identified by Moses and Elijah, identify the context and the conditions of Israel's and through Israel of all mankind's, participation in the humanizing activity of God in the world. The context was a pattern of relationships, freely offered and freely taken up in election and covenant, in calling and commitment to the foundational, liberating, and fulfilling purposes for which the world was purposed. In that context, law expressed the dynamics and the direction of the divine will toward boundaries of freely accepted limits within which the practice of humanness was certain to become "a thing of beauty and a joy forever." In that context, the Prophets, from Moses to Elijah, from the Lawgiver to the Law-fulfiller, were the divinely appointed guardians of the righteousness of God in action. "In the Old Testament," says von Rad, "there is no concept (*Begriff*) of such absolutely central significance for all the relationships of human life as is that of the *tsedaqah* (righteousness)."[37]

Von Rad goes on to remark that there has been a long-standing theological misinterpretation of the Old Testament meaning of righteousness, owing to an ingrained habit in Western thought, which searches for "an absolute idea of righteousness" that func-tions as "an absolute ethical norm." The search is foredoomed to fruitlessness because there is no such idea, no such norm, in Old Testament experience and thought. On the contrary, righteousness is a relational term that refers to the social reciprocities in which man acts, which actually function in a directional way, and at the same time in very diverse ways. The key relationship, determinative of the meaning of righteousness, is "the relationship of fellowship that Jahweh has offered Israel and that was principally nurtured in the cult. Here, too, reciprocity is called for: righteous is he who is right with the particular claims that this fellowship-relation with Jahweh makes upon him. . . . Jahweh's righteousness was no norm, but deeds, and really demonstrations of salvation."[38] The righteousness of God, then, means God's presence in the midst of his people, as help and salvation.[39] So when Matthew tells us that Moses and Elijah are the conversation partners of Jesus on the Mount of Transfiguration, he affirms that with Jesus of Nazareth a new Moses has come, that the prophetic guardianship and lifestyle have begun to take human shape in human life, that the practice of love is the fulfillment of the Law and the Prophets, and that the concrete focus of the practice of love is righteousness.[40]

## C. THE VOICE FROM THE CLOUD: POLITICAL MESSIANISM OR MESSIANIC POLITICS

There is one further point to be made about the paradigmatic significance of the Transfiguration for politics. It emerges from Peter's vocalization of the awesome experience of those who were caught up in that dazzling interpenetration of presences and could not hear a word. And it seems to have been confirmed by the identifying voice from the cloud, declaring that there could no longer be any doubt about "who's who and what's what."

> Then Peter spoke: "Lord," he said, "how good it is that we are here! If you wish it, I will make three shelters here, one for you, one for Moses, and one for Elijah." While he was still speaking, a bright cloud suddenly overshadowed them, and a voice called from the cloud: "This is my Son, my Beloved, on whom my favour rests; listen to him." At the sound of the voice the disciples fell on their faces in terror. Jesus then came up to them, touched them, and said, "Stand up; do not be afraid." And when they raised their eyes they saw no one, but only Jesus. (vv. 4–8)

Peter's understandable desire to hold things fast was a mistaken assessment of the dynamics unloosed "when heaven tries earth if it be in tune," with no warm ear, softly overlaid, but instead, with a ringing declaration that "the ax is laid to the roots of the trees," that the moment of truth has arrived in Jesus' human and destined embodiment of the righteousness of God.[41] Baltensweiler's declaration that "the rejection of political messiahship is the essential meaning of the Transfiguration" makes the right point with dubious reasons.[42] It is not necessary to take up the belief that Elijah's role as eschatological restorer would find him completely changed in character, a mild and gentle figure instead of the firebrand who taunted the priests of Baal. There is a readier intratextual clue to the political thrust of the Transfiguration pericope. The dating does it, as Baltensweiler himself has also pointed out.[43] The phrase "six days later," with which the pericope begins, strikingly correlates with the Feast of Tabernacles (or Booths, or Shelters, as the NEB gives it) at which the rites of the seventh day tended to arouse hopes of national deliverance that God would soon bring to pass by inaugurating an age in which the Law would be gladly and fully observed. Moses' presence in the conversation, as well as Peter's proposal to build the shelters, point in the same direction. If this be allowed, the crucial question arises: Why did Jesus go up the mountain instead of to the city to celebrate the Feast?

This question has already been partly answered by the convergence of the resurrection and redemption themes in the dazzling light of transfigurement. Since the annual observance of the Feast of Tabernacles (Sukkoth) kept alive the expectation that God would once again dwell with his people in tabernacles, or booths, as he had in the Exodus wanderings, Jesus' own keeping of the Feast on the mountain seems designed by the Evangelists to underline the imminence of the end-time through his own imminent exodus. Yet, if this were all, the Synoptic authors would seem to have ill-protected themselves against the awkward possibility of leaving Jesus, and Peter, James, and John on that mountain, with an exposed left flank. While the Zealots were doing their organizational best with a bid for political messianism in Jerusalem, Jesus and his disciples simply withdrew to the top of a mountain. Although the move was scarcely "East Village," it would have been more than scarcely "Qumran-ish."[44] Indeed, between membership in Qumran and membership in the Zealot political party, Jesus is having a bit of a time of it these days, with his "associations for purposes of identification only."[45]

The historical question eludes verification beyond a doubt. Yet in view of the concurrence of two competent New Testament scholars, such as Brandon and Cullmann, that there were unmistakable affinities between Jesus and the Zealots, we may discount Qumran and face the political question head-on. Jesus' stricture against violent men who seek by violence to seize the kingdom of heaven may have been directed against the Zealots (Matt. 11:12). But then, as surely, his warning not to seek after the Messiah by running off into the wilderness may be taken as more than a hint of his hesitations toward Qumran (Matt. 24:23–27). The minimal facts seem to be that Jesus' sympathies were largely with the Zealots, that some of his disciples were Zealot sympathizers, perhaps even members, and that Jesus was accused and condemned to death because he was suspected of fomenting and planning a Zealot revolt.[46] ". . . Jesus found himself in a certain sense close to the Zealots—as also to the Pharisees. There was for him a Zealotist temptation."[47] At the Feast of Tabernacles, he resisted this temptation and went to the mountain instead. Why did he do this?

Brandon has once more, and rightly, shattered a still too widely held Jesus stereotype. If Jesus was no demagogue (Renan), neither was he a bearded Horatio Alger, after the manner of that highly heretical, almost blasphemous, *Head of Christ* by Sallman, which hangs *ad nauseam* in church parlors and educational buildings across the United States. The "gentle Jesus, meek and mild" is as alien to the gospels, as he ought to be, but still is not, to the piety and sensibility of the Christian chuch. The "pacifist" Jesus is not the Jesus of the New Testament, including the writers of the gospels, even (*contra* Brandon) Mark. He is certainly not the Jesus who was transfigured. On the contrary, the Jesus who went up the mountain, rather than into Jerusalem, is the Jesus for whom Zealotism was a cause—and a temptation—; but still a cause. The cause was zeal for, and dedication to the imminent arrival of the kingdom of God, the rule of God in and over human societies in this world, and according to the expectations and conditions set out by Moses and the prophets. The temptation was the confusion of God's initiative with man's, the outrunning of God's patience by man's eagerness, the substitution for God's time of man's timetable. Programs neither capture nor fulfill the promises of God. Baltensweiler's reading of the Transfiguration as an emphatic rejection of political messianism not only finds support from a formidable consensus of New Testament scholarship but faithfully accords with the politics of confrontation that we have been exploring in these pages.[48] Thus one answer to the question why Jesus avoided Jerusalem on the Feast of Tabernacles is that he wished clearly to dissociate himself from Zealotist passions and practices.

But is this the whole answer? I think not; and principally because the pericope of the Transfiguration includes a paradigmatic political thrust. Not only does Jesus not stay on the mountain but before the descent, his disciples have to come to terms with "only Jesus," and with his injunction, in the power of his divinely attested messianic presence and errand in the world. "This is my Son, my Beloved, on whom by favour rests; listen to him. . . . Stand up; do not be afraid" (vv. 6–7). The battle with the Establishment is being neither circumvented nor concluded. Instead, it is being joined. There is a difference between *political messianism* and *messianic politics*.[49] There is a difference between the foreshortening of the eschatological radicalism of Jesus' messianic presence and power in and over the world and the faithful adherence to his radical relativization "of all realities in this world" (Cullmann) until a truly God-man shape of things coming to pass has moved from promise and possibility to experienced happening. There is a difference between the seizure of power by force in order to establish a new order and the unyielding pressure upon established power, already under judgment for its default of order, in response to the power already ordering all things in a new and humanizing way.

This power is the authentic *force-majeure* that carries revolutionary promises to victory over revolutionary perils. It shatters all surrogates, however divinely sanctioned or fanatically masked as *forces-humaines* they may be. Cullmann rightly rejects the simplistic alternative according to which Jesus must be either a revolutionary or a defender of existing institutions. There is a dialectical complexity in Jesus' thinking derived "from his expectation of the end."[50] But then Cullmann appears to espouse an oversimplification of his own by resting Jesus' case against the Zealots upon the link between Jesus' expectation of the end and the rejection of force. ". . . The *love of one's enemy* which he Jesus required in the name of the kingdom of God," Cullmann writes, "places him beyond the warring political forces. He excludes every use of force as it was preached by the Zealots."[51] Then he goes on to repeat the ethically time-worn and threadbare distinction between goals and means. On the basis of Jesus' teaching and example, the Christian "is to work together with them (i.e., with 'worldly,' non-Christian groups) where he shares their goals and methods. But . . . he will dare to give a decisive 'No' where goals are pursued and methods employed which are contrary to the gospel."[52]

If we have rightly understood the political thrust of the Transfiguration pericope, particularly as it concludes, it may be suggested that both goals and means belong to the complexity of that eschatological radicalism that emerged for Jesus from his single-minded obedience to the kingdom of God and to his role in its inauguration. Consequently, Jesus was and remained a truly radical revolutionary. He never was a defender of existing institutions. His invitation to discipleship included the fearless standing up in acknowledgment of his messianic Sonship to God, in "condemnation of legalism, hypocrisy and injustice" (Cullmann), and in the rejection of force "as the Zealots preached it." But it seems to us to go beyond both the New Testament record and the relativization to which Jesus' eschatological radicalism led him, to conclude that the use of force has no place in Jesus' purview or in the messianic politics in which he engaged and bids his disciples to engage.

The "one important point" at which Cullmann expressly considers "a translation . . . as plainly impossible" is the very point at which the Transfiguration pericope points to the transfiguration of the political messianism of the Zealots into the messianic politics of Jesus. "It is certain," writes Cullmann, that Jesus did not reckon with the continuation of the world for centuries."[53] On the contrary, Jesus reckoned with the imminence of the new order of God to which the revolutionaries of his day aspired. The violent use of force in such a context would have signaled a loss of confidence in God's action and a disobedient repudiation of Moses and the prophets. Since the world obviously has continued for centuries, where does that leave us? With the conversion of the heart? And with the ultimately stultifying or frustrating distinction between goals and methods? Certainly with no less than these! But just possibly also with much more than these: with a politics of transfiguration that still involves us in the responsibility to "listen to him . . . my Son, . . . on whom my favour rests"; who, "in their presence . . . was transfigured" (vv. 5, 3). With the dynamics and the implications of such a politics of transfiguration, we shall need to reckon before we conclude these reflections.

Meanwhile, we shall have to attend, however briefly, to the revolutionary goings on, which, on the surface at least, make our world even more distinct from Jesus than did his own apparent failure to reckon with the centuries. It might just be that in that mountain conversation in the dazzling light, Moses and Elijah were on top of the whole timing affair in a way that commentators have hitherto failed to notice. "Six days later" signaled a seventh day as different from an occasion for a national uprising against the world's then most intransigeant Establishment as was Jesus' zealot-oriented refusal to celebrate the Feast. In the brightness of that light, the world was being made all over again, and an invitation was being heralded abroad to join in a new celebration of the Sabbath when God looked upon everything that he had made and called it "Good!" and the whole human running race shouted in reply: "It is very good indeed!" The old creation transfigured in and by the new creation prefigures the Sabbath launched in the exodus of the Christ. The descent from the mountain meanwhile takes us from the time spent with him into the times he spends with us. Turning from the account of the Transfiguration into the revolutionary turmoil in which we are, there is a sustaining discovery at our disposal made available by John Calvin as he turned toward the account of the Transfiguration from where he was. He declared:

> We know the truth of the common proverb that to one in expectation even speed looks like delay; but never does it hold

more true, than when we are told to wait for our salvation till the *coming* of Christ. To support his disciples in the meantime, our Lord holds out to them, for confirmation, an intermediate period; as much as to say, "If it seem too long to wait for the day of my coming, I will provide against this in good time; for before you come to die, you will see with your eyes that kingdom of God, of which I bid you entertain a confident hope."[54]

CHAPTER 8

# REVOLUTION AS TRANSFIGURATION

In the literature of revolution the word *transfiguration* can scarcely be said to appear with notable or even noticeable frequency. The gap between transfiguration and revolution thus seems as great as the gap between transfiguration and politics. If, in the immediately foregoing pages, we have managed to narrow the distance between politics and transfiguration, should we not be content and forbear the still more problematical attempt to narrow the distance between revolution and transfiguration? The question is spared a disavowal as rhetorical by a curious double coincidence. The co-incidence may expose nothing so much as the patent folly of the whole course of the argument upon which we have embarked. On the other hand, "in a world where nothing is as it seems," as Alice was to learn about Wonderland, we may, as did she, come quite coincidentally to some discoveries of our own, of the secrets and senses of the goings-on around us into which we seem increasingly to have fallen without prospect of egress. A part of what Alice found "Through the Looking-Glass" concerned her encounter with the Red Queen in "the Garden of Live Flowers." The Queen and Alice had been running faster and faster for quite some time, 'til suddenly, just as Alice was getting quite exhausted, they stopped, and she found herself sitting on the ground, breathless and giddy.

The queen propped her up against a tree, and said kindly, "You may rest a little, now."

Alice looked round her in great surprise. "Why I do believe we've been under this tree the whole time! Everything's just as it was!"

"Of course it is," said the Queen. "What would you have it?"

"Well, in *our* country," said Alice, still panting a little, "you'd generally get to somewhere else—if you ran very fast for a long time as we've been doing."

"A slow sort of country!" said the Queen. "Now, *here*, you see, it takes all the running *you* can do, to keep in the same place. If you want to get to somewhere else, you must run at least twice as fast as that."[55]

On 6 August 1945, a bomb carrying a nuclear warhead was dropped upon the Japanese city of Hiroshima. In a blinding flash of light, "with a whiteness no bleacher on earth could equal" (Mark 9:3), the face of earth and sky were so profoundly and radically changed, not only so as never to be the same again, but so as to make the destruction of that city the point of departure for the blazing of a trail either of darkness and death or of life and light for the whole of mankind, perhaps even of the world itself. A transfiguration of presence and power, of reality and redemption, had happened, which signaled that the operation of power in human affairs had reached a point of no return. Its moment of truth had arrived in the imminence, urgency, and inescapability of an ultimate perspective and direction for power according to which the dynamics of power and the human reality and purpose of power correspond. Politics in a more or less familiar sense had run headlong into the possibility and power of making room for freedom in so unfamiliar a sense as to take nothing less than a totally other foundation and style, for moving from rhetoric to action, from the possession of power to the practice of love "where the action is." A power revolution had revolutionized the purpose, possibilities, and possession of power in the world.

No longer could the "principalities and powers" (RSV), "the authorities and potentates of this dark world" (NEB), or even "the superhuman forces of evil in the heavens" (NEB; Eph. 6:12–13), prevent or temporize with the breaking out of old and dehumanizing confinements in the direction of new, untried, and liberating possibilities for giving human shape to human life. Phoenixlike, from the ashes of the "age of humanity," the revolution of humanity was rising up to take its place. Yet it may scarcely be gainsaid that no one (or almost no one) in the bodies politic of the world, or even among the churchmen of the world, and least of all President Truman and his political and military advisers, was aware that 6 August 1945 was the day of the Feast of Transfiguration.

This is the first coincidence. The second has to do with the coincidental use of the word *transfiguration* in the literature dealing with revolution. We have come upon but a single instance. The usage in point clearly seems more inadvertent than deliberate. Yet this very inadvertence goes to the core of the dynamics of revolutionary aspiration and action. Consider the following passage from Crane Brinton's masterful analysis of *The Anatomy of Revolution*. He writes:

> Men may revolt partly or even mainly because they are indeed hindered, or, to use Dr. George Pettee's expressive word, *cramped*, in their economic activities; but to the world—and, save for a very few hypocrites, also to themselves—they must appear *wronged*. "Cramp" must undergo moral transfiguration before men will revolt. Revolutions cannot do without the word "justice" and the sentiments it arouses.[56]

Brinton does not pause over the phrase *moral transfiguration*. In the light of the medical analogy of a fever, to which his painstaking effort to achieve the objectivity of scientific method in the description of a sociohistorical phenomenon has led, such a phrase seems strangely out of key and to call for an elucidation, however brief. On the other hand, the absence of elucidation inadvertently suggests that the story of revolution as a whole is to be understood as a documentation of transfiguration. Revolutions, as we have already noted, happen; they are not made.[57] They happen because, sooner or later, revolutions cannot do without justice. They cannot do without justice because, sooner or later, "cramped" is experienced as "wronged"; "wronged" is experienced as "injustice"; and "injustice" is experienced as dehumanization. Just as a fever signals that the health of the body can no longer be ignored but must be remedied, so revolutions signal that the health of society can no longer be deferred but must be set right. The "moral transfiguration" that engenders revolution is the conversion of the social and power conditions under which men live to the human and humanizing purposes for which these conditions were designed. The single use of this phrase in Brinton's brilliant analysis of the "anatomy of revolution," with its studied avoidance of philosophical, ethical, and theological evaluations, suggests a kind of "freudian slip" that brings the phenomenological and the human meaning of revolution together.

The chink in the armor of this resolute pursuit of a *vis medicatrix naturae,* with its equally resolute rejection both of God and Freud, is its inadvertent allusion to the congruence of the dynamics of revolution with a politics of transfiguration.[58] The distance between "cramped" and "wronged," between economic hindrances because of which "men *may* revolt" and "moral transfiguration" that men must undergo before they "*will revolt,*" is paralleled by the distance between Hiroshima and the Feast of Transfiguration in the revolutionary ferment of our present "time of troubles" (Toynbee). The double coincidence into which our present concerns have stumbled underlines, without intending to do so, the conjunction of reality and redemption, of presence and power, of truth and life, in the struggle of men to be, become, and end up as human beings in the world. It suggests the fundamental sense in which the dynamics of revoluton and the dynamics of transfiguration are reciprocal. The power revolution unveiled in the destruction of Hiroshima on the Feast of Transfiguration is congruent with the moral transfiguration of human affairs unveiled in the revolutionary struggle to humanize the possession, the uses, and the purposes of power. President John A. Mackay of Princeton Theological Seminary was wont to say that "he who does not believe in God is unprepared to take account of undesigned coincidence." The remark springs, of course, from a Calvinistic perception of providence in and over the affairs of men. As such, it readily courts a skeptical, if not cynical, dismissal in a "world come of age." But the dismissal cannot exile a profoundly historical and human resonance that ever and again echoes in the remark, and in the unlikeliest of times and places.

From Neuchâtel, Switzerland, for example, the Swiss playwright and philosopher, Friedrich Dürrenmatt, recalls that a Czech author once told him that "he understood Kafka only since his country turned Communist." He then goes on to note:

> Kafka is a religious author: the fact that he can be understood politically today is symptomatic of our time. The parallels are dismaying. In his novel, *The Castle*, for instance, Kafka uses the parable of heaven as a kind of inscrutable Administration. This picture today is one of political reality. . . .
>
> For Kafka, as for other religious thinkers, the meaning of this world lies with God, which is beyond this world. Therefore the meaning of this world is incomprehensible to Kafka. All that God does, therefore, seems to be senseless: senseless his justice, and senseless the mercy of heaven. God is the absurd. Man neither knows of what he is guilty, why he is put to trial, why he is condemned to death and executed, nor how to obtain clemency.
>
> Kafka does not reject belief in God, but belief in the possibility of recognizing God. Therefore, for Kafka the question is irrelevant, whether God is fair or unfair, merciful or unmerciful, or whether the world has meaning or no meaning. Man must subjugate himself to God's absurdity, or he is condemned to ask senseless questions for which there is no answer.
>
> Man is not only religious or non-religious. He is also political or non-political. And here it seems to me of fundamental importance that man should be religious, but not religious-political. Man can subjugate himself to an absurd God, but not to an absurd government. . . . Not for nothing is Kafka in Communist nations a much disputed and often still-forbidden author—because of fear that Kafka's religious unreality may be mistaken for political reality.[59]

With the confidence in man and rationality characteristic of the Enlightenment, and with a strangely secularized Lutheran twist,

Dürrenmatt deems it important that man be religious but irrelevant and political but irreligious. When religion goes political, it fortifies the inscrutability and uncontrollability of government through fatalistic piety. "Intellectual enlightenment," on the other hand, "is without effect if it is not political at the same time." According to Dürrenmatt, the recent publication of *The Pentagon Papers* shows that "Kafka's combination of religion and politics joins unreality and reality in such a way as to deprive his castle of its only possible exit."[60] The publication symbolizes man's indispensable struggle against the unreality and falsehood both of God and of government. Thus it was not treason but "a necessity. Kafka's absurd castle politically can only be led *ad absurdum* through 'News from Kafka's Castle.' "

With this concluding note, Dürrenmatt seems to have left his Czech author as far behind as the distance separating Neuchâtel from Washington. The press is indeed a slender reed on which to lean when religion and politics, reality and unreality, are to be sorted out and assigned their proper spheres of pertinence and responsibility. It is no derogation of the *Times'* astute and courageous challenge to government by secrecy, in the name of the guarantees of freedom affirmed and safeguarded by the First Amendment, to recall that the *Times* was no early critic of the Vietnam war or of the system of "leaks" by which secrecy in government is both pursued and suspended. I. F. Stone has trenchantly observed that "the press, too, has been corrupted in its own way by the web of secrecy woven by imperialism. . . . (This partly) explains why the establishment press, despite so much first rate reporting from Viet Nam, has taken so long to disengage from the 'party-line' on the war. . . . No small part of what is now coming to light was visible years ago, for those who cared to look. . . ."[61]

A press sensitive of its *ad absurdum* responsibilities might have aided a Czech author's grasp of the world of Franz Kafka. But the absence of such a press was scarcely the key to Kafka's religious assessment of the relations between reality and unreality, piety and politics. The Soviet Union's "incursion" into Prague (1968) was a revolutionary political thrust that closed some castle doors while opening others, lowered some drawbridges while raising others.

That it failed of its transfiguring occasion and possibility, and ended by substituting one castle for another, is a tragic consequence for which intellectual enlightenment gone political is scarcely adequate. Against this exchange of castles, artists and writers are increasingly in revolt at a much profounder human level, at Kafka's level of depth discernment of Establishment absurdity, whether cosmic or social, religious or political. When "cramped" is experienced as "wronged," a moral transfiguration is in the making that sooner or later will out. Conscience in revolt against injustice become intolerable!—it is *this* that underlies the world of Kafka, of Daniel Ellsberg's success, at long last, in goading the press into action, and of the shattering of Establishment securities. It is all one world, not two, as Dürrenmatt wistfully believes. An absurd system that has exiled God as absurd is God's absurd way of making the system a surd.

The dynamics of Jesus' Transfiguration, to which our double concidence points, unveils an absurdity-surdity syndrome as a providential rejection of the fatalism and futility intrinsic to Establishment politics. The bombing of Hiroshima on the Feast of Transfiguration, like the "freudian slip" of a moral transfiguration in an analysis of the anatomy of revolution, means that revolutions are best and rightly understood as signs of transfiguration. In their absurdity lies at once their divine occasion and their happening on every frontier of power where the conjunction of reality and redemption is being resisted and forged. As *vis medicatrix naturae,* revolutions do not confine social and political reality to a cosmic inscrutability that makes Hobbes' bitter dictum *bellum omnium contra omnes* inevitable but bearable.[62] On the contrary, as *vis medicatrix naturae,* revolutions herald the profound wisdom of the classical dictum: *Quos deus perdere vult, prius dementat,* and, owing to a providential transfiguration of this surd-absurdity, they make room for a *novus ordo saeculorum* in a God-man world.[63] A striking contemporary instance of the convergence of these dicta in a kind of proleptic transfiguration, e.g., a foretaste of the judgment visited upon the pretensions of self-justifying power under the dynamics of messianic politics, is described by Ralph L. Stavins, of the institute of Policy Studies in Washington, D.C. An article, at least coincidentally related to the Pentagon Papers, deals with "Kennedy's War," and in the course of the account the following paragraph appears:

> Once in Vietnam, Taylor and Rostow explored ways of introducing US ground troops. They had decided that Diem needed them to preserve his rule, but they also recognized that such a course would damage America's image as a peacekeeper. The general and the professor wondered how the United States could go to war while appearing to preserve the peace. While they were pondering this question, Vietnam was suddenly struck by a deluge. It was as if God had wrought a miracle. American soldiers, acting on humanitarian impulses, could be despatched to save Vietnam not from the Viet Cong, but from the floods. McGaar, the Chief of MAAG, stated that Taylor favored "moving in US military personnel for humanitarian purposes with subsequent retention if desirable." He added, "This is an excellent opportunity to minimize adverse publicity."[64]

Of course, it takes the Bible to clue one in on the pace and point of things in a God-man world. But Pharaoh's troubles with Moses come rather immediately to mind. Only in Vietnam the waters did not engulf the pursuing armies. They merely provided a deluge for the shielding of the people of promise and the further "despoiling of the Egyptians" already under way. According to the logistics of messianic politics, the first exodus continues to illuminate and be illuminated by the second exodus, the exodus of promise, covenant, and liberation by the exodus of transfiguration, suffering, and vindication.

## CHAPTER 9

# A TYPOLOGY OF CURRENT REVOLUTIONS[65]

In a providential as well as in a sociopolitical sense, revolutions are not "as plentiful as blackberries." So to regard them is to cheapen the meaning of revolution by the notion of quick changes in technical procedures and social policies. It is also to overlook the fact that the Marxist theory that mankind goes from revolution to revolution needs and presupposes a broader context that Marxism was partly able and partly unable to supply.[66] Contemporary revolutionary experience has been forged by the Marxist assessment of the concrete mode of injustice and the realities of power. Yet this experience has been increasingly freed of an ideological bondage to Marxism, owing to diverse historical and pragmatic conditions, which exhibit a deeper root and a farther horizon. This does not mean that ideological factors and functions have been exiled from revolutionary passion and practice. They have, instead, been disciplined by the priorities of revolutionary experience itself, and by the mounting importance of strategy for revolutionary purposes and possibilities. Marxism-Leninism, as we have already observed, is still the bearer of the revolutionary dynamics of our times.[67] Yet the notable fact about revolutions, since the Bolshevist accession to power in Russia in 1917, is that the teachings of Marx and Lenin, together with their implementation in the Soviet Union, are instrumental rather than normative in the theory and practice of revolution.

We are all, Marxism included, beholden to the French Revolution as the point of departure for the understanding and evaluation of the phenomenon of revolution. This, too, we have already noted.[68] But the sense in which this indebtedness identifies the meaning of revolution has become increasingly apparent. It is instructive that Rosenstock-Huessy's massive study of revolution (1931) and Jean-François Revel's recently published analysis of revolution in the United States make the same point although in different ways.[69] The former is a cultural-historical account; the latter, a socio-political one. According to Rosenstock, World War I marks the turning point in the dynamics of revolution from a sporadic, geographically limited phenomenon to a worldwide phenomenon. A *Gärungszustand* (a condition of fermentation), which, under the prophetic iconoclasm of Voltaire and Beaumarchais, spelled the end of the "Bourgeois Gentilhomme" and the beginning of the first revolutionary orthodoxy of modern times, has burst the boundaries of nation-states, and even continents; of races and classes, and even sexes; and has become a world phenomenon. Indeed, revolution has displaced war, and functions as "a kind of economy of history" (Rosenstock). The revolutionary creed then was: liberty, equality, fraternity, and the rights of man.[70] The creed now is: justice, human rights, the liberation of all mankind, and power to the people! As Revel puts it, a movement is now on from "the first global revolution" to "the second global revolution."[71] The first revolution effected

the displacement of authority thenceforth to those subject to it, or at least who delegate it; the substitution of the notion of contract for divine right, or the right of the strong, of the right of legal power for personal power; the substitution of an egalitarian society for an hierarchical one; the separation of state and church (*du civil et du religieux*); the accreditation (*l'affranchissement*) of knowledge and of culture in general by consensus rather than by political or ecclesiastical control. These achievements, however precarious, however hypocritically applied or brutally suspended, have at least reshaped the political traits of the planet.[72]

The second revolution "can only have one goal, upon which all other goals, however numerously they may be proposed, will depend: the establishment of a world government."[73] The first revolution has crossed the Rubicon at World War I, and ever since revolution means "the will to introduce into world history once for all a new principle of life, a total upheavel (*eine Totalumwaelzung*)."[74] The second revolution exhibits the dynamics and the components of this total upheaval. M. Revel has identified these components as broadly five in number:

1. the criticism of injustice in economic, social, and eventually racial structures (*rapports*);
2. the criticism of operability (*la gestion*) or effectiveness. It focuses upon the waste of material and human resources and the extent to which injustice involves faulty organization, declining productive capacity, and the misuse of technical progress by devoting it to the production of what is useless or even harmful to man;
3. the criticism of political power: its source and foundation, its technics and the conditions of its exercise;
4. the criticism of culture: morality, religion, dominant beliefs and customs, philosophy, literature and art; of the ideologies that support them; and of the function of culture and of intellectuals in society and in the diffusion of culture:
5. the criticism of the past (*de l'ancienne civilisation*) for its censure or violation of the liberty of the individual. In this context, revolution aims at the liberation of personal creativity and the reanimation of individual initiatives against repressive societies.[75]

Quite apart from the conclusions that Revel himself draws from his "five points" of "the second global revolution," they do express the operational phase of the current revolutionary creed: justice, human rights, the liberation of all mankind, and power to the people! In so doing, they serve as a framework within which a typology of current revolutions may be identified and explored. Typologies are, at best, rubrics of interpretation for dynamic and complex happenings that illuminate what is going on within acknowleged limits. The limits are inherent in the phenomena to which the typologies refer. These happenings seem to resist schematization as readily as they suggest it. There are always exceptions that do not neatly fit the rubric; and there is always the possibility of a more satisfactory typological arrangement. Nevertheless, the revolutions now under way do exhibit, in Brinton's phrase, "uniformities" and "variables" that lend themselves to typological analysis.[76] More especially is this the case when one considers these revolutions as signs of a politics of transfiguration. In quite different ways and under quite different conditions, current revolutions are united by the passions and purposes symbolized in the revolutionary creed. They are divided by various foci of total upheaval, by variant strategies, and by differing ideological patterns and practices.

Among these uniformities are:

1. a relentless mobility and urgent movement: the time for change is *now*, and *grosso modo*;
2. a confidence that revolutionary conditions, being present, call for making revolutions happen;
3. a revolutionary leadership capable of combining charisma with conviction in the nurture of hope and for the shaping of personal lifestyles and patterns of social reconstruction, neither expecting too much nor succumbing to defeats;
4. a pragmatic and flexible ordering of priorities and strategies in implementing revolutionary goals and actions;
5. an instrumental, in distinction from a dogmatic, appropriation of Marxism-Leninism; and as its corollary:
6. an instrumental, in distinction from a dogmatic, appropriation of ideology;
7. a realistic and functional (i.e., nonideological) assessment of the relations between violence and power;
8. an informed and formative awareness of the psychology of revolutionary experience.

Among the variables of contemporary revolutionary theory and practice are:

1. the identification of the major counterrevolutionary realities and patterns of power;
2. the relations between leadership and the people, especially with reference to guerrilla warfare and contradictions in society; and as its corollary:

3. the uses of ideology;
4. the inevitability of violence;
5. the relation of religious resources to revolutionary endeavor.

In a world indifferent to the presence of Jesus of Nazareth, and to the messianic story centered in him, these uniformities and variables are sufficient for identifying and charting the course and the crises of the "fever" afflicting the global body politic. But they are less than sufficient for identifying the root occasion, the intensity and pervasiveness of the fever, or the prospects for its surcease and replacement by a reassuring measure of human and social health. Indifferent to the presence of Jesus of Nazareth and to the messianic story, one may indeed take account of the fact and the pattern of revolutionary experience but scarcely of the dynamics and the depth of revolutionary passion and promise. In a world, however, to which Jesus of Nazareth has not been indifferent, and into which he has released a messianic story, exposing the direction, the possibilities, and the power of human liberation and human fulfillment, the uniformities and variables of current revolutionary experience are notably illumined by "Jesus and his story," and symbolically confirm it.

Current revolutions, in all their concreteness and ambiguity, are a sign of the eschatological pressure of revolutionary reality, zeroing in upon a moment of truth, at which a liberating presence heralds and pioneers a humanizing lifestyle and an ultimate agony of suffering and vindication. The power of this presence is such as to put to flight existing principalities and powers, and existing patterns of injustice and oppression, and to make room for a new order of righteousness and freedom, peace and reconciliation, whose time is at hand. This is the agenda of a messianic politics, launched with the Transfiguration of Jesus of Nazareth, for the transfiguration of humanity in humanness and of power by truth and life.

One may arrive at this agenda by way of a symbolization nurtured by the biblical story and nourished by biblical language, as we have mainly done. Or, as has been pointed out in passing, one may arrive at this agenda by the language and life of the community of faith, which is the church. Revelation and eschatology,

creation and providence, incarnation, crucifixion, and resurrection, justification and sanctification, judgment and reconciliation—are the recurrent symbols through which the vast panorama of the divine economy is unfolded as a testimony to the transfiguration of history and nature, of humanity and society, and as an invitation to revolutionary involvement in the dynamics and direction of what God is doing in the world. Admittedly, the Christian experience of reality, and the commitment of Christians to the truth and the life that are in Jesus of Nazareth, the Christ, more often than not have been diverted to counterrevolutionary establishment purposes and policies. But such diversion is a perversion of obedience, and can be regarded only as a crucifixion of "the Lord of glory" (I Cor. 2:8). The power of biblical and theological symbolization calls it into question, and awakens a redemptive sensitivity to the "signs and wonders and mighty works" (Acts 2:22) of human liberation and formation that are making room in the world for the righteousness of God in action.

Howsoever one way arrive at the agenda of a messianic politics, "he who runs may read" (Hab. 2:2 RSV) as follows:

1. let the oppressed go free—"the poor have the gospel preached to them" (Isa. 61:1; Luke 4:18);
2. the world, including institutions, is made for man not man for the world—"therefore the Son of Man is sovereign even over the Sabbath" (Mark 2:28); God "has chosen what the world counts weakness . . . He has chosen things low and contemptible, mere nothings to overthrow the existing order" (I Cor. 1:28);
3. existing powers are being called into question by the risks of power —"Elijah has come already" (Matt. 17:11);
4. a new order of human fulfillment is at hand! The time of a liberating presence has come!—"This is My Son, my Beloved . . . listen to him" (Matt. 17:5);
5. death is the frontier of resurrection, suffering of vindication, redemption of reconciliation—"My task is to bear witness to the truth. For this was I born; for this I came into the world, and all who are not deaf to truth listen to my voice. . . . We have a law; and by that law he ought to die, because he has claimed to be the Son of God" (John 18:37; 19:7). "Leave no claim outstanding against you, except that of mutual love. He who loves his neighbor

has satisfied every claim of the law. . . . therefore the whole law is summed up in love" (Rom. 13:8, 10).

In short, in a world lived in, and lived and died for, by Jesus of Nazareth, current revolutionary experience signals the righteousness of God in action, freeing human beings for being human in *that* world and in the world to come. "Jesus then came up to them, touched them, and said, 'Stand up; do not be afraid.' . . . I tell you this: if you have faith no bigger even than a mustard-seed, you will say to this mountain, 'Move from here to there!', and it will move; nothing will prove impossible for you" (Matt. 17:20).

The typology of current revolutions, at work on this agenda, may be formulated in terms of three interrelated movements, each directed against a particular mode of power whose dehumanizing injustice has reached its moment of truth. The interrelations of these movements exhibit the uniformities of the revolutionary creed in operation. The variables in this operation mean that the power focus of each movement does not exclude the other forms of dehumanizing power and that quite concrete and diverse social and historical conditions are being transfigured by the dynamics of revolutionary aims and strategies. Each of these movements in itself, and all taken together, mean that a line is being drawn in the present course of human events between a self-justifying perpetuation of power at the service of the established order of things and a revolutionary use of power for the liberation of human beings for human fulfillment. The current revolutions are the bearers of this moment of truth because they expose the falsehood and death in established forms and structures of power, and at the same time, the points at which room is being made (space for freedom) for the correspondence between the dynamics of power and the human reality and purpose of power. The three movements to which we may briefly attend, as signs of transfiguration, are:

A. A movement from Marx to Mao and Ho Chi Minh
B. A movement from Fidel and Che Guevara to Camilo Torres and Nestor Paz Zamora
C. A movement from Frantz Fanon to Martin Luther King, Jr., Malcolm X, and the Black Panther Party.

The principal revolutionary thrust of the first movement is: in the name of the people, against *colonialist imperialism*. The principal revolutionary thrust of the second movement is: in the name of the people, against *imperialist colonialism*. *Colonialist imperialism* may be described as the conquest of, and rule over, foreign places and peoples intrinsic to the expansionist policies of powerful states. By contrast, *imperialist colonialism* may be described as the domination of foreign places and peoples by powerful expansionist states in ways other than conquest or annexation. The principal revolutionary thrust of the third movement is: in the name of the people, against *racism*. Power to the people!—people "claimed by God for his own, to proclaim the triumphs of him who has called (them) out of darkness into his marvellous light"; people "who once were not his people" but "are now the people of God"; people who "outside his mercy once, . . . have now received his mercy" (I Pet. 2:9, 10; parenthesis mine).[77]

### A. FROM MARX TO MAO AND HO CHI MINH

When the hauteur of a Western intellectual acquires a gallic accent, it comes to expression with notably biting disdain. Thus Revel's derogation of Mao Tse-tung is in the best tradition of Voltaire but in the worst perception of the revolutionary realities of the world today. Rather more suited to the reinforcement of the stereotypes by which American power perpetuates its counterrevolutionary course than suitable to these realities, Revel plays into the hands both of the Americans whom he celebrates and of the intrepid "savior" of the Chinese people whom he deprecates. "But the study of the texts," Revel writes, "obliges one to say that, philosophically, the little red writer is nonexistent. He is only a 'Chinese version' of marxism. There is no 'thought of Mao.' "[78] The architects of American foreign policy, at least since the refusal to sign the Geneva Accord (1954), can only welcome every encouragement to "one-upmanship," even an implicitly philosophical one. Mao Tse-tung, on the other hand, can scarcely be other than content with what he does not need, namely, a further confirmation of his conviction and policy designed to keep intellectuals and peasants creatively together in the theory and practice of social reality. "The theories of Marx, Engels, Lenin and Stalin can be applied to the whole universe. Their theories are not to be looked upon as dogma but as a guide to action." So Mao wrote in a report to the Sixth Plenum of the Sixth Central Committee, in October 1938. Four years later, in a speech, delivered at the opening of the Party school in Yenan on 1 February 1942, he declared:

> If a man read ten thousand volumes by Marx, Engels, Lenin and Stalin, and read each volume a thousand times so he could recite every sentence from memory, he still could not be considered a theoretician. . . . We need theoreticians who base their thinking on the standpoints, concepts, and methods of Marx, Engels, Lenin and Stalin, who are able to explain correctly the actual problems issuing from history and revolution, who are able to give a scientific interpretation and theoretical explanation of the various problems of Chinese economics, politics, military affairs, and culture. . . . We consider it entirely necessary to hold the intelligentsia in esteem, for without a revolutionary intelligentisia the revolution cannot succeed. However, we know that there are many intellectuals who consider themselves very learned and who make a great display of their knowledge, not realizing that this attitude is harmful and obstructs their progress. . . . One truth that they should realize is that a great many so-called intellectuals are actually exceedingly unlearned and that the knowledge of the workers and peasants is greater than theirs.[79]

Jesus made the same point against "the wise and understanding" of his day, and in sharper terms.[80] Obviously, the argument on Mars Hill is still going on.[81]

## 1. Mao's Formation as a Marxist

On 1 October 1949, in an unforgettable ceremony, Mao Tse-tung declared: "The Central Governing Council of the People's Government of China today assumes power in Peking. . . ."[82] It was no accident that he used the old imperial name for the city rather than the name *Peiping*, bestowed by the Kuomintang in 1927, at the end of its northern march. *Peking* means "northern capital"; *Peiping* means "northern peace." For the Kuomintang, the "northern peace" meant the continuation of Western imperialism in China and the war against the people. For Mao Tse-tung and the Central Governing Council, the "northern capital" meant that the Chinese people had been returned to their ancient birthright and liberated for the dawning of their day of promise. Robert Payne says:

> In effect, both Mao and Chiang had summoned up the past in order to help them wage their war in the present; but they had conjured up different pasts. Chiang saw himself as a Chou dynasty prince leading his feudal armies to battle, like any one of the princes described so brilliantly in the *Tso Chuan*. Mao saw himself as one of the heroes of *All Men Are Brothers*. Both employed ancient rituals, Chiang Kai-shek even going so far as to encourage his lieutenants to present him with copies of the ancient bronze tripods traditionally presented to victorious emperors. . . . Mao resurrected the ancient peasant brotherhoods who took to the woods and defied the Emperor on the grounds that the Mandate from Heaven had lapsed, and he was never so innocent as to believe that the Chinese peasants were powerless.[83]

Mao is himself a peasant and has remained so. Born in a small village in Hunan province, from which the best scholars and the best soldiers are reputed to have come, he absorbed, as it were by osmosis, the intimate and inseparable bond between power, culture, and the peasantry. The soil of China has been the principal base of social reality from time immemorial; and peasant wisdom, compounded of simplicity and shrewdness, has combined with sheer numbers to make of peasants at once the principal focus of social stability and the major force of social change. Long before Marx, Lenin, and Stalin gave conceptual form and ideological power to the social struggle in an industrial and technological age, the Chinese peasants had been schooled by secret revolutionary societies in the planning and implementation of resistance to oppression and exploitation by existing power structures. Long before the historic Long March, from October 1934 to October 1935, and from Fukien in the Southeast over 6,000 miles to Yenan in the central north, made Mao Tse-tung the unchallenged military, political, and intellectual leader of the People's Revolution, he had learned from China's sages, poets, and novelists the subtle, at once profound and practical, insights and counsels through which sustaining and creative links are forged between patience and persistence, between the long view and the short run, between an indefatigable endurance and an indomitable will in the making of an old society into a new one.

By this same knowledge and wisdom he was readied for leadership in the transformation of a once fearsome imperium on the grand scale into a dynamic and awesome people's democracy bidding for recognition as one of the three or four great powers of the earth. There are echoes of Confucius, whom Mao learned in his youth and learned to despise, and whom in his prime and his age he learned to draw upon and even emulate, in the epigrammatic style and cryptic wit that have poured forth into countless speeches and treatises, reports and slogans, maxims and manifestoes, from the mind and pen of the Teacher, Sage, and acknowledged Ruler of the most populous nation in the world today. "There is a saying in China," Mao said in a speech in Moscow during the winter of 1957, " 'If the east wind does not prevail over the west wind, then the west wind will prevail over the east wind.' I think the characteristic of the current situation is that the east wind prevails over the west wind."[84]

It would be very misleading, however, to suppose that "the little red writer" does not exist; or, since he does exist, that he is merely the source and purveyor of boring and borrowed Marxist slogans. On the contrary! Mao Tse-tung combines a lifelong passion for the liberation of the Chinese people from exploitation, oppression, and deprivation with an uncommonly gifted and intense intelligence and passion for learning. This passion, far from generating romanticist social and political enthusiasms and expectations, "was tempered by an astonishing regard for facts."[85] During the bitter ordeal of the Long March, with its deprivation, discouragement, and the companionship of the ever-present specter of defeat, his personal courage and commitment, intellectual powers, and sheer physical energy and endurance not only outdistanced his companions in the struggle, but severely tested and proved his own competence for leadership. We are told:

> As usual, he worked at night, poring endlessly over newspapers, books, and captured documents, marking important passages in red pencil. The Red Army was constantly on the move, and he travelled with it, but every night he would find somewhere to work, setting up a lamp and a table and then busying himself with the documents which poured out of the capacious knapsack he carried on his shoulders when on the march. The knapsack was divided into nine compartments: one for maps, another for newspapers, another for books, and so on. The knapsack he regarded as his most important possession, and he liked to have it in view. His other possessions were few. . . . Possessing so little, he was able to move at a moment's notice.[86]

But this discipline and concentration were not acquired on the Long March. They had been nurtured and husbanded from his youth up. Born in 1893, Mao was thirteen in 1906, when a severe famine faced him for the first time with the problems of poverty and insurrection. A year later, he arrived at a middle school, some fifteen miles upriver from his birthplace. Alone and poverty-stricken, he was given the worst food and sleeping quarters, performed menial services for some of the wealthy students, generally hating his fellows who referred to him as "the dirty little peasant from Shao Shan." But "he studied hard, melted down old candles to fashion new ones, hid at night over his books while the other students were asleep, and was soon at the head of his class, only to discover that he was now even more despised for being diligent."[87]

This ravenous intellect devoured not only the Chinese classics, the literature of the revolutionary societies, and the Three Principles of Sun Yat-sen, but Western political literature as well. In the *Great Learning,* Confucius had underlined with approval the maxim "Everything must be made anew." During the year 1906–9, under the influence of the Reformist passions and pamphleteering of Liang Ch'i-ch'ao, Mao shared the convictions and expectations of Chinese youth for "making a new people." Liang's vision of a new China, emerging as a constitutional monarchy under laws modeled on England, was informed particularly, if not always entirely accurately, by Montesquieu, and as regards the nature of society and of social change by Darwin and Spencer. It was from Spencer, rather than from Marx, that Mao first took up the conviction that the individual must be sacrificed to society, social survival being a greater good than the survival of the individual. What an odd coincidence it seems that these social and political analyses should have reached these passionate reformers by way of a very dull book about basic sociology by a very minor Western sociologist.

Experience with Western civilization these Reformers knew at firsthand. But *The Principles of Western Civilization* they eagerly appropriated from Benjamin Kidd. Liang Chi'i-ch'ao found Kidd more stimulating than Marx and more intriguing than Huxley. He was destined, as Liang put it, "to influence all the races of the world, to be a great light to the future."[88] If one remembers that Kidd was the mediator of Spencer and Marx, and of a theory of social evolution that dominated the nineteenth century, and still reaches into the twentieth, Liang's judgment is less extravagant than at first it seems. The social and cultural distance between East and West narrows significantly.

Here is yet another coincidence in the story of revolutions as signs of transfiguration. One is tempted to coin a Confucianism of one's own, in an "East-West" version of the Chinese sage and American revolutionary homespun: as "tall oaks from little acorns grow,"[89] from small coincidences momentous consequences flow. At all events, Mao was prepared long before Marx for the theory and practice of revolution. His espousal of Marxist-Leninist dogmatics and tactics is fundamentally instrumentalist and characteristically Chinese. They fit the Chinese experience of colonialist-imperialist practice of the "principles of Western civilization." It is the West rather than the East that is materialist. It is the West rather than the East that is driven by an internal energy (*dynamis,* dynamic) toward a globalization of a mechanistic-organizational-technological lifestyle. The computer having displaced the machine as a model, the statistical has become one vanguard of the positivistic mentality in the ordering, valuation, and control of human affairs. Echoes of Oswald Spengler whisper through the melancholy suggestion of Lewis Mumford that the havoc of heliocentrism has eclipsed the promise of it in the regions of the setting, not the rising, of the sun.[90] Under the aegis of the rising sun, amidst its own full share of imperialist rivalries and conflicts, heaven still battles with earth and earth with heaven for the making of a highway for the humanity of people and for people in their humanness. If in the East colonialism has been the harbinger of imperialism, in the West imperialism seeks the hegemony of neocolonialism over states and peoples whose history and destiny have been designed for human freedom and fulfillment. The power realities are the same; it is the resistance to them that has begun to claim its birthright.

If Mao's version of dialectical materialism seems to Western eyes and minds to be more Marxist than Chinese, it is prudent to consider whether this could be due at least as much to Western ignorance of Chinese ways of being human in the past and present as to simplistic redaction and repetition on the part of Mao Tsetung. It is true that Mao's exposition of dialectical materialism is Marxist-Leninist through and through. It is true also that Mao adopts the Marxist reading of history and social development. Mao never loses sight of the specific realities of the Chinese people in their struggle against poverty, exploitation, and injustice. He declares:

> The chief conflicts in the present Chinese society are the conflict between imperialism and the Chinese nation, and the conflict between the remains of the feudal elements and the Chinese people. . . . The chief enemies of the Chinese revolution at its present stage . . . are none other than imperialism and semi-feudalism, in other words, foreign bourgeoisie and the Chinese land-owning class, because these two classes are oppressing and retarding the development of the Chinese society. . . . The extreme hardships and oppressions of the Chinese people are not to be found elsewhere in the world. . . . The tasks of the Chinese revolution (are): externally it must carry out a national revolution to overthrow the oppression of imperialism, whilst internally it must carry out a democratic revolution to overthrow the oppression of remaining feudal elements. . . . The leadership of this

two-fold revolutionary task rests upon the shoulders of the poltical party of the Chinese proletariat—the Communist Party, and without the leadership of the Chinese Communist Party, no revolution can succeed.

On the other hand,

Theory and practice can be combined only if men of the Chinese Communist Party take the standpoints, concepts and methods of Marxism-Leninism, apply them to China, and create a theory from conscientious study of the realities of the Chinese Revolution and Chinese history. . . . (x) Not only are the Chinese people well known for endurance and tenacity, but they are also a people who love liberty and possess revolutionary traditions.[91]

Thus Mao's passion for freedom from oppression, and for a life of human fulfillment for the great masses of his countrymen, combined with his remarkable intellectual and human gifts for revolutionary leadership to bring him to the pinnacle of power and to the nearer edge of immortalization as the *Teacher and Savior* of the Chinese people.[92]

In my judgment, Mao Tse-tung belongs with Marx and Lenin as one of the great formative minds and decisive shapers of human events in the twentieth century. He stands in the succession of those who have pioneered a new order of human affairs and a new consciousness of the dynamics and the dimensions involved in being human in a world in which power continually threatens freedom with the denial of *Lebensraum*. It may be, as W. H. Auden has remarked, that "the social and political history of Europe would be exactly the same if Dante and Shakespeare and Mozart never lived."[93] But we should rather think that in a world in which Jesus Christ has brought the realities of power under the transfiguration of truth and life, and made revolutions the signs of this transfiguration, Marx and Lenin and Mao are the shapers of a world in which Dante and Shakespeare and Mozart still live, and under the prospect of a fuller human participation in the wonder, the reality, and the joy of being human, which they all died beholding as yet a great way off. The world would indeed be exactly the same; but with the sameness that makes the difference. The question is whether politics make poets (and prophets) expendable or whether transfiguration makes politics and poets (and prophets) the pioneers of what being human in the world means.

As for Mao Tse-tung, there are perhaps two writings from his vast published output that above all others bring concretely into contemporary focus the dynamics and the dimensions of what being human in the world involves. These writings are *On Contradiction* and *On Guerrilla Warfare*.[94] The first piece exhibits the fundamental thrust of Mao's dependence upon, and independence of, Marxism-Leninism over the significant two decades of his revolutionary struggles and development. The second tract exhibits Mao's pragmatic skill in the application of his conviction that revolutions can be brought about, even against great power odds. Both pieces exhibit with special vividness and force that combination of "passion, imagination as well as shrewd political analysis" that is "Mao . . . in his element," together with a clue to the secret of Mao's rule over one-fourth of all humanity and the long shadow of his ideological influence from Indonesia to Albania, from Africa to Latin America, as well as all over Asia.[95]

## 2. Mao's Analysis of Contradictions

*On Contradiction* sets out from Lenin's dictum that "In its proper meaning, dialectics is the study of the contradiction within the very essence of things" (128). Hegel, of course, had made the point first, in order to describe the dynamics in reality according to which the fundamental unity in things unfolds through relations of opposition, gathered then into a higher unity and its succeeding opposition. As is well known, "the very essence of things" was, for Hegel, defined by the dynamics of Spirit (*Geist*), whereas Marx, and Lenin after him, inaugurated a momentous and radical inversion (*metabasis eis allo genos*) and affirmed the material basis of the social, productive, and cultural relations of human life in history. Thus Mao declares:

> The basic cause of things does not lie outside but inside them, in their internal contradictions. . . . Similarly, social development is chiefly due . . . to the development of the internal contradictions in society, namely the contradiction between the productive forces

and the relations of production, the contradiction between the classes, and the contradiction between the old and the new; it is the development of these contradictions that propels society and starts the process of the supersession of the old society by a new one. . . . (129)

With particular reference to China, and with due regard for the reluctance of historical and human reality to yield at every point to the dogmatics of Marxist orthodoxy, Mao goes on to note certain external and internal contradictions in the national development (itself revolutionary) of China as well as in China's world relations. Except for the Marxist language, they sound almost like leaves from the Pentagon Papers. He declares:

> We often say: "The Chinese Government is the countinghouse of our foreign masters." Perhaps there are some who don't believe this. We also say: "The false show of friendship by foreigners (especially Englishmen and Americans) is merely a pretense of 'amity' in order that they may squeeze out more of the fat and blood of the Chinese people." Perhaps there are some who do not believe this either. Ever since the prohibition against the export of cotton was repealed owing to the opposition of the foreigners, it has been impossible not to believe what we have just said to some extent. (142)

The historic mission of the Chinese people thus becomes that of opening "a new era through revolutionary methods, and to build a new nation" (142). The mission is Chinese. But the sociological reality of the struggle is worldwide. Mao identifies five social classes whose attitudes toward the national revolution affect their participation in it. The "big bourgeoisie, middle bourgeoisie, petit bourgeoisie, semi-proletariat, and proletariat" exhibit a mentality in accordance with their economic position and a wide spectrum of response to the revolution, including complete opposition, partial opposition, neutrality, participation in the revolution or being the principal force in the revolution (144). Mao declares:

> The attitude of the various classes in China toward the national revolution is more or less identical with the attitude of the various classes in Western Europe toward the social revolution. This may seem strange, but in reality it is not strange at all. For basically

today's revolution is the same everywhere, its goals and its techniques are similar—to overthrow world capitalist imperialism and to unite the exploited peoples and classes to wage war. This is the unique feature which distinguishes today's revolution from all other revolutions in history. (144–45)

Correlative with this sociological realism is the realism about what the social struggle involves. The focus of this realism is contradiction. Externally, these contradictions are endemic to imperialism. Internally, these contradictions are endemic to the exploitation to which disproportionate economic ownership and social status give rise. Mao observes:

> Since contradictions are developing internationally between the imperialist countries, between the imperialist countries and their colonies and between imperialism and the proletariat in these countries, the imperialists feel all the more urgently the need to contend for China. As the imperialists' contention for China intensifies, . . . the contradictions within the ruling class also develop daily. . . . The dumping of commodities by imperialism, the corrosion by Chinese mercantile capital, and the increase of taxation by the government bring about the sharpening of the contradiction between the landlords and the peasantry, and the exploitation through rent and usury becomes heavier. . . . Once we understand all these contradictions, we shall see in how desperately precarious a situation and how anarchic a state China finds herself. . . . The proverb "A single spark can start a prairie fire" appropriately describes how the current situation will develop. (148–49)

Plainly, in the West, the tinder is not that dry. Irrigation facilities, if not always readily available, have so far managed to be sufficiently at hand to prevent a general conflagration. However greatly a Marxist-Leninist analysis may have miscalculated both the tempo and the inflexibility of these contradictions in the West, their operation has not, on that account, been invalidated; nor has their price in human suffering and deprivation been prevented or paid. The mills of God grind slow, but they grind exceeding small; especially of the God with whom a thousand years are as one day, and one day as a thousand years (Ps. 90). The prevalence of the east wind over the west wind is not a foregone conclusion. But the east wind still blows, as the long shadow cast by Mao Tse-tung and Ho Chi Minh over the May (1968) barricades in Paris, the campuses in Berlin and Berkeley in the same year, and over the Himmler-like figure of the Attorney-General of the United States, astride the balcony of the Department of Justice in Washington, D.C., in May 1971 attest.

Meanwhile, the single spark has caught fire in China. After two decades of struggle, "the victories of the bourgeois-democratic revolution and the socialist revolution, coupled with our achievements in socialist reconstruction, have rapidly changed the face of old China. . . . However, this does not mean that there are no longer any contradictions in our society" (236–37). It is possible now to adapt Lenin's distinction between antagonism and contradiction and speak of antagonistic and nonantagonistic contradictions. "We are confronted by two types of social contradiction," says Mao, "—contradictions between ourselves and the enemy and contradictions among the people" (237). It also becomes possible to draw a sharper line between friends and enemies. Among friends, contradictions are nonantagonistic. "These include contradictions between the interests of the state, collective interests, and individual interests; between democracy and centralism; between those in positions of leadership and the led; and contradictions arising from the bureaucratic practices of certain state functionaries in their relations with the masses. All these are contradictions among the people" (237–38). But underlying all these contradictions "is the basic identity of the interests of the people" (238). On the other hand, "the term 'the people' has different meanings in different countries and in different historical periods in each country. . . . At this stage of building socialism, all classes, strata, and social groups that approve, support, and work for the cause of socialist construction belong to the category of the people, while those forces and groups that resist the socialist revolution and are hostile to and try to wreck socialist construction are enemies of the people" (237).

Here the going gets very rough indeed, as regards the dynamics and the dimensions of what being human in the contemporary world really involves. At what point do nonantagonistic contradictions become antagonistic ones? At what point does hesitation about the course of the revolution become hostility to it? Mao's analysis identifies a correct and crucial problem. But it scarcely composes a criterion for a reliable, in distinction from a ready-made, differentiation between revolutionary criticism and criticism of the revolution. Instead, Mao's account of contradictions offers an instructive Maoist confirmation of the Marcusian espousal of repressive tolerance—a thrust directed with all the hauteur of Marcusian intransigence particularly at the descendants of John Stuart Mill (and *mutatis mutandis* of John Locke). Behind both Mao and Marcuse, of course, is the brilliant and bitter thrust of Marx against Hegel, taking the grim shape of grimmer consequences before our very eyes and ears. "The weapon of criticism," Marx declared, "cannot . . . replace the criticism of weapons."[96] Even if the suppression of dissent did not cut so fiercely to the Right as to the Left, the way seems terrifyingly short between a draconian replacement of "the weapon of criticism" as a revolutionary policy and an "up against the wall" criticism of weapons as a revolutionary necessity.

It is a tragic irony of the revolutionary story that the "moment of truth" for the revolutionary is the opposite side of the power coin by which the Establishment is judged as having had its day. The irony is, perhaps, second only to the tragedy whereby both the revolutionary and the Establishment reject the transfigured and transfiguring Presence whose power liberates as it binds and binds as it liberates. The bitter experience of the revolutionary is that established power never yields; hence it must be seized. The bitter experience of established power is that once established, it justifies itself as necessary and earned. The truth about power, e.g., the messianic reality of it, is that power is a gift that can never be earned but sometimes may be seized, and in the seizing of it, transfigured for the freedom wherewith, in the dynamics and direction of messianic politics, man has been set free in truth. Since the French Revolution, an important correction in revolutionary theory and practice has come about. This is that freedom is not *liberty* but *liberation*. It is the struggle for liberation that involves a total change in the existing order of things because, as Marcuse has put it with a strong assist from Hegel ,"it is the whole which determines the truth—not in the sense that the whole is prior or superior to the parts, but in the sense that its structure and function determine every particular condition and relation."[97]

The historicization and humanization of this truth about power is one of the major—if not *the* major—permanent contributions of Marxism to the dynamics and dimensions of what being human in the world involves. The roots of this achievement lie deep in the matrix of that conversation of Jesus of Nazareth with Moses and Elijah on the Mount. And just as the Marxian inversion of Hegel does not dispose of Hegel, so the Hegelian inversion of the incarnation does not dispose of the transfiguration of the relations between power and truth effected by the presence and the lifestyle of Jesus of Nazareth in the world. It is not accidental that the movement from Lenin's democratic centralism to Mao's assessment of the relations between freedom and contradiction to Marcuse's repressive tolerance should sooner or later stand or fall on the boundary between freedom and tolerance, where the sheep are separated from the goats and enemies from friends. Mao declares:

> Our constitution states that citizens of the People's Republic of China enjoy freedom of speech, of the press, of assembly, of association, of procession, of religious practices, and so on. . . . Our socialist democracy is democracy in the widest sense, such as is not found in any capitalist country. . . .
>
> But this freedom is freedom with leadership and this democracy is democracy under centralized guidance, not anarchy. Anarchy does not conform to the interests or wishes of the people. (238)

In marked contrast, Marcuse finds that

> in our advanced industrial society . . . the realization of the objective of tolerance would call for intolerance toward prevailing policies, attitudes, opinions, and the extension of tolerance to policies, attitudes, and opinions which are outlawed or suppressed. In other words, today tolerance appears again as what it was in its origins, at the beginning of the modern period—a partisan goal, a subversive liberating notion and practice. Conversely, what is proclaimed and practiced as tolerance today, is in many of its most effective manifestations serving the cause of oppression. . . . Generally, the function and value of tolerance depend on the

equality prevalent in the society in which tolerance is practiced. . . . Tolerance is an end in itself only when it is truly universal, practiced by the rulers as well as by the ruled, by the lords
as well as by the peasants, by the sheriffs as well as by their victims. And such universal tolerance is possible only when no real
or alleged enemy requires in the national interest the education
and training of people in military violence and destruction. As
long as these conditions do not prevail, the conditions of tolerance
are "loaded": they are determined and defined by institutionalized
inequality (which is certainly compatible with constitutional
equality), i.e., by the class structure of society. In such a society,
tolerance is *de facto* limited on the dual ground of legalized violence or suppression (police, armed forces, guards of all sorts)
and of the privileged position held by the predominant interests
and their "connections."[98]

We cite this passage at some length, and in relation to Mao's statement, because it so precisely and concisely identifies the actualities
of revolutionary and counterrevolutionary experience and confrontation. In so doing, the passage also underscores the enormous
difficulty of sorting out friends and enemies in the revolutionary
struggle and of achieving power by revolutionary means without
losing the purposes, promises, and achievements to which revolutionary passion and effort have been directed. Indiscriminate
tolerance means *de facto* restrictive freedom. The way toward
authentic freedom is the way of restrictive, and eventually repressive, tolerance. Unless the "soft" revolution becomes the "hard"
revolution, no effective correlation of freedom with justice, and of
power with order, has a chance. The *via dolorosa* leads through
the *via guillotina* to the *via humana humanorum*.

But does it? Just here the question of Jesus Christ and the question of revolution are impaled upon the agonizing dilemma of
violence. To this dilemma we shall need to return below. Meanwhile, it is pertinent to note that the *via guillotina* is the route both
of revolution and of counterrevolution whereas the *via dolorosa*
is the route along which counterrevolution comes to grief and
revolution moves toward the reconciling solidarity and power of a
liberating comradeship. Everything depends upon whether and

in how far revolutionary passion and purpose are transfigured as liberation—liberation *from* oppression and *for* being human in the world, liberation *of* all that being human in the world requires. In short, when the transfiguration of which revolutions are a sign happens to the revolutions in the making, then revolution is liberated from itself for itself, and the *via dolorosa* bypasses the *via guillotina* and enters the *via humana humanorum* directly.

Two well-known epigrams of Mao Tse-tung express the agonizing dilemma of revolutionary activity, with its high and subtle stakes, in the context of Chinese experience and the Chinese struggle. In November 1938, in the course of his concluding remarks at the Sixth Plenum of the Central Committee, Mao remarked: "Every Communist must understand this truth: political power grows out of the barrel of a gun."[99] In the speech of 27 February 1957, from which we have already quoted, Mao voiced his confidence that in a socialist society, antagonistic contradictions will disappear and nonantagonistic contradiction will continue as a salutary ferment. "Let a hundred flowers bloom," he declared; and "let a hundred schools of thought contend" (240). Clearly, the first of these epigrams gathers up the bitter experience of prerevolutionary China and of the long struggle of the Revolution. The second looks back upon the achievement of power and ahead toward the achievement of a creative conjunction of freedom and tolerance as the fruit of an altered mentality in a new society. The second epigram became the signal and the watchword of the Cultural Revolution.[100] The first was a watchword of the social revolution that had established, by military triumphs, the groundwork for the Cultural Revolution.

Both watchwords lend themselves to cynical interpretation that tells at least as much about the cynics as about the Maoist enterprise. On the cynical view, the "hundred flowers" were a calculated trap to ensnare and eliminate the last vestige of "the weapon of criticism," that is, intellectual and political freedom in the Western democratic sense, and enforce more absolutely than ever "the criticism of weapons," that is, the leadership of the Communist Party in China. On the cynical view, the power of the gun solemnizes the comradeship of Mao with Stalin and Lenin in the exaltation of violence and terror as the necessary and continuing condition of revolutionary tactics and triumph. Such judgments, however, are not only gross distortions of Mao's meaning and of the Chinese revolutionary experience. They are symptomatic as well of a congenital counterrevolutionary blindness to the messianic reality of revolutions as signs of transfiguration.

If there is any absolutism in Mao's leadership of the Chinese Revolution, it lies embedded in his personal admiration "for the martial spirit, courage, and violence" (9 ff., 193). Chinese legendary history and the recurrent, if abortive, exploits of the revolutionary societies were amply formative of these inclinations. In moments of critical decision, it would be strange indeed if ever and again they did not tip the balance in their favor. But this is by no means a proof of violent power as a power policy. Mao's expressed judgment is that the world is molded and managed by *imperialist* power that can be "remolded only with the gun." In this same context, he goes on immediately to say: "as advocates of the abolition of war, we do not desire war; but war can only be abolished through war—in order to get rid of the gun, we must first grasp it in hand" (209–10). Mao had learned this grim reality the hard way. If we turn now from his thoughts *On Contradiction* to his pamphlet on *Guerrilla Warfare*, we shall perhaps be able to follow, at less remove, Mao's own tracing of the way from "gun power" to "flower power" in the still unfinished Chinese Revolution.

## 3. On Guerrilla Warfare

The brief pamphlet on *Guerrilla Warfare* can be briefly summarized.[101] Drawn from the wisdom of an ancient Chinese military philosopher and the shrewdness of the great Marxian architect of applied power, Mao's analysis of guerrilla warfare was hammered out in the bitter struggle against the Japanese imperialist invasion of China during World War II. Two thousand four hundred years ago, Sun Tzu had noted in *The Book of War* that "speed, surprise, and deception were the primary essentials of the attack" (37). From Lenin, Mao had learned that "a people's insurrection and a people's revolution are not natural but inevitable. (41–42) . . . Evil does not exist in guerrilla warfare but only in the unorganized and undisciplined activities that are anarchism" (46).[102] Thus guerrilla warfare is "a weapon that a nation inferior in arms and military equipment may employ against a more powerful aggressor nation. When the invader pierces deep into the heart of the weaker country and occupies her territory in a cruel and oppressive manner, there is no doubt that conditions of terrain, climate, and society in general offer obstacles to his progress and may be used to advantage by those who oppose him" (42).

As a revolutionary instrument, guerrilla warfare depends not upon size but upon mobility and above all upon political and military leadership. It does not aim at a rival army but at what we have come increasingly to call a "paramilitary force." Mao does not use the phrase. He notes, however, that there must be easy passage between guerrilla units and what he calls the *orthodox army*. The importance and effectiveness of alertness, mobility, and attack are vividly indicated in a passage that declares that "the enemy's rear, flanks, and other vulnerable spots are his vital points, and there he must be harassed, attacked, dispersed, exhausted, and annihilated. . . . Guerrilla units . . . may be compared to innumerable gnats, which, by biting a giant both in front and in rear, ultimately exhaust him" (46, 54). In distinction from orthodox warfare, which aims at positions, guerrilla warfare aims at no positions but solely at a war of movement, and this in continuous and close contact with the masses of the people whose revolutionary instrument the guerrillas are.

Although guerrilla warfare has a considerable history, which Mao digresses to sketch, it is uniquely suited to the present social state of China and to the presence upon Chinese territory of a vastly superior invader. "China is a country half colonial and half feudal; it is a country that is politically, militarily, and economically backward. . . . It is a vast country with great resources and tremendous population, a country in which the terrain is complicated and the facilities for communication are poor. All these factors favor a protracted war; they all favor the application of mobile warfare and guerrilla operations" (68). The pamphlet goes on to specify the logistics of guerrilla warfare, with careful attention to the formation and organization of guerrilla bands, to the methods of arming them, to the relations between officers and men in the guerrilla army, and to the relationship between politics and military affairs. In an almost eschatological passage, Mao almost lyrically affirms the positive and promising human meaning of the conjunction of guns and power and revolutionary purposes. He writes:

> It is to be hoped that the world is in the last era of strife. The vast majority of human beings have already prepared or are preparing to fight a war that will bring justice to the oppressed peoples of the world. No matter how long this war may last, there is no doubt that it will be followed by an unprecedented epoch of peace. The war that we are fighting today for the emancipation of the Chinese is a part of the war for the freedom of all human beings, and the independent, happy, and liberal China that we are fighting to establish will be part of that new world order. (89–90)

*Yu Chi Chan*, as the Chinese title of the pamphlet on Guerrilla Warfare reads, is a manifesto on the making of a revolution when all the major social conditions for a revolution are present. Among these are: a long history of imperialist exploitation; a vast disproportion between the power and privilege of the ruling groups and the possibility and power available to the masses of the population for a human level of existence and development; an effective conjunction of national and revolutionary aspirations, of the unfulfilled ideals of the past and the participation in those ideals through a new order of life on the part of those who literally have nothing to lose but their chains; the impact of a revolutionary vanguard of dedicated leaders, politically astute, socially sensitive, and militarily tested and tried; the imminent emergence of a revolutionary consciousness, that is, of a fundamentally altered political, social, valuational—in short, of a human mentality. There can be little doubt that these conditions were dramatically present in and around the confrontation in China between a highly disciplined, technologically organized, military invasion from without and an arrogant, divided, moribund political and social establishment within. The Long March, undertaken by Mao and about twenty others in the vanguard of some eighty-five thousand soldiers and thirty-five women,[103] has become a legend of political, military, personal, and revolutionary achievement. At the cost of a staggering loss of life and against incredible odds of terrain and sheer power ranged against them, the Red Army came into being as a result of the experience and tactics set down two years later in *Yu Chi Chan*. Time and again outnumbered, disciplined and purposeful bands of guerrillas routed superior enemy positions, acquired abandoned enemy material, and enjoyed the virtually miraculous protection of mountainous terrain, hastily improvised river crossings, and above all, the unfailing support of the masses of the population. It was as though

> the stars fought from heaven
> the stars in their courses fought against Sisera.
> (Judg. 5:20)

At least, so a politics of transfiguration may regard it. Perhaps the most striking thing about the Long March, second only to the victory of the Red Army, is the blindness with which Western imperialism, including the United States, was smitten. It poured vast quantities of funds and supplies into the opulent obsolescence of the Kuomintang, only to have them fall like manna from heaven into the hands of Mao's increasingly effective guerrilla units and thus to facilitate the forging of the national army of the new China. Small wonder that Mao could say to Anna Louise Strong in August 1946: "The atom bomb is a paper tiger used by the U.S. reactionaries to scare people. It looks terrible but in fact it isn't. Of course, the atom bomb is a weapon of mass slaughter, but the outcome of a war is decided by the people, not by one or two new types of weapon. All reactionaries are paper tigers."[104] A year later he wrote, "This is the historic epoch in which world capitalism and imperialism are going down to their doom and world socialism and democracy are marching to victory. The dawn is in sight, we must exert ourselves" (281). Whether or not history will adjudge Mao Tse-tung as one of the world's great military strategists must for the moment remain open. There can be little doubt, however, that the defeat of the Kuomintang and the Japanese and the socialist liberation of China are in a major way due to the indomitable spirit, the remarkable theoretical and practical intellect, and the personal example of conviction, courage, and suffering on behalf of a new and human order of life for his people of Mao Tse-tung.

Two decades after the victorious application of the principles of guerrilla warfare came the year of the "hundred flowers." The Cultural Revolution was as suddenly aborted as it had been begun. A test was being made of the critical issue whether victory over the Kuomintang and the Japanese and the inauguration of a "People's Democracy" in China had been matched by the formation of a revolutionary consciousness adequate to that human future. Prepared for according to the pamphlet on *Guerrilla Warfare*, projected according to the analysis of *Contradictions*, and symbolized in the epigrammatic movement from "gun power" to "flower power," the test failed. It signaled a social convulsion rather than a dependable social development. The Red Guards, as one observer reports, seem to have disposed of the last vestiges of anti-communist activity in the People's Democracy, or at least driven it deeply underground.

Yet the price of this achievement seems to have been a China "weakened . . . economically, politically, militarily, no matter what course the crisis takes, and no matter who winds up holding the reins of power."[105] The single certainty is that "communism in China is there to stay."[106] The disorganization of agricultural and industrial production has not prevented the detonation of a hydrogen bomb; nor has it deterred the determination of the government to achieve top membership in the nuclear club of the world's great powers. The Cultural Revolution seems to have affected neither foreign policy nor the stockpiling of armaments. China has moved up to third place, overtaking France, despite industrial backwardness and domestic disorders. Indeed, the paramount question now seems to be the consolidation of revolutionary power, with less attention to the consolidation and development of a revolutionary consciousness. Like Jacob and Esau, the heirs of revolutionary destiny and promise are more fiercely poised against each other than against their once-common imperialist enemies in the capitalist world. Within and without, the line between revolutionary orthodoxy and revolutionary heresy threatens to become a fortified wall dividing friends from enemies, as the struggle for succession within and for the leadership of the world revolution goes on.

## 4. Ideology, Power, and the Future of China

It will be recalled that Robespierre ultimately abandoned his own "despotism of liberty" before "the much more powerful conspiracy of necessity and poverty" that exalted the contentment of the people over the freedom that being human takes, as the ultimate goal of the Revolution.[107] "We shall perish," he had declared in his last speech, "because, in the history of mankind, we missed the moment to found freedom."[108] At the pinnacle of power, and on the nearer edge of whatever immortality may be reserved to him, Mao Tse-tung finds himself in a strangely similar case. The dynamics of humanization are the same, but the context and complexity of giving personal and institutional shape to them have drastically altered. Once again, the issue is joined between ideology and power, between the continuing implementation of revolutionary goals and the maintenance of revolutionary gains.[109] A knowledgeable and sober estimate of the greatness and the tragedy of Mao has put the questions of the future of Mao and the future of China in this way:

> . . . The leap from guerrilla warfare in the countryside to the building of a modern industrial economy was a very great one indeed, an overwhelming challenge to Mao's flexibility. . . . Mao's tragedy is that of a man who has striven all his life to adapt to new and strange conditions and ideas, who has succeeded in doing this far better than most of his contemporaries, and who then discovers that the world with which he has sought to come to terms for half a century no longer exists, or in any case has been so profoundly modified that old formulas and old ideas are no longer applicable. . . . Mao Tse-tung began his career as an iconoclast struggling against the restraints imposed on the individual by traditional society. He now finds himself grappling with the problems of organized and rationalized production in the era of automation. . . . He shares the Leninist prejudice according to which the organization of the economy is a mere matter of detail once the basic question of the locus of political power in society is easily resolved. Like Lenin, he thinks that the tasks of adminis-

tration are easy; but whereas Lenin's answer was to get them out of the way in the most inconspicuous way possible . . . , Mao's solution is to dramatize everything, including scientific research, in political terms. . . . Mao Tse-tung places the political criteria of doctrinal purity—which for him are also moral criteria—ahead of mere economic necessity. . . . He refuses to recognize that economics has its own logic, partly independent of any broader criteria; for him, . . . practical activity must be penetrated from beginning to end with moral values.[110]

If this be indeed the greatness and the tragedy of Mao Tse-tung, it is, in a still more fundamental sense, the tragedy of revolution in a society in which "technological rationality has become political rationality" (Marcuse). In such a society, the autonomous logic of economics steadily deepens and widens the cleavage between power and value and transposes the crucial issue between ideology and power into the more complex one between the *power of an ideology* and an *ideology of power*. The *power of an ideology* is the power of a humanizing vision to shape values and of values to shape the organization of a social order in which freedom has the space to undergird the people's happiness. An *ideology of power*, on the other hand, is the self-justifying defense and expansion of existing power through a subtle and pervasive invasion of the people's consciousness in order to achieve an identification between the happiness of the people and the security guaranteed by the very power that seeks to justify itself. Within this vicious circle, the exchange of freedom for security occurs.

As of this writing, it would appear that Mao's skill and achievements as a guerrilla strategist are being devoted to the ideological attempt to bring technology and morality together in order that the human fruits of the Chinese Revolution might be nourished and sustained. The political revolution having been achieved, the consciousness revolution is in full swing. In the second of his *Letters from China*, James Reston, reporting on his visit to Peking, writes:

> . . . It is a bit of a shock to discover that your good Maoist not only believes in struggle and revolution but in plain living and high thinking. . . . The similarities with the dogmatism of the Protestant ethic are not only unmistakable but unavoidable. . . .

There is something about these serious revolutionary chairmen that persuades you that they are telling the truth, and . . . the atmosphere of intelligent and purposeful work is impressive.

More important, it is clear that you are in the presence not merely of industrial or agricultural technicians but of true believers in the gospel according to Mao Tse-tung.

They don't talk production but the Spartan philosophy of Chairman Mao, and it is fairly obvious that they believe the production will never be achieved without the philosophy. . . . The main thing is to get the purpose straight, to mobilize the people even if they have to move mountains with teaspoons and to find a common philosophy which the people believe. And that they seem to be doing, ironically by adopting many aspects of the old faiths which the West has dropped along the way.[111]

The West has indeed dropped many aspects of the old faiths along the way. Given its vast technological advantage over the remolded society in China, it is doing less well in the human task of making space for freedom. Western technology is altering Western mentality and values. In the China of Mao Tse-tung, the link between production and philosophy (in Mao's words, between practice and theory) may be shattered by the technological development and education necessary to a modern industrial society —and so undo the revolution in society and consciousness now under way. In the West, at least in the United States, the marked surrender of the humanistic tradition to the statistical and organizaional mentality, the increasing dependence of university and theological faculties and administrations and even churches upon the expertise of consultants (witch doctors for sick institutions), and the addiction of the search for personal identity and meaning to the rising egocentrism of psychedelic and group dynamics underline the magnitude of a counterrevolutionary, systemic dehumanization rushing into the vacuum left by the effective exclusion of morality (not to mention piety) from technics. It may be that in the West, at least in the United States, there is a revolution in consciousness in the making, as Charles Reich has been arguing;[112] and it may be that this revolutionary consciousness will find its way by an inverse direction to a companion political and social reconstruction, which in China has come first. But until such an inverse course for "Consciousness III" (Reich) is more clearly and firmly apparent, it would be premature to assume that the increasingly technocratic society of the West is being transfigured by the dynamics of a revolutionary humanization; and a mistake to assume that Mao Tsetung has missed the moment to found freedom.

If it should turn out that an ideology of power should overtake the power of an ideology and bring the Maoist achievement to a stop before a recrudescence of China's immemorial nationalism and imperialism, the gains of the revolution would remain, though unfulfilled. The calendar of revolutions assigns them a short lifespan but does not thereby invalidate them. The People's Republic of China may have reached a plateau of uncertain horizon on which a power struggle will be fought and a succession of cultural revolutions make its intense and fitful way. The passion and vision of a new order of human affairs, an order of freedom and justice, of liberation from bondage and oppression, may abate; but they will not cease. In a world fundamentally and ultimately the theater of messianic politics, the moment of truth for colonialist-imperialism has arrived, and until its doom has been accomplished, signs of transfiguration will not be wanting. Elijah's mantle could fall again upon Elisha. The line from Ahab to Jehu is a line of battle between the prophets and the kings, between revolution and counterrevolution (I Kings 17—II Kings 11). The Maoist revolution was no sooner on its way than the front line of combat shifted. The battle is now joined between Washington and Hanoi; and the prophetic mantle has fallen upon Ho Chi Minh.

## 5. Ho Chi Minh and Mao Tse-tung: The End of Colonialist Imperialism

A foremost instance of ideological blindness in the Western sense has marked the foreign policies of five Presidents of the United States and their military advisers in the Pentagon, ironically enough for almost half the life-span of the revolution in China under Mao Tse-tung. The well-known historic enmity between the Chinese people and the Vietnamese people, and the fierce nationalism of the Vietnamese, have been effectively disregarded by the shapers of American policy, in the arrogance of American power. At a fateful meeting in Geneva in 1954, the wide gulf between a messianic understanding of the divine economy and a rigid Calvinist understanding of the morality of politics stood exposed. A politics of transfiguration and a politics of moral order have been as far apart, then and since, as were the world of Jesus of Nazareth and the religious and Roman authorities before whom the showdown came. The failure of the United States to sign the Geneva Accord proved to be more than the trifle of a missing signature. It heralded more than a decade and a half of the crudest and cruelest forms of imperialist destruction and dehumanization only to end in bitter and ignominious disengagement.

The clue to this humiliating checkmate, amounting to defeat, is the transfiguration of the poverty and exploitation, of the suffering and the weakness, of the dehumanizing victimization by power, of a people thus destined for colonial injustice and bondage, through the instrumentality of Ho Chi Minh. Through him the power of the things that are not, to bring to naught the things that are, began to take the shape and direction of a human future. The people that were no people, the strength that was no strength, the possibilities that were no possibilities, had come under the dynamics of the political realism of a messianic politics released by the presence and power of Jesus of Nazareth in the world for the humanization of all mankind. At Dien Bien Phu (1954), in the Tet offensive (1965), and at Paris (since 1967), the signs of this transfiguration have appeared to all who have had eyes to see and ears to hear. Colonialist imperialism has been weighed in the balance and found wanting. The peoples of Asia, in a floodtide of passion for their humanness, have been claimed by a revolutionary vision and by revolutionary possibilities for a new and human order of freedom, justice, and peace.

Bernard Fall has observed that

> more than most other colonial revolutionaries, Ho Chi Minh understood that Vietnam's case as a colonial country was not exceptional but rather was typical of the whole colonial system. In his writings, Ho was to show a constant concern for other colonial struggles in Africa, the Middle East, and Latin America.

His early writings also clearly reflect the personal humiliations he must have suffered at the hands of his colonial masters—not because they hated him as a person, but simply because, as a "colored" colonial, he *did not count as a human being*. This intense personalization of the whole anticolonial struggle shines clearly throughout Ho's writings.[113]

It was this personalization that first turned Ho toward Lenin and the Communist movement. In an article on "The Path Which Led Me to Leninism," written in April 1960, Ho stated: "At first, patriotism, not yet Communism, led me to have confidence in Lenin, in the Third International. Step by step, along the struggle, by studying Marxism-Leninism, I gradually came upon the fact that only Socialism and Communism can liberate the oppressed nations and the working people throughout the world from slavery" (6, 7).

The pilgrimage of Ho to revolutionary leadership in Vietnam is strikingly similar to that of Mao Tse-tung. Mao did not study abroad, as Ho did. His bitterness toward the West was thus secondhand, not firsthand. Ho's firsthand experiences in France and in the United States left upon him the indelible impression that in these centers of culture, power, and advanced development, the prospects of a human future for all mankind were frustratingly blocked by imperialism, colonialism, and racism. Mao's more distant experience of the same was destined sooner or later to make them companions in the commitment to a new and intrinsic human future for their own and all the deprived peoples of the world. Like Mao, a pragmatist and nationalist who found in Marxism-Leninism the instrument of theory and practice for the implementation of revolutionary conviction, Ho Chi Minh became a Communist because he was a revolutionary. He did not become a revolutionary because he was a Communist.

In the stress upon the repudiation of colonialist imperialism; upon the instrumentality of Marxism-Leninism, especially of its doctrine of the inseparability of theory and practice; upon raising the level of ideological understanding (in the Maoist, not in the Western sense) of the party leadership and of the people; and in the confidence that the social revolution under way in China embraces national and international aspirations and achievements of a human future for all the deprived peoples of the earth—the thoughts and efforts of Ho Chi Minh are strikingly parallel to those of Mao Tse-tung. China and the Soviet Union are the great models of the path and the power of this new future. This does not mean the abandonment of historic national and cultural differentiations, and even enmities between the Chinese and the Vietnamese. Nor does it mean a slavish adherence to Soviet power and policy. It means that although "the Chinese Communist Party also made mistakes in its line and suffered losses from dogmatism," nevertheless "in the fight against it, the Chinese Communist Party, under Mao Tse-tung's leadership, succeeded in combining the universal truth of Marxism-Leninism with the revolutionary practice of China, thereby taking steps proper to the Chinese society, and made a great contribution to the treasure-house of Marxist-Leninist ideology and experience" 320–21).

Ho's admiration for China and the Soviet Union means that "the October Revolution brightened the history of mankind with a new dawn. . . . (It) has shattered the fetters of imperialism, destroyed its foundation, and inflicted on it a deadly blow. Like a thunderbolt, it has stirred up the Asian peoples from their centuries-old slumbers. It has opened up for them the revolutionary anti-imperialist era, the era of national liberation" (323, 326). It means that "the October Revolution gave an impetus to the movement of national liberation, which has become a surging wave in all Eastern countries: China, India, Indonesia, Vietnam, etc. After World War II, many colonial and semicolonial countries have shattered imperialist chains" (332). It means that "the victory of the Chinese revolution was a historical event of great significance. It struck a new blow against the imperialist system, the severest since the October Revolution" (332–33). It means that "in a short space of history, socialism has become a world system, now embracing twelve countries with more than 900 million people" (326).[114]

From the point of view of *Realpolitik*, the movement from Marx to Mao to Ho Chi Minh is a movement in the course of which the power of ideology (in the Western sense) has become an ideology of power. Consequently, a worldwide imperialism, unable to cope with its contradictions, is being confronted by a rival imperialism, whose contradictions are still able to be coped with. But from the point of view of the political realism of a messianic politics, the movement from Marx to Mao to Ho Chi Minh is a revolution best understood as a sign of transfiguration. The transfiguration is the unveiling of the imminence of an ultimate judgment upon the established power of colonialist imperialism whose moment of truth has arrived; and of a presence in the world whose sovereign life and spirit are at work bringing power and truth together for the conversion of suffering into reconciliation under the promise and possibility of a new and human order of freedom and fulfill-ment already breaking in and under way.

### B. FROM FIDEL AND CHE GUEVARA TO CAMILO TORRES AND NESTOR PAZ ZAMORA

On 18 April 1959, in an interview in Havana, Ernesto Che Guevara made public acknowledgment of his own indebtedness and that of the Cuban Revolution to Mao Tse-tung. "We have always looked up to Comrade Mao Tse-tung," he said. "When we were engaged in guerrilla warfare we studied Comrade Mao Tse-tungs' theory on guerrilla warfare. . . . We studied this little book carefully and learned many things. We discovered that there were many problems that Comrade Mao Tse-tung had already sys-tematically and scientifically studied and answered. This was a great help to us."[115] We turn to the revolutionary movement from Fidel and Che Guevara to Camilo Torres and Nestor Paz Zamora, via this reminder of the revolutionary movement from Marx to Mao and Ho Chi Minh, for two reasons. One reason is to keep us from forgetting that the east wind also blows in the West; the other is to indicate that the west wind blows with certain revolutionary currents of its own. We have dealt at some length with the move-ment from Marx to Mao to Ho Chi Minh because it exemplifies the purpose, pattern, and power of revolutionary aspiration and achievement, the magnetism of which fascinates and challenges at least half the continents of earth. As such a "field of force," Marxism-Leninism provides both a model for, and a confirmation of, revolutionary possibilities for the other revolutionary movements in the current scene.

This is particularly the case in the matter of the organization and tactics of guerrilla activities. But it is also evident in the stress upon the close relation between theory and practice, upon the central importance of a mass basis and support of revolutionary leadership, and in the thoroughly instrumental relation of Marxism-Leninism to the specific social, national, and cultural conditions from which a given revolution springs and can be made. Fidelism is the next most conspicuous case in point. As one of its brilliant theoreticians has put it: "Fidelism is only the concrete process of the regeneration of Marxism-Leninism in Latin American conditions and according to the historic traditions of each country. . . . The lesson of Fidelism is that a genuine nationalism in Latin America implies the final overthrow of the semi-colonial state, the destruction of its army, and the installation of socialism."[116]

It will be recalled that in the early dawn of 26 July 1953, a group of men under the leadership of Fidel Castro attacked the Moncada Barracks in Oriente Province of the island of Cuba. The attack failed. Its survivors were imprisoned only to resume the revolutionary struggle after an amnesty had been granted. The 26th of July Movement, however, was to become the point of departure for, and the symbol of, a fundamental shift of power and of consciousness that within five years brought Fidel Castro, together with his brother Raul and Ernesto Che Guevara, to the effective leadership of the Cuban Revolution. Between the failure of the 26 July attack and the departure on 31 December 1958 of Fulgencio Batista from Cuba, there had been counterrevolutionary harassment, exile, and arrest in Mexico; a dangerous return voyage on their yacht, the *Granma*, on the part of eighty-two men; furious battles from their hideout in the Sierra Maestra mountains; and a precarious but ultimately potent new alliance between the peasants and a vanguard military and political force that opened the way in Cuba for a new era of freedom and opportunity for the great majority of the population.

### 1. Fidelism As Judgment upon Imperialist Colonialism

This précis of how it began is familiar enough. What is less familiar, or at least less carefully attended to, is that "this is the first time—ever, anywhere, that a genuine socialist revolution has been made by *non*-communists."[117] Fidelism is a deep-rooted Cuban movement that, by secular standards, *happened* because the dehumanizing reality of an old social, economic, and political order had arrived at its moment of truth and point of no return. In a world under the dynamics of messianic politics, Fidelism was called to displace an establishment, incapable of the practice of love (Rom. 13), of the exercise of power in truth (John 18, 19), whose day was done. "One of the supreme ironies of the revolution is that the social and economic programs of the Batista government closely resembled those of Castro's 26th of July Movement: both focused on structural problems of the economy, and both held out promises to nearly every socioeconomic group in Cuba" (0, 7, 8). But beneath this irony was the inescapable fact that "Cuban socialism was inevitable in the sense that it was necessary if the island was to be rescued from permanent economic stagnation, social backwardness and degradation, and political . . . corruption" (0, 6).

Thus one may go further and say that in a world under the dynamics of messianic politics, the Cuban Revolution is a sign of transfiguration. In and through it, a human future has broken in upon a moribund past, fresh possibilities of freedom and justice, of hope and fulfillment, have become imminent exactly where old and dehumanizing patterns and practices of human existence had played themselves out. Indeed, so imminent was this future that its inbreaking could be heralded by a handful of dedicated revolutionaries and, like the Russian October Revolution, the actual transfer of power could be effected without violence. The fury of battle had gone before; and, as in China, guerrilla experience had forged a rebel army capable of leadership, and of holding power once transferred. "The social revolution was peaceful and orderly," however, "because the political revolution transferred economic power from one small group of men to another . . . and because the nationalization of agriculture and industry won the consent and support of the majority of the Cuban people" (0, 8).

If economic stagnation, social backwardness and degradation, and political corruption were the internal dynamics making the Cuban Revolution inevitable, the external dynamics of the revolution were spearheaded by imperialist colonialism. We have ventured to distinguish between *imperialist colonialism* and *colonialist imperialism* in order to underline the difference between the imperialist thrust in Central and South America and the imperialist thrust in Asia and Africa. In both cases, colonialism, with the full measure of its psychological and sociopolitical ambiguities and variations, is the purpose and consequence of imperialism. Imperialism is the psychological, socioeconomic, and political domination of a weaker power by a stronger power. It has displaced the conquest, occupation, and exacting of tribute that once characterized the subjugation of peoples and powers by a more subtle deployment of political, military, and socioeconomic dominance through an absentee administration and a limited degree of self-determination. This more subtle deployment of power, administration, and limited self-determination is colonialism.

In Asia and Africa, colonialism is the consequence of economic domination in the wake of military conquest and occupation. It is *overt* colonialism, the direct possession of territories, resources, and peoples by reason of disproportionate and expansionist power. Hence it may be described as *colonialist imperialism*. In Latin America, colonialism is *covert*, the indirect exercise of political and economic hegemony over territories, resources, and peoples by reason of disproportionate and expansionist power, always with the threat of military occupation lurking in the wings. Hence it may be described as *imperialist colonialism*. In short, *colonialist imperialism* is *de facto* and *dejure* possession of colonies; *imperialist colonialism* is the exercise of political, socioeconomic, and psychological domination without either *de facto* or *de jure* possession of colonies. The pattern of imperialism in the nineteenth century was largely *colonialist imperialist*; in the twentieth century, the pattern is largely *imperialist colonialist*. In the nineteenth century, imperialist domination was exercised from and by western

European powers. In the twentieth century, imperialist domination is being exercised chiefly from and by two powers: the United States and the Soviet Union.

The Chinese Revolution is a direct challenge to, and judgment upon, the imperialism of both these powers. The Cuban Revolution is an explicit challenge to, and judgment upon, the imperialism of the United States, implicitly upon that of the Soviet Union. In any case, imperialism in both its colonialist forms is the Establishment whose day is done. Of this judgment, in a world under the dynamics of messianic politics, the Chinese and the Cuban Revolutions are the bearers. They are the bearers too of new and humanizing possibilities, breaking in upon old and dehumanizing ones, possibilities for freedom and justice, for power at the disposal of truth, and for suffering as the prelude to the healing of enmity by reconciliation. As such, they are signs of transfiguration.

## 2. Love and a Revolutionary Vocation: Che Guevara

At the conclusion of Part Two, we referred to Moltmann's paraphrase of a remark of Che Guevara's concerning the vocation of a revolutionary.[118] We return to this remark now because of the remarkable comradeship between Fidel Castro and Che Guevara in the leadership of the Cuban Revolution and because this leadership is so revealing of the human and, *pari passu*, of the messianic significance of what is now going on on that island. What Che actually says about the relation between the vocation of a revolutionary and love is set down in a letter addressed to Carlos Quijano, editor of *Marcha* (Montevideo), in March 1965. Che writes:

Let me say, with the risk of appearing ridiculous, that the true revolutionary is guided by strong feelings of love. It is impossible to think of an authentic revolutionary without this quality. This is perhaps one of the greatest dramas of a leader; he must combine an impassioned spirit with a cold mind and make painful decisions without flinching one muscle. Our vanguard revolutionaries must idealize their love for the people, for the most sacred causes, and make it one and indivisible. They cannot descend, with small doses of daily affection, to the places where ordinary men put their love into practice.

On these conditions, one must have a large dose of humanity, a large dose of a sense of justice and truth, to avoid falling in dogmatic extremes, into cold scholasticism, into isolation from the masses. Every day we must struggle so that this love of living humanity is transformed into concrete facts, into acts that will serve as an example, as a mobilizing factor. . . .

The Revolution is made through man, but man must forge day by day his revolutionary spirit.

Thus we go forward. At the head of the immense column . . . is Fidel, followed by the best party cadres and, immediately after, so close that their great strength is felt, come the people as a whole, a solid conglomeration of individualities moving toward a common objective: individuals who have achieved the awareness of what must be done, men who struggle to leave the domain of necessity and enter that of freedom. (Ch, 167–68)

An earlier passage in this letter speaks of "the culpability of our intellectuals and artists" as lying "in their original sin" (Ch, 166). It is not entirely clear whether this "original sin" consists in the fact that "they are not authentic revolutionaries" (Ch, 166), or whether they are prevented from being "authentic revolutionaries" by an "original sin" of some other genre, such as having stopped "where the anguish of alienated man shows through" and failing to press forward to a more positive and human "relation between form and content" (Ch, 165). In any case, "the new generation will arrive free of original sin . . . and revolutionaries will come to sing the song of the new man with the authentic voice of the people. It is a process that requires time" (Ch, 166). Again and again, the refrain runs through the thoughts and writings of Che Guevara that socialism can, must, and will build a new man. This is humanistic messianism with all the fire of a passionate and purifying vision. It informed his admiration for, and loyalty to, Fidel, his tireless efforts in and on behalf of Cuba's revolutionary government both at home and abroad, and sustained him in his sufferings, imprisonment, torture, and assassination in the wake of the abortive uprising in which he lost his life in Bolivia on 9 December 1967.

In a letter to Castro, on 3 October 1965, Che writes:

Reviewing my whole life, I believe I have worked with sufficient honesty and dedication to consolidate the revolutionary triumph. My only shortcoming of some gravity was not to have trusted in you more from the first moments in the Sierra Maestra and not to have understood with sufficient celerity your qualities as a leader and a revolutionary. . . .

Few times has a statesman shone more . . . ; I am proud, too, of having followed you without hesitation and of identifying myself with your way of thinking, of seeing, and of assessing dangers and principles.

Other hills of the world demand the aid of my modest efforts. I can do what is denied you because of your responsibility as the head of Cuba, and the hour for us to separate has come. . . .

On the new battlefields, I will carry the faith which you instilled in me, the revolutionary spirit of my people, the sensation of fulfilling the most sacred of all duties—to struggle against imperialism wherever it may be. This in itself heals and cures my laceration. (Ch, 422–23)[119]

Eight years earlier, in recalling his first meeting with Fidel, Che had described what led him to those first moments in the Sierra Maestra:

I spoke with Fidel a whole night. At dawn I was already the physician of the future expedition. In reality, after the experience I went through, my long walks throughout all of Latin America and the Guatemalan closing, not much was needed to convince me to join any revolution against a tyrant; but Fidel impressed me as an extraordinary man. He faced and resolved the impossible. He had an unshakable faith that once he left he would arrive in Cuba, that once he arrived he would fight, that once he began fighting he would win. I shared his optimism. (Ch, 364)[120]

Perhaps the most touching indication of the integrity and intensity of "the strong feelings of love" that inform the vocation of a revolutionary is given in Che's last letter to his children, written from Bolivia.[121] The letter begins:

To my children:
. . . if one day you read this letter it will be because I am no

longer with you. You will almost not remember me and the littlest ones will not remember me at all.

Your father has been a man who acts as he thinks and you can be sure that he has been faithful to his convictions. Grow up to be good revolutionaries. . . . Remember that the Revolution is what matters and that each one of us, alone, is worth nothing. Above all, always be capable of feeling deeply any injustice committed against anyone anywhere in the world. That is the most beautiful quality of a revolutionary.

Farewell, children, I still hope to see you. A big hug and kiss
from Papa (Ch, 426)

"Feeling deeply any injustice committed against anyone any- where in the world"!—and laying one's life on the line in order to achieve the eradication of the same! In obedience to this feel- ing and in the pursuit of this vocation, Che has been described as a "revolutionary purist," in distinction from Fidel Castro, who is a "revolutionary pragmatist" (Ch, 27). Between them, they worked out a theory and practice of revolution that combined a humanistic vision with the realities of power and of the organization and implementation of policies; a national base with international solidarity; and a unification and mobilization of resources—human and cultural, socioeconomic and political—with a resolute identi- fication of the enemy whom the dynamics of history and the divine economy had brought to judgment. That enemy is the im- perialist colonialism as practiced by the United States of America.

In a statement on 8 August 1961, as Chairman of the Cuban delegation at the Fifth Plenary Session of the Organization of American States, in Punta del Este, Uruguay, Che explained the Cuban Revolution as "an agrarian, antifeudal, antiimperialist revo- lution, transformed by its internal evolution and by external aggres- sion into a socialist revolution. . . . It is a revolution with humanistic characteristics. It feels solidarity with the oppressed peoples of the world" (Ch, 274–75). The same statement includes a strong con- demnation of the Alliance for Progress, different only in its word- ing from what informed people in government, university, press, and the church, both Catholic and Protestant, in Brazil had told him a decade earlier. "We have denounced the Alliance for Progress," Che declares, "as an instrument designed to separate Cuba from the other countries of Latin America, to sterilize the example of the Cuban Revolution, and then to bend the other countries to the wishes of the imperialists" (Ch, 290). The statement then proceeds to a Bill of Particulars. Two and one-half years later, at the United Nations Conference on Trade and Development (25 March 1964), the Bill of Particulars gets more specific and the denunciation more explicit. "The so-called Alliance for Progress is another clear demonstration of the fraudulent methods used by the United States to maintain false hopes among nations while exploitation grows worse" (Ch, 321). Writes Régis Debray: "To sum up: the Alliance for Progress regulates, conceals and reinforces the process whereby the undercapitalized countries of South America nourish and increase the accumulation of capital in the United States of America" (D, 121).

"Feeling deeply any injustice committed against anyone anywhere in the world"! As in China, so in Cuba, the terms for understanding the intensity and the enormity of the task of setting such injustice right were discovered in Marx and Lenin. And this in the most general sense that Marx and Lenin had grasped the dynamics of social reality and social change since the industrial revolution with a depth and accuracy that, despite errors of detail, made them the architects of a combination of theory and practice that could not be ignored by anyone sensitive enough to injustice and exploitation to look facts in the face. "Our position, when asked whether we are Marxists or not," says Che, "is the same as that of a physicist when asked if he is a 'Newtonian' or a biologist if asked whether he is a 'Pasteurian.' There are truths so evident, so embedded in the people's knowledge, that they are now useless to discuss. One should be a 'Marxist' as naturally as one is a 'Newtonian' in physics, or a 'Pasteurian' in biology . . ." (Ch, 49). That was in 1960. Four years later, in an interview with Maurice Zeitlin of the University of Wisconsin, Che adheres to the same point. "We regard Marxism as a science in development, just as, say, biology is a science." As for Lenin,

> the value of Lenin is enormous—in the same sense in which a major biologist's work is valuable to other biologists. He is prob-

ably the leader who has brought the most to the theory of revolution. He was able to apply Marxism in a given moment to the problems of the state, and to emerge with laws of universal validity. For example? His theory of imperialism, of the state and revolution, of the work of the party through the stages of the revolution, of his studies of the material development of production. (Ch, 394)[122]

Thus the Cuban Revolution is Marxist in a fundamentally non-ideological sense; and in an ideological sense only in the sense of the discovered pertinence to Cuba of Lenin's assessment of the realities of power and the machinery of the state in a capitalist and imperialist world.[123]

In such a world, the dynamics of the Cuban Revolution are bound to attract the revolutionary aspirations and struggle of the wider Latin American world. This does not mean a proliferation of revolutions Cuban-style from Mexico to Argentina. Nor does it mean an imminent and unified uprising of the whole South American continent. It means that the tide is beginning to run, and with gathering force, against North American imperialist colonialism. It means that the impoverished and oppressed agrarian and urban masses are beginning to find their way toward a revolutionary vanguard aware of Lenin's dictum that "without a revolutionary theory there is no revolutionary movement," and mindful of the lessons in guerrilla warfare taught by Mao Tse-tung and Che Guevara. It means that the "northern colossus" is an increasingly fragile reed upon which to lean in the endeavor to checkmate intensifying contradictions of a technocratic society. As the Second Declaration of Havana states:

> In many Latin American countries revolution is inevitable. This fact is not determined by the horrible conditions of exploitation under which the American people live, the development of a revolutionary consciousness in the masses, the world-wide crisis of imperialism, and the universal liberation movements of the subjugated nations.
>
> Today's restlessness is an unmistakable symptom of rebellion. The entrails of the continent are stirring after having witnessed four centuries of slave, semi-slave, and feudal exploitation of man

by man, from the aborigines and slaves brought from Africa to the national groups that arose later—whites, blacks, mulattoes, mestizos, and Indians—who today share pain, humiliation, and the Yankee yoke, and share hope for a better tomorrow. (Ch, 80)

The question is not whether—but when; when the day of liberation breaks, the hour of transfiguration strikes.

But established power does not yield easily; indeed, except to a force majeure, as Marx said, not at all. Meanwhile, as Régis Debray has axiomatically put it: "Revolution also revolutionizes counter-revolution" (D, 124).[124] "To sum up," he goes on to say, "the door which Cuba opened by surprise, under the very nose of imperialism . . . has been solidly bolted from within by the national oligarchies and from without by imperialism, always ready to intervene" (D, 124). From the Bay of Pigs to the invasion of the Dominican Republic, from the training of counterrevolutionary guerrillas in Guatemala, to the Alliance for Progress to the Shylockian negotiations over expropriation, and not least, to the murder of Che himself—United States imperialism offers a counter-revolutionary confirmation of Debray's axiom that can be regarded with charity rather than with cold contempt only under the rubric of Romans 13.

On the other hand, there is a poignant tragedy and a powerful paradox in the life and death of Ernesto Che Guevara. His revolutionary vision and passion overreached the realistic complexity and pace of social change. His own theory of the foco may not have underestimated the cold cunning of enemies but did underestimate the fractionalism and elemental human weaknesses of friends, including rival revolutionary groups. His own guerrilla activities in Bolivia were a casualty to multiple blunders. As a sympathetic critic has remarked: "Guevara had too much iron will and too little political sophistication" (Ch, 36). At the same time, "his death represents a great paradox: the failure of his political strategy is also the victory of his example. His military defeat gave him an existential victory" (Ch, 38). One thinks, almost without thinking, of the confrontation between Jesus and Pilate (John 18, 19). There was no military defeat, of course; but there was an obvious failure of political strategy and a victory of Jesus' example.

Yet it was precisely the obvious that was being transfigured. The quickening pace connecting an earlier transfiguration with an earlier and more literal crucifixion echoes strangely in the capture and assassination of a contemporary and committed revolutionary. To anyone tutored in a politics of transfiguration, it is all somehow reminiscent of the fascination and the freeze of the echoes in the whispering gallery in London's old St. Paul's. Whether Che himself was animated by even a subliminal attachment to Jesus of Nazareth, we do not know enough to know. But there is a certain, not entirely coincidental, yet thoroughly heretical similarity between the image of Che and the tonsorial reduplication of Jesus and Che that leads the alienated, yet strangely committed youth of these days to the too literal imitation of the redemptive revolutionary and the too wistful imitation of the revolutionary redeemer.

### 3. Revolution As Efficacious Charity: Camilo Torres and Nestor Paz Zamora

There were, however, revolutionary companions of Che who were more than subliminally attached to Jesus of Nazareth. In nearby Colombia, and indeed, in Bolivia itself, there were apostolic revolutionaries called to the struggle against poverty and persecution. In the exercise of that vocation, they were prepared for the discovery of a liberating brotherhood with Marxist revolutionaries. In Camilo Torres and Nestor Paz Zamora, Jesus and Marx meet face-to-face in the revolutionary movements now current, through a comradeship of differing perspectives and dedicated concern for what it takes to be and to stay human in the world and in the sharing of suffering and death. The "Revolutionary Priest," as a recently published edition of his writings and messages calls him, is perhaps second only to Che Guevara as a hero on the way to sainthood of the revolutionary struggle. "Francisco," as Nestor Paz Zamora was trustfully known by his companions in a guerrilla band of short duration (July to October 1970) in Bolivia's Department of La Paz, was an almost unknown Christian mystic. Like Camilo Torres, Francisco gave up his life for his vocation as a revolutionary. Like Che, Francisco left a diary, although a briefer one, through and between the lines of which the depth and integrity of his commitment both to Jesus Christ and to the revolutionary struggles of the poor and the persecuted of his native country become unmistakable and—to any fellow Christian, revolutionary or not—compelling. In a *Letter to God*, dated 12 September 1970, Francisco writes:

> Dear Lord:
>
> It has been a long time since I wrote to you. Today I feel a real need for you and your presence, perhaps because of the nearness of death or the relative failure of the struggle. . . . Perhaps today is my Thursday and tonight my Friday. Because I love you I surrender everything into your hands, without limit. What hurts me is the thought of leaving those I most love—Cecy and my family—and perhaps not being here to participate in the triumph of the people—their liberation. We are a group full of true, "Christian" humanity and I think we will change the course of history. The thought of this comforts me. . . . No one's death is meaningless if his life has been charged with significance; and I believe this has been true of us here. Chau, Lord! Perhaps until that heaven of yours, that new world we desire so much![125]

An entry in the *Journal* seems to complete the Passion theme of this letter in a strikingly revolutionary "remythologization" of the reality of the resurrection:

> The resurrection now has a real meaning in my life and is no longer simply a "truth." I want to grow down and penetrate deeply in the "life" of man. I want to reach a total humanization. That is the vocation of my life, and it is our true fulfillment. (Z, 3)

The priest and the mystic, the ordained and the unordained Christian, are significant for this account of the phenomenology of current revolutions not only because of the fact that, like Che, they exemplify the vocational meaning of being a revolutionary; but also, and not least, because they express the conjunction of the messianic humanism of Christianity, whose reach and range have been pointedly illuminated by the Transfiguration of Jesus, with the humanistic messianism of Marxism. In Rubem Alves' cogent formulation:

> Humanistic messianism is a new type of messianism, which believes that man can be free by the powers of man alone. . . .

Messianic humanism, on the contrary, believes, from its historical experience, in the humanizing determination of the transcendent. When it pronounces the name "God," it is referring to the power for humanization that remains determined to make man historically free even when all objective and subjective possibilities immanent in history have been exhausted. . . . Humanistic messianism is born out of a historical experience in which only the statistically and quantitatively tangible resources of man's freedom and determination are available, whereas messianic humanism was created by the historical reality of liberation in spite of the collapse of all human resources.[126]

It is not accidental that Alves, too, is a Latin American. When one recalls that Camilo and Francisco were exploring what later came to be called "Christian-Marxist dialogue," some time before the spirit and the efforts of the Christian Peace Conference began to move beyond the boundaries of that body, and into western Europe and the United States, their own attempts to break down "the middle wall of partition" (Eph. 2:14) between these two revolutionary humanisms becomes a pioneering enterprise in the intersection of Jesus Christ with the question of revolution. In a forceful passage, combining a succinct summary of his personal, scientific, and priestly training and commitments with a clarification of the constructive relations between Christians and Communists in the revolutionary task, Torres declares:

The relations that have traditionally existed between Christians and Marxists, between the church and the Communist party, may give rise to doubts and misunderstandings about the relations taking shape within the United Front between Christians and Marxists and between a priest and the Communist party. . . .

I have said that as a Colombian, as a sociologist, as a Christian, and as a priest I am a revolutionary. I believe that the Communist party consists of truly revolutionary elements, and hence I cannot be anti-Communist either as a Colombian, a sociologist, a Christian, or a priest.

As a Colombian I am not an anti-Communist because anti-Communism hounds nonconformists among my compatriots regardless of whether they are Communists or not. Most of them are simply poor people. As a sociologist I am not an anti-Communist because theses concerning the fight against poverty, hunger, illiteracy, lack of shelter, and absence of public services offer scientific solutions to these problems. As a Christian I am not an anti-Communist because I believe that anti-Communism implies condemnation of everything that Communists stand for.

As a priest I am not an anti-Communist because among the Communists themselves, whether they know it or not, there may be many true Christians. . . . I am prepared to fight together with the Communists for our common goals: against the oligarchy and United States domination; for the winning of power by the people. I do not want to be identified with the Communists alone and hence, I have always sought to work together not only with them but with all independent revolutionaries and revolutionaries of other convictions. (T, 370–71)

A few months earlier, he had said in an interview:

. . . In Christianity the principal evil is the lack of love, both for other Christians and for non-Christians, including Communists. Communism as a solution, with all its wisdom and its fallacies, comes from the lack of real love applied in temporal structures in a scientific form by Christians.

From the scientific point of view, the position of the Christian should not be anti-anything but pro-humanity. If this good of all mankind cannot be achieved except by changing the temporal structures it would be sinful for Christians to oppose change. (T, 313)[127]

These passages look back more than a decade upon the anti-Communist hysteria in North America in the 1950s, which the Latin Americans learned to call *Macartismo*, after the then Junior member from Wisconsin of the United States Senate, Joseph R. McCarthy. The perspective and the points of Torres' position were and still are pertinent to North as well to South America, to the postrevolutionary corruptions of power in the Marxist-Leninist contexts of the Cultural Revolution on the precipitous edge between the liberation and the repression of a revolutionary consciousness. Torres' position was and still is pertinent to the Soviet destruction of the Spring in Prague in 1968, as well as to the anti-humanist and anti-Marxist contexts of the *Syllabus of Errors* (1864) and of

*Humani Generis* (1950). Torres wanted to remain a priest, and never thought of himself as other than a priest. "I took off my cassock to be more truly a priest," he declared: words often echoed afterward by Daniel Berrigan in the United States.[128] He wanted, as a priest, to be a part of a Christian-Marxist effort to change the center and the structures of power in his native country.

Continuation in the priesthood was denied to him by his bishop.[129] The protracted and bitter nature of the power struggle denied him the realization of his revolutionary hope. On 15 February 1966, the guerrilla detachment of which he had become a member ambushed a military patrol. In the course of the counter-attack that ensued, Torres did not hear the order to retreat, continued firing, and fell in the battle (T, 30–31). Less than a year earlier, he had told an assembly of Union delegates and the general public (mostly workers) gathered at the headquarters of the Bavarian Union in Bogata:

> I considered it indispensable to my vocation as priest and my vocation as revolutionary that I prove my willingness to serve the cause of the people. When I was faced with the dilemma, forced to choose whether I would follow the discipline of the clergy or continue in the revolutionary struggle, I could not hesitate. Otherwise I would have betrayed the revolution by betraying you. (T, 344–45)

That was in July 1965. One month earlier, as we have noted, Camilo's laicization had been ordered by Cardinal Concha. On the following 18 October, he left his official priesthood together with his bourgeois connections behind and took to the mountains. Five months later, Camilo had given his life to the revolution (T, 28–31). "The Catholic who is not a revolutionary," he had come to believe, "is living in mortal sin" (T, 29).

The passion and the pace of Camilo's vocational development as a revolutionary seem to find him at the very antipodes of that mountain on which Jesus was transfigured. Mountains were involved; but the doings on them were the signs of another world altogether. As surely as Jesus turned aside from the politics of Zealotry, so surely does Camilo Torres seem to have turned into the Zealot path to power. His superiors in the Church, and certainly those whom he himself had identified as "the privileged minorities," who hold power in the state, so regarded him. Nothing is easier than to find in Torres' course his own particular version of Latin volatility—inherited from his mother no less (T, 15 ff.)—and his own version of the political and military mistakes of Che Guevara. Such *ad hominem* factors plague every revolutionary as soon as he begins to think and speak and write about the humanly intolerable contradiction in society between the powerlessness of the poor and the power of the privileged.

When the revolutionary comes to regard his conscience as a calling and begins to translate his convictions into action, the plague becomes an accusation. However great the distance may be between the mountains that sheltered Camilo Torres and the mountain of Jesus' Transfiguration, that distance cannot be measured by the difference between *ad hominem* factors that plague and those that accuse; and still less by the difference between a "soft" revolution and a "hard" revolution. There are more than hints in the New Testament that Jesus himself suffered both the plague and the accusation of *ad hominem* rejection of what he was about. He was even suspected of being on Camilo Torres' path from "soft" to "hard" revolution. Was it not said that he was subversive (Luke 23:2)? that he was out of his mind (Mark 3:22)? that he was demonic (Luke 11:15)? even that he had blasphemed (Matt. 26:65–66)?

And why else would the authorities take counsel together how they might destroy him (Matt. 27:1–2; Mark 3:6; 12:2; 14:2)? The interrogative rhetoric here is designed not to evade the *ad hominem* caveat to which every revolutionary consciousness and lifestyle are subject. The rhetoric is designed instead to underscore the extent to which *ad hominem* rejections of revolutionary aspiration and commitment conceal a self-justifying insensitivity to the collision course between the poor and the powerful that current revolutionary movements have unmasked; and no less an insensitivity to the conflict of worlds unveiled in the Transfiguration of Jesus. Between that momentous conversation with Moses and Elijah and that nocturnal confrontation between Jesus and Pilate, the established powers of this world were being judged and brought low. Time was even shorter than space; for nothing less than the death and resurrection of mankind in its humanity, and of the humanity of mankind, was involved.

The rhetoric rests upon a record that, in a world of messianic politics, it would be irresponsible to ignore. The rapidity of the radicalization of Camilo Torres' may, as in the case of Che Guevara, call into question the accuracy of his assessment of the realities of the power struggle. But there can be no question of the integrity of his revolutionary commitment as a Christian. The crucial year spanned September 1964 to October 1965. In September, Torres read a long essay at the Second International Congress of *Pro Mundi Vita* at Louvain. Its published title is *Revolution: Christian Imperative*, its theme was the revolutionary reality of the Christian Apostolate (T, 261–94). The piece is a combination of Dominican and socioeconomic learning at its best.

The theological analysis of the mandate of Christ "to establish and extend the kingdom of God" (T, 261) explores the Scriptures, together with familiar Catholic distinctions between the supernatural and the natural life, between faith and good works, and leads to the conclusion "that there is no supernatural life in persons who have the faculty of reason if good works in helping our neighbor are lacking" (T, 263). Questions of grace in relation to faith, of supernatural to natural life, of sacraments to ethics, of who is a Christian and who is not, are not to be played off against each other in a mutually exclusive way. The problem is not one "of exclusion, but rather of priorities in policies and procedures in apostolic action. In a word, it is a problem of pastoral methods" (T, 264). The responsibility for the *determination* of priorities is a *theological* one. The responsibility for the *identification* of the priorities is a *historical* one. Torres the Dominican priest joins up with Torres the social scientist in risking the judgment that the priorities become "more clearly apparent when considered in the light of two historical circumstances of our time: the social problem and pluralism. These are the circumstances which should orient pastoral action" (T, 265).

What follows is a careful assessment of the social problem in terms of its economic factors, of these in terms of the task and the possibilities of planning in capitalist contexts and in the context of underdevelopment, and of the relation between leadership and power in effecting essential social and structural change. In the underdeveloped countries, the "popular class" is at a power disadvantage in relation to the "ruling class" at the level of leadership, both as regards its quality and its availability (T, 281–83). In view of this power disproportion, effective structural social change will not come about without pressure from the popular class. Whether this pressure erupts in violence, or will be peaceful, depends upon the foresight of the ruling class. But violent revolution "is a quite probable alternative, because the ruling classes lack foresight" (T, 283). According to Torres, the apostolic rubric for effective structural social change is "the attainment of charity which is really efficacious for all men, without distinction of creeds, attitudes, or cultures" (T, 284). "If Christians assumed the leadership in the matter of change and in planning, it is possible that the ultimate ends might be quite compatible with a more integral humanism and that the chosen means would be less traumatic, especially in relation to certain spiritual values" (T, 285). Owing to a lack of technological competence and a certain "monolithic dogmatism," it is scarcely likely that Christians will manage to provide a successful leadership (T, 286). Hence the problem of efficacious charity ultimately encounters the question of pluralism in the form of cooperation with Marxist leadership. And it encounters the thorny question of morality and tactics in the power struggle in the familiar form of the question of ends and means (T, 288).

The essay addresses itself at the close to the question of "the Christian attitude towards efforts to bring about structural changes . . . favorable to the majorities." The presentation shows how carefully and cautiously Torres endeavored to avoid the rejection of these efforts, or abstention from them, by a Marxist collaboration that moved beyond the paralyzing sorting out of ends and means and beyond the alternative of calculated violence as well. He believed that it is possible for Christians simply to disregard the question of evil ends and means, because "revolution is such a complex undertaking that it would be deceitful to classify it within a system of causality and finality that is wholly evil" (T, 289). His hope is that "since the greatest authority accepted by a society that needs structural change is the authority of revolutionary commitment, which for the Christian should be a commitment in charity," this authority will permit us to demand concessions in the event that the Marxist have some share of power" (T, 289–90).[130]

Eleven months later, the convulsive course of political, social, and religious events had brought Camilo's careful caution to an end. In *A Message to Christians* (26 August 1965), he explored the relations between charity, or love, and revolution in a Christian context in terms very similar to those of Che Guevara's Marxist humanism (T, 367–69). He takes off from the injunction of Romans 13:8, concerning the practice of love as the fulfillment of the law.

> For this love to be genuine, it must seek to be effective. If benefice, alms, the few tuition-free schools, the few housing projects—in general, what is known as "charity"—do not succeed in feeding the hungry majority, clothing the naked, or teaching the unschooled masses, we must seek effective means to achieve the well-being of these majorities. These means will not be sought by the privileged minorities who hold power, because such effective means generally force the minorities to sacrifice their privileges. . . . Thus, power must be taken from the privileged minorities and given to the poor majorities. If this is done rapidly, it constitutes the essential characteristic of a revolution. The revolution can be a peaceful one if the minorities refrain from violent resistance. Revolution is, therefore, the way to obtain a government that will feed the hungry, clothe the naked, and teach the unschooled. Revolution will produce a government that carries out works of charity, of love for one's fellows—not only for a few but for the majority of our fellow men. This is why the revolution is not only permissible but obligatory for those Christians who see it as the only effective and far-reaching way to make the love of all people a reality. . . . After the revolution we Colombians will be aware that we are establishing a system oriented toward the love of our neighbor. The struggle is long; let us begin now. (T, 367–69)

On the same day, Torres published a statement explaining his own decision to abstain from the electorial process (T, 364–66). It carried the force of a manifesto intended for the Colombian situation but was readily taken up as a programmatic proposal beyond the boundaries of that country, not least among students, and not least in the United States among students disillusioned by the war in Vietnam and the increasing gulf between poverty and privilege there.

Two months later (October 1965), amidst Camilo's own decision to leave his bourgeois past behind and commit himself to revolutionary activity as a guerrilla, came *A Message to Students* in which he urges a serious vocational self-examination on the part of students, each in his own country, about his social responsibilities and vocational commitments. Once again, the intensity of his own commitment to the revolution led him to address the Colombian students, among whom he had worked as a university chaplain, in terms which focused upon Colombian reality but were insufficiently protected against transposition as revolutionary policy to other situations, in which attention to *their* revolutionary reality was inadequate. In a statement that in context can scarcely be understood as other than a serious vocational appeal, to the exclusion of all play at revolution, Torres declares:

> The student's revolutionary convictions must lead to real commitment taken to the ultimate consequences. *Poverty and persecution should not be actively sought after, but they are the logical consequence of total struggle against the existing system.* Under the present system they are signs that authenticate a revolutionary life. The same convictions should lead the student to participate in the economic hardships and social persecution which workers and peasants suffer. Therefore, commitment to the revolution passes from theory to practice. If it is total, it is irreversible, and the professional cannot renege without betraying his conscience, his historical vocation, and his people.
>
> At this moment of revolutionary opportunity, I do not want to preach. I want only to encourage students to make contact with authentic sources of information to determine their responsibility and their necessary response. (T, 404–05; italics mine)

The significance of this passage does not lie in the question whether it is to be limited to the revolutionary situation in Colombia, or is generalizable to revolutionary possiblities in Latin America and elsewhere. Its significance lies in its clear call to revolutionary discipleship intrinsic to a Christian apostolate. The call evokes a diverse array of reminiscence and comradeship from those near at hand and from those afar off. Six months after the death of Camilo Torres, it was written:

> This is what we wish to reflect: the meaning, the urgency, the means, the movements of the commitment of Christians in the revolution.
>
> In sum, for all revolutionaries, the option of the Last Day of the Gospel forces upon us our daily task as a fundamental imperative because only revolution can feed the hungry, house the homeless, care for the sick, bring dignity to the dispossessed, freedom to the exploited, life to the drowning, calm to the frightened, happiness to the miserable, the earth to the meek. Only revolution can recreate faith in life and in man and realize the commandment of fraternity through solidarity among peoples. This revolution, though at times necessarily violent, because some hearts are so callous, is not one of despair: it is the only way that humanity may once again hope and love.
>
> And so we begin. (T, 34)

In honor of the memory of Néstor Paz Zamora, a Christian, the Vice Rector of the University of La Paz, a Marxist declared:

> . . . the figure of "Francisco" the guerrilla inspires a profound respect. . . . There is a truth which hammers at our conscience: a certain Christian refused to ignore Marxists. As a result, Teoponte refused to ignore the believers. Our history becomes fuller and America is grander because a handful of heroes understood that to fight to change the destiny of the poor is more important than to enjoy life. . . .
>
> "Francisco" the guerrilla; Néstor the Christian; Paz the Bolivian —a hero dignified by human love. . . .
>
> Neither Marxists nor Christians want violence for violence's sake. We want power for the people. Let us remember the Christian precept, that we will be judged by our deeds, not by our intentions. Deeds in the name of Christ by Christians should be those which help our neighbors. For us Marxists, this is not the time to discuss ideological differences about eternal truth. . . .

Néstor Paz, "Francisco," the guerrilla, you exalted the Christian faith. While your body knows the rush of tormented rivers, from your voice come springs of faith and justice. (Z, 5–8; Teoponte is a gold-mining camp in the jungles of Larecaja Province.)

As for those afar off, it is difficult not to remember the reflections of Dietrich Bonhoeffer on the call to discipleship and on the Sermon on the Mount in *Nachfolge*; or the commitment, sufferings, and power of lifestyle of Francis of Assisi; or, perhaps most of all, the bewilderment and agony of Jesus' own disciples between the Transfiguration and the Crucifixion, as they tried to sort out the line and the limits of their own involvement with Jesus in his attempt to put the existing poor and existing power humanizingly together. Of such is the communion of saints. For of such is the kingdom not of this world.

### 4. The Crucial Question of Violence

As with Che, so with Torres and Néstor Paz Zamora, the revolutionary confidence and expectation put forward in *A Message to Christians* and in a *Message to Students* are exactly the confidence and expectation that every revolution sooner or later disappoints, including what contemporary American power has done and is doing to the social and human implementation of those self-evident truths and precariously wrought checks and balances of power affirmed and struggled for by the Founding Fathers of the Republic. But to ignore or to dismiss these "heroes" (if one is a Marxist) or "martyrs" (if one is a Christian) of the revolution as proselytizers and romanticists or as fomenters of violence is at once to scorn the integrity of humanistic messianism and of apostolic faithfulness, to disregard the reality of messianic politics that makes the dynamics and destiny of current revolutions into signs of transfiguration, and to court the company of those "who eat up the property of widows and make long prayers for appearance' sake" (Luke 20:45–46), only to be numbered in the end with those who crucified him whose life was committed to, and given for, the liberation of power by truth for the humanization of human life.

Whether Ivan Ilich's conviction that "the proper way to force an upheaval in society is through a revolution in the educational process" is more or less romantic than the revolutionary vocation of Camilo Torres, whom he knew as "an adorable drinking companion" but never invited to his Cuernevaca Institute (CIDOC), or merely a further crypticism peculiar to Ilich's personal style, remains to be seen.[131] Che and Torres and Francisco have not been the only revolutionary martyrs in Latin America. But they have been and are in the vanguard of those who have sensed and responded to an intensifying revolutionary urgency in Latin America, and have inspired an increasingly aroused mass of the oppressed and an increasingly aroused Catholic Church. Meanwhile, the exemplary try at a revolutionary restructuring of society on the island of Cuba continues to haunt, though not to hasten, revolutionary development. Indeed, under the incipient continental leadership of an ascendant demo-technocracy in Brazil, a level of political and economic stability of indefinite duration, coupled with the most brutal Leavenworth-conceived and trained ways of crushing dissent, appears to have driven revolutionary commitment and organization underground and postponed indefinitely the realization of revolutionary hopes.

Consequently, the question of violence is more urgent than ever. Not only has the Marcusian distinction between "systemic violence" and "countervailing violence" acquired a horrendous confirmation, but these "heroes" and "martyrs" of the revolutionary movement in Latin America have also articulated in theory and practice a reconsideration of the meaning and role of violence in social conflict and social change. They have carried the question of revolutionary violence beyond its long-standing acceptance or rejection on ethical grounds by underlining its sociological reality in terms of the distinction between "official violence" and "counter-violence" (T, 456) and its function as a revolutionary risk.[132] In doing so they have pressed the question of the social efficaciousness of love to that point of ultimacy at which the fate and the function of revolutions, as signs of transfiguration, stand or fall.

The revolutionary judgment upon imperialist colonialism and the revolutionary judgment upon colonialist imperialism thus come upon a common point. The point is whether revolutionary passion and purpose are foredoomed by the violent seizure of power to their own undoing or whether there is an authentic revolutionary alternative to violence in order to effect a change in social consciousness and social power adequate to the liberation of people from oppression and for the freedom to be human in the world. In either case, is the vocation of a revolutionary, owing to the risk of violence that it entails, adverse to, or incumbent upon, the vocation of a Christian? In short, is it or is it not, in Torres' vigorous epigram—theologically, not ecclesiastically, understood—"the duty of every Catholic to be a revolutionary, the duty of every revolutionary to make the revolution" (T, Frontispiece)? We must defer once more the consideration of these ultimate questions and turn now to the third revolutionary movement under the typology upon which we have ventured.

## C. FROM FRANTZ FANON TO MARTIN LUTHER KING, JR., MALCOLM X, AND THE BLACK PANTHER PARTY

The revolutionary ferment of the present time has been both broadened and narrowed by the advent of black people upon the current stage of revolutionary struggle and development. The broadening occurs through the addition of another continent to the stirrings of "the Wretched of the Earth," as Frantz Fanon has called them, against the bondage and exploitation of colonialism and imperialism. Along with Asia and South America, Africa too is on the move to full participation in the human fullness of life for all mankind. The momentum of the movement, on what never really was the "dark continent," from tribalism to nationalism to personal and social identity through self-determination, is pressing with increasing insistence and acceleration hard against the once axiomatic domination by "settlers" from without, and the diminishing if stubborn domination internal to that bastion of *apartheid* within.[133] The narrowing focus of the black revolutionary struggle occurs in the United States through the increasing tension and confrontation between two communities above all others: the one black, the other white. Indeed, the dual hegemony of established power in the world exhibits a racial thrust that erupts in various ways with varying intensities. In the Soviet Union, the virus bears the mark of anti-Semitism; in the United States, it poisons the body politic against the black people. In the Soviet Union, the dynamics of a revolutionary society encounter a racial *factor*; in the United States, the dynamics of a society in revolution encounter a racist *focus*.

In any case, the established powers of the present world are being weighed in the balance and found wanting because of a triple violation of human reality and possibility in the world. Colonialism, imperialism, and racism are under the judgment of history. Their moment of truth has come and they have reached their point of no return. In a world of messianic politics, the Establishment has had its day. It has come under the judgment of the Maker of heaven and earth and the Head of all principality and power. In the transfiguring light of that judgment, the power of the Establishment is being exposed as falsehood by the power of the truth that sets men free.

In two notable respects, the Black Revolution varies from the Chinese and the Latin American movements toward a new order of freedom and justice in human affairs. The first, and more important, is the unveiling of the *depth*, in distinction from the *range*, of dehumanization effected by the power dominance of colonialist and imperialist economics and politics. One could formulate this depth distinction by saying that, whereas the economics and politics of colonialism and imperialism pursue and achieve dehumanization by deprivation, the racist factor of colonialism and imperialism achieves dehumaniaztion by *de-identification*. The preceding account of the phenomenon of revolution in Asia under the leadership of Mao Tse-tung and Ho Chi Minh, and in Latin America under the inspiration of the Cuban achievement, has focused upon the denial of the freedom to be human through the injustice of social and material exploitation and oppression. The revolution in which the black people are engaged, however, erupts from a still deeper level of what is involved in being human. This is the psychological level of personal and social identity. Here the havoc wrought by exploitation and oppression upon their victims is the denial of the possibility of self-evident self-identification inherent in belonging to a group whose identity in the total human community is axiomatic and plain. What the group *achieves* is valuable and valued because of what the group *is*; and conversely, what the group *is*, is valuable and valued because of what the group *achieves*. An unimpeded reciprocity obtains between identity and creativity that functions as the womb and matrix of individual personhood.

If the *exterior* injustice of colonialism and imperialism is the deprivation of the *opportunity* of being human in the world, the *interior* injustice of this exploitation and oppression is the de-identification that prevents the *possibility* of being human in the world. Indeed, the difference between the *fact of race* and the *factor of racism* in social behavior and organization emerges precisely at this point. *Race* refers simply to the fact that there are peoples in the world who may be differentiated according to the superficial feature of color; or, as in the singular instance of the Jews, by separatist cultural self-consciousness. Insofar as color operates adversely in the relations between peoples, it does so by superficially rooted prejudice. At bottom, prejudice is the corruption of difference by preference. The fundamental question whether race is a valid anthropological category is moot. But it does not alter the sociological reality that is the transposition of the fact of race into the factor of racism. *Racism* is the social attitude and behavior that make of color, regardless of its superficiality, the effective source and justification of preferential valuation in intergroup relations. Consequently, racism is the denial, to the group so devalued, of the reciprocity between identity and creativity essential to personal and group self-identification. Thus racism is a pivotal dehumanizing form of group and personal behavior, according to which some "colored" peoples humanly devalue other "colored" peoples; or, more pertinently, according to which "non-colored" people devalue "colored" people, depending upon one's physics of color. The critical contemporary case in point is, of course, the prejudice of the "white" people against the "black" people; of the peoples of "Caucasian" against the peoples of "Negroid" stock, to put it technically.

The second respect in which the Black Revolution varies from the revolutionary movements in Asia and Latin America concerns the relation to Marxism. We have seen that, in the latter instances, Marxism provided a theoretical instrument for the clarification and guidance of revolutionary experience and practice. Neither Mao Tse-tung nor Fidel Castro became revolutionaries because they were Marxists. They became Marxists because they were revolutionaries. Marxism, particularly in its Leninist version, provided an ideology of power that illuminated the experienced realities of the power struggle and tended to be confirmed by them. In the case of the Black Revolution, however, the relation to Marxism-Leninism seems either altogether negligible or altogether co-incidental. Fanon explains that, owing to the racist factor in colonialism, "Marxist analysis should always be slightly stretched every time we have to do with the colonial problem. Everything up to and including the very nature of pre-capitalist society, so well explained by Marx, must here be thought out again."[134] Similarly, Martin Luther King, Jr., "was simultaneously drawn to and repelled by Marx" (LB, 20).[135] He was pained by Marxism as a Christian heresy, and not so much because it was a heresy as because it underlined the social failure of the Christian church (LB, 35-36). Although King's economic orientation may have been Marxist, "one need not . . . attribute" his later radicalism "to Marxian predilections. Martin's fascination for the socialist ideas implicit in the Social Gospel was probably more relevant. . . . Almost until the end, the meliorism of the Social Gospel—and, more viscerally, that of the Black bourgeoisie—stayed with Martin, despite the instructive lessons in Marx and Niebuhr" (LB, 354, 394-95).

It is instructive that C. Eric Lincoln's able and facinating account of the Black Muslims contains no index reference to Marx or to Marxism, an absence amply confirmed by *The Autobiography of Malcolm X*. Patently, what Marx and Lenin had done for Mao, Ho, Fidel, and Che, Christianity had done for King, and Islam for Malcolm X. With the radicalization of the Black Revolution, however, the general cultural significance of theoretical Marxism takes a familiar ideological turn. Unlike Maoism and Fidelism, for which movements Marxism-Leninism provided, as we have seen, a conceptuality for the clarification of revolutionary experience, as well as an ideology of power, the Black Panthers have found in Marxism-Leninism chiefly a tactical instrument for the power struggle. This discovery has come about through the mediation of Mao Tse-tung. As with Che Guevara, so with Eldridge Cleaver and Huey P. Newton, it is the impact of Mao's treatise on *Guerrilla Warfare* that has made the Black Revolution aware of its kinship with the world revolutionary struggle at the level both of consciousness and of strategy.

Eldridge Cleaver writes:

> In economics, because everybody seemed to find it necessary to attack and condemn Karl Marx in their writings, I sought out his books, and although he kept me with a headache, I took him for my authority. I was not prepared to understand him, but I was able to see in him a thoroughgoing critique and condemnation of capitalism. It was like taking medicine for me to find that, indeed, American capitalism deserved all the hatred and contempt that I felt for it in my heart. (CSI, 24)[136]

In February 1967, three months after his release on parole from California's unconscionable Soledad Prison, Cleaver began working with the Black Panther Party whose Minister of Information he now is.[137] From his own involvement in the power struggle comes an expressed respect for Karl Marx, "using the fruits of his wisdom, applying them to this crumbling system" (CPP, 145), but an emphatic recognition of the guerrilla character of the Black struggle and its indebtedness to Mao Tse-tung. "We have to have solidarity with the most extreme enemy they pose for you, the People's Republic of China. Mao Tse-tung, baby, you've done a beautiful job" (CPP, 129). "In our epoch, guerrilla warfare is the vehicle for national liberation all around the world" (CPP, 70). In this struggle, Mao is "the Prophet of the Gun" (CPP, 71). Back in prison again, after the Oakland shoot-out (this time at the State Medical Facility at Vacaville), Cleaver managed to smuggle out a letter, dated 15 June 1968, in the course of which he described his first meeting with the Black Panthers and the deep impression made upon him by Huey Newton. "The only culture worth talking about," Huey had said, "is a revolutionary culture. So it doesn't matter what label you put on it, we're going to talk about political power growing out of the barrel of a gun" (CPP, 31).[138]

Thus, for the Black Revolution (when compared with the revolutionary movements discussed above), as radicalization overtakes what began under specific, diverse, and local conditions, Marxism-Leninism provides to a lesser extent a theoretical conceptuality and to a like extent an ideological and tactical guide for the struggle for power. At stake is a protest against oppression and injustice that have become humanly intolerable, and an organized attempt to make time and space make room for freedom. The struggle sharpens a revolutionary consciousness, and in so doing, forges a sense of comradeship in a worldwide repudiation of the principal modes of established power: colonialism, imperialism, and racism. In their own terms, this revolutionary consciousness and worldwide comradeship find the tides of history running mightily with the goals and aspirations of a totally new human order of affairs. In terms of the power realities of a world under the dynamics of messianic politics, however, what is going on is the steady pressure of truth upon power, which signals that the countdown of the Magnificat has already begun. He whose "name is Holy":

> the deeds his own right arm has done
>   disclose his might:
> the arrogant of heart and mind he has put to rout,
> he has brought down monarchs from their thrones,
>   but the humble have been lifted high.
> The hungry he has satisfied with good things,
>   the rich sent empty away.
>
> (Luke 1:50–53)

Owing to the presence in our history of Jesus of Nazareth, the Christ, whose power liberates as it binds and binds as it liberates, the Black Revolution means that one more sign is at hand of the transfiguration of a dehumanizing present under divine judgment through the imminence of a new and humanizing future on earth as it has been taking shape in heaven. A foretaste is breaking in of that human fulfillment promised and purposed from before the foundation of the world. "It was hidden for long ages in God the creator of the universe, in order that now, through the church, the wisdom of God in all its varied forms might be made known to the rulers and authorities in the realms of heaven. This is in accord with his age-long purpose, which he achieved in Christ Jesus our Lord" (Eph. 3:9–11).[139] For the author of Ephesians, the "church" (*ekklesia*) means the visible community, called together in the world, to be the vanguard of the presence of Christ in his purposed liberation (or, salvation) of all people for full participation in human fulfillment. In this sense, "the church" is understood as a revolutionary community, not as an institutional or bureaucratic structure, whatever the sociological and/or historical pertinence of such structures might be. When James Cone writes that "the church means the people who make the world more amenable to black self-determination by forcing rulers to decide between blackness and death," he is not only expressing the emerging revolutionary reality and consciousness of black people in the world today but he is also faithful to the fact and the gospel of the presence of Jesus of Nazareth in the world, to which the Ephesian letter refers. For "the world," as Cone rightly sees and says, "is where white and black people live, encountering each other, the latter striving for a little more room to breathe and the former doing everything possible to destroy black reality."[140]

It cannot be too strongly emphasized that Professor Cone is not making a chromatic separation of the world into "black" and "white." He is on the contrary, making a chromatic identification of the frontier of truth and life in the world. It is Jesus of Nazareth, whose presence and transfiguration in that world transfigure and define that frontier of truth and life as a frontier of human reality. On that frontier the black struggle for liberation is a revolutionary struggle to extend that frontier until the whole of humanity is encompassed by it. "The wisdom of God has been made known" or "unveiled (*gnōristhe*) to the rulers and authorities in the realms of heaven" (Eph. 3:10), that is, to the uttermost reaches of established power whose rebellion against God's purpose of human fulfillment has been unmasked by Jesus Messiah. And this "unveiling" has "achieved" contemporary concreteness in the revolutionary struggle for black liberation.

So let us briefly try to follow the course of this revolutionary un-veiling, as it seems to have been signaled in

1. The Racist Core of the Current Revolutionary Struggle: Frantz Fanon;
2. The Radicalization of a Dream: Martin Luther King, Jr.;
3. The Human Meaning of Blackness: Malcolm X;
4. The Ax at the Root of the Tree: The Black Panthers.

## 1. The Racist Core of the Current Revolutionary Struggle: Frantz Fanon

Frantz Fanon's searing psychosociological exposure of the de-humanization wrought by colonialism and imperialism upon *The Wretched of the Earth* has added a further dimension to the dynamics of the current revolutionary struggle. As a practicing psychiatrist, he has observed and concluded on clinical grounds that the ruinous human effects of the operation of established power are racist at the core. Fanon writes:

> When you examine at close quarters the colonial context, it is evident that what parcels out the world is to begin with the fact of belonging to or not belonging to a given race, a given species. . . . It is neither the act of owning factories, nor estates, nor a bank balance which distinguishes the governing classes. The governing race is first and foremost those who come from elsewhere, those who are unlike the original inhabitants, "the others." (F, 40)

The colonial world is divided between "settlers" and "natives." The "settlers," even if they should wish to do so—which they do not—can never become "natives." The "natives," except by the ugly path to, and exercise of, violence, can never come into what is humanly and rightfully their own, into what "the foreigner coming from another country (had) imposed (as) his rule by means of guns and machines" (F, 40; parentheses mine).

The socioeconomic and political bifurcation of the colonial world exhibits, however, a deeper cleavage still. "The colonial world is a Manichean world." (F, 41). The psychodynamics of a sociological division that began with conquest and continues by military and enconomic power have an ultimate intensity and self-justifying falsity about them. "As if to show the totalitarian character of colonial exploitation, the settler paints the native as a sort of quintessence of evil." (F, 41). The racial factor of group and cultural differentiation becomes a racist focus that insists that the "native" not only lacks values but that he is incapable of them. The "settler," by contrast, is the bearer of values, in his own eyes inherently humanizing, and justifying his "civilizing" mission beyond the borders of his homeland. "At times," says Fanon, "this Manicheism goes to its logical conclusion and dehumanizes the native, or to speak plainly, it turns him into an animal. . . . When the settler seeks to describe the native fully in exact terms he constantly refers to the bestiary." (F, 42). Thus, color and culture and country, i.e., native land, which function as the matrix of a concrete and humanizing reciprocity between identity and creativity, become the self-justifying monopoly of the "settler" and the dehumanizing fate of the "native."

In an earlier writing, called *Black Skin, White Masks,* Fanon has described more fully the humanly fateful operation of this Manichean world.[141] Its importance in this connection arises from its kinship with Eldridge Cleaver's *Soul on Ice.* In the Introduction to *Soul on Ice,* Maxwell Geismar has noted that "in both books, the central problem is (one) of *identification* as a black soul which has been 'colonized'—more subtly perhaps in the United States for some three hundred years, but perhaps even more pervasively—by an oppressive white society that projects its brief, narrow vision of life as eternal truth." (SOI, 9; paranthesis added; italics Geismar's). Although Geismar does not say so, one might take another step and note that just as Fanon has moved in *The Wretched of the Earth* beyond the earlier work, and from a description of the way the Manicheism of racist colonialism works, to a consideration of the path to liberation from this oppression, so Cleaver's *Post-Prison Writings and Speeches* move beyond the baring of a soul in its search for identity to the marshaling of forces for a power struggle to put an end to this Manichean de-identification once for all. As Fanon puts it in the later book, the native "knows that he is not an animal; and it is precisely at the moment he realizes his humanity that he begins to sharpen the weapons with which he will begin to secure its victory." (F. 43).

There is thus an ineluctable psychodynamics in the racist character of colonialism that has drawn black people everywhere in the world into the struggle for their own identity as black people. The achievement of this identity is the certification of membership in the human race. The risk of a reverse Manicheism is a calculated one with which the Black Revolution is destined to deal along the way. But for the moment that is not where the action is. The action is against the operation of power, at once dehumanizing and heretical, whose time has come. In uncovering the racist core of colonialism, Fanon has uncovered a yet greater shame of the Christian church in its practice of Christian faith. This is the failure to discern that the church's rejection of cosmic and ethical Manicheism as heretical necessarily involved the rejection of political and social Manicheism as well. In a bitter passage of rebuke to "the Christian religion," Fanon declares:

> The recession of yellow fever and the advance of evangelization form part of the same balance sheet. But the triumphant *communiqués* from the mission are in fact a source of information concerning the implantation of foreign influences in the core of the colonized people. . . . The Church in the colonies is the white people's Church, the foreigner's Church. She does not call the native to God's ways but to the ways of the white man, of the master, of the oppressor. And as we know, in this matter many are called but few chosen. (F, 42; italics Fanon's)

"Who said that?" one is tempted to ask, as does the almost Restoration Countess, in Christopher Fry's *The Dark Is Light Enough*: "I thought it was a quotation."[142] With that combination, at once poignant and pathetic, of wistfulness and triviality, which voices confusion as a cliché, the Countess does not even pause for an answer to her own question. She garrulously proceeds to answer it herself. And thereby she shows that she has missed the point. Just so, the Chief of State of the most powerful imperialist nation in the world today has also missed the point. Self-styled global emissary of peace, he journeys to the capitals of powerful ideological and revolutionary repudiations of colonialism with a survival invitation to join in making the world safe for the "national (international) bourgeoisie." With the garrulity of epoch-making insensitivity, both to the heights of human creativity and to the depths of human suffering, he reduces both the Great Wall of China and the Diary of Little Tanya to a ceremonial cliché.[143] Writes Fanon:

> The capitalist regime must not try to enlist the aid of the socialist regime over "the fate of Europe" in face of the starving multitudes of colored peoples. . . . For some time past the statesmen of the capitalist countries have adopted an equivocal attitude toward the Soviet Union. After having united all their forces to abolish the socialist regime, they now realize that they'll have to reckon with it. So they look as pleasant as they can, they make all kinds of advances, and they remind the Soviet people the whole time that they "belong to Europe." (F, 105–06)

So "the west wind" continues to spend its waning force in lulling "the European peoples" to continue "playing the stupid game of Sleeping Beauty" as "the east wind" gathers its prevailing strength in "an obstinate refusal to enter the charmed circle of mutual admiration at the summit."[144]

Fanon has no time for mere quotation; not even for an indirect quotation. The bitter irony of his allusion to the Gospel unmasks not only the garrulity with which established power conceals from itself and its adherents the judgment intensified by its every exercise. It unmasks as well the painful reality to which the revolutionary struggle points. The question whether or not the allusion to the Gospel was intentional does not disallow a serious pause over the "moment of truth" hidden within it. The conjunction of the unveiling of what another translation of the Ephesian passage calls "the complex wisdom of God" (RSV) and Fanon's proverbial appropriation of the Gospel unmasks the racist core of the conflict between domination and liberation, and their concomitant mentalities. The truth is that the human reality purposed in and by the wisdom of God and the "native reality" purposed in and by "decolonization" are identical. The truth is that the identities and the relations between the many who are called and the few who are chosen are being transfigured. The identification of the wisdom of God with the revolutionary rejection of colonialism is inherent neither in social and historical reality nor in a one-to-one correlation between Gospel and world. It is the gift of a politics of transfiguration according to which truth and life are one in the freedom wherewith Christ has set us free. Fanon writes:

> The truths of a nation are in the first place its realities. (F, 225) . . . In every age, among the people, truth is the property of the national cause. . . . Truth is that which hurries on the break-up of the colonialist regime: it is that which promotes the emergence of the nation; it is all that protects the natives, and ruins the foreigners. (F, 50) . . . Political education . . . as Césaire said, . . . is "to invent souls." (F, 197)[145]

Unlike the Aristotelian context, in which politics could be defined as the science of human community because a correlation between the consciousness of being human and the experience of community could be presupposed, the colonial context exhibits a radicalization of political theory and practice, which defines politics as the effective bond between consciousness and action. Common to Aristotle and to Fanon is the recognition that politics have to do with what it takes to make room in the world for the freedom that being human takes. The revolutionary reality of the colonial context, however, is that a political consciousness must first of all be developed if a humanizing bond between consciousness and action is to give effective shape to human freedom. In short, politics is indeed "the invention of souls" because souls have first of all to be "invented." Fanon writes:

> Colonialism is not satisfied merely with holding a people in its grip and emptying the native's basin of all form and content. By a kind of perverted logic, it turns to the past of the oppressed people, and distorts, disfigures, and destroys it. . . . The colonial mother protects her child from itself, from its ego, and from its physiology, its biology, and its own unhappiness which is its very essence. (F, 210–11)

This radicalization must be recognized and understood, if one is to understand Fanon's remark, born of the Algerian struggle, that "we

have watched a man being created by revolutionary beginnings . . ."
(F, 191).

So deep is the racial Manicheism of colonialism that such revolutionary beginnings are launched by violent confrontation. The Colombian study of the sociological reality of violence, so carefully documented by Monsignor Guzmán and his colleagues,[146] finds impressive confirmation in Fanon's analysis of the depth-psychological and sociological reality of colonialism. The shocking conclusion is that violence is a necessary first step in the decolonization that is the fundamental precondition of black liberation. Indeed, this shock of recognition is the concrete mode of that shock of recognition which, as Kierkegaard has already taught us, is the precondition of the liberating acknowledgment of the paradox of the incarnation in which the secret of human identity and freedom is unveiled. A conflict of worlds has broken out, a conflict that is the harbinger of the judgment upon power by truth. As Fanon puts it:

> The natives' challenge to the colonial world is not a rational confrontation of points of view. It is not a treatise on the universal, but the untidy affirmation of an original idea propounded as an absolute. (F, 41)

> Decolonization never takes place unnoticed, for it influences individuals and modifiies them fundamentally. It transforms spectators crushed with their inessentiality into privileged actors, with the glare of history's floodlights upon them. It brings a natural rhythm into existence, introduced by new men, and with it a new language and a new humanity. But this creation owes nothing of its legitimacy to any supernatural power; the "thing" which has been colonized becomes man during the same process by which it frees itself. . . .

> If we wish to describe it precisely, we might find it in the well-known words: "The last shall be first and the first last." Decolonization is the putting into practice of this sentence. That is why, if we try to describe it, all decolonization is successful.

> If the last shall be first, this will only come to pass after a murderous and decisive struggle between the two protagonists. That affirmed intention to place the last at the head of things, and to make them climb at a pace (too quickly, some say) the

well-known steps which characterize an organized society, can only triumph if we use all means to turn the scale, including, of course, that of violence. . . .

The native who decides to put the program into practice, and to become its moving force, is ready for violence at all times. From birth it is clear to him that this narrow world, strewn with prohibitions, can only be called in question by absolute violence. (F,36–37)

As we have noted, Fanon admits the "reverse Manicheism" expressed in this assessment. But unless we are prepared to begin at this point in our assessment of the Black Revolution, we shall not only never understand it as a judgment upon, and liberation from, white domination and oppression; but once again, we shall have missed the moment to found freedom. We shall have missed the moment because we shall have failed to discern that this "reverse Manicheism" signals a movement from animality to humanity, from anonymity to identity, which marks the beginning of yet another journey from Exodus to Easter, in which he is present and over which he presides, whose prodromal *via dolorosa* sets the *via guillotina* free for a more promising passage into the *via humana humanorum*.[147] Even if we should suppose that Fanon's recollection of the Gospel (see Matt. 20:16; Luke 13:30) is merely a proverbial coincidence, the ironic force of the bitter passage just cited can scarcely be less than reminiscent of the providential coincidence of those signs that seal a bond between revolutionary movements and a politics of transfiguration. When "cramped" is experienced as "wronged," to paraphrase Brinton, a moral transfiguration is under way that makes men revolt and revolutions the harbingers of a long-overdue justice in the affairs of men.[148] As the earliest account of the Transfiguration reports it:

And in their presence he was transfigured; his clothes became dazzling white, with a whiteness no bleacher on earth could equal. . . . And now suddenly, when they looked around, there was nobody to be seen but Jesus alone with themselves. . . . On their way down the mountain, he enjoined them not to tell anyone what they had seen until the Son of Man had risen from the dead. They seized upon those words, and discussed among themselves what this "rising from the dead" could mean. And they put a question to him: "Why do our teachers say that Elijah must come first?" He replied, ". . . I tell you, Elijah has already come and they have worked their will upon him, as the scriptures say of him." (Mark 9:2, 3, 8, 9–11, 13)

The question whether violence may or must be reckoned as part of the story of this Transfiguration, is still to be faced.[149] Meanwhile, it is clear that, according to Fanon's very secular gospel, violence is simply a hard-core fact of the revolutionary struggle against colonialism. The racist core of that struggle requires it as a factor both of consciousness and action.

> It is clear that in the colonial countries the peasants alone are revolutionary, for they have nothing to lose and everything to gain. . . . The exploited man sees that his liberation implies the use of all means, and that of force first and foremost. . . . Colonialism only loosens its hold when the knife is at its throat. . . . Colonialism . . . is violence in its natural state, and it will only yield when confronted with greater violence. (F, 61)

Nonviolence, on the other hand, is "a creation of the colonial situation." It is "an attempt to settle the colonial problem around a green baize table . . . before any blood has been shed" (F, 61).[150]

But Fanon is not unaware of the risks of this intrinsic violence. Indeed, however indispensable violence is as a starting point for the achievement of racial identity in the struggle against colonialism, the resort to violence cannot be allowed to dispense with the question of strategy and tactics. The perennial questions that haunt revolutionary movements also haunt movements of national liberation. The more genuinely revolutionary these movements become, the more urgent become the questions whether and when the social situation is ripe for revolutionary action; and by what means are the revolutionary goals to be achieved? Lacking a coherence between violence and tactics, "there is only a blind will toward freedom, with the terrible reactionary risks which it entails" (F, 59). In the course of a perceptive and precise analysis of the strengths and weaknesses of spontaneity and of the pitfalls of the national consciousness, Fanon outlines the perils and possibilities of a revo-

lutionary movement that begins with the recovery by decolonization of racial identity and takes the route of national liberation both
of consciousness and action toward a new order of humanization
for the whole of mankind.

The intensity, complexity, and magnitude of the Black Revolution require a bond of solidarity and trust between intellectuals and
peasants, exactly as with Fidelism and with the Chinese Revolution
under Mao Tse-tung. The temptations of the national bourgeoisie
to succumb to the compromise with colonialism must be resisted
and overcome. The "mystifications" inherent in the dubiously humane logic of colonialism, as well as in the revival of the tribal
fantasies of any people undergoing an awakening of national consciousness, must be rejected. A reversal and redirection of the relations between the countryside and the towns, between the masses of
the people and the people in the urban centers, between the *Lum-
penproletariat* (F, 129 f.) and the revolutionary leadership, must
and will occur. The achievement of the necessary coherence between revolutionary aspiration and the organic realities of national
development presupposes the insight and the skill to convert hatred
into patience and to combine the organic character of social change
with the tasks of building a new order of life. The problem now,
says Fanon,

> is to lay hold of . . . violence which is changing direction. When
> formerly it was appeased by myths and exercised its talents in
> finding fresh ways of committing mass suicide, now new condi-
> tions will make possible a completely new line of action. (F, 58)

But

> racialism and hatred and resentment—"a legitimate desire for
> revenge"—cannot sustain a war of liberation. (F, 139)
>     . . . The national government, before concerning itself about
> international prestige, ought first to give back their dignity to all
> citizens, fill their minds and feast their eyes with human things,
> and create a prospect that is human because conscious and sov-
> ereign men dwell therein. (F, 204–5)[151]

There is no contradiction between nationalism and humanism.
The development of a national consciousness leads to a national

culture as the slowly maturing fruit of a racial identity born of the revolutionary struggle for decolonization. The Black Revolution is, in truth, the practice of the Gospel saying that "the first shall be last and the last shall be first" (Matt. 19:30). But this is no literalistic correlation designed either to prove the social relevance of the Gospel or to lend religious sanctification to a revolutionary movement informed by other purposes and by another spirit. On the contrary, the correlation is a sign of the messianic reality and pattern characteristic of current revolutionary movements and exhibited by the Black Revolution with singular clarity and force. "The colonized man who writes for his people," says Fanon, "ought to use the past with the intention of opening the future, as an invitation to action and a basis for hope" (F, 232). This almost eschatological saying finds its confirmation in the emergence and in the fate of the storytellers. "The formula 'This all happened long ago' is substituted with that of 'What we are going to speak of happened somewhere else, but it might well have happened here today, and it might happen tomorrow'" (F, 240). And the messianic precedent for the fate and the future of the tellers of a revolutionary story illuminates their role and destiny in the struggle for the liberation of the people—of their people, of all the people.

> Colonialism made no mistake when from 1955 on it proceeded to arrest these storytellers systematically. . . . Every time the storyteller relates a fresh episode to his public, he presides over a real invocation. The existence of a new type of man is revealed to the public. The present is no longer turned in upon itself but spread out for all to see. . . . The story teller replies to the expectant people by successive approximations, and makes his way, apparently alone but in fact helped on by his public, toward the seeking out of new patterns. . . . (F, 241)

And

> he went round the whole of Galilee, teaching in the synagogues, preaching the gospel of the Kingdom, and curing whatever illness or infirmity there was among the people. (Matt. 4:23) . . . The people were astounded at his teaching; unlike their own teachers

he taught with a note of authority. (Matt. 7:28–29) . . . The disciples went up to him and asked, "Why do you speak to them in parables?" He replied, "It has been granted to you to know the secrets of the kingdom of Heaven; but to those others it has not been granted. For the man who has will be given more, till he has enough and to spare; and the man who has not will forfeit even what he has. That is why I speak to them in parables; for they look without seeing, and listen without hearing or under-standing. . . . But happy are your eyes because they see, and your ears because they hear! Many prophets and saints, I tell you, desired to see what you now see, yet never saw it; to hear what you hear, yet never heard it." (Matt. 13:10–13, 16–17)

"Today," Fanon writes, "we are at the stasis of Europe." His is the voice and conscience of the Third World in distinction from the colonial and imperialist world of Europe and North America. He declares:

> Let us flee from this motionless movement where gradually dialectic is changing into the logic of equilibrium. Let us recon-sider the question of mankind. Let us reconsider the question of cerebral reality and of the cerebal mass of all humanity, whose connections must be increased, whose channels must be diversified and whose messages must be rehumanized. . . . For Europe, for ourselves, and for humanity, . . . we must turn over a new leaf, we must work out new concepts, and try to set afoot a new man. (F, 314, 316)

In Jesus of Nazareth, the new man has already happened. His presence in the human story has released a power that binds as it liberates and liberates as it binds. This is the dialectic that shapes the course of human events, making room for revolutionary renewal, even as it rescues revolutions from the fate of their own undoing. The question of mankind has been reconsidered. The enterprise of revolution is the unveiling of mankind's visibility.

## 2. The Radicalization of a Dream: Martin Luther King, Jr.

Although David Lewis' *Critical Biography* of Martin Luther King, Jr., omits the name of Frantz Fanon from its index of persons, places, and movements significant for understanding King's life and work, there is nevertheless a significant if paradoxical relation between them.[152] The paradox of the relation between Fanon and King is that their respective assessments of the social, political, psychological, and human reality and evil of racism are virtually identical, but their proposals for the revolutionary triumph over racism are radically contradictory. Fanon derives the role of violence in the struggle against racism from its reality as a positive as well as a negative factor in that struggle. King is fully aware of the intensity, complexity, obduracy, and brutality of the black revolutionary struggle but as fully committeed to the strategy and the goals of nonviolence in bringing the struggle to a victorious end. The sobering truth is that the relation between Frantz Fanon and Martin Luther King, Jr., shows that the dynamics and the meaning of the Civil Rights Movement in the United States and of the Black Revolution in Africa are one and indivisible. The relation shows further—and this in a strikingly paradigmatic way—how the radicalization of the dilemma of the Black Revolution unites it with the fate of all revolutions whose aim is freedom.

As we have noted, the fate of all revolutions is that they devour their own children, because sooner or later revolutionary promises and passions fail to coincide and cancel each other out.[153] In the case of the Black Revolution, the dilemma between passions and promises, between patience and power, erupted in a vividly concrete and focal way in the Civil Rights Movement in the United States. From Montgomery in 1954 to Memphis in 1968, the decade and a half of the struggle for human rights against racist demonry and dehumanization witnessed Martin Luther King, Jr.'s rise to decisive leadership and directional control of the battle.[154] The course of the conflict simultaneously exhibited the radicalization of a Dream through "Crisis and Compromise," until, shortly after 6:00 P.M. on Thursday, 4 April 1968, an assassin's bullet brought the dreamer's life to a close, exposed the implicit and explicit sadism with which "the Killers of the Dream" had been granted a sacrificial victim, and all but shattered the Dream itself in a nightmare of despair and retaliatory power.[155] At least since Socrates, and expressly since Jesus, in every confrontation between truth and power, there is "no authority . . . if . . . not . . . granted . . . from above; and therefore the deeper guilt lies with the (men) who handed (the dreamers) over . . ." (John 19:11).

The Dream of Martin Luther King, Jr., took the epochal shape of words on 28 August 1963, as the climax of the March on Washington, D.C., which brought an estimated 250,000 people to the Mall and to the base of the Lincoln Memorial in the capital of the nation. Approximately 75,000 to 95,000 participants in the march were white (LB, 224). The purpose of the march was to arouse the conscience of America, and consequently the Congress of the United States to enact into law a Bill of Civil Rights.[156] King's address on that occasion seemed strikingly parallel to another unforgettable "civil rights" speech in the annals of the nation's history. Once again the question of the unity or disunity of the American nation was at issue; and the scars of bitterness and battle, of hatred and mistrust, had become open wounds whose healing could no longer be delayed. It was altogether natural that the speech itself should have interlaced its "I have a Dream" refrain with allusions to the Gettysburg Address.[157]

There is some difference of judgment between Coretta King and her husband's biographer, David Lewis, as to the genesis of the "Dream Speech." It is clear from both accounts that the address was "more carefully prepared than any he had made before" (LB, 227); also that the dream theme had first come to utterance in Cobo Hall, after the march down Woodward Avenue in Detroit on 23 June 1963. Detroit turned out to be a mid-point in a triumphal journey across the country in the wake of the Birmingham breakthrough for the civil rights of blacks in public facilities and public transportation. According to Coretta King, however, her husband had worked especially hard to avoid a repetition of the dream theme, planning instead to speak to the theme of a "bad check," which the black people had received from America (CK, 236). "We are here today," Dr. King had said, "to redeem that check, and we will not accept the idea that there is no money in the Bank of Justice" (CK, 239). As the speaker began to articulate his demands for "freedom *now*," for "jobs *now*," the intense exultation of the crowd's response moved him to discard his prepared speech and to take up the Dream again (CK, 239). He said:

> I say to you today, even though we face the difficulties of today and tomorrow, I still have a dream. It is a dream that is deeply rooted in the American dream. I have a dream that one day this nation will rise up, live out the true meaning of its creed: We hold these truths to be self-evident, that all men are created equal.
>
> I have a dream that one day on the red hills of Georgia the sons of former slaves and the sons of former slave-owners will be able to sit down together at the table of brotherhood. I have a dream that even the state of Mississippi, a state sweltering with the heat of oppression, will be transformed into an oasis of freedom and justice.
>
> I have a dream that my four little children one day will live in a nation where they will not be judged by the color of their skin but by the content of their character.
>
> I have a dream that one day every valley shall be exalted, every hill and mountain shall be made low. The rough places will be made plain and the crooked places will be made straight. . . . With this faith we will be able to hew out of the mountains of despair the stone of hope. With this faith we will be able to work together, to pray together, to struggle together, to go to jail together, to stand up for freedom together, knowing we will be free one day.
>
> This will be the day when all of God's children will be able to sing with new meaning "Let freedom ring." . . . When we allow freedom to ring from every town and every hamlet, from every state and every city, we will be able to speed up the day when all of God's children, black men and white men, Jews and Gentiles, Protestants and Catholics, will be able to join hands and sing in the words of the old Negro spiritual, "Free at last! Free at last! Great God A-mighty, we are free at last!" (CK, 239–40)

Reading the "Dream Speech" now is to relive the day of its utterance for all who heard it, on the Washington Mall or through the media. And in so doing one can affirm again Mrs. King's report that "it seemed to all of us there that his words flowed from some higher place, through Martin, to the weary people before him.

Yea—Heaven itself opened up and we all seemed transformed" (CK, 239). "Transfigured" is perhaps the truer word. And this, not only because another exodus was in the making, but also because a moment of truth had broken in from which there could be no turning back. Moses and Elijah were in the wings. Righteousness and resurrection were on the move. And there were yet great sufferings to be endured (Mark 9:12). It is understandable that "a day of heroic fantasy" is the best that David Lewis can ascribe to that memorable event (LB, 229). For he has been able to turn aside from the biblical vistas and images that had unmistakably nurtured the words at Gettysburg and of that spoken Dream. How else could one reduce the lofty cadences of an Isaianic vision to "rhetoric almost without content" (LB, 228)? As though aware of some misbegotten secular improverishment, King's otherwise impressively gifted biographer seems himself unable to ignore the power of the closing peroration, and hastens reluctantly to appropriate another's assessment of such happenings. "If Gustave Le Bon is correct, 'The memorable events of history are the visible effects of the invisible changes of human thought' " (LB, 229).[158]

There were incredulous observers who missed the point of what was going on in the agony of that first transfiguring confrontation of truth with established power. In what may well be the replacement by the author of the Fourth Gospel of the Synoptic accounts of the Transfiguration of Jesus, it is recorded that "the crowd standing by said it was thunder, while others said, 'An angel has spoken to him.' Jesus replied, 'This voice (i.e., from heaven) spoke for your sake, not mine. Now is the hour of judgment for this world; now shall the Prince of this world be driven out. And I shall draw all men to myself, when I am lifted up from the earth.' This he said to indicate the kind of death he was to die" (John 12:29–33; parenthesis mine).

Echoes of the Dream took the shape of the dreamer's words again and for the last time at Clayton Temple in Memphis on 3 April 1968, the night before Martin Luther King's untimely death. Disaster had overtaken the carefully planned nonviolent march in support of the black sanitation workers. A militant organization, calling itself The Invaders and purporting to speak for the teenagers, had resisted all attempts by Dr. King and the staff of the Southern Christian Leadership Conference (SCLC) "to give nonviolence a chance to prove itself in Memphis" (LB, 384). A federal court injunction against demonstrations had been granted to the city of Memphis and the National Guard was at hand to enforce the injunction, if necessary. Violence did erupt, and much against his will, King agreed to leave the march in order to alleviate genuine fears for his life. "I don't know what will happen now," King said to a packed and expectant audience. "The mantle of prophecy seemed to descend upon Martin," his wife reports (CK, 316). "We've got some difficult days ahead," King continued. "But it really doesn't matter to me now. . . . I just want to do God's will. And He's allowed me to go up to the mountain. And I've looked over, and I've seen the Promised Land. I may not get there with you, but I want you to know tonight that we as a people will get to the Promised Land. So I'm happy tonight. I'm not worried about anything. I'm not fearing any man. Mine eyes have seen the glory of the coming of the Lord . . ." (CK, 316). Coretta King notes that the response of the audience was so intense and Martin's exaltation so high that he was overcome. "He broke off there. I believe he intended to finish the quotation—'His truth is marching on.' But he could not" (CK, 316).

It is well known that the Dream of Martin Luther King, Jr., and his efforts at its social and political implementation were rooted in biblical and Christian faith and the pragmatic nonviolence of Mahatma Gandhi. The former is attested not only by his family influences, his college, seminary, and university education, and his vocation as a Baptist minister and preacher. It is attested more persuasively by the strong sense of a life lived as an instrument of the divine will and under a providential destiny. "It was in Montgomery," writes Coretta King, "that . . . we felt a sense of destiny, of being propelled in a certain positive direction. We had the feeling that we were allowing ourselves to be the instruments of God's creative will" (CK, 97). Although the call to the ministry of the Dexter Avenue Baptist Church was the immediate occasion for these reflections, Mrs. King supplies more than one moving glimpse into the inner confidence and trust in God's will and purpose for their lives that they shared together. Thus it was not pretense but simple candor that prompted King's reply to the query of a puzzled newsman after a singular news conference at the height of the tension in Memphis fourteen years later. "Dr. King, what has happened to you since last night? Have you talked with someone?" "No," came the reply. "I haven't talked with anyone. I have only talked with God" (CK, 311).

In *Strive Toward Freedom* (1958), which tells the Montgomery Story, King notes that "not until I entered Crozer Theological Seminary in 1948, . . . did I begin a serious intellectual quest for a method to eliminate social evil" (LB, 34). At that time, Professor George Davis had lectured on Gandhi's conception of *Satyagraha* (nonviolence). But it was really Mordecai Johnson, then President of Howard University, through whose uncommon gifts of mind and eloquence "Gandhi's spiritual leadership and pacifist techniques attained an immediate and luminescent dimension that Martin might otherwise never have apprehended" (LB, 34). This intellectual and psychological facination with *Satyagraha* underwent a deepening transformation in the wake of the Montgomery Boycott of 1956. August of the following year brought a visit to Montgomery of the Gandhian disciple and scholar, Ranganath Diwakar, who "convinced Martin that he, too, must set an example of physical suffering" (LB, 96). Consequently, "Martin resolved that, if the opportunity again presented itself, he would accept imprisonment rather than compromise with an evil law." And "he could be fairly certain that Montgomery would not deny him the opportunity" (LB, 96). Two years later (1959), a trip to India virtually finalized the Gandhian strain in King's developing convictions. In India, he met Diwakar again and was explicitly reminded of Gandhi's own description of *satyagraha*. Gandhi had said it

differs from passive resistance as the North Pole from the South. The latter (i.e. passive resistance) has been conceived as a weapon of the weak and does not exclude the use of physical force or violence for the purpose of gaining one's end, whereas the former (i.e. *satyagraha*) has been conceived as a weapon of the strongest and excludes the use of violence in any shape or form. (Quoted, LB, 103; parentheses mine)

Upon this instruction, King remarked "that he had perceived during the Montgomery struggle the near identity of *agape* and *Satyagraha*: '*Agape* was love seeking to preserve and create community' " (LB, 103).

These recollections are indispensable to a proper assessment of the crisis that had beclouded and afflicted the Dream between the March on Washington in 1963 and the March in Memphis in 1968. It was this crisis that exposed at once the radicalization of the Dream already under way in King's own mind and activity, and the uttermost limit of that radicalization, which threatened to deprive a decade of civil rights achievement of a formative future. King himself has dated the characteristic and critical decade of the Civil Rights Movement from "the Montgomery Bus Boycott of 1956 to the Selma movement of 1965."[159] His last published book surrounded this assessment with a succinct summary of his own understanding of the Black Revolution and of his commitment to it. King wrote:

> Before this century, virtually all revolutions had been based on hope and hate. The hope was expressed in the rising expectation of freedom and justice. The hate was an expression of bitterness toward the perpetrators of the old order. It was the hate that made revolutions bloody and violent. What was new about Mahatma Gandhi's movement in India was that he mounted a revolution on hope and love, hope and nonviolence. This same new emphasis characterized the civil rights movement in our country. . . . We maintained the hope while transforming the hate of revolutions into positive nonviolent power. As long as the hope was fulfilled there was little questioning of nonviolence. But when the hopes were blasted, when people came to see that in spite of progress their conditions were still insufferable, when they looked and saw more poverty, more school segregation and more slums, despair began to set in. Unfortunately, when hope diminishes, the hate is often turned most bitterly toward those who originally built up the hope. (CC, 51–52)

What was the crisis? And how did it erupt? In a word, the crisis that brought the radicalization of a dream to a fateful revolutionary juncture was the dilemma between freedom and power. More insistently and concretely, it was the dilemma between freedom *now* and power *now*. From without, the Civil Rights Movement was beset by a slackening pace of achievement in the struggle for justice against racism in the United States. From within, the movement was beset by the emergence of a young, impatient, and militant black leadership. The freedom movement and the Black Power movement entered upon a collision course in the battle against "internal decolonization" and for the "deracination" of America. The crisis is still going on.

It is often suggested that Martin Luther King, Jr.'s leadership of the Civil Rights Movement came to a foreseeable end. His simplistic adherence to a religiously inspired idealism of nonviolence proved to be no match for the recalcitrance of racist power in American political and economic institutions and the white backlash of a middle-class society. The decade of boycotts and mass marches had breached the walls of the hitherto impregnable racist fortress that was the United States. But the SCLC, under King's direction, lacked the sober pragmatism and the resolute will-to-power required for effective racial justice and freedom in the land. Clearly on the Petrus Bridge on the outskirts of Selma, the words of a favorite marching song had been unforgettably turned back upon themselves. "Ain't Nobody Gonna Turn Me Round" reverberated with more than an echo as "Ain't Nobody Gonna Turn America Around."

But such a simplistic assessment of King's part and place in the Black Revolution overlooks both the fact of his own radicalization and the complexity of the confrontation between freedom and power. King had always seen "a close relationship between the black struggle in America and the struggle for independence in America" and "often compared European colonialism with Negro oppression" in the United States (CK, 154). He had never underestimated the entrenched racism in America or the difficulties of unseating it. Indeed, the third chapter of King's last book, *Where Do We Go from Here: Chaos or Community?* deals with "Racism and the White Back Lash" and reads as though it were excerpted for American conditions from Fanon's essay on "The Pitfalls of National Consciousness" in *The Wretched of the Earth*. "There has never been a solid, unified and determined thrust to make justice a reality for Afro-Americans," King declared (CC, 80). "Ever since the birth of our nation, white America has had a schizophrenic personality on the question of race," he remarked. "The 'congenital deformity' of racism has crippled the nation from its inception" (CC, 80–81).

For King, the question "Chaos or Community?" with which his last book concludes, was no merely rhetorical question. The author's intention was "to answer for himself and his critics some of the divisive questions that afflicted the black man as well as American society" (LB, 364). It may be that David Lewis correctly regards "these pastiche materials" as a regrettable repetition of previous sermons and speeches and as the effort of "obviously a tired man. His originality seemed spent" (LB, 364). On the other hand, the weariness may attest King's own deepening awareness that the Black Revolution in America was being carried inexorably by the conjunction of social and political responses, which are always too little and too late, with the internal dynamics and divisions within the revolution itself, toward a fateful decision between freedom and power. Already in 1964 King had declared that "white Americans must be made to understand the basic motives underlying Negro demonstrations. . . . It is not a threat but a fact of history that if an oppressed people's pent-up emotions are not nonviolently released, they will be violently released. So let the Negro march. For if his frustrations and despair are allowed to continue piling up, millions of Negroes will seek solace and security in black-nationalist ideologies" (LB, 369). A year later, he characterized the paralysis of the American schizophrenia between democracy and racism with a catalogue of fateful lassitude.

> Just as an ambivalent nation freed the slaves a century ago with no plan or program to make their freedom meaningful, the still ambivalent nation in 1954 declared school segregation unconstitutional with no plan or program to make integration real. Just as the Congress passed a civil rights bill in 1868 and refused to enforce it, the Congress passed a civil rights bill in 1964 and to this day has failed to enforce it in all its dimensions. Just as the Fifteenth Amendment in 1870 proclaimed Negro suffrage, only

to permit its *de facto* withdrawal in half the nation, so in 1965 the Voting Rights Law was passed and then permitted to languish with only fractional and half-hearted implementation. (CC, 95)

However, the external and internal pressure upon Martin Luther King's leadership of the Civil Rights Movement, far from detaching him from his adherence to nonviolence, radicalized it instead. The religious and idealistic matrix of this adherence was not abandoned. It was subordinated to a stress upon the pragmatism of nonviolence as a method of social change. Marches and demonstrations designed to correct specific and local injustices were to give way to a unified, massive, second march on Washington. At an SCLC meeting in Atlanta in December 1967, King presented his plan for a "Poor People's Campaign." He strongly urged that, if the summer of 1968 were not to see a repetition of the disasters of the summer of 1967, a nonviolent demonstration on a much grander scale must be launched.[160] "I think we have come to the point," he declared, "where there is no longer a choice between nonviolence and riots. It must be militant, massive nonviolence, or riots" (LB, 368–69). In the subsequent Massey Lectures, recorded for the Canadian Broadcasting Corporation, he went one step further: "Nonviolent protest must now mature to a new level to correspond to heightened black impatience and stiffened white resistance." This "high level is mass civil disobedience" (LB, 370).

Then came what King's biographer has aptly described as the "Memphis Donnybrook" (LB, 382). Not only had "Martin's spiritual resiliency declined sharply" (LB, 382). But the failure of Memphis had given the white power structure and the black militants a common cause against the nonviolent option, however pragmatic, and however radicalized it had become. President Johnson appeared on national television on 28 March 1968 to condemn "mindless violence," voicing thereby the abhorrence on the part of "the *bien pensant* coalition of white prelates, civic leaders, businessmen, intellectuals, and news commentators (of) the invitational violence of Martin's activities" (LB, 383; parenthesis mine). The most pragmatic argument that King had been using against the black militants had thereby been turned against him. In their turn, "the Black militants took the failure of the Memphis demonstration as an incontrovertible sign of the impotence of nonviolence" (LB, 383). The radicalization of a dream had reached the limits of its pertinence to the realities of the Black Revolution.

For two years—between the shooting of James Meredith on 6 June 1966 and the Memphis march on 28 March 1968 directly preceding King's death—Martin Luther King, Jr., had been aware of the serious threat to the internal unity of the Black Revolution posed by the advocates of Black Power. His own account of this "widening split in our ranks" (CC, 35) in the course of the chapter on "Black Power" in *Where Do We Go From Here: Chaos or Community?* shows not only how clearly and agonizingly he understood and sympathized with the Black Power movement, with its genesis and with its aims, but also how deeply convinced he was that the implicit and explicit espousal of violence, intrinsic to the semantics and tactics of the militant leadership of the Congress of Racial Equality (CORE) and the Student Nonviolent Coordinating Committee (SNCC,) could only bring the Black Revolution to its own undoing.

In a five-hour discussion with Stokley Carmichael and Floyd McKissick "in a small Catholic parish house in Yazoo City," Mississippi (CC, 35), King argued that "while the concept of legitimate Black Power might be denotatively sound, the slogan 'Black Power' carried the wrong connotations" (CC, 35).[161] To these representations Stokely replied, according to King, that "the question of violence versus nonviolence was irrelevant. The real question was the need for black people to consolidate their political and economic resources to achieve power. 'Power,' he said, "is the only thing respected in this world, and we must get it at any cost'" (CC, 35; see also LB, 325 f.). For the purposes of the march in support of James Meredith, the leaders of CORE and SNCC agreed to refrain from the use of the slogan "Black Power!" and the SCLC leadership agreed to abstain from shouting the slogan "Freedom Now!" But the impasse between freedom and power had been defined, and the dream of a revolution without violence initiated by the revolutionaries had been shattered. The radicalization of the dream had not been adequate to the power realities of the black struggle. As the *ultima ratio* of the Black Revolution, the dream had reached its ultimate limit.

The crisis of decision between freedom, achieved by the power of nonviolence, and power, violent or nonviolent, as the precondition of the freedom to be achieved by and for black people, was forced by events. It was a crisis of priorities rather than of goals. But as events compel decisions, decisions expose the judgments that inform them. And a crisis of decision, compounded by a crisis of judgment, exposes the ambiguities and frailties of revolutionary leadership. The historical and human stakes are higher for a revolutionary bid for power than for established power, because the revolutionary future is the human future and because, as we have already noted, the revolutionary is nearer the heart of God than are the "law-and-order people."[162] There is a parabolic pathos in that conversation between Martin Luther King, Jr., and Stokely Carmichael as they walked along that Mississippi road on behalf of James Meredith and the ongoing struggle for black freedom and black civil rights. According to Coretta King's account, Carmichael said: "Martin, I deliberately started the Black Power thing to get you committed to it." To this Martin smilingly replied: "That's all right. I've been used before. One more time won't hurt."[163]

"Being used!" or "Being right!"—that was the agonizing dilemma that haunted the crisis of decision and of judgment that shattered the dream of Martin Luther King, Jr. One may accept Carmichael's disclaimer of any premeditated intention to discredit King and the SCLC at Greenwood, Mississippi (LB, 325). In a cohesive context of comradeship and trust, such an interplay of policy and jest would be readily understandable. In the shadow of an emerging crisis, however, a harmless conversation has a way of becoming a portent of turmoil and tragedy ahead. In retrospect, it appears that every achievement of the Dream was shadowed by an incipient corruption, if not capture, of its vision and its goal. There was B-Day on 3 April 1963, which brought the desegregation of Birmingham, Alabama. "We are going to make Birmingham the center of anti-discrimination in the nation," King declared (LB, 178–79). The bitter struggle marked a precarious coexistence between "violent tension" and "nonviolent tension." There was the "Letter from a

Birmingham Jail," completed on 16 April, a document second only to the "Dream Speech" as a charter of the vision and goal of freedom to be achieved by the power of nonviolence. If civil disorders erupted, nevertheless, King found that regrettable. Yet it was far more regrettable that "Birmingham's white leaders 'left the Negro community with no alternative'" (LB, 189). Most compromising of all, perhaps was "the regnant preoccupation of the Kennedy Administration (with) the quick restoration of civil peace in Birmingham. The legitimacy of black demands . . . clearly enjoyed a second priority in the Kennedy brothers' political universe" (LB, 196; parenthesis mine). The ground was thus already prepared for the laggard implementation of the Civil Rights Bill which, on 11 June 1963, President John Kennedy publicly requested of the Congress in a speech that turned out to have but deepened the gap between noble promises and their fulfillment.

With the Voting Rights Bill, signed into law by President Lyndon Johnson on 6 August 1965, the ambiguities of Birmingham were virtually replayed. King's patient and pragmatic attempt to correlate freedom demonstrations and political calculus had suspended the protests, lest Kennedy fail of election in 1960, and again in 1964, in order to take no chances with the election of President Johnson. The latter judgment is the more problematical in view of Johnson's opposition to Selma in 1965 and his increasing alienation from King, owing to King's commingling of the racial struggle and the war in Vietnam, since the Spring Mobilization speech in New York in 1966 (LB, 310). If Johnson mistrusted "the political judgment of Martin . . . " (LB, 311), there were those in the black community who did likewise (LB, 303). When, then, the confrontation with Mayor Daley in Chicago over Cicero in the summer of 1966 took the civil rights leader to the mass rally that he had called for Soldier's Field instead of to the streets in an act of massive civil disobedience, the crisis of decision and of judgment seemed to have broken "the last straw." As Lerone Bennett said at the time, "the pity is that Martin never went as far as his mentor, Gandhi" (LB, 334). The bitter irony with which Adam Clayton Powell took to referring to "Martin 'Loser' King," and Roy Wilkins' lost confidence in "Martin's demonstrated ability to mount peaceful rallies" (LB, 383), surely reached a point of heartbreak with the admission on the part of King's own alterego, Ralph Abernathy, that "if Dr. King had lived, there would never have been a Poor People's Campaign" (LB, 385).

Thus *ad hominem* judgments deepen the ambiguity of strategic judgments and becloud yet more the integrity of revolutionary dreams, commitments, and purposes. Not least among these *ad hominem* judgments is the possibility that the mounting burden of revolutionary leadership had overtaken even the peerless integrity and spirit of Martin Luther King, Jr., with a paralysis of self-criticism that prevents a liberating recognition of the fact that the rightness of past achievements does not guarantee the rightness of present and future judgments and decisions.

The dream of Martin Luther King, Jr., rooted as it was in Christian faith and experience, and in the ethos of the black community in the United States, an ethos shaped by the Christian church, is the most explicit instance of a revolutionary effort expressly responsive to Jesus of Nazareth. Accordingly, the radicalization and shattering of that dream seem to establish nothing so plainly as the fact that Jesus Christ is no more promising and persuasive an answer to the question of revolution than any other presence is. King and Gandhi, Torres and Nestor Paz, as proximate and confessed Christians, seem to join with Lenin, Trotsky, and Bucharin, Mao and Ho, Fidel and Che, in a cloud of witnesses to the overshadowing of revolutionary expectation and integrity by revolutionray zeal, discord, and mistrust. Jesus, too, has missed the moment to found freedom. The power of a presence that liberates men as it binds them to a humanizing loyalty and direction, and in so binding them, sets them free from the corrosive consequences of revolutionary crises of judgment and decision, has encountered once again the default of impotence. Once again, the freedom for the vision and sensitivity that know how to discern the difference between obedient surrender and obedient waiting has failed. Once again, the power of weakness turns out operationally to be weaker than the weakness of power; and the refusal of power functions as a counsel of confusion when the exercise of power is the unmistakable next step.

Jesus of Nazareth may be clearly against the Establishment; but he is not, on that account, clearly on the side of revolution. Indeed, he darkens counsel by confusing obedient waiting with disobedient surrender, by fortifying the hopelessness of truth before power, and, perhaps worst of all, by enervating every "hard" revolution called for by events, by the "soft" revolution of a "Kingdom not of this world" that can only evaporate as a shattered dream *in* this world. Christianity is thus the ally of every Establishment, and most of all in this, that Christianity ultimately offers to every challenge to the Establishment compassion and crucifixion as the mystery of ultimate victory. It is not strange that Nietzsche, and following him Jean-Paul Sartre, should be convinced that Christianity beguiles men with the morality of slaves and diverts them from the spirit of being creators who hold within themselves the keys to power, truth, and freedom.

The shattered dream of Martin Luther King, Jr., leaves us at the critical juncture between "obedient surrender" and "obedient waiting." Before crossing that border into the land of promise heralded by Nietzsche and Sartre, we must briefly consider yet a further phase of the Black Revolution. This is its present situation under the aegis of two alternate and less than compatible faiths. The one is the revolutionary freedom that Islam brought to Malcolm X. The other is the faith implicit in the secular, humanistic fury of the Black Panthers.

### 3. The Human Meaning of Blackness: Malcolm X

From the point of view of the Black Revolution, Malcolm X and Martin Luther King, Jr., were distantly related. The ties that bound them together, yet kept them apart, were ties of birth and kinship, not according to the flesh, but according to the spirit. As black men, they were born into the dehumanizing environment of white racism in America; and their spiritual calling turned out to be a calling to pilgrimage and leadership of the struggle of black people for freedom and dignity, for human rights and civil rights, for their humanity as black people. The pursuit of their spiritual calling took them by markedly different routes toward an identical vision of a black and human future for the people from whose stock they were sprung. Martin Luther King, Jr., was a child of the manse; and from the relative security and privilege of culture and opportunity which that fact made possiblt, he spent himself in struggle and in suffering with and for his people, in and out of prison, under calumny and praise, claimed and nourished by Christian faith and hope, and dedicated to a revolution of love in nonviolent action. Malcolm X was also a child of the manse (Baptist, as was the case of Martin Luther King, Jr.). But the difference between Atlanta, Georgia (1929), and Omaha, Nebraska (1925), was the difference between being the "beneficiary of that lavish love," as President Benjamin Mays of Morehouse put it (LB, 7), and being the unwilling and fated victim of what Malcolm X himself referred to as a "Nightmare."

Via ghetto and prison, and a Muslim Community and Mecca, Malcolm journeyed from survival by belligerence and wit, through hatred and violence and passionate separatism, to find in Islam the experience, vision, and power of black humanity freed for reconciliation with white humanity in the United States and in the world. Both Malcolm X and Martin Luther King, Jr., learned to live with a premonition of death and fearlessness before it. As Martin Luther King, Jr., discovered and died for the dream of "the day when all of God's children . . . will be able to join hands and sing . . . Free at last! . . . ," Malcolm X discovered and died for the human meaning of blackness.

It is not an unreasonable conjecture—although it is only a conjecture—that Malcolm X and Martin Luther King, Jr., would have joined in a reconciling brotherhood on behalf of the Black revolution had not an assassin's bullet brutally intervened to deprive that revolution of the leadership of both. Apparently, in the course of the struggle for the freedom and humanity of black people, they met only once. The place was Washington, D.C.; the time, 26 March 1964. The purpose was the maximization of public pressure upon the Congress for the enactment of pending Civil Rights legislation (LB, 271). In early February of the following year (1965), they might have met again had Martin not been behind bars in a Selma, Alabama, jail for his march from Brown's Chapel, A.M.E. Church to the Selma courthouse in the drive for black voter registration. Malcolm had come to Selma, as Coretta King tells us, not "to make his (i.e., King's) job difficult. I really did come thinking that I could make it easier" (CK, 258; parenthesis mine). He had planned to visit Martin in jail but was prevented by a commitment to an African Students' Conference in London. His declaration of purpose was part of the message that he sent through Coretta to Martin in prison. Before the month of February had ended, Malcolm was killed. It was Sunday, 21 February 1965, in the Audubon Ballroom on West 166th Street, between Broadway and St. Nicholas Avenue in Harlem.

Five years earlier, "the gulf of misunderstanding" between the two leaders "appeared to be practically unbridgeable" (LB, 125). In addition to the advocacy of violence and the rhetoric of hate, King found in Malcolm's espousal of the Muslim program of "a black nation within a larger nation . . . some kind of strange dream" (LB, 125). Accordingly, he declined an invitation to speak at a Muslim Education Rally in 1960, as he had also done three years before in 1957. Malcolm, in turn, entertained "dark predictions" of the course and outcome of King's efforts for black civil rights. He was sure that King, "like Walter White, a man of unquestionable courage, . . . would relish first-name intimacy with the nation's white leaders, water his fiery rhetoric to suit the banquet-table, and begin to appreciate the 'complexities' that delayed immediate racial justice" (LB, 239).

On the other hand, Martin and Malcolm seem to have been drawn to each other by a kind of subliminal attraction to, and respect for, each other's leadership. The unfolding dynamics of the movement in which they were caught up might even have converted into cooperation. Alex Haley, writing the Epilogue to *The Autobiography of Malcolm X*, reports an interview with Martin Luther King, Jr., in the course of which

he was privately intrigued to hear little-known things about Malcolm X that I told him: . . . he discussed him with reserve, and he did say that he would sometime like to have an opportunity to talk with him. Hearing this, Malcolm X said drily, "You think I ought to send him a telegram with my telephone number?" (But from other things that Malcolm X said to me at various times, I deduced that he actually had a reluctant admiration for Dr. King).[164]

As for Martin Luther King, Jr., it is not too much to affirm a similar regard for Malcolm X. Despite their differences,

> Martin firmly agreed with certain aspects of the program that Malcolm X advocated. . . . He shared with Malcolm the fierce desire that the black American reclaim his racial pride, his joy in himself and his race—in a physical, a cultural, and a spiritual rebirth. He shared with the nationalists the sure knowledge that . . . in so many respects, the quality of the black people's scale of values was far superior to that of the white culture which attempted to enslave us. Martin too had a close attachment to our African brothers and to our common heritage.
>
> And, on the other side, Martin too believed that *white* Christianity had failed to act in accordance with its teachings. (CK, 256-57; italics Ms. King's)

Coretta King further records that

> the death of Malcolm X affected me profoundly. . . . Martin and I had reassessed our feelings toward him. We realized that since he had been to Mecca and had broken with Elijah Muhammad, he was moving away from hatred toward internationalism and against exploitation. In a strange way, the same racial attitude which killed others who were working for peaceful change also killed Malcolm X. (CK, 258)

Indeed, it may be note that the unfolding dynamics of the movement in which they were caught up carried Martin Luther King, Jr., from passive resistance to nonviolent protest to militant nonviolence, as almost concurrently Malcolm X was carried from hatred and violence to separatism to nonviolent militancy.

*The Autobiography of Malcolm X* is a documentary of the personal dynamics and dimensions of the struggle of black people, all around the world and especially in the United States, against imperialism, colonialism, and fascism, but especially against racism. As an inset photo illuminates, in depth and intensity, a segment of a panoramic exposure of a happennng or a landscape, so this life story of an intensely gifted black person, whom neither circumstance nor death could deprive of his destiny as a human being, illuminates in depth and intensity what the struggle for justice, freedom, and creativity on the part of any person or any people means in concrete human terms of pain and agony, bitterness and humiliation, of capacities, opportunities, and achievements denied. What Frantz Fanon has done on a sociopsychological scale of historic proportions for the revolutionary struggle of a continent, Malcolm X has done on a psychopersonal scale of intense interiorization and transformation. The destructive demonization effected by racism upon social relations and social institutions so vividly analyzed by Fanon is companioned by Malcolm's unforgettable account of the demonic dehumanization with which a racist society afflicts and destroys an individual human being.

Taken together, *The Wretched of the Earth* and *The Autobiography of Malcolm X* are the primers of the Black Revolution: of its dynamics and dimensions, of the reality of dehumanization from which it springs, of its humanizing directions and purposes, and of its ultimate victory over every Establishment that ignores or obstructs it. To paraphrase Crane Brinton, when "cramped" is experienced as "wronged," a "moral transfiguration" occurs and "men will revolt."[165] To fail to take account of these documents as testimony to this transfiguration is to remain in self-willed darkness, and to fall under the judgment of the divinely ordained Transfiguration of Jesus, of which that "moral transfiguration" is a sign.

Whenever a culture and society transform the self-evidence of human identity into a question, that culture and society are in violation of the reality, direction, and dynamics disclosed in Jesus' Transfiguration. An obedient involvement in what God is doing in the world to make and to keep human life human leaves neither time nor room for self-conscious preoccupation with the question who one is. When the alienation and anonymity underlying the question of identity become the focus of attention and attack, the messianic center and sense of human existence have been replaced by a positivistic self-confidence and self-justification that generate a dehumanizing conflict between vitality and form, between responsibility and discipline, between imagination and truth, between liberation and freedom. In Ruben Alves' suggestive symbolic ocr-relation, "the child" is being devoured by "the dinosaur" on the way to extinction.[166] It is no accident that the Black Revolution has unmasked these identity preoccupations as the pretensions of a white society corrupted both by affluence and by racism.[167] Black people have neither time nor space for enervating existentialist diversions. Theirs is a genuinely revolutionary agenda, wholly dedicated to "freedom now," and wholly absorbing. Perhaps it is worth pondering that *liberation* is a word characteristic neither of Fanon nor of Martin Luther King, Jr., nor of Malcolm X (See F, 246). For all three, however, the struggle for justice aims at freedom and a new humanity—for black people, certainly; but, beyond them, for the whole of humankind.

The suggestion that the principal significance of Malcolm X for the Black Revolution is his discovery of the human meaning of blackness does not imply that this insight was absent from other leaders of the movement or from the black people themselves in their struggle against racism. The battle for civil rights is rooted in the emerging and increasingly articulate conviction among black people of their rights as human beings. Malcolm declares:

> The American black man is the world's most shameful case of minority oppression. What makes the black man think of himself as only an internal United States issue is just a catch-phrase, two words, "civil rights." How is the black man going to get "civil rights" before first he wins his *human rights*? If the American black man will start thinking about his *human* rights, and then start thinking of himself as part of one of the world's great peoples, he will be a case for the United Nations. (AX, 179; italics Malcolm's)

The human meaning of blackness is at once the precondition of the revolutionary struggle for justice and freedom and the passion and point of the odyssey of Malcolm X. It is this passion that dominates Malcolm's bitter alienation from white society, his furious and even fanatical commitment to hatred and separatism, his conversion to Islam and his post-Islamic vision of reconciliation between black people and white people, sharing creatively in the humanness of all people. He writes:

My thinking had been opened up wide in Mecca. . . . In the long letters I wrote to friends, I tried to convey to them my new insights into the American black man's struggle and his problems, as well as the depths of my search for truth and justice.

"I've had enough of someone else's propaganda," I had written to these friends. I'm for truth, no matter who tells it. I'm for justice, no matter who it is for or against. I'm a human being first and foremost, and as such I'm for whoever and whatever benefits humanity *as a whole*. (AX, 366; italics Malcolm's)

The negative side of Malcolm's discovery emerges in the course of his painfully vivid and frank description of the dehumanization that white racism inflicts upon a human being whose color happens to be black. The ghetto is the focal point of these disclosures. Malcolm writes:

. . . Almost everyone in Harlem needed some kind of hustle to survive, and needed to stay high in some way to forget what they had to *do* to survive. (AX, 91; italics Malcolm's)

But the middle-Harlem narcotics force found so many ways to harass me that I had to change my area. I moved down to lower Harlem, around 110th Street. There were many more reefer smokers around there, but these were a cheaper type, this was the worst of the ghetto, the poorest people, the ones who in every ghetto keep themselves narcotized to keep from having to face their miserable existence. . . . Some of those reefer smokers who had the instincts of animals, . . . followed me and learned my pattern. They would dart out of a doorway, I'd drop my stuff, and they would be on it like a chicken on corn. When you become an animal, a vulture, in the ghetto, as I had become, you enter a world of animals and vultures. It becomes truly the survival of only the fittest. (AX, 102)

It takes no one to stir up the sociological dynamite that stems from the unemployment, bad housing, and inferior education already in the ghettoes. This explosively criminal condition has existed for so long, it needs no fuse; it fuses itself; it spontaneously combusts from within itself . . . (AX, 366)

Malcolm X would agree with the Governor of the State of New York "that actually the most dangerous black man in America (is) the ghetto hustler" (AX, 311; parenthesis mine). But when Gov-

ernor Rockefeller included in his annual message to the state legis-
lature for 1973 a resounding recommendation for the incarceration
of drug pushers without parole, the absence of an equally resounding recommendation for the excarceration of the ghetto unmarked
his proposal. He seemed not only to have missed the point of
what Malcolm "knew better than all whites knew" (AX, 310–11).
The Governor had also missed the moment of truth unveiled in
the Transfiguration of Jesus, "with a whiteness no bleacher on earth
could equal" (Mark 9:3). The truth is that in this world—our
world—political messianism has been displaced by messianic politics. In such a world, the self-justifying pretensions of established
authorities sooner or later bring men under the judgments of their
own divine ordination. They pass the point of no return and are
passing away before the new order that is coming to be.

Similarly, when the President of the United States, on 20 January 1973, on the occasion of his Second Inaugural, can ignore the
realities of the Black Revolution in the United States as conspicuously as the absence of black citizens from that occasion signaled
the silence of divine judgment in the wings, "the supreme authóri-
ties" would seem to have discerned the truth in their power with
the insensitivity (minus the bewilderment) of Pilate, and through
the hollow solemnity of their words hastened upon themselves the
awesome judgment of their own dispatch. "Government must learn
to take less from people so that people can do more for themselves,"
said ex-President Nixon. And with an individualism more rugged
than any since President Hoover summoned the troops into the nation's capital to crush a riot born of hunger and despair, the Second
Inaugural took up the theme again: "In our own lives, let each of
us ask not just what will Government do for me, but what can I
do for myself?"[168] "Then, if anyone says to you, 'Look, here is
the Messiah,' or, 'There he is,' do not believe it," said Jesus of
Nazareth. "Imposters will come claiming to be messiahs or
prophets, and they will produce great signs and wonders to mislead
even God's chosen, if such a thing were possible. . . . Wherever the
corpse is, there the vultures will gather" (Matt. 24:23, 24, 28).[169]
Or, as Romans 13:8–10 has put it, "Leave no claim outstanding
against you, except that of mutual love. . . . Love cannot wrong

a neighbor; therefore the whole law is summed up in love."[170]

As the ghetto was the focal point of Malcolm X's discovery of the human meaning of blackness through the bitter experience of negation, Mecca was the focal point of the positive implications and possibilities of that discovery. The turning point came in prison. Here the long human journey to Mecca began. In the Norfolk Prison Colony in Massachusetts, Malcolm tells us:

> I had my first experiences in opening the eyes of my brain-washed black brethren to some truths about the black race. . . . I have to admit a sad, shameful fact. I had so loved being around the white man in prison I really disliked how Negro convicts stuck together so much. But when Mr. Muhammad's teachings reversed my attitude toward my black brothers, in my guilt and shame I began to catch every chance I could to recruit for Mr. Muhammad. (AX, 182)

Through his brother Reginald, Malcolm had first come under the spell of Elijah Muhammad and through him of the teachings of Islam. "The white man is the devil," Elijah Muhammad had taught (AX, 183). And this doctrine accorded well with the realities of black prison experience. Malcolm notes:

> The black convict is the most perfectly preconditioned to hear the words, "the white man is the devil." . . . Usually the convict comes from those bottom-of-the-pile Negroes, the Negroes who through their entire lives have been kicked about, treated like children—Negroes who have never met one white man who didn't either take something from them or do something to them.
> You let this caged-up black man start thinking, the same way I did when I first heard Elijah Muhammad's teachings: let him start thinking how, with better breaks when he was young and ambitious he might have been a lawyer, a doctor, a scientist, anything. You let this caged-up black man start realizing, as I did, how from the first landing of the first slave ship, the millions of black men in America have been like sheep in a den of wolves. That's why black prisoners become Muslims so fast when Elijah Muhammad's teachings filter into their cages by way of other Muslim convicts. (AX, 183)

In prison, Malcolm reports, "reading . . . changed forever the course of my life. . . . Not long ago, an English writer telephoned me from London, asking, . . . 'What's your alma mater?' I told him, 'Books.' You will never catch me with a free fifteen minutes in which I am not studying something I feel might be able to help the black man" (AX, 179). Looking back upon his conversion and, in the light of it, over the course of his life, we learn that Elijah Muhammad had touched the core of Malcolm's *human* being.

> When I was a foul vicious convict, so evil that other convicts had called me Satan, this man had rescued me. He was the man who trained me, who had treated me as if I were his own flesh and blood. He was the man who had given me wings—to go places, to do things I otherwise never would have dreamed of. (AX, 298)
>
> Sometimes, recalling all of this, I don't know, to tell the truth, how I am alive to tell it today. They say God takes care of fools and babies. I've so often thought that Allah was watching over me. Through all of this time of my life, I really *was* dead—mentally dead. I just didn't know that I was. (AX, 125; italics Malcolm's)

Islam had freed Malcolm X for humanizing leadership in the Black Revolution. "I felt a challenge," he declares, "to plan, and build, an organization that could help to cure the black man in North America of the sickness which has kept him under the white man's heel" (AX, 312). "The *color-blindness* of the Muslim world's religious society and the *color-blindness* of the Muslim world's human society: these two influences had each day been making a greater impact, and an increasing persuasion against my previous way of thinking" (AX, 338–39; italics Malcolm's). On his way to Mecca, his experience of brotherhood across all barriers, especially of course the barrier of color, was at once exalting and profound.

> I tucked it into my mind that when I returned home I would tell Americans this observation: that where true brotherhood

existed among all colors, where no one felt segregated, where
there was no "superiority" complex, no "inferiority" complex—
then voluntarily, naturally, people of the same kind felt drawn
together by that which they had in common. (AX, 344)

Indeed, the human meaning of black reality and black revolutionary experience and aspiration was precisely not the amalgamation
of the races but the justice and freedom that made room for a
reconciliation through which the light of the Creator's own joy
in his creation shone. In that light, difference has been purged of
its destructive operation as an occasion of preference and power.
It has indeed been restored to its original design, according to
which difference is, in truth, a thing of beauty and a joy forever.

In *his* autobiography, Augustine of Hippo recalls that when
Faustus, the great teacher of the Manichees, could not, with clarity
and candor, convincingly reply to the searching questions of an
eager disciple, he was shaken by the disparity between knowledge
and virtue that had thus been exposed, and turned to other options
in his intense quest for human meaning.[171] Similarly, Malcolm's
own disenchantment with Elijah Muhammad was occasioned by
the disparity between life and teaching. This disillusionment might
well have turned Malcolm X toward a repudiation of Islam had
not the Hajj to Mecca enriched and fortified him with a vision of
black separatism without rancor, of revolutionary commitment
without hatred and violence, of the reconciling reciprocity of difference for the salvation of America's soul. He tells us:

> Asked about my "Letter from Mecca," I was all set with a
> speech regarding that:
> I hope that once and for all my Hajj to the Holy City of Mecca
> has established our Muslim Mosque's authentic religious affiliation
> with the 750 million Muslins of the orthodox Islamic World. And
> I *know* once and for all that the Black Africans look upon Amer-
> ica's 22 million blacks as long lost *brothers*! They *love* us! They
> *study* our struggle for freedom! They were so *happy* to hear how
> we are awakening from our long sleep—after so-called "Christian"
> white America had taught us to be *ashamed* of our African
> brothers and homeland! (AX, 361–62; italics Malcolm's)
> . . . The white man is not inherently evil, but America's racist

society influences him to act evilly. . . . Where the really sincere white people have got to do their "proving" of themselves is not among the black *victims*, but out on the battle lines of where America's racism really is—and that's in their own home communities. . . . We will completely respect our white co-workers. . . . We will meanwhile be working among our own kind, in our own black communities. . . . Working separately, the sincere white people and sincere black people actually will be working together.

In our mutual sincerity we might be able to show a road to the salvation of America's very soul. It can only be salvaged if human rights and dignity, in full, are extended to black men. Only such real, meaningful actions as those which are sincerely motivated from a deep sense of humanism and moral responsibility can get at the basic causes that produce the racial explosions in America today. Otherwise the racial explosions are only going to grow worse. (AX, 371, 376–77; italics Malcolm's)

It is not accidental that in this very context, Malcolm X should acknowledge his relationship to Martin Luther King, Jr. Their approaches were as different as the "nonviolence of marching" is different from the "rhetoric of hate," rooted in outraged fury at the unyielding dehumanization of black people at the hands of white people. But "the goal has always been the same," Malcolm declares, and with almost premonitory sobriety, goes on to remark: "It is anybody's guess which of the 'extremes' in approach to the black man's problems might *personally* meet a fatal catastrophe first—'non-violent' Dr. King, or so-called 'violent' me" (AX, 377–78; italics Malcolm's). For Martin Luther King, Jr., it was the presence of Jesus of Nazareth in the human story that made the difference. For Malcolm X, it was the absence of this presence from Christianity, as he experienced it, that made the difference. And contrariwise, it was in Islam that Malcolm X experienced the vision, the power, and the reality of the human meaning of blackness. Very early in his account of himself, he remarks: "All praise is due to Allah that I went to Boston when I did. If I hadn't, I'd probably still be a brainwashed black Christian" (AX, 38). In a central and summary passage, the larger meaning of this defacement becomes sharp and plain:

The black man in North America was spiritually sick because for centuries he had accepted the white man's Christianity—which asked the black so-called Christian to expect no true Brotherhood of Man, but to endure the cruelties of the white so-called Christians. Christianity had made black men fuzzy, nebulous, confused in their thinking. It had taught the black man to think if he had no shoes, and was hungry, "we gonna get shoes and milk and honey and fish fries in Heaven." (AX, 313)

It should surprise no one that out of this distortion of the Christian gospel, one of its ablest and most sensitive victims could assert that "the Bible . . . has enslaved the world" (AX, 185); and that as far as the black man was concerned, "the religion of Christianity had failed him" (AX, 365).

One could, of course, conclude from the shattered dream of Martin Luther King, Jr., and from Malcolm X's agonizing and humanizing development as a Muslim, that Christianity and revolution are either irrelevant to each other or incompatible. The Black Revolution, unlike its revolutionary companions in the contemporary world, was cradled in the Christian church and in a society whose religious ethos has been shaped by Christianity. The Church provided the messianic story, with its images, symbols, and memories of a people, chosen for freedom and fulfillment, delivered from oppression, and sustained through suffering and hope by the vision of a promised land where righteousness and peace and gladness dwell.[172] The racist society against which the Black Revolution is directed is a house divided against itself, at least on two fronts. There is the rift within the religious community between those who find in the messianic story a sanction for racism, and those who find in that same story the mandate for joining with the black community in its revolutionary struggle. There is also the deepening cleavage, both within the black community and in the larger society, between those who are convinced of the revolutionary thrust of the messianic story, and those who are driven to repudiate the Church and all its works in their rage against racism and in the fury of their passion for freedom and for a new beginning toward a new order in human affairs.

Meanwhile, it must not be overlooked that insofar as the black community in the world is not increasingly secular—that is, non-religious as well as antireligious—it is largely Muslim. The importance of this consideration is that the religious matrix of Malcolm X's discovery of the human meaning of blackness is effectively Islam; whereas the shattered dream of Martin Luther King, Jr., is a Christian failure. On the record, the community shaped by the messianic story turns out to have been a community burdened by its own racial sin and guilt as well as in default of a revolutionary challenge. It failed to discern the biblical matrix of the alienation and dehumanization that Marx had rightly discerned as intrinsic to a capitalist economy. In consequence, the integrity and power of a prophetic judgment upon the colonialism, imperialism, and racism of an industrial and increasingly technological society was more than muted. It was simply missing.

Martin Luther King's attempt to hold to the distinction between the example and teaching of Jesus, on the one hand, and a racist church that claimed his name and society, on the other, was too slender a reed on which to depend for a continuing confidence in the revolutionary pertinence of Jesus Messiah. Similarly, Malcolm X's liberating discovery of the color blindness of Islam scarcely establishes the revolutionary thrust of Muslim piety and practice. To discredit the dream because it failed to bring the Black Revolution through to its appointed goals is as speciously *ad hominem* as would be the contention that Malcolm's break with Elijah Muhammad aborted the truth and the power of his discovery of the human meaning of blackness. The complexities of social change and the tragic irony of history seem to have found a melancholy convergence in an assassin's bullet. Whatever may have been the operative connection between Islam and the death of Malcolm X,[173] the dynamics of the Black Revolution seem to have overtaken Malcolm's labors by a confidence strangely like a replay of the one that confronted Martin Luther King, Jr., at the time of his death.

About a year before his murder, Malcolm had announced a new *Organization of Afro-American Unity* (OAAU) for the purpose of a "constructive program for the attainment of human rights" (AX, 416). The tone of the OAAU "appeared to be one of militant black nationalism" (AX, 416). At the press conference called to receive the OAAU announcement, Malcolm had cryptically replied to a questioner: "Whether you use bullets or ballots, you've got to aim well; don't strike at the puppet, strike at the puppeteer. . . . I'm going to join in the fight wherever Negroes ask for my help" (AX, 416). One sensed a mounting irritation in the mounting rhetoric of fury, the stigma of which Malcolm could never quite elude. Two complaints against him seemed to come up again and again. "One was that actually Malcolm only talked, but other civil-rights organizations were *doing*." " 'CORE and SNCC and some of them people of Dr. King's are out getting beat over the head,' " the gossip went (AX, 420). The second complaint was that Malcolm was "too confused to be seriously followed any longer. 'He doesn't know *what* he believes in' " (AX, 420; italics are Malcolm's). As Alex Haley was en route to Kansas City to attend the swearing-in of his brother as a member of the Kansas State Senate, Malcolm told him to tell his brother "that he and all the other moderate Negroes who are getting somewhere need to always remember that it was us extremists that made it possible" (AX, 423). Later, as he talked about his pressures and frustrations, Malcolm told Haley that "no one wanted to accept anything relating to him except 'my old *hate* and *violence* image.' He said 'the so-called moderate' civil rights organizations avoided him as 'too militant' and the 'so-called militants' avoided him as 'too moderate.' 'They won't let me turn the corner!' he once exclaimed. 'I'm caught in a trap!' " (AX, 423–24; italics mine).

The trap is the tension between moderation and militancy, between pressure and progress, between violence and nonviolence. It has become familiar to us as the fate of all revolutionary aspiration and action. The crisis of confidence from which both Martin and Malcolm were removed by an assassin intensifies and becomes the crisis of all revolutionary confrontations with the established order of things. At stake is the integrity of the revolution on the threshold of the realization of its promises. On that threshold, *submission* and *silence* become the code words of the imminence of a new order of human affairs and the criterion of revolutions as signs of transfiguration. The impasse at which the Black Revolution had arrived with the deaths of Martin Luther King, Jr., and of Malcolm X is the impasse between taking the kingdom of heaven by force and violence (Matt. 11:12; Luke 16:16) and in patience possessing one's soul (Luke 21:19 av). As Martin and Malcolm were removed by death from the leadership of the Black Revolution, impatience, rhetoric, and violence seemed to be taking the revolution over.

## 4. *The Ax at the Root of the Tree: The Black Panthers*

Toward the close of his instructive and fascinating account of the Black Muslims, C. Eric Lincoln has summarized the dynamics and the direction of this revolutionary take-over in words at once dispassionate and sobering. They underline the grim prospect of the transformation of the avoidable into the inevitable. Lincoln writes:

> So there has developed, in the last decade, a wide and dramatic spectrum of extralegal protest. The passive Negro, who trusts that God and the NAACP will salvage his dignity while he concentrates on avoiding trouble, is rapidly becoming extinct. Those Negroes (most of them young) who still believe in the possibility of peaceful change have developed a bold but gentle technique to quicken the white man's conscience. They simply ignore restrictive laws and go wherever they know they have a moral right to be. . . . These are not "angry young men"; they are not "bitter." They are just tired of waiting.
>
> At the opposite end of the spectrum are the Black Muslims. They *are* angry; they *are* bitter; and they are also tired of waiting. . . . Today's generation of Negro youth are not afraid. They are determined to change the Negro's status *now*—by nonviolent action, if nonviolence will work. So long as they have a vestige of faith in the white man's latent decency, their strength will be exerted through integrative organizations to shape an integrated society. But if that flickering faith is allowed to perish, black nationalism may feed sumptuously on their despair.[174]

In October 1966, the Black Panthers erupted from the depths of the struggle of black people against racism in the United States.[175] The tumultuous, uneven, and uncertain course of the Party marks the contest between hope and despair in the Black

Revolution. The Black Panther Party also exposes the truth about power in the Establishment.

*The Black Panther Party for Self-defense,* as it was initially called, was organized by Bobby Seale and Huey P. Newton in Oakland, California. Within six months, the phrase "for self-defense" was dropped from the name, largely owning to the dawning awareness "that a broader political offensive was necessary to realize the self-defense they sought" (F, xviii). The immediate occasion for the organization of the Party was the intensifying struggle between the residents of Oakland's black ghetto and Oakland's police. The confrontation, direct or indirect, between the ghetto and the police occasioned the Party's name, identified the principal enemy, and symbolized the deepening power struggle between black people and the white power structure in the United States.

Originally, the "Black Panther" was the emblem of the Freedom Party organized in Lowndes County, Alabama, in 1965 (F, xv). Its appropriation by Seale and Newton was designed to affirm that—like the panther, reputed never to make an unprovoked attack but to defend itself ferociously whenever it is attacked —black people were no longer going to accept the deprivations and dangers of their ghetto existence (F, xv). Instead, they were going to organize for their own defense. As with the panther, so with the symbol of the "pig," the Black Panthers popularized the symbol, but they were not the first to use it.[176] The "pig" identified the police as the paramilitary arm of the white power structure against which the time had come to revolt. The degree to which this struggle simmered in the ghetto, gathering energy for a revolutionary explosion, is acknowledged in a report of the *National Commission on the Causes and Prevention of Violence,* under the chairmanship of Milton S. Eisenhower. The commission set about its work at the Center for the Study of Law and Society in Berkeley, California, on 28 August 1968 and submitted its report on 21 March 1969. Foner has excerpted the following passage from the report:

> . . . For the black citizen, the policeman has long since ceased to be—if indeed he ever was—a neutral symbol of law and order.

Studies of the police emphasize that their attitudes and behavior towards blacks differ vastly from those taken towards whites. Similar studies show that blacks perceive the police as hostile, prejudiced, and corrupt. In the ghetto disorders of the past few years, blacks have been often exposed to indiscriminate police assaults and, not infrequently, to gratuitous brutality. . . . Many ghetto blacks see the police as an occupying army. . . .

In view of these facts, the adoption of the idea of self-defense is not surprising. . . . (F, xvii)

Although the Panthers were not the first blacks in the United States to defend themselves against the oppression and injustice of the white society in the midst of which blacks live, they were the first to do so as a separate organization in a sustained and organized way. "The Black Panthers, though favoring Socialism and coalitions with other oppressed groups, retain their separate identity as a revolutionary movement" (F, xix). Repeatedly, says Foner, the Black Panthers "reminded black Americans that their future was linked to their past, to the experience of such slave rebels as Toussaint L'Ouverture, Gabriel Prosse, Denmark Vesey, and Nat Turner, who did not hesitate to use revolutionary violence in their efforts to free their people from slavery" (F, xvi).

When Bobby Seale met Huey P. Newton, he tells us that "the experience of things I'd seen in the black community—killings that I'd witnessed, black people killing each other—and my own experience, just living, trying to make it, trying to do things, came to the surface" (S, 12). That was in the early sixties. In the late sixties, Seale's judgment is that "Huey is still the philosophical theoretician, the practitioner, the head director, and top official spokesman of the Black Panther Party. It is impossible to talk about the Black Panther Party without first talking about Huey P. Newton, because brother Huey put it all into motion. We sometimes talk about 'the genius of Huey P. Newton' " (S, 13). The phrase is not an exaggeration, for "the motion" was the response of black individuals and of crowds of black people alike to the charismatic gift of leadership by word and energy, by fearlessness and facts, always readily at his command, by suffering and by the passion of a single-minded commitment to the liberation of black people from oppression and for the freedom and integrity of their inalienable humanity.

As is well known, Bobby Seale became the Chairman of the Black Panther Party, Huey P. Newton became the Party's Minister of Defense, and, with Eldridge Cleaver's affiliation with the Party in 1967, he became with impressive alacrity the Party's Minister of Information. Cleaver had just been released from California's Soledad Prison (where George Jackson was later to meet a brutal and untimely death) after serving nine years of a fourteen-year sentence on a conviction for assault with intent to murder. On 6 April 1968, the night of the infamous "shoot-out" with the Oakland police that resulted in the death of Bobby Hutton, Cleaver was arrested again. On appeal, his parole status was restored; but when he was ordered back to prison, and when the U.S. Supreme Court refused to stay the order, a few days before the deadline of 27 November 1968 Cleaver quietly dropped form sight and made his way via Cuba to Algiers.[177]

The triumvirate—Seale, Newton, Cleaver—has provided the Black Panther Party with a remarkably effective leadership. This triumvirate has also borne the burden of the power and the peril of the Party's present course. The passion for human freedom and dignity that sparked Bobby Seale's resistance to the deprivation of his youth opened his mind and imagination to Huey Newton's call for unity, organization, and self-defense. This same passion and Newton's tutelage sustained him in the unconscionable humiliation and suffering in Judge Hoffman's Courtroom in Chicago (1969) and equipped him for dedicated revolutionary leadership (S, 3–56; 289–361). The book in which Seale attempts to set the record of the Party straight is a personal odyssey as well. In the Foreword, Seale writes:

> . . . The demagogic politicians have lied about the Party and have lied about who the real enemy is. . . . This book shows the chronological development of our Party and how it grew out of the social evils of an unjust, oppressive system. It also shows that repression is a natural product of this wealthy, technological society, owned and controlled by a small minority of the people. (S, ix)

The book concludes:

> We are not trying to be supermen, because we are not supermen. We are fighting for the preservation of life. . . . The only way the world is ever going to be free is when the youth of this country *moves* with every principle of human respect and with every soft spot we have in our hearts for human life, in a fashion that lets the pig power structure know that when people are racistly and fascistically attacked, the youth will put a foot in their butts and make their blood chill. . . .
>
> The time is *now* to wage relentless revolutionary struggle against the fascist, avaricious, demagogic ruling class and their low-life sadistic pigs. Power to the People! Seize the Time! (S, 429; italics Seale's)

It remained for Huey P. Newton, however, to galvanize the Party into a revolutionary identity. Seale records a vignette "to show Huey's humanism toward all other human beings; this is the way he is" (S, 23). The incident concerns Huey's vigorous rejection of a rebuke by the black cultural nationalists because he had opened a door for a black sister to pass through and had held the door open for a white girl, following immediately behind, also to pass through. "Look man," he said, "I'm a human being and I'm not a fool" (S, 23). Seale's comment is:

> When I look back at some of the things that Huey was thinking at that time, and a lot of the things that Huey understood then, I know that I didn't understand them at the time; but I followed Huey because he clarified these things to me. (S, 23)

The real measure of Newton's humanism and its skillful conjunction with political action is attested, however, by the ten points of the *Black Panther Party Platform and Program*, which he essentially wrote. The platform is plainly modeled on the Bill of Rights of the United States Constitution and expresses the determination of black people to take up "their Right," indeed "their Duty," "when a long Train of Abuses and Usurpations . . . evinces a Design to reduce them under absolute Despotism, . . . to throw off such Government, and to provide new Guards for their future Security," as the Declaration of Independence itself declares. Pursuant to these aims and obligations, the platform of October 1966 demands, among other things, "freedom for black people to determine the destiny of the black community; full employment; decent housing, fit for shelter of human beings; exemption of black people from military service; an immediate end to police brutality and murder of black people; trial of black people by juries of their own peers; land, bread, housing, education, clothing, justice and peace" (F, pp. 2, 3). Appended to this program are rules of discipline, violations of which bring as a penalty expulsion from the Party. The rules come down hard against the use or distribution of narcotics; against drunkenness; against stealing; against killing of Party members and black people as such; against using or firing weapons unnecessarily or accidentally at anyone; and the like (F, 4–6).

Eldridge Cleaver's poetic imagination and passion for human meaning and fulfillment have lifted the Party's revolutionary purposes and actions to symbolic proportions. It belonged to Newton's genius to create a living image of the Black Panther in his black pants, black leather jacket, black beret, and black gun. It belonged to Cleaver's genius and destiny to incarnate "the anti-hero" of the colonial, imperialist, racist, technological society that is the United States today. Of Commander Alan Bean, "clambering over the moon," and of Eldridge Cleaver, "in unhappy political exile," Lee Lockwood has perceptively noted:

> . . . Two men as unalike as the uniforms they wear, are both logical end products of the American system. Bean, heroic in his silvery-white space suit and helmet, represents the best that America can accomplish when she harnesses vast portions of her technology and wealth to a single purpose. Cleaver, the anti-hero in . . . the Panther uniform, . . . embodies the victim's inevitable response to a society willing to invest billions of dollars in space exploration and bloody war while millions of its citizens continue to be afflicted by hunger, poverty, racism, exploitation and repression.
>
> It is this sense of imbalance and injustice in America, an injustice experienced at first hand and every day, that ultimately impels men like Eldridge Cleaver, who would much rather be doing something else, to become revolutionaries. (LCC, 4)

Cleaver himself has put it this way:

> What the white man in America must be brought to understand is that the black man in America today is fully aware of his position, and he does not intend to be tricked again into another hundred-year forfeit of freedom. Not for a single moment or for any price will the black men now rising up in America settle for anything less than their full proportionate share and participation in the sovereignty of America. The black man has already come to a realization that to be free it is necessary for him to throw his life—everything—on the line, because the oppressors refuse to understand that it is now impossible for them to come up with another trick to squelch the black revolution. The black man can't afford to take a chance. He can't afford to put things off. He must stop the whole show NOW and get his business straight, because if he does not do it now, if he fails to grasp securely the reins of this historic opportunity, there may be no tomorrow for him. (SOI, 119)

The Black Panthers regard themselves as the successors of Malcolm X.[178] Malcolm's *Organization of Afro-American Unity* impressed Huey Newton with the necessity of organization if the Party's platform and program were to be effective, and when the Party was formed, watchfulness over the safety of Malcolm's wife and children became a special privilege of the Party's disciplined revolutionary responsibility. Moreover, as with Malcolm X, so with the leaders of the Black Panthers, Frantz Fanon was their inspiration and guide (S, 1, 25–34.) Fanon clarified for them the intimate interconnection between racism, colonialism, and imperialism, together with the positive role of violence in the revolutionary struggle. Unlike Malcolm, the Panthers did not find their way to a vision of human brotherhood and reconciliation through Islam. Unlike Malcolm, and unlike Fanon as well, the Panthers found that vision in Marxism-Leninism and in the teachings of Mao Tse-Tung, especially his treatise *On Guerilla Warfare*. The Panthers became convinced, in the hard and bitter school of experience, that the time had come for a world dominated by colonialism, imperialism, and racism—a dominion now under American hegemony—to give way before the imminence of a new order of human affairs. Correspondingly, the urgency of decision has carried the Panthers beyond Martin Luther King, Jr., and beyond Stokely Carmichel, from *Freedom Now* to *Power Now*; and from non-violent confrontation, nonmilitant or militant, to the Black Liberation Army. (See F, 41–45 on "The Correct Handling of a Revolution," from *The Black Panther* May 18, 1968.)

The language of the Panthers is replete with three- and four-letter words. They are the metaphors of animal husbandry that strike the eyes and ears of readers and hearers in the white community—even those in sympathy with their cause—with ominous and alienating resonance. Actually, the language is the dialogue of the ghetto, and its use is not only altogether natural to the dehumanizing animal existence that, as Malcolm X has already reminded us, is imposed by the ghetto, but it also heightens the intense seriousness with which the Panthers pursue their revolutionary commitments and purposes. Only the most humanly insensitive and unyielding of those at some remove from the immediacy of the black revolutionary struggle can fail to discern the outrage of a righteous fury in the Panthers' revolutionary rhetoric. But when the rhetoric is joined with guns, an oppressive white society is quick to mask its guilt-ridden fears behind its own self-justifying rhetoric of law and order, of "social change takes time," of "things are so much better now and getting better all the time."

At long last it would seem that, at least on the surface, the surface logic of submission set down in Romans 13 had gone into reverse. The Bolshevist victory over Czarist imperialism and the long march to power by Mao Tse-tung and his comrades were the overripe fruit of a moribund Establishment under the judgment of a war that accelerated that Establishment's demise. The Franco-Algerian accommodation of 1962, at Evian-les-Bains, looked back upon the fall of Dien Bien Phu (1954), and in Cuba internal corruption in government combined with economic deteriorization to bring the "existing authorities" to book. Thus, as we have argued, *submission* is that revolutionary practice of love that seals the doom of the powers that be, already far advanced toward their own divinely ordained retribution. But the Panthers seem to have turned all this around. They have resisted by word and by deed, and through this resistance they have brought the "authorities" to a crisis of conscience to which their own temporizing and rhetoric bear witness.

Should such a reversal be the gift of the future to the Black Revolution in its American Panther phase, historians of that future will make it a matter of record that the Black Revolution is the second American Revolution, and that this was what the Bicentennial of 1976 was really all about. In the wake of that future, the self-justifying rhetoric of law and order would have been overtaken by a reconciling struggle to find an order for law, and the precarious vision of Eldridge Cleaver and the power pragmatics of Bobby Seale would have arrived at the nearer edge of realization despite all the difficulties of these days.[179] Thus Bobby Seale may be and must be taken seriously when he declares that

> The Black Panther Party is not a black racist organization, not a racist organization at all. Our Minister of Defense, Huey P. Newton, has taught us to understand that we have to oppose all kinds of racism. . . . What the Black Panther Party has done in essence is to call for people and organizations who want to move against the power structure. . . . It is obvious that trying to fight fire with fire means there's going to be a lot of burning. The best way to fight fire is with water because water douses the fire. The water is the solidarity of the people's right to defend themselves together in opposition to a vicious monster. . . . We do not fight racism with racism. We fight racism with solidarity. We do not fight exploitive capitalism with black capitalism. We fight capitalism with basic socialism. And we do not fight imperialism with more imperialism. These principles are very . . . practical humanistic and necessary. . . . Ours is not a racist organization but a very progressive revolutionary party. (S, 69–71)

And Eldridge Cleaver may be and must be taken seriously, as he puts hopes and deeds together:

> We are not nihilists. We don't want to see destruction, so then we have to have an alternative. We're talking these days about an alternative, perhaps the last alternative, the last go-round. We go back to basic principles and we say that, in order for this situation to be salvaged, we need sane people in this country;

we need sane black people, and we need sane white people. . . .
the Black Panther Party can't do it by itself, black people can't
do it by themselves. It's going to take white people who recognize
the situation that exists in this world today, to stand up, yes, to
unite with their black brothers and sisters. We're dealing with a
situation where they've become estranged from each other, they've
become hostile to each other, and they've painted themselves into
various corners. . . .

There is no contradiction between what we say and what we do.
We are for responsible action. . . . We are not about to engage in
the kind of random violence that will give the pigs an opportunity
to destroy us. We are revolutionary, but that means we're disciplined, that we're working out programs, that we intend to create
a radical political machinery in coalition with whites that will
uproot this decadent society, transform its politics and economics
and build a structure fit to exist on a civilized planet inhabited by
humanized beings. (CPP, 117, 198)

At this writing, however, it is this very future that is critically at
stake. The ruthlessness of the police, from the Federal Bureau
of Investigation to the local precinct, has intensified. Paramilitary
operations have undertaken by ruse and by relentlessness to deci-
mate the Panther Party. Its leaders have been arrested and imprisoned, with erratic disregard of even minimal civil rights. Protracted
trials, attended by bitter struggles over excessive bail, and by humiliating conditions of detention, have practiced the shadow of
justice in, with, and under the maximalization of injustice. Shoot-
outs in Oakland and gaggings in Chicago are only indicators of a
frontier justice and a Kangaroo Court.[180] They point not only to a
deepening cleavage between justice and law but to an existing order
of human affairs being weighed in the balance scales of history and
found wanting.[181]

Upon one point the Panthers and the established authorities
together with the society whose victims the Panthers are, agree.
This is that *the time is now!* "I believe that our time has come,"
Eldridge Cleaver declared on 22 November 1968, five days before
his scheduled surrender to prison authorities in California, and in
face of which he chose an Algerian exile instead (CPP, 147, 152).
Less than a year and a half later (5 March 1970), as "the Nixon-

Agnew-Mitchell administration . . . moves closer and closer to open fascism," Bobby Seale explained, "we know that, as a people, we must seize our time. . . . The time is *now*. . . . Power to the People! Seize the Time!" (F, 428–29; italics Seale's). The leadership of the Party was still together then. But there were slowly gathering disagreements and tensions over policies and practices that from the summer of 1970 onward brought the Party itself into the vortex of a deep and bitter and enervating schism.

The story is still to be told. Meanwhile, its tangled course is as obscure as it is complex. But the time that is now regrettably finds the Panthers less than united in a revolutionary struggle against the power structure against whom the time is to be seized. They are locked instead in an internecine conflict between the pragmatic militancy of Huey P. Newton and Bobby Seale and the ghetto militancy of Eldridge Cleaver. Personal rivalries and fiscal recriminations (which appear to have included killings), have erupted in a jurisdictional struggle between the West Coast and the East Coast of the United States and in a decimating ideological battle between Newton and Seale on the one side and Cleaver on the other. For Newton and Seale, the time that is now calls for a politics of education and of communalism in the face of the existing power structure. For Cleaver the time that is now calls for a continuing politics of confrontation through guerrilla action. Newton and Seale have become steadily concerned about the gulf between the leadership of the Panthers and the black people who are the daily victims of poverty and repression and without whose loyalty and participation the revolutionary goals and actions of the Party cannot be brought to victory. In their view, these revolutionary aspirations and purposes must be pursued along a slower course of cultivated connections with the historical experience and social institutions and patterns of black people—most notably perhaps the Black Church. Cleaver, as Lee Lockwood reports his development, has become at one and the same time more radicalized ideologically and more Americanized by his exile. He "has no intention of 'dropping out of history.' " He is absorbed with the theory and practice of revolution, "specifically . . . the *American* revolution, why it should be made and how it will be made, and the role that Cleaver intends to play in making it. . . . It is an uncompromisingly grim vision indeed: in order to have Utopia, we must suffer Armageddon first."[182]

It would be premature to conclude from the present crisis of the Black Panther Party that its doubtful future heralds the victory of *freedom now* over *power now* in the struggle for a new order of human affairs in the United States. A politics of transfiguration means that the subordination of power to freedom is the vocation and destiny of politics, both in history and beyond history. The dynamics and direction of a politics of transfiguration, however, confirm neither the wisdom and justice of existing authorities nor the repudiation of revolution owing to its ideological and human idolatry and fury. On the contrary, in a world in which the silence of Jesus before Pilate is the critical instance of a politics of transfiguration, the critical future of the Black Panther Party signals the fact that the *time now* is the *end-time* of imperialism, colonialism and racism, and that this *end-time* has come home internally to the United States of America. The present crisis of the Black Panthers shows once again that the hard reality of history schools the revolutionary in the *submission* and *silence* required by the rightness of his cause and his calling, even as it exposes the point of no return and the moment of truth at which all holders and wielders of power have, by divine appointment, arrived. As John Adams observed: "This is the established order of Things, when a Nation has grown to such an height of Power as to become dangerous to Mankind, she never fails to lose her Wisdom, her Justice and her Moderation, and with these she never fails to lose her Power; which however returns again, if those Virtues return."[183]

That was 1778, as the first American Revolution was beginning to assume the political responsibilities of its triumph. Hannah Arendt's reading of the revolutionary record could yet be confirmed by the tribunal of history. Under that judgment, the American Revolution would have emerged once again as the shining exception to the fate that otherwise has overtaken revolutionary aspiration and action for a *novus ordo saeclorum*.[184] But this prospect depends decisively upon the return of those virtues heralded by

President John Adams through the painful struggle of the second American Revolution, that is, through the Black Revolution.

Although Cleaver's self-imposed exile has scarcely resolved the struggle over the leadership of the Black Panthers, his absence has meant that the present phase of the Party's future has come firmly under the guidance and direction of Newton and Seale, with Newton in the principal position. It is not surprising that exile—self-imposed or not—should bring with it a waning effectiveness in a political struggle, particularly one separated by the wide expanse of an ocean and continuing on another continent. But what may be surprising is the extent to which Newton and Seale are giving themselves to the search for a creative alignment of wisdom with power, and of justice with moderation, in the struggle for a new order of freedom and humanness for all oppressed peoples of the world.[185] A shift in policy and strategy is under way, the architect of which is Huey P. Newton. The shift does not mean an alteration of goals and hopes. It means, instead, a displacement of the rhetoric of urgency and action by a clearer and profounder grasp of the realities of revolutionary struggle and of the importance of widening participation in it. On the surface, the change is marked by the abolition of titles of leadership, which characterized the founding phase of the Black Panther Party; by the abandonment of "the filthy-speech movement," which it lately appears that Newton never liked, and which, according to Newton, was "an infantile diversion from Mario Savio's 'Free Speech movement' " (P); and by an expansion of community programs, which now include, besides food distribution, also health clinics and, above all, the *Samuel Napier Intercommunal Youth Institute*.

Newton's rise to leadership of the Panthers is the result of unmistakable intellectual capacities combined with a passionate, even ascetic, dedication to the cause of justice and freedom for black people in the United States, as the vanguard of liberation for oppressed peoples everywhere. The conversations with Erik Erikson, "in search of common ground," provide impressive substance to the biographical indications of native and emerging competence. Bobby Seale's awesome fascination with Huey rests upon more than the youthful adulation of a shared cause. However disquieted one may be over the incongruity between the luxury level of Huey's present domestic lifestyle and his revolutionary commitments, one cannot fail to give due recognition to the perceptive and incisive grasp of the goals, issues, complexities, and difficulties of the revolution in process or to the risks of dying daily to which his leadership of the Party exposes him. "We are neither dead nor lying down," Huey replied to Lee Lockwood's question about the meaning of the current "low profile of the Panthers." "We are becoming better established in our own community—and hence potentially more powerful—than ever" (P). Commenting upon Newton's apartment, "elegant and expensive . . . twenty-five floors above the streets where (he) grew up and lived most of his years" (E, 95–96; parenthesis mine), Kai Erikson has written that "what is not said in the press, however, is that the apartment is almost as spare as a cell. . . . Both literally and figuratively this is a high price to pay for security, and most of the people who have felt disappointed or irritated because a revolutionary leader lives in such expensive circumstances have not really given much thought to what they mean" (E, 95–96).

Be that as it may, the present low profile of the Panthers is the consequence of a deliberate obedience to Huey's revolutionary vision (E, 133 f.). It is a vision of "intercommunalism," as he calls it. To state the vision as he states it is at the same time to understand where the Black Revolution is now and why. Huey declares:

> We say that the world today is a dispersed collection of communities. A community is different from a nation. A community is a small unit with a comprehensive collection of institutions that exist to serve a small group of people. And we say further that the struggle in the world today is between the small circle that administers and profits from the empire of the United States, and the peoples of the world who want to determine their own destinies.
>
> We call this situation intercommunalism. We are now in the age of reactionary intercommunalism, in which a ruling circle, a small group of people, control all other people by using their technology.

At the same time, we say that this technology can solve most of the material contradictions people face, that the material conditions exist that would allow the people of the world to develop a culture that is essentially human and . . . in a way that would not cause the mutual slaughter of all of us. The development of such a culture would be revolutionary intercommunalism. (E, 30–31)

It is obedience to this vision that informs Huey's insistent judgment that there is no significant split in the Black Panther Party (P). This vision and obedience inform also the quiet yet determined confidence that history is on the side of the Black Revolution and that "obedient waiting" is the revolutionary order of the day.

One is reminded of the combination of patience with revolutionary involvement that informed Marx and Lenin, and Chairman Mao on the Long March and after; and of the remarkable resistance of the North Vietnamese army and people to vastly superior military power under the vision and leadership of Ho Chi Minh. "Intercommunalism" has carried Huey Newton beyond the struggle between colonialism and nationalism (and even beyond racism), which was as far as Franz Fanon could see. It has translated Martin Luther King, Jr.'s vision of a nonviolent victory in the struggle for civil rights into a discerning sociopsychological assessment of the transfiguration of social relations and political power through the dialectical dynamics of revolutionary reality and a highly disciplined perception of the use and the limits of violence. "The death of any man diminishes me," Newton affirms, "but sometimes we have to be diminished before we can reconstruct" (P). Here is the twin recognition of violence as endemic to humanization and also as a risk that is never to be converted into policy, a risk by which revolutions themselves stand or fall. It parallels the psychoanalytic insight, as Erik Erikson put it, that "only people with equal dignity can love each other, and this point sometimes has to be made by fighting the other—fighting him with a defined purpose and an acknowledged discipline—until he is forced to see. You see what I mean? I fight him to bring out the angel in him, so that the angel can bless both of us" (E, 79).

Thus the third option with its heroic story that has provided the flexibility and reciprocity necessary to the exercise of power within humanizing limits, and that to date has made the first American Revolution the shining exception to revolutionary fate, is on trial before the second American revolution. This revolution is confident that the American empire is a necessary stage in the dialectical materialism through which history makes way for humanization by overcoming the negative contradiction of reactionary intercommunalism. This revolution is also confident that through the positive and creative contradiction between small communities and the universal community that includes all the peoples of the world, revolutionary intercommunalism will come about. There is a story here too. For, as Erikson has pointed out, "historical here means the universal actualization of new images and symbols" (E, 48).

Reminding us of the fact that Huey traveled "equipped not only with a gun but with a law book" (E, 46), Erikson goes on to say: "the book and the fire—it cannot escape us what an elemental pair of symbols this has been in revolts as far removed from each other as that of the Germans in Luther's day and that of the Zionists in our own" (E, 46). Huey's vision and action have implied a "transvaluation of identity . . . for generations of young blacks" (E, 54). In "all true transvaluation of values . . . there is a genuine religious element, . . . especially where it concerns a faith in the God-given gifts of an exile or a suppressed people" (E, 49). As for Huey, he thinks "that after the dialectical process has run its course, man will reach a state of godliness—and that's because I think God is mostly what man has said, 'I am not.' " And he adds, characteristically, "that's just long-range specualtion, of course. We'll have to live with dialectics for awhile yet" (E, 109–10).

Once again, the story does make all the difference in the world where the boundary is drawn between revolutionary fate and a revolutionary future. Especially is this the case when on that boundary all the people have become heroes. Not least significant in Newton's vision of the world as it is and as it is coming to be is a correlative confidence. On the one hand, there is his confidence that the dynamics of dialectical materialism have already signaled the demise of American world hegemony for which discerning readers have been, or at least could have been, prepared by Romans 13. On the other hand, there is his confidence that the course of history leads intrinsically from the liberation of the oppressed to the god-manhood of "the whole human running race" in an inter-communal world already under way, a world in which freedom and justice are indeed enough for being human in. Huey has said:

> I will fight until I die, however that may come. But whether I'm around or not to see it happen, I know we will eventually succeed, not just in America but all over the world, in our struggle for the liberation of all oppressed peoples. The revolution will win. . . . All we can do as individuals is try to make things better now, for eventually we all die. I think Mao's statement sums it up best: "Death comes to everyone, but it varies in its significance. To die for the reactionary is as light as a feather. But to die for the revolution is heavier than Mount Tai." (P)

Pending the realization of that prospect, however, we would do well to ponder the parabolic implications of Eldridge Cleaver's apocalyptic vision of the choice before us. It is, he has said, "the most important thing, at least the thing that sticks in my mind most when reading Che Guevara or thinking about him":

> Wherever death may surprise us, let it be welcome, provided that this, our battle cry, reaches some receptive ear, and that another hand reaches out to pick up our weapons and other fighting men come forward to intone our funeral to the staccato of machine guns and new cries of battle and victory.

Central to this battle

> is the wisdom, when laying an ambush, of shooting the first man, and the position this places the second man in. . . . The importance of shooting that first man (is) that when the sergeants and the lieutenants and the generals order another reconnaissance, then problems develop about who's going to be the first man out. It's not so much the killing of the first man; the point is that it makes the other soldiers think about what is their relationship to the war, and who is it that has the right to send them out there to give up their lives, and for what?
> I think this is part of the guerrilla's bag, and to me . . . that's

where it is—the guerrilla fighter and the first man out there, and
what he is doing out there? (LCC, 92–94; parenthesis mine)

In the Gospel of Matthew, it is written that

> John the Baptist appeared as a preacher in the Judaean wilder-
> ness; his theme was: "Repent; for the kingdom of Heaven is upon
> you!" . . .
> When he saw many of the Pharisees and Sadducees coming for
> baptism he said to them: "You vipers' brood! Who warned you
> to escape from the coming retribution? Then prove your repent-
> ance by the fruit it bears; and do not presume to say to your-
> selves, 'We have Abraham for our father.' I tell you that God
> can make children for Abraham out of these stones here. Already
> the ax is laid to the roots of the trees; . . ." (Matt. 3:1, 2, 7–10)

That too is a parable to ponder; and in a world caught up in
a politics of transfiguration, more than a parable. In a world lived
and died in by Jesus of Nazareth, and under his sovereign authority
and liberation, the revolutionary meaning of these revolutionary
times is that the fate of revolutionary aspiration and action has
been overtaken by a humanizing destiny. "In him everything in
heaven and on earth was created, not only things visible but also
invisible orders of thrones, sovereignties, authorities, and powers:
the whole universe has been created through him and for him. And
he exists before everything, and all things are held together in
him" (Col. 1:16, 17). Consequently, *transfiguration* belongs with
*submission* and *silence* as the code words of revolutionary aspiration and action that no longer need to devour their offspring. They
have become instead the vanguard of a liberating presence in the
world of time and space and things, who makes time and space
make room for human freedom and fulfillment. The dynamics of a
politics of transfiguration are the harbingers of this formation. They
may be discerned in certain liberating accents that signal the inbreaking in the established order of things of a new order of human
affairs and ultimately the transfiguration of revolution itself.[186]

# PART FOUR

# THE TRANSFIGURATION OF POLITICS

## CHAPTER 10

# THE BIBLICAL AND THE
# HUMAN MEANING OF POLITICS

The thesis of the foregoing pages is that the pertinence of Jesus Christ to the question of revolution is evident from the conjunction of revolution and humanization that generates a dynamics and direction in human affairs, requiring a liberating or "saving" story. The Christian story records the presence and power of Jesus of Nazareth in and over human affairs, coordinates the human meaning of reality with a humanizing experience and perception of it, delivers revolutionary passion and prospects from a self-destroying fate, and transfigures revolution as the harbinger of a human future through a new beginning of a divinely appointed order of human freedom and fulfillment in this world and the next.

The explication of this thesis has involved certain exegetical interpretations of paradigmatic biblical texts and a typological analysis of current revolutionary movements. In the course of these reflections, four corollary considerations have emerged in confirmation of the thesis. These corollaries engage us now as a concluding indication of the salient facets of the biblical and human meaning of politics and of the fundamental revision of political priorities that, in Christian perspective, are the point and purpose of the happening called "revolution." The corollaries focus upon:

A. Biblical politics and an incarnational hermeneutics;

B. The correspondence between the biblical and the human meaning of politics;

C. The parabolic and kairotic significance of revolutions as signs of transfiguration;

D. The story by which revolutions are saved.

A. BIBLICAL POLITICS AND AN INCARNATIONAL HERMENEUTICS

William Stringfellow's recently published, trenchant prophetic commentary upon the Book of Revelation affirms "the empirical integrity of the biblical witness."[1] By this witness, Christian apperception, Christian sensibility, and a Christian way of thinking are formed and informed. This apperception, sensibility, and way of thinking do not interpret the goings-on in the world of time and space and things "off the pages of the Bible," as it were. Nor do they interpret the Bible "off the pages" of the daily goings-on in the world of time and space and things. There is a more appropriate hermeneutical option. This option is derived from an insight of faith nurtured in the Christian community in the world. The insight takes the shape of words and thoughts centered upon the presence of Jesus of Nazareth in the human story and upon the difference that his presence makes in and to the human story. In theological shorthand, the present essay presupposes a theology of the incarnation and undertakes to explore the pertinence of a theology of the incarnation to politics.

A theology of the incarnation affirms that the presence of Jesus of Nazareth in the human story opens up a way of perceiving the world of time and space and things that gives primacy and priority to the human sense and significance of what is going on. In the jargon of the Schools, a theology of the incarnation alters the priorities in the possibility and the order of inquiry. The science of "human things" takes precedence over the sciences of knowing and of being; in short, anthropology is the clue to, and the criterion of, epistemology and ontology (or metaphysics). Feuerbach correctly discerned that all theology is anthropology.[2] But the iconoclastic thrust of his proper criticism of the incarnational theology that had come down to him combined with the anti-Hegelian matrix of his thought to produce an arrested development. Feuerbach's familiar dictum requires a supplement, according to which it would read: "All theology is anthropology as a reflex of Christology." Amplified in this way, Feuerbach's inversion of Hegel becomes also an inversion of Calvin, who claimed that "true and substantial wisdom consists principally in the knowledge of God and of ourselves."[3] As Calvin read the Bible amidst the ferment and fomentation of his days, he reports his conviction that the discernment of wisdom involved a movement from the Scriptures to the knowledge of God in Christ without disallowing the possibility of setting out from the knowledge of human things. Beginning with "the knowledge of ourselves," as Feuerbach did, does not necessarily exclude a livelier appropriation of Scripture, as Feuerbach appears to have done. Indeed, a knowledge of ourselves includes a movement from the Scriptures to the knowledge of human things in Christ, precisely so that we do not lose our way amidst the ferment and fomentation of what we can join with Calvin in recognizing as "the melancholy desolation of these days."[4]

If a name for it helps, the hermeneutical option, derived from the incarnation, and indicative of the conjunction of Jesus Christ and the question of revolution in these pages, is one familiar to the early Fathers of the Church.

The nonliteral interpretation of texts was widespread in the Hellenistic world. Christian theologians drew particularly upon hermeneutical practices long familiar in rabbinic Judaism and from the Stoic interpretation of Homer. By the third century, the theological responsibility of bringing some clarity and order to a considerable hermeneutical variety, and even confusion, became at once urgent and unavoidable, as Origen's notable discussion shows. Origen's distinction between the "literal" and the "spiritual" sense of Scripture was further refined in Augustine's recommendation that the Scriptures should be read *tropically*. "A trope is a form of figurative speech involving the use of a word in a different sense from that which is proper to it"; that is, from its literal sense.[5] A distinction was made between *simple tropes*, based upon the resemblance of properties; and *metaphors*, based upon the resemblance of relations. Accordingly, the paradigmatic interpretation of certain New Testament passages in the course of the present analysis is *tropic* in character, and may be regarded as an attempt at an incarnational hermeneutics. An incarnational hermeneutics seeks to discern the word and will of God in, with, and under the discernment of the times in which we live; and, in turn, to discern "the meaning of this time"[6] in, with, and under the word and will of God. The knowledge of God and the knowledge of ourselves are thus reciprocally and revelationally joined; and the point of intersection, at which the point of no return is disclosed as the moment of truth, is Jesus of Nazareth: his Abrahamic and prophetic lineage; his messianic mission and destiny; his life and death; his resurrection and ascension; his dominion over and consummation of all things visible and invisible in this world and the next. As William Stringfellow has pungently put it:

> Incarnational theology regards this world in the fullness of its fallen estate as *simultaneously* disclosing the ecumenical, militant, triumphant presence of God. It esteems that which is most characteristic of Jesus Christ as the incarnate Word of God as also inherent in the whole of Creation. It is the incarnational aspect of biblical faith with its exemplary affirmations about time and history, and with its radical and preemptive concern for life in this world, from which the viable ethics and political action of the gospel issue.[7]

This remark is virtually an analytical paraphrase of an occasion, recorded in Luke's gospel, on which Jesus, in the course of his journeyings, engaged in conversation alternately with his disciples and with the people. We are told:

> He also said to the people, "When you see cloud banking up in the west, you say at once, 'It is going to rain,' and rain it does. And when the wind is from the south, you say, 'There will be a heat-wave,' and there is. What hypocrites you are! You know how to interpret the appearance of earth and sky; how is it you cannot interpret this fateful hour?" (Luke 12:54–56)

B. THE CORRESPONDENCE BETWEEN THE BIBLICAL AND THE
HUMAN MEANING OF POLITICS

Given, then, "the empirical integrity of the biblical witness,"
incarnationally understood and tropically interpreted, there is a
correspondence between the biblical and the human meaning of
politics. This correspondence is neither accidental nor incidental.
It expresses the characteristic will and purpose of God,[8] according
to which the Creator and Redeemer of the world brings the world,
and all things in it, to their appointed and freeing fulfillment. The
will and purpose of God are that the creature who, as male and
female, bears God's likeness and singular favor, shall find in
privacy and in society the fulfilling joy and freedom of reciprocal
creaturehood and creativity. The discovery of self-identity, in and
through the self-giving of and to an Other, of each in the Other,
of all in each and each in all—is the hidden and the open experience of humanness in a world in which time and space and things
are chiefly meant for being human in. For the world is "the theatre
of the divine glory" (Calvin); and creation, despite its fallen state,
is, in Bonhoeffer's arresting phrase, "the natural," that is, "the form
of life preserved by God for the fallen world and directed towards
the justification, redemption and renewal through Christ." Correspondingly, "the unnatural is that which, after the Fall, closes
its doors against the coming of Christ."[9]

Thus piety and politics belong intrinsically and inseparably together. Piety is the compound of reverence and thankfulness that
forms and transforms the reciprocity between creaturehood and
creativity, in privacy and in society, into the possibility and the
power of fulfilling human freedom and joy. Politics is the compound
of justice, ordination, and order that shapes, sustains, and gives
structure to a social matrix for the human practice of privacy and
for the practice of humanness in community. In such a matrix,
justice is the reciprocity of differences in creaturehood and creativity, experienced as enrichment rather than as a threat;[10] ordination is the insistent priority and pressure of purpose over power

in the practice of the reciprocity between creaturehood and creativity; and order is the possibility and the power of so living in one time and place as not to destroy the possibility of other times and places.[11] So piety apart from politics loses its integrity and converts into apostasy; whereas politics without piety subverts both its divine ordination and its ordering of humanness, perverts justice, and converts into idolatry.

To read and understand the Bible *politically* and to understand and practice politics *biblically* is to discern in, with, and under the concrete course of human events the presence and power of God at work, giving human shape to human life. The human meaning of politics is to the biblical meaning of politics as the Fall is to the creaturehood and destiny of humanity in a world that has been created and redeemed. In such a world—our world—the face of reality undergoes a transfiguration, and "with a whiteness no bleacher on earth could equal" (Mark 9:3). Consequently—in a vivid phrase of Horace Bushnell's—"there is a vast analogy in things"[12] that, to those who have eyes to see and ears to hear, points to the steady pressure upon the shape of things to come of the sovereign, freeing, and fulfilling purpose and power of God. Indeed, in the context of biblical politics, the word *God* acquires a specific and humanizing referentiality. The word *God* refers to him who, in the power of a future that is coming to be, picks up the humanizing pieces of the past and makes a humane and humanizing present. Thus the human meaning of reality is a compound of this divine pressure upon the dynamics and the shape of things, experienced as the moment of truth and the point of no return; *and* its metaphorical description and communication.

## C. THE PARABOLIC AND KAIROTIC SIGNIFICANCE OF REVOLUTIONS AS SIGNS OF TRANSFIGURATION

There is a *kairos* in human affairs, as Paul Tillich perceptively noted many years ago.[13] The presence and power of Jesus of Nazareth in the human story transformed this *kairos* from a moment of fate into a moment of destiny. Consequently, the goings-on in time and space are no longer experienced as an inexorable necessity, ultimately foredooming to futility all human creativity and hope. Instead, the goings-on in time and space may be and are to be experienced as occasions for actions designed for making room for the freedom that being human takes. Such actions are *kairotic* actions. They break through the enervating intransigeance of possibilities, powers, and structures that ever and again overtakes the long course of human events; and they mark the point of entry for new possibilities, powers, and structures as liberating instrumentalities of human destiny. *Kairotic* actions "zero in" upon the freedom without which there is and can be no order, upon the justice that defines the legitimate order in law; and they signal the revolutionary character of politics that ultimately unmasks "*Realpolitik*" as a denial of political reality.

The revolutionary character of biblical politics is intrinsic to the divine pressure upon the dynamics and the shape of things and to the human meaning of reality in a fallen world. It also follows from the correspondence between the biblical and the human meaning of politics that the metaphorical indication of break-through happenings varies in accordance with the *kairotic* dynamics of human affairs. Just as revolutions are not made but happen, so the metaphors that break open the break-throughs of the divine presence and pressure upon the shape of things to come vary in their parabolic power to take paradigmatic form. Moreover, just as faith is a risk and not a formula for unanimity or uniformity, so a proposal of paradigmatic metaphors, which illuminate and are in turn illuminated by the *kairotic* actions of a revolutionary time, involves a corresponding risk. The "order of times" is such that, at other times and seasons, other actions will happen as *kairotic* break-throughs, and other metaphors take on the parabolic power of a paradigm.

In these pages it has been argued that revolutions happen in human affairs whenever established patterns and possibilities, powers and structures of action, fail to make time and space make room for the freedom that being human takes. In short, revolutions happen whenever an existing order subverts its divine ordination and obstructs the emergence of a *polis*. In so doing, the existing order exhibits an antipolitical ethos and dehumanization becomes the order of the day. The revolutionary ferment and fomentation

of our times—from the French Revolution onward—have exposed
the moment of truth and the point of no return for existing holders
and structures of power through a rising tide of *"forces-humaines"*
against colonialism, imperialism, and racism. The pivotal case in
point is the power of the state and its military-industrial-technologi-
cal satellites; and the critical question is whether the passion of
revolutionary movements for freedom, a new beginning, and a
new order of human affairs will survive or succumb to the fate that
has beset all revolutions to date, namely, that they devour their
own children.[14]

### D. THE STORY BY WHICH REVOLUTIONS ARE SAVED

Revolutionary aspiration, struggle, and action are nourished by
and generate a rhetoric of promises, goals, and directions. The
rhetoric, in turn, feeds upon a saving story. And the power of the
story to "save" is drawn from the appropriateness of the metaphorical indication of the correspondence between the biblical and
the human meaning of politics.[15]

The pertinence of Jesus Christ to the question of revolution is
that he stands at the juncture of revolutionary freedom and fate.
His presence in the human story transforms revolutions from
harbingers of futility, violence, and death into signs of transfiguration in the power of a saving story. The Christian or messianic story
documents its "saving reality and power" in a paradigmatic movement from a politics of confrontation to a politics of transfiguration
whose code words are: *submission*, *silence*, and *transfiguration*
itself. These code words identify the boundaries toward which and
within which the dynamics of revolutionary passion, promise, and
struggle are liberated from self-destruction and shaped instead for
a new and divinely appointed order of human affairs in which time
and space are ordered so as to make room for freedom. The code
words mean that a break-through possibility and power are at hand
in relation to which the question may be decided: "whether societies
of men are capable or not of establishing good government from
reflection and choice, or whether they are forever destined for their
political constitutions on accident and force."[16]

This exploration of biblical politics has tried to show that the revolutionary movements of the present time have brought the established power and order of colonialism, imperialism, and racism under a divinely appointed judgment. Established power and order are in violation of human freedom, human history, and human destiny. These same revolutionary movements hold within their trust and practice the secret and the power of submission, silence, and transfiguration, in the sovereign exercise of which the impatience and failure of revolutionary passion and promise may be overtaken by the inbreaking and formation of a new order of human affairs. A paradigmatic reading of Romans 13:1–10; of the Fourth Gospel's account of the nocturnal conversation between Jesus and Pilate (18:33–40; 19:1–16); and of the account of the Transfiguration of Jesus, according to Matthew 17:1–9, provides a parabolic indication of the terms on which the revolutionary struggle for freedom, justice, and order may undergo a transfiguration that will signal the imminence of the political realization of revolutionary hopes. Transfiguration is the happening according to which the providential-eschatological pressure of reality upon human affairs gives political shape to a divinely appointed new and freeing and fulfilling human order. As signs of transfiguration, revolutions are the happenings that mean that a long-overdue revision of political priorities can no longer be deferred.

## CHAPTER 11

# A REVISION OF POLITICAL PRIORITIES

Revolutionary challenges to established social and cultural patterns and values, institutions and structures of power, call into question the foundational logic by which existing authorities shape policy and justify the possession and the use of power. Conversely, revolutionary commitments and energies, directed toward a new beginning and a new order of freedom in human affairs, are called into question by the question whether revolutions can themselves achieve the revision of political priorities that they demand. The logic of the Establishment is that order is the presupposition and the condition of freedom; that law is the foundation and the criterion of justice; and that the radical rejection of this logic, and of the institutions, structures, and powers that practice it, is fundamenally inimical alike to freedom and to order, to law and to justice. The critical instance of this hostility is the violence with which revolutions are inbred, which is intrinsic to their practice, and the ultimate outcome of their endeavors. It must be admitted that violence *is* the critical instance of revolutionary passion, promise, and fate. The typology of current revolutions that has engaged the present analysis has come in each instance to the stark realiy of violence as a kind of Rubicon of revolutionary theory and practice.

238

A biblical politics, however, radically revises the meaning and practice of violence. The saving story that describes and consummates the correspondence between the biblical and the human meaning of politics confronts and is available to existing authorities and powers, as well as to revolutionaries. The story is designed to identify and to enable the revision of political priorities that existing authorities have been ordained and authorized to practice but have inverted. In the power of the saving story, the self-justification by which existing authorities deceive themselves about their doom is adjudged idolatrous and unnecessary. It stands exposed as a lie. For the revolutionaries, the saving story identifies and enables the transfiguration of revolution, and this carries the revision of political priorities that revolutions demand across the boundary dividing revolutionary fate from a revolutionary future. The fact that existing authorities are unable to abandon the self-justifying exercise of their power does not invalidate the saving story. It confirms, instead, the radicality and the rightness of the revolutionary challenge to established power. On their part, revolutionaries bear a similar burden of guilt for their own undoing. The rightness intrinsic to the radicality of their humanizing vocation and destiny intensifies the displacement of the patience required for the possession of their souls (Heb. 2:14–18; 10:39) by the fury to process the future for which suffering, oppression, and deprivation have prepared their souls. Caught in the dilemma between a premature seizure of power and a convulsive adherence to power seized, revolutionaries are no less vulnerable than are existing authorities to their own brand of ideological self-justification. Nevertheless, as the thirteenth chapter of Romans has instructed us, they are nearer to the purposes of God for human fulfillment, and consequently they bear a righteousness not their own.[17]

In the power of this righteousness, the logic of revolutionary politics compels a revision of political priorities. The revision goes to the roots of the logic by which existing authorities justify the power that they hold and exercise, and inverts it. In so doing, the meaning and the role of violence in revolutionary theory and practice are altered. And in the radicality of that alteration, the meaning and the role of revolution in the human story is transfigured, "with a whiteness no bleacher on earth could equal" (Mark 9:3). According to the logic of revolutionary politics, freedom is the presupposition and condition of order: order is not the presupposition and the condition of freedom; justice is the foundation and the criterion of law: law is not the foundation and the criterion of justice; violence is the sign that politics have arrived at an apocalyptic moment of truth and point of no return: violence is not the endemic nemesis of revolution, which disbars revolutions and denies them vindication before the court of human history and destiny. A biblical politics discerns in the story by which revolutions are saved the possibility and power of a transfiguration through which revolutions become more than the midwives of history, shattering the dead fossilized forms of the past. They become instead the catalysts of the new and human future that God through them is already making present.

A. FREEDOM IS THE PRESUPPOSITION AND THE CONDITION OF
ORDER: ORDER IS NOT THE PRESUPPOSITION AND
THE CONDITION OF FREEDOM

The current phase of the American Revolution is precariously poised against the revision of political priorities required by the biblical and the human meaning of politics and urged upon existing authorities and structures of power by a world-wide rejection of colonialism, imperialism, and racism. A vivid, more than coincidental, and virtually verbatim case in point is provided by a reverse Agnew-ism. One may allude to it, admittedly with malice aforethought; indeed, with a holy malice. For the Creator and Fulfiller of human life and destiny in the world does not deny such a response to those who distort his will and purpose for the body politic.[18] The reverse Agnew-ism declares that freedom is the presupposition and condition of order: order is not the presupposition and condition of freedom.[19]

The former Vice-President of the United States was, of course, giving utterance to a rationale of power that goes back at least as far as the mentality of the "law-and-order people" against whom, among others, the thirteenth chapter of Romans was directed. In disregard of apostolic insight and subtlety in the matter of the use and abuse of power by existing authorities, the law-and-order rationale for power expressed itself in Christian political theory in terms of a neat division and distribution of power between church and state, pope and emperor, spiritual and temporal authority, on the model of the relations between soul and body; or, more awesomely, if not more luminously, between the sun and the moon. Consequently, political theory in the West has fostered, and has been fostered by, an ingrained habit of mind that insists that order is the precondition of any possibility of being and staying human in the world. Accordingly, freedom is the fruit of order. Any departure from this foundational logic of power courts the inadmissible risk of anarchy and chaos. This risk, whatever its secular perils and penalties may be, involves the ultimate impiety of seeking to circumvent the original and originating act of creation that was and is God's purposed way of setting limits to chaos.

A biblical politics finds in this law-and-order rationale for existing power and authority a vast theological distortion. The distortion not only subverts the dynamics and direction of a politics of transfiguration but violates the sabbath celebration that followed the sixth day of the work of creation. The celebration marks the joy and peace of the Creator with the world wrought of his freely purposed will and power henceforward to be himself in reciprocal giving and response toward an other than himself. Indeed, creation means a world that has come to be in the sovereign freedom of the Creator, whose electing action signals a continuing and ultimate, but no ulterior, purpose than the drawing of this world, of this other-than-God, into the sustaining and fulfilling purposes of God himself. It is this electing action of the Creator toward the creation that gives foundational priority to freedom over order, purpose over policy, future over past, and destiny over devices, in the world of time and space and things, and of people in community and in their privacy. Indeed, "world" is the fruit of God's own freedom in pushing back chaos and the void, in checking whatever in the world cuts across purposefulness and possibility and new beginning, in setting and sanctifying change and chance and motion and meaning within the boundaries of his will and ways. Accordingly, freedom is a way of being in the truth, and the truth is the reality in relation to which, as gift and response, all created things are free.[20]

There is, then, a radical permissiveness intrinsic to the givenness of things. Its charter declares of every creature according to its kind: "You may be who or what you are! Be, then, who or what you are!" Far from haunting the world of time and space and things and people with the aimless arbitrariness of license that declares that "might is right!" and "to the victor belong the spoils!", and far from harboring a capriciousness that knows neither order nor direction, this radical permissiveness makes ultimate purposes the measure of penultimate possibilities and policies, and gratitude the secret of the human sense of things in privacy and in community. On its positive side, freedom is the experience of this givenness of things as good, i.e., as foretaste and avenue of fulfillment for every creature according to its kind; as the time and space and matrix of relatedness for being, in fact and in prospect, who or what one was meant to be and to become. In short, freedom is the opportunity and occasion for discovering *who* and *why* one is, *as* and *who* one is, amidst the whole panorama of the divine economy, and saying "Yes!" to it. On its negative side, freedom is the experience of the givenness of things as a liberating limit, within which every creature according to its kind finds the fulfilling direction and order of its own time, in the world of time and space and things and people. Thus there is a paradox of being free and being bound, of liberation and limitation, that ordains freedom as the presupposition and condition of order and order as the practice of freedom. As freedom is the affirmation of the givenness of things as fulfilling, so order is the enabling possibility, pattern, and power through which the lifetime of creatures in one time and place and culture and society may be so lived, not only so as not to destroy the possibility of other times and places and cultures and societies, but so as to make one's own and given time and space and culture and society make room for freedom.

The default of the passion and the confidence of the law-and-order people is the addiction to the notion that order is the presupposition and the condition of freedom. Whenever a society begins to reverse the creative, ongoing, and dynamic reciprocity between freedom and order in the givenness of things by insisting upon the priority of order over freedom, that society has embarked upon a politics, ethics, and lifestyle of self-justification. This self-justification is in direct contravention of the free gift of God that there be a world in which his human creatures may and are to express their humanness in both the naming of, and the caring for, all the works of the Creator's will and purpose. Thus a politics that assigns priority to order over freedom in the shaping of privacy and of community violates the celebration of difference as a thing of beauty and a joy forever. It exalts instead the power of preference in and by which the creature exults in rivalry with the Creator and sets all creation at enmity with itself. When God adjudged the world of his making to be "very good!" he did not mark it as a place of tedium, in which nothing ever afterward was to happen that was humanly exciting and fulfilling. On the contrary, the world is good because, from its creation to its consummation, it is purposed as the theater of divine and human gladness and glory.

The priority of freedom over order affirmed by a biblical politics and confirmed by the phenomenon of revolution corresponds with the human meaning of politics. An instructive indication of this correspondence is provided by the foundational theoretical analysis of social interaction on the part of two influential contemporary sociologists. I owe to Professor Peter M. Blau of Columbia University the following passage from *The Sociology of Georg Simmel*:

> All contacts among men rest on the schema of giving and returning the equivalence. The equivalence of innumerable gifts and performance can be enforced. . . . The legal constitution enforces and guarantees the reciprocity of service and return service—social equilibrium and cohesion do not exist without it. But there are also innumerable other relations to which the legal form does not apply, and in which the enforcement of the equivalence is out of the question. Here *gratitude* appears as a supplement. It establishes the bond of interaction, of the reciprocity of service and return service, even when they are not guaranteed by external coercion.
>
> Beyond its first origin, all sociation rests on a relationship's effect which survives the emergence of the relationship. . . . *Gratitude* is definitely such a continuance. . . . *If every grateful action, which*

*lingers on from good turns received in the past,* were suddenly eliminated, society (at least as we know it) would break apart.[21]

Although acknowledging that "not all human behavior is guided by consideration of exchange" (5), Blau argues that "social exchange directs attention to the emergent properties in interpersonal relations and social interaction" (4). These properties "cannot be accounted for by the psychological processes that motivate the behavior of the partners" (4). They show that exchange "is the joint product of the actions of both individuals, with the actions of each being dependent on those of the other" (4). Furthermore, social exchange underlies "relations between groups as well as those between individuals; both differentiation of power and peer group ties; conflicts between opposing forces as well as cooperation; both intimate attachments and connections between distant members of a community without direct social contacts" (4). Eventually, "group norms to regulate and limit the exchange transactions emerge, including the fundamental and ubiquitous norm of reciprocity, which makes failure to discharge obligations subject to group sanctions" (92). The "norm of reciprocity" is Blau's elaboration of what Simmel identifies as "gratitude." Recognizing that there are "some individuals who selflessly work for others without any thought of reward and even without expecting gratitude" (6), Blau notes that these individuals "are virtually saints, and saints are rare. The rest of us also act unselfishly sometimes, but we require some incentive for doing so, if it is only the social acknowledgment that we are unselfish" (16–17). Whether on the level of sainthood, or on the more widely discernible level of human social interaction, on which selfishness and unselfishness are ambiguously mixed, "the gradual expansion of mutual service is accompanied by a parallel growth of mutual trust. Hence, processes of social exchange, which may originate in pure self-interest, generate trust in social relations through their recurrent and gradually expanding character" (94).

The dynamics of this recurrent and gradually expanding character of social relations result in "a wider social context," gradually acquired by "interpersonal relations" and relations between "face-to-face groups" (7). Accordingly, the "strain toward imbalance as well as toward reciprocity in social associations" (26) increases in complexity as well as in precariousness. Social interaction is a process of exchange directed toward integration. But intrinsic to this process is a paradox that, on the one hand, shows that psychological dispositions are insufficient to account for the dynamics and complexity of social exchange (4) and, on the other hand, that "exchange processes . . . give rise to differentiation of power" (22). The paradox of social integration is "that the impressive qualities that make a person a particularly attractive and valuable group member also constitute a status threat to the rest" (44). In short, integration and opposition, attraction and threat, are concomitant and thus paradoxical factors in social interaction. This paradox of social integration exhibits also a paradox of power. One might say, although Blau does not put it this way, that the paradox of power is the concomitance of gratitude and coercion in the emergence and operation of power. Following Max Weber and R. H. Tawney, Blau notes that power "broadly defined . . . refers to all kinds of influence between persons or groups, including those exercised in exchange transactions, where one induces others to accede to his wishes by rewarding them for doing so" (115). What Reinhold Niebuhr taught us long ago to recognize as the paradox of power between equilibrium and coercion, here finds sociological refinement and confirmation in the paradoxical relation between positive and negative sanctions in the use of power.[22] The power of attraction and its concomitant in the power that threatens is paralleled, in the dynamics of social exchange, by the power of positive and negative sanctions, of inducement and coercion.

An important consequence of this refinement is that Niebuhr's relative differentiation between the morality of individuals and the immorality of groups, especially nations, becomes a differentiation between what Blau calls "microstructures" (composed of interacting individuals) and "macrostructures" (composed of interrelated groups) or collectives (24). Common both to "microstructures" and to "macrostructures" is the factor of structure. This means that structuralization is a determining characteristic of social interaction and thus of the reality of being human in the world. To this commonality belong certain parallel processes, such as differentiation between individuals and groups, bonds of integration between individuals and groups, institutionalization and even valuation. But these parallels "must not conceal the fundamental differences between the processes that govern the interpersonal association in microstructures and the forces characteristic of the wider and more complex social relations in macrostructures" (24). Most significant among these differences are: the social values and norms "that must complement the analysis of exchange transactions and power relations but must not become a substitute for it"; and perhaps, most crucially, the process of institutionalization. Intrinsic to this process is the stabilization and the redirection of social interaction with enormous consequences for the personal as well as the external conditions of human existence (25).

These consequences arise because of the enormous differences in the dynamics of power within microstructures and within macrostructures, as well as between collectivities. The critical instance of these differences is the legitimization of power. In microstructures, Blau notes that "the weakness of the isolated subordinate limits the significance of his approval or disapproval of the superior" (23), an observation that is reminiscent of Augustine's remark that "the weakness, then, of infant limbs, not its will, is its innocence."[23] But in the case of macrostructures, "the agreement that emerges in a collectivity of subordinates concerning their judgment of the superior . . . has far-reaching implications for developments in social structure" (23). We come here upon the critical divide between stability and change, conformity and dissent, legitimacy and revolution, in human affairs. Writes Blau:

> Collective approval of power legitimates that power. People who consider that the advantages they gain from a superior's exercise of power outweigh the hardships that compliance with his demands imposes on them tend to communicate to each other their approval of the ruler and their feelings of obligation to him. . . . Collective disapproval of power engenders opposition. People who share the experience of being exploited by the unfair

demands of those in positions of power, and by the insufficient
rewards they receive for their contributions, are likely to communi-
cate their feelings of anger, frustration, and aggression to each
other. There tends to arise a wish to retaliate by striking down the
existing powers. (23)

Retaliation is nurtured by a double outrage: against oppression, and
against injustice. And since there are few other advantages to be
gained from participation in a revolutionary challenge to power
that has been legitimated, retaliation must be regarded as a sign
that established power has breached the human limit of legitimation. Revolutions are a barometer of the bankruptcy of gratitude
because coercive power has overdrawn its *account-ability*. As
Blau, perhaps too cautiously, puts it: "There is some empirical
evidence in support of the thesis that extremist opposition is often
not a calculated means to gain explicit rewards but an expressive
action signifying antagonism against existing powers, stemming
from feelings of deprivation, powerless and alienation" (237).

Some empirical evidence indeed! As a statistical verification of
the correlation of opposition, antagonism against existing powers,
and the transcendence of calculated gain, the data seem less pertinent to the shaping of institutionalization than to the illumination
of the sociology of revolution. However, taken together with the
"anatomical"-descriptive evidence to which Crane Brinton's analysis of revolution has pointed, one arrives at the threshold on which
the sociohistorical reality of revolution and the story by which
revolutions are saved meet. When "cramped" appears as
"wronged," a "moral transfiguration" has occurred, and "men will
revolt."[24] This transfiguration is the breaking in upon the dynamics
of institutionalization of the reversal of the relations between order
and freedom in human affairs. When order has ceased to be the
presupposition and the condition of freedom, and freedom has been
glimpsed and grasped as the presupposition and condition of order,
the risks of new institutional rigidities, "creating needs for fresh
oppositions" (25), are patently worth the taking. The risks are
worth taking because in and under that same freedom, justice is the

foundation and the criterion of law. "Revolutions cannot do without the word 'justice' and the sentiments it arouses" (Brinton).

The revolutionary reversal of the relations between freedom and order opens the way for the experience and practice of freedom that are occasioned and nurtured by story. The story bears the secret and the power of the truth that makes people free in the freedom that being human takes. Karl Mannheim has pointed out that "there is neither freedom nor discipline (order?) in the abstract but only in concrete forms that depend on the cultural context."[25] Like Peter Blau, Mannheim is aware that "the ultimate integration of the social order . . . what holds society together—whether it is power, the division of labor, or a spiritual bond—is one of the most profound questions the sociologist has to answer" (285). Blau's exploration of a theory of social structures is paralleled and to some extent anticipated by Mannheim's assessment of the significance of religion for social integration. At the profoundest level, the capstone of a theory of social structures, as of an adequately integrative cultural context, is the reciprocity between sociological reality and a saving story. A story that saves is a story that offers insight and language, and through these a power of symbolization and structuralization through which the tension, and ultimately the conflict, between gratitude and power in social interaction are overcome in a social order that is instrumental to the freedom that being human takes. Aware of the present cultural context as one of transition from an age of laissez-faire to an age of planning, and profoundly discerning of the impact of this transition upon ways of thinking, of valuation, and of believing, Mannheim underlines the unifying and freeing function of religion in the achievement of social integration. In a culture marked by "the delocalization of the mind" (294), the depersonalization of human privacy and of community alike (298), the manipulative transformation of rationality (297 f.) and of moral sensitivity (305 f.), a unifying and freeing "spiritual bond" is as urgent as it is hard to come by. In a telling passage, Mannheim declares:

> We now realize that a social order can only maintain itself satisfactorily on the basis of a sound statement of belief that performs in a new way the role of the old dogma. . . . The idea of a

religious society with a fundamental belief in tolerance is the paradoxical pattern that has emerged from the history of the Anglo-Saxon countries. . . . It is one of the great paradoxes of our age that the more our technical skill permeates the details of everyday life, where we seek for purposeful arrangements, the more our philosophy tends toward the idea that purpose as a concept does not apply to Nature as such: even those things that seem to be purposeful are the result of selection, the chance product of endless variety and forms of adaptation. *Such an idea can be conceived, but it can hardly be lived.* It is like admitting in theory that the earth moves around the sun while still experiencing the sun as a rising disc that radiates light day by day. In the same way, calm assurance that the highest thing in life is communion with One to whom we can speak and who will respond with unfailing understanding and forgiveness is so deeply ingrained that despondency would reign if this religious belief were lost. Only through satisfaction of these deep-rooted aspirations (that there is a Purpose in what we are doing, and that there is a Personal Power to whom man can appeal) can man develop the sense of belonging in a world where he can find his place and where there is an order that supports him and dispels his anxieties. (287, 289; parenthesis Mannheim's; italics mine)

As we have seen, this is exactly what biblical politics are about. They identify the perspective and the purpose, the matrix and the direction, of the freedom and the order that being human in the world requires. Biblical politics affirm that there is a freedom for order in the world in and through which gratitude presupposes and nurtures trust, and power is the instrument of the justice that ultimately makes retaliation and revolution unnecessary. Penultimately, however, the revolutionary reversal of the relations between freedom and order effects a reversal of the relations between justice and law. Some attention to this reversal will carry us one further step toward that transfiguration of revolution in which *a* saving story becomes *the* saving story. The story by which revolutions are saved is the story in the reality and power of which revolutions are freed from their fate and freed for the pursuit of their appointed end: the making room for freedom and a new beginning and a new order of human affairs.

B. JUSTICE IS THE FOUNDATION AND THE CRITERION OF LAW: LAW
IS NOT THE FOUNDATION AND THE CRITERION OF JUSTICE

Established collectivities, especially governmental ones, have a way of subverting the ordination according to which they are destined to shape order as the practice of freedom. The rationale of this subversion is that law is the foundation and the criterion of justice. The rationale is sprung from roots as deeply embedded in the human story as are those that warrant the preeminence of order over freedom. At issue is, in Karl Barth's pungent phrase, *die Richtigkeit der Stetigkeiten* (the rectitude of the reliabilities);[26] or, as we have tried elsewhere to explore the problem, at issue is the reciprocity between the responsible life and human life.[27] Law is the nexus of this reciprocity, and as such, the fulcrum of the human in the dynamics of exchange and power. To put it another way: Law defines and directs the operation of gratitude in society. In so doing, it marks what is right in the interrelations between and among individuals and groups. Whether as precedent or as statutory, as common or as positive, as divine or as natural, law is the guarantor of what it takes to keep human life human in the world. What it takes is justice; and as the guarantor of justice, law functions as its foundation and criterion. Or so the argument runs.

In ancient Greece, as Hannah Arendt has noted, law was prepolitical. It antedated the city-state and was given or laid down by a legislator outside the body politic but neither above the law nor divine. Despite a considerable variety in the uses of the word *nomos* in Greek civilization, a semantic constant was never lost. *Nomos* was the opposite of *phusis*, man-made as against what is natural, i.e., in the nature of things. The original significance of *nomos* was spatial and expressed "the notion of a range or province, within which defined power may be legitimately exercised."[28] Among the Romans, *lex* was, from the first, political. The root sense of the word is "intimate connection" or relationship, linking "two things or partners whom external circumstances have brought together" (188). Although the existence of a people as an ethnic unity was thought to be independent of all laws, the dynamics of social interaction all but inevitably overtook that almost primordial condition, so that in Rome as in Greece law functioned differently, but toward the same end. The end was the rectitude of the reliabilities, whether as a guarantor of space for freedom, or as a contractual instrument, either for establishing peace after conflict or for extending the *societas Romana* "to the provinces and communities which belonged to the Roman system of alliances" (188–89).

At this point, however, Arendt's account of these beginnings seems moot. The record itself signals the subversion that has afflicted the reciprocity between law and justice in the theoretical and practical search for "a well-ordered society."[29] Arendt cites Virgil's reference to "Saturn's people whom no law fettered to justice, upright of their own free will and following the custom of the gods of old" (188).[30] But she contents herself only with the point that, unlike the Greeks, Virgil affirms the Roman tradition that *lex* was political and "not coeval with the founding of the city" (188). The companion consideration that Virgil takes note both of the priority of justice over law and of "the custom of the gods of old" is passed over. It is difficult to accept the assertion that "Roman law . . . still needed no transcendent source of authority" and that the gods gave merely "a nodding affirmation," if any at all, to "the act of legislation" as to "other important political acts" (188). To be sure, from Socrates to Lucretius a steady criticism of religion had reshaped Homeric piety and had made the gods increasingly problematical, if not expendable. But this is not the same thing as a repudiation of a transcendent source of authority. Indeed, Cicero, whose conception of the relation between law and justice formatively influenced legal and political theory in the West, himself introduced "a transcendent authority," once supplied by the gods, in the form of the natural law (*lex naturae*), whose primary and principal content was the *suum cuique*. "Law," Cicero, declared, "is the highest reason, implanted in nature (*insita in natura*), which commands what things are to be done, and which forbids the contrary."[31] Foremost among the things that are to be done, and of which the contrary is forbidden, is "to give every man his due."[32] One need not go so far as did the jurists and theologians of the Middle Ages in declaring God to be the Author of the natural law. It is sufficient to note that a divine sanction, however minimally or variously conceived, was regarded as indispensable to the right relations between law and justice, and thus to a well-ordered society. One should add, following Rawls: at least until Rousseau.

But we have already had occasion to note Rousseau's unease about the intrinsic effectiveness of law in achieving a humane society. The problem is akin to that of squaring the circle in geometry, he had observed. And for *that*: *il faudrait des dieux.*[33] Montesquieu may be the exception among prerevolutionary theorists in using "the word *law* in its old, strictly Roman sense," as Arendt has noted. It is one thing, however, to refuse the idea of an absolute power in the political realm, whether divine or despotic, and to regard laws essentially as "the *rapports* subsisting between the Creator and the creation, or between men in the state of nature," as no more than "rules" or "*régles*" that determine the government of the world and without which a world would not exist at all" (189; italics Arendt's). But it is another thing, and this more than a matter of indifference, or of a casual appropriation of traditional usage, that Montesquieu should assume a "Creator and Preserver of the universe," speak of a "state of nature," and of "natural laws"; and above all, that he should call his work *l'Esprit des Lois* (the spirit of the laws). One need not insist upon a "higher law" as a necessary presupposition of a well-ordered society. But one does not thereby escape the critical issue that arises for the reciprocity between law and politics.

This is the issue of sovereignty, of the power by which the law is established and fulfills its function as the nexus of the reciprocity between rectitude and reliability, between the responsible life and human life. It is more than quixotic, or merely coincidental, that revolutionary experience should have discerned the critical instance of sovereignty, where law and politics, or law and an order appropriate to freedom and justice, are concerned. As Robespierre put it, in a speech to the National Convention on 7 May 1794: "The idea of a Supreme Being and the immortality of the soul is a constant recall to justice; thus it is social and republican" (314). Two decades earlier, Thomas Jefferson had made the same point more cautiously through an ambivalent appeal, on the one hand, to "the Laws of Nature" and "of Nature's God," and, on the other hand, to truths that are "self-evident." Such truths, he said, were "the opinions and beliefs of men (which) depend not on their own will, but follow involuntarily the evidence proposed to their minds."[34] Revolutionary experience describes an arc connecting maximal with minimal transcendence indispensable to a well-ordered society, to which Hobbes' grim dictum that in politics "authority, not wisdom, makes the law" would otherwise apply.[35] For revolutions "cannot do without the word, 'justice,' and the sentiments it arouses."[36]

"Authority, not wisdom, makes the law" whenever and where-ever a rule of reason—a priori or hypothetical, commanded or intuited—functions as a rule of power in determining and applying the law as the nexus of the reciprocity between rectitude and reliability, between the responsible life and human life. A subversion of the ordination has occurred according to which order is the practice of the freedom that being human takes and justice is the foundation and criterion of law. At the level of conceptuality, this subversion is signaled by a shift from rationality to ideology. At the level of structuralization, the subversion is signaled by a shift from the self-evident to the self-justifying legitimation of power in social interaction. At both levels, false consciousness (Marx) displaces wisdom, and authority of problematic if not spurious legitimacy makes the law. The subversion begins with the criticism of religion, which Marx rightly identified as "the beginning of all criticism." Its culmination—though not a necessary one—is a humanistic displacement of transcendence by self-evidence, with the result that sovereignty is deprived of a religious matrix that, in turn, nourishes the nurture of sovereignty by justice; and justice is bereft of the piety without which justice can neither undergird nor shape the law.

From Socrates and Solon, via Cicero and Ulpian, to Grotius and Hobbes, Rousseau and Rawls, the uneasy equilibrium between the divine and the human resources for a human reciprocity between rectitude and reliability, between the responsible life and human life, has netted the gradual erosion of wisdom by reason and of the power of sovereignty by the sovereignty of power in a society increasingly haunted by the extremes of tyranny and anarchy, of repression and revolution. Chile, Greece, and the paranoia leading to the Watergate, *sic*![37] Consequently, order has become the presupposition and the condition of freedom, and law has become the foundation and the criterion of justice. The idea of "a religious society with a fundamental belief in tolerance" (Mannheim) has taken the shape of a technological collectivity of "repressive tolerance," and man has been deprived of "the sense of belonging in a world where he can find his place and where there is an order that supports him and dispels his anxieties" (Mannheim).[38]

The crisis of sovereignty, to which the subversion of the ordination according to which justice is the foundation and criterion of law leads, is a negative instance of the correspondence between the human and the biblical meaning of politics. The positive instance is the persistent perception of the primacy of justice in political theory and practice, and the confirmation of this perception by revolutionary expectation and action. As Rawls has succinctly put it: "Justice is the first virtue of social institutions, as truth is of systems of thought" (3). The explication of this "virtue" is pursued by Rawls, with the pivotal assistance of the distinction between "the concept of justice" and "conceptions of justice," in order to take account of the diversity of notions, interpretations, and applications of the concept of justice in political theory and practice. As for the concept of justice itself, it refers to "the basic structure of society, or more exactly, the way in which the major social institutions distribute fundamental rights and duties and determine the division of advantages from social cooperation" (7). For Rawls, the search for a theory of justice in our time involves "an alternative systematic account to the dominant utilitarianism of the tradition" (viii), and a refinement of "the traditional theory of the social contract as represented by Locke, Rousseau and Kant" (viii), in the interest of a more precise conceptuality for the shaping of a well-ordered society. At issue is the social cohesiveness and applicability of the *suum cuique* in an increasingly unified world caught in a crisis of sovereignty.

It lies beyond the scope of this book to attend to the ways in which the *suum cuique* has been explicated in the theory and practice of politics. Pertinent to the correspondence between the biblical and the human meaning of politics is the recurrent insistence upon the primacy of justice in human social interaction and upon a transcendent referentiality as the ultimate foundation upon yhich the *suum cuique* rests. Upon the indispensability of this referentiality, poets and dramatists, philosophers and theologians, join in a chorus of assent to what it takes, at the structural level, to keep human life human in the world. Plato quotes Simonides as having been the first to voice the insight that was to take the verbal shape of the *suum cuique*.[39] In the *Nichomachean Ethics*, Aristotle applies the *phusei dikaion* (the just by nature) as the criterion of human law; and in the *Rhetoric*, he emphasizes the theological dimension of this criterion, with an assist from a line of Sophocles to the effect that to be just by nature is "the unwritten, irrefragable law of the gods."[40]

It is well known that, under the aegis of Stoicism and Christianity, the religious matrix and sanction of justice as the foundation and the criterion of law took the form of a reciprocity between "the law of reason and nature" and the Decalogue. "The model in whose image western mankind had construed the quintessence of all laws," writes Hannah Arendt, "even those whose Roman origin was beyond doubt . . . , was itself not Roman at all; it was Hebrew in origin and represented by the Divine Commandments of the Decalogue" (190). The great achievement of this reciprocity was the wisdom, nurtured by an insight of faith, that in a world created and governed by divine will, ordination, and purpose, the likenesses and differences, equalities and inequalities, in nature (cosmic as well as human) and in human communities were designed for freedom in reciprocity. In such a world, human creativity, enrichment, and fulfillment were expressed through mutual rights and obligations, which did indeed give to each his due. These rights and obligations were safeguarded by the inviolability of each human person and practiced through the measure of human gifts and resources in a shared community of concern. The Decalogue defined the boundaries and directions of this reciprocity; as law it expressed the divine will that also was its sanction.

In the immediate aftermath of World War II and the struggle

against the totalitarian disregard of "the foundations of faith, on which the European idea of justice is based," Emil Brunner summed up the achievement of a biblical politics in making justice the foundation and criterion of law. Brunner wrote:

> The Christian religion is the only one in which the idea of justice is inherent, which combines with the recognition of the equal, unconditional dignity of persons the recognition of responsibility to society as a duty and privilege of mutual dependence and service, which emphasizes equally the equality and inequality of human beings and recognizes the independence of the individual as well as his subordination to a social whole as anchored in the will of God. Hence Christianity alone can protect men from the demands both of one-sided individualism and one-sided collectivism.[41]

Not only medieval political and legal theory were informed by this achievement, but the reciprocity between the natural law and the Decalogue informed also the thinking of the Protestant Reformers.[42] Even as late as the seventeenth and eighteenth centuries, when "the natural law stepped into the place of divinity" (190), it was not easily possible to provide for a substitute sanction. As Arendt succinctly says: "The point of the matter has always been that natural law itself needed divine sanction to become binding for men" (191).

The failure of this achievement to prevent the decay that has steadily overtaken it since the Enlightenment invalidates neither the priority that it assigned to justice over law nor the bond between piety and politics that both the biblical and the human meaning of politics tend to confirm. When, however, this failure is viewed in the light of the reversal that the logic of revolutionary politics requires in the political priorities of established authorities, an internal defect in the reciprocity between the natural law and the Decalogue is exposed. This defect is the excessive stress in the tradition of Christian political theory upon the commandment as the bearer of the divine sanction necessary to the legitimation of justice as the foundation and criterion of law. As Arendt pointedly puts it: "Only to the extent that we understand by law a commandment to which men owe obedience regardless of their consent and mutual agreements, does the law require a transcendent source of authority for its validity, that is, an origin which must be beyond human power" (190). On the record, this is the way the validation of law was understood and applied. And on this record, Hobbes' dictum correctly summarizes the state of the matter: "Authority, not wisdom, makes the law." Hobbes' experience is the polar opposite of the experience reported by the Apostle Paul, who wrote to the church at Rome: "There was a time when, in the absence of law, I was fully alive; but *when the commandment came, sin sprang to life and I died.* The commandment which should have led to life proved in my experience to lead to death, because sin found its opportunity in the commandment, seduced me, and·through the commandment killed me" (Rom. 7:9–11; italics mine).

Exactly so! The heteronomy of the commandment is the deceptive expedient through which the law is understood and applied as a check against anarchy. Consequently, the law subserves order rather than affirms justice and destroys rather than serves the freedom that being human takes. Against the heteronomy of the commandment, both biblical politics and revolutionary experience, passion and purpose, protest. Biblical politics protest in the name of a theonomus derivation and direction of justice that excludes both heteronomy and autonomy from the human meaning of politics. The logic of revolutionary politics protests in the name of a human derivation and direction of justice that excludes both the primacy of order over freedom and of law over justice from the political options through which time and space are to be shaped for a new beginning and a new order of human affairs. Biblical politics and revolutionary politics are conjoined in the conviction that only insofar as order is the practice of freedom and law is a function of justice can the human meaning of politics be nurtured and assured. Biblical and revolutionary politics are in tension, if not at odds, over the piety that justice requires if there is to be a humane society at all.

As for biblical politics, justice is derived not from God's will as commanded, but from God's will as covenanted. The incarnational reality, to which biblical politics are a response, affirms a primordial rightness or fitness of things that is expressed in the creation of the world and in the destiny of a human people through whose story all people are sustained and fulfilled in the trust and openness, the caring and the responsiveness, that make for humanness. This rightness or fitness of things is the human side of the righteousness of God. As we have already noted, this righteousness is pivotal in the gospel account of the Transfiguration of Jesus. The paradigmatic role of Moses and Elijah in that account is that in them the righteousness of God attested in the law and the prophets is disclosed as present both in judgment upon the established order and authority before the bar of reality, and in the imminent inbreaking of a new and human future. The Old Testament underlines the righteousness of God as the single most important affirmation about God in his covenant relations with his chosen people in the world.[43] This righteousness is a commandment in the imperative sense only insofar as such an imperative signals the foundational and purposed fitness of things. The quintessence of the Decalogue is the *indicative* reality whose direction and boundaries are defined in covenantal, that is, personal terms through the commandment form. The reality is God's presence in the midst of his people as help and salvation.[44] This help and salvation are concretely and specifically evident in the deliverance of the poor who are the test case of the practice of justice in human society. The poor are the deprived, the outcasts, the oppressed— in short, all those without status and without power in the world and in the society that God has called into being for the humanization of human life. Thus the poor are the bearers of the battle between freedom and order, justice and law, humanization and dehumanization, true and false piety, in the world.

In the midst of this battle, the Transfiguration of Jesus occurs as its moment of truth and point of no return. This paradigm of a politics of confrontation joins the New Testament with the Old Testament in the crucial affirmation of the interchangeability of righteousness and justice in what God is doing in the world to make and to keep human life human.[45] This interchangeability has been weakened in the course of the story of justice in the Western tradition, owing to the commingling of the concept of justice with notions of equity and equality according to a rule of reason that has lost the wisdom nurtured by faith's insight into the height and breadth and length and depth of the human fitness of things. A legalistic reading of the commandments has obscured an existential response to them (Rom. 7, *sic!*), an authoritarian understanding and application of law has obscured the human reality and dimensions of justice, and authority, devoid of divine as well as human sanction, not wisdom, makes the law.

The doings of Philip and Daniel Berrigan and their companions in Catonsville and the proceedings in the trial of the Chicago Eight, to which we have already referred,[46] are among the more acute if predictable instances of the crisis of sovereignty that the revolutionary movements of our times have torn open and brought to the threshold of violence. If we are to be able to look forward to a reversal of the Hobbesian dictum, so that wisdom, not authority, makes the law, the revolutionary reversal of Establishment priorities must find a way beyond the violence that aborts the vicarious righteousness of revolutionary promise, commitment, and action and delivers revolutions over to their fate. The prospect of finding such a way, and the power to take it, are the ultimate sense and significance of a biblical politics for the question of revolution. A biblical politics change the human and operational meaning of violence, and in so doing make available to the revolutionary passion for freedom, for a new beginning, and for a new order of human affairs, the liberation from its own undoing in a transfiguration of its unavoidable and warranted occasion.

## C. THE APOCALYPTIC SIGNIFICANCE OF VIOLENCE

It is more than coincidental that the crucial question dividing revolutionary possibility and promise from revolutionary fate and the critical pertinence of Jesus Christ to the question of revolution should intersect. The intersection is providential; and the discernment and explication of this providence is the contribution of a biblical politics, centered upon transfiguration, to revolutionary theory, practice, and hope. At stake is the integrity of revolution on the threshold of the realization of its promises. On that threshold, *submission* and *silence*, together with *transfiguration*, become the code words of the imminence of a new order of human affairs and the criteria of revolutions as signs of transfiguration.[47]

Frequently in the course of the foregoing analysis, we have encountered the factor of violence, as the *ultima ratio,* determinative of a revolutionary future as against the revolutionary fate. By this determination, as Camilo Torres faced it, the social effectiveness of love seemed to stand or fall. In the context of the Latin American experience of imperialist colonialism, the crucial question posed is whether revolutionary passion and purpose are foredoomed by the violent seizure of power to their own undoing, or whether the sociological reality of violence points to an authentic revolutionary alternative to violence, adequate to the social reality of power and to the struggle for liberation from oppression and for the freedom to be human in the world.[48] As Frantz Fanon puts it, in the context of colonialist imperialism, the problem now "is to lay hold of . . . violence which is changing direction. . . . Now new conditions will make possible a completely new line of action."[49] But can one "let a hundred flowers bloom" unless the gun has done its work of power successfully?[50] What are Fanon's "new conditions" that "will make possible a completely new line of action"? Do they herald the displacement of the gun by psychological and technological violence alternatives? Or have these "new conditions," together with Lenin's confident assessment of "the new class smashing (the state) machine and commanding, governing with the aid of a *new* machine,"[51] been overtaken by Marcuse's grim insistence that we live in a world in which "technological rationality has become political rationality" and "repressive tolerance" has become the order of the day?[52]

In such a world, the violence that under revolutionary conditions once changed the direction of things, however temporarily, would indeed be "changing direction." It would be a technological phenomenon too, the sociological reality of which would be the achievement of a precarious equilibrium between "systemic violence" and "counter-vailing violence" (Marcuse).[53] In such a world, the bitter struggle of the Black Revolution over "freedom now" or "power now," and the shift in policy from passive resistance to nonviolent protest to militant nonviolence produced by that struggle, would also have been overtaken by events. It would turn out to have been scarcely more than a squall over an ocean of dehumanizing futility.[54] Perhaps the revolutionary ferment and fomentation of the twentieth century have become but the most tragic victims of "the moral reality named death," which alternately bewitches and paralyzes us all, "full of sound and fury/Signifying nothing."[55] And William Stringfellow is profoundly right! There is "an inherent inefficacy in classical revolution because of its reliance upon the very same moral authority as the regime or system which it threatens to overthrow and succeed—death—. . . ."[56]

As an ultimate assessment of "the impotence of revolution," this is a judgment, based upon biblical politics, that is both factually and politically correct. "Biblical politics . . . as it manifests resistance to the power of death is, at once, celebration of human life in society."[57] There is, however, a penultimate assessment of revolutionary politics, precisely in the light of biblical politics, that cannot be overlooked without disregarding the factual and political significance of revolutions as signs of transfiguration. To do so risks compounding the confusion over the relations between power and violence, and thus intensifying the ideological self-justification to which, as we have noted, revolutionaries are no less vulnerable than are existing authorities. The "ubiquity and versatility of violence," so aptly described by Stringfellow, and to which both a premature seizure of power and a convulsive adherence to power seized are subject, must not be allowed to obscure the fact that biblical politics discern revolutions as signs of transfiguration, and as such as bearers of a righteousness not their own.[58]

In the power of this righteousness, the logic of revolutionary politics compels a revision of political priorities also at the juncture of power and violence, so critical for a revolutionary future as against a revolutionary fate. In a world under "the moral reality named death" by technological rationality become political rationality, violence undergoes a double transfiguration. At the level of revolutionary politics, violence is unveiled not as the endemic nemesis of revolution but as a sign that politics have arrived at an apocalyptic moment of truth and point of no return. At the level of biblical politics, violence as the *ultima ratio* of a fallen world, in which civilization rests upon a primal crime, is exposed as the *ultima ratio* of a world already lost, in the act of being displaced by a new and human world already on the way. In short, the apocalyptic significance of violence is the talisman of its transfiguration.[59]

The paradigmatic significance of the pericope of the Transfiguration of Jesus now reaches the threshold of its most momentous consequences. It has already been remarked that this happening points to the immediate confrontation of a commanding Presence with an inescapable present. What is going on is the pressure of the end-time upon times already coming to an end. The messianic dynamics of reality are on the nearer edge of the exposure of its "messianic secret." At stake are the revolutionary character of reality and the revolutionary response to this reality in a world once lived and died in by Jesus of Nazareth, the Christ, and over which he still presides.[60] In a telling phrase of Dietrich Bonhoeffer's, "the world ever and again opens itself up anew . . . through the formative presence of Jesus Christ, which so permeates us on its own initiative as to mark the form and structure of our life as his own."[61]

The consequences of a biblical politics, centered upon the Transfiguration, are a shift in the understanding and practice of the relation between power and violence. The shift is the recognition and assessment of violence not in primarily ethical (moral), or legal, or even sociological terms; but as an apocalyptic phenomenon. The ethics of good and evil, of legality and illegality, of value and disvalue, of the ideal and the real, of perfection and compromise, are transfigured by the dynamics of life and death, of humanity and inhumanity, of reconciliation and judgment, of a new order against an established order in and through an apocalyptic moment of truth. On the threshold dividing revolutionary possibility and promise from revolutionary fate, biblical politics discerns an accelerating tempo, which carries the sociological reality and inevitability of violence in a world of power beyond all established patterns and structures toward the concreteness of a new thing that God is about to do in the midst of his people, and for the sake of the world which he has reconciled to himself in Jesus Christ. On the apocalyptic level of sensitivity, insight, and expectation, the critical question erupts with an ultimate urgency: Is God upholding the world by changing it, or is God changing the world by upholding it? If God is doing the second, then the given patterns and structures are the fundamental supports indispensable to having any world at all; then order has taken priority over freedom and law over justice. Then too, violence is the endemic nemesis of revolution, an insubordinate violation of the divinely established existing order. But if God is doing the first, then the concrete realities are those *not yet given* patterns and structures that are displacing patterns and structures that have been taken for granted; then freedom is the presupposition and condition of order, and justice is the foundation and criterion of law. Then also, violence is a sign that politics have arrived at an apocalyptic moment of truth and point of no return, and of a transfiguration already under way.

Some indication of the implications of such an apocalyptic understanding of the relation between power and violence may be derived from two recent statements addressed to the question. The statements are plainly occasioned by the intensification of violence amidst the revolutionary struggles that have engaged our attention; and they put the issue in a precise and sharply contradictory way. The authors are concerned not only about revolutionary violence but about the involvement in violence of Christians who are informed by biblical faith and politics. One statement comes from a concise and vigorous book by my colleague, James Cone, called *Black Theology and Black Power*. The other statement comes from an equally concise and vigorous book by Jacques Ellul of the Faculty of Law at the University of Bordeaux. Ellul's book is called simply *Violence*.[62] We turn first to Professor Cone.

Cone sets out from the claim that God's self-identifying activity in the world is the liberation of his people from slavery, oppression, and injustice. Under given historical and sociological conditions, the form and structure (*Gestalt*) of God's people under slavery changes; and, in consequence, the focus of liberation changes. In our time, and especially in the United States, the black people are the bearers of God's liberating activity in the world. Since Christian theology is intrinsically an analysis of God's liberating activity in the world—the primary accents of which are suffering, deliverance, and reconciliation—Christian theology is Black Theology. Blackness is significant theologically as a color solely because the *sociological* reality of blackness is that it identifies the people whom God is liberating from oppression. "Black Theology," Cone writes, "will not respond positively to whites who insist upon making blacks as white as possible by de-emphasizing their blackness, and stressing the irrelevance of color, while really living as racists. As long as whites live like *white* people, . . . black people must use blackness as the sole criterion for dialogue. Otherwise reconciliation will mean black people living according to white rules and glorifying white values, being orderly and calm, while others enact laws which destroy them" (147–48; italics Cone's). From this systemic reality, Cone moves on to face the difficult decision with which this reality confronts the Christian. "The Christian," he declares, "does not decide between violence and non-violence, between evil and good. He decides between the lesser and the greater evil. He must ponder whether revolutionary violence is more detrimental to man in the long run than systemic violence. But if the system is evil, then revolutionary violence is both justified and necessary" (143).

As we have seen, the human depth and range of the concrete experience of systemic violence have been documented psychologically by Frantz Fanon and sociologically by Monsignor Guzmán and others in Colombia. From these analyses, it appears that the concrete reality of violence is that it is indigenous to the humanization of human life in a world of power. As the problem of power is the problem of its human and humanizing use, so the problem of violence is the problem of a human and humanizing response to power. There is a *systemic* violence and there is a *counterviolence*; and in the dynamics of the relation between power and violence, *counterviolence* is *revolutionary* violence and *systemic* violence is *counterrevolutionary*. Cone has clearly discerned the necessity of violence; but the necessity of violence is not its justification, as he seems to suggest. The justification of violence is neither a sociological nor an ethical question. It is an apocalytic question; and that means that the question of the justification of violence is a question out of court. Ever and again, violence is unavoidable;

but violence is never justifiable. Biblical politics, centered upon transfiguration, have no place for a justification of violence. They do, however, make room for the inevitability of violence in the course of the revolutionary struggle for humanization. In that struggle, violence is part of the apocalyptic threshold dividing revolutionary fate from a revolutionary future. It too belongs to the transfiguration under way. In Bonhoeffer's language, the question of violence and of the justification of violence must be viewed in the light of the relations between the ultimate and the penultimate dimensions and decisions of life in this world as christologically structured and experienced.[63]

Jacques Ellul's discussion of violence is diametrically opposite to that of Cone. Ellul acknowledges that "violence is the condition of human existence . . . the form that human relations normally and necessarily take" (87). In this minimal sense, Ellul would agree with Cone that the reality of black-white relations is that the black person is violated by the white person. In this concrete context, it becomes quite clear what violence is. *Violence is the violation of the humanity of my neighbor, by whatever means—military, psychological, moral, medical, institutional, religious.* Violence is not exhausted by the use of a hammer, or a gun, or a knife upon and against my neighbor. Violence is neither confined to, nor exclusively defined by, the killing of somebody, whether by accident or deliberately. Violence is what I do to my neighbor insofar as my involvements make it impossible for him to be a human being. Ellul would admit all this. He does not deny that we all live violently. It is not, he says, "the acceptance of violence that I am against. It is the justification of violence that the Christian must oppose" (140). The reason for this resolute opposition of the Christian to violence is, according to Ellul, that the Christian is called to break the vicious circle of necessity occasioned by the fact that violence inevitably breeds violence (129–30).

How, it may now be asked, are we to live within, or break out of, the vicious circle of necessity that hangs like a Damocles' sword over the relation between power and violence and makes violence endemic to power? The sharp juxtaposition of the views of Cone and Ellul seems virtually to expose the Christian to a schizophrenia that, sooner or later, makes him either a fanatic or paralyzes his ethical sensitivity to his involvement in violence and brings him out on the side of systemic violence.

In a world in which revolutions are signs of transfiguration, owing to the correspondence between the biblical and the human meaning of politics, biblical politics discern also the transfiguration of the relations between power and violence. There is a third option open to the Christian and to the revolutionary alike, which the counterrevolutionary violence of existing authorities has already refused. This is the form that Jesus himself gives to violence in his own confrontation of power with truth in the course of his affirmation of the God-man structure of the world. According to Jesus, violence is an apocalyptic happening that erupts whenever, in the dynamics of the world's formation for freedom over order and justice over law, the power of systemic violence has provoked the counterviolence of the concrete responsibility for setting right what is not right, for setting aside what is dehumanizing, and setting straight what is humanizing in the world. The apocalyptic character of violence means that violence is a sign of the imminent breaking in of the divine judgment upon an established order of power and life that has been weighed in the balance and found wanting. Violence, apocalyptically understood, is the *mene, mene, tekel upharsin* (Dan. 5:25–28) of a systemic default upon the use of power for the humanization of human life.

As an apocalyptic reality, the endemic sociological reality of violence is not a sign of the necessity of violence but of the dehumanizing dynamics of the society in which violence has become endemic. This is why the question of the justification of violence is an inappropriate question. Violence can never be justified any more than the disestablishment of one order through the inbreaking of a new order is a matter for justification. The inbreaking of a new order is indeed a judgment upon an old order on the way out. The new order, however, is not on that account justified. Apocalyptic reality is beyond justification in the ethical or even in the religious sense. *What is happening with the outbreak of violence is the pressure upon the powers of this world of the God-man structure of the world in making room for the freedom and fulfillment of being human in the world.* The apocalyptic character of violence means that violence is a sign of the radical penultimacy under which nothing and no one are justified in themselves but all things depend upon the merciful and favorable providence of God making all things new, setting all things right, and making the world safe and glad for being human in.

Biblical politics discern in the apocalyptic character of violence that conjunction of revolutionary and messianic politics that sets revolutionary promises free from revolutionary fate and transfigures the futility of the things that are through the presence and power of the things that are not, proleptically experienced as already taking shape in a new and humanizing ordering of human affairs. It is the apocalyptic character of violence that shatters its vicious circle of necessity (*contra* Ellul) and disallows its justification (*contra* Cone). Apocalyptically understood, the difference between systemic violence and revolutionary counterviolence is unveiled as the difference between violence that has converted risk into calculated policy and violence as a calculated risk always threatened by conversion into policy. At the juncture of revolutionary and messianic politics, however, violence is always a risk but can never become a policy or program. Just as violence is always an ultimate recourse of established power and authority, so violence is ever and again a penultimate resource of revolutionary challenge and confrontation.

In a forceful passage, Rubem Alves has described the historical concreteness of violence as a risk involved in a lifestyle shaped by biblical politics and at the same time by the commitment to being socially real and responsible in the world, that is, revolutionary. Alves writes:

> God's politics . . . is subversive of the stability created by the violence of the old. The false peace of unfreedom is put out of balance and its walls of defense are made to crumble.
>
> There is violence involved in the process. God does not wait for the dragon to become a lamb. He knows that the dragon will rather devour the lamb. It (i.e., the dragon) must be opposed and defeated by the power of the lamb. . . . (God) does not wait for the master to decide freely to liberate the slave. He knows

that the master will never do that. So, he breaks the yoke and the erstwhile master can no longer dominate. The power of God destroys what makes the world unfree. This use of power looks like violence because it destroys the equilibrium and peace of the system of domination. But, . . . what looks like the violence of the lion is really the power of counter-violence, that is, power used against those who generate, support, and defend the violence of a world of masters and slaves. Violence is power that oppresses and makes man unfree. Counter-violence is power that breaks the old which enslaves, in order to make man free. Violence is power aimed at paralysis. Counter-violence is power aimed at making man free for experimentation.[64]

Thus violence is that apocalyptic possibility that thrusts all who are caught up in the correspondence between the biblical and the human meaning of politics—the true revolutionaries called to "true worldliness" (*echte Weltlichkeit*: Bonhoeffer)—into the agony and abandon of "a life of absolute insecurity . . . and safety" (Bonhoeffer)[65] in which all idolatry and self-justification crumble and the freedom of the divine ordination shapes once again the involvement in a world that God is making over and making new.

It is reported in the Gospel according to Luke that

Some people were talking about the temple and the fine stones with which it was adorned. He said, "These things which you are gazing at—the time will come when not one stone of them will be left upon another; all will be thrown down." "Master," they asked, "when will it all come about? What will be the sign when it is due to happen?"

He said, "Take care that you are not misled. For many will come claiming my name and saying, 'I am he,' and, 'The Day is upon us.' Do not follow them. And when you hear of wars and insurrections, do not fall into a panic. These things are bound to happen first; but the end does not follow immediately." Then he added, "Nation will make war upon nation, kingdom upon kingdom; there will be great earthquakes, and famines and plagues in many places; in the sky terrors and great portents.

"Before all this happens they will set upon you and persecute you. You will be brought before synagogues and put in prison;

you will be haled before kings and governors for your allegiance to me. This will be your opportunity to testify; so make up your minds not to prepare your defense beforehand, because I myself will give you power of utterance and a wisdom which no opponent will be able to resist or refute. . . . By standing firm you will win true life for yourselves.

". . . When all this begins to happen, stand upright and hold you heads high, because your liberation is near." (Luke 21:5-16, 19, 28)

The testimonial integrity of a biblical lifestyle is exposed on the threshold dividing revolutionary promise and possibility from revolutionary fate. This is the threshold of violence as an apocalyptic happening. When the risk of violence has withstood its conversion into policy, the moment of truth and point of no return has arrived. For established collectivities, at the apex of which stands the power of the state, such an ultimate moment means that the time of their providential disavowal and historical repudiation has come, no matter how long it takes. In an unforgettable remark of Reinhold Niebuhr's: "History, like nature, never buries what it kills!" For revolutionary movements, such an ultimate moment brings the prospect of revolutionary fulfillment transcending revolutionary failure. Such a moment unveils the possibility and power of a biblical lifestyle as the secret of revolutionary commitment and achievement. When this happens—and political reality in distinction from *Realpolitik* forbids an *a fortiori* exclusion of such a possibility—the happening called revolution is undergoing a transfiguration of its own. Sooner or later, we noted at the outset, the question of Jesus Christ runs headlong into the question of revolution, and the question of revolution runs headlong into the question of Jesus Christ. [66] The *ultima ratio* of this encounter is the coinherence of biblical and revolutionary politics as the human meaning of politics.

Such an *ultima ratio* is high on the agenda of a revolutionary future. It must be admitted, however, that on the threshold of violence one sees "through a glass, darkly" (I Cor. 13:12 AV); perhaps too darkly. For the piety without which there can be no justice and the justice without which there can be no society may require another way toward the future altogether. There is the piety of naturalistic humanism in J. Glenn Gray's deeply moving vision of a reconciliation between the human ∂nd the nonhuman orders of life through which enmity and conflict and war shall be no more, and God and nature and humanity are joined together in the fulfillment of healing and of hope.[67] There is the piety of charismatic discernment and sacramental participation in "the biblical life-style," in the power of which William Stringfellow sees the possibility and sense of a testimonial "No!" to all "the principalities, . . . and powers, . . . (and) spiritual hosts of wickedness" (Eph. 6:12 RSV; parenthesis mine) who nurture, perpetuate and preside over "the moral reality named death."[68] There is the piety of the poetic sacramental realism of Daniel Berrigan, which seems, for the sake of justice, to turn aside from the struggle for the justice without which there can be no society, and to invite an individual participation in a neomonastic brotherhood of dedication to the reclaiming of the human in and for us all, in a world already redeemed and renewed by God in the sacrificial self-immolation of Jesus Christ.[69] In politics, as in ethics, the power to shape action is the test of credibility as well as viability in the search and struggle for a new and fulfilling order of human affairs—as surely as "you will recognize them by their fruits" (Matt. 7:20).

The present account of the phenomenon of revolution and its contemporary dynamics and shapes is intended rather as a critical consideration addressed to these serious and sensitive probings of what we all see dimly than as a rejection of their wisdom. If in the paradigm of the Transfiguration a certain light upon the darkness of the gospel has been discerned, in the rays of which *submission* and *silence* become code words of revolutionary freedom beyond revolutionary futility, the reason lies in the central and inescapable place of justice in the piety required by society and nurtured by the coinherence of biblical and revolutionary politics.[70] On the threshold of violence, and very much "through a glass, darkly," it is fitting to conclude with a very exploratory indication of what the transfiguration of revolution could mean for revolutionary passion and expectation, logic and practice.

## D. THE TRANSFIGURATION OF REVOLUTION

Biblical politics identify transfiguration as the happening according to which the providential-eschatological pressure of reality upon human affairs gives political shape to a divinely appointed new and freeing and fulfilling human order. As signs of transfiguration, revolutions herald a long overdue revision of political priorities that can no longer be deferred.[71] Sooner or later, however, the dynamics of revolutionary passion and expectation bring the logic and the practice of revolutionary commitment and purpose under the shattering strain of an unbearable tension. The sign of this tension is the conversion of violence from a risk into a policy. Should this conversion occur, revolutions would have succumbed to the logic and practice of Establishment politics and have defaulted upon their destiny as signs of transfiguration. Should this conversion have been resisted, revolutions would have managed to "make their calling and election sure" (II Pet. 1:10). Their destiny as signs of transfiguration would then have been confirmed in a transfiguration of revolution itself. Bearers of a righteousness not their own, the sign and the thing signified (*signum signans et signum signatum*) would so have converged as to liberate revolutions from their own undoing and to inaugurate through them a new order of freedom for being human in the world.

Transfiguration is the unveiling of the hidden destiny of revolution in the miraculous inversion of its dynamics from self-justifying self-destruction to the concrete practice of an order whose presupposition and condition is freedom, of law whose foundation and criterion is justice, and of the displacement of the love of power by the power of love in the societies of humankind. The transfiguration of revolution makes plain to "the whole human running race" that

> The miracle is the only thing that happens,
>> but to you it will not be apparent,
> Until all events have been studied and nothing
>> happens that you cannot explain;
> And life is the destiny you are bound to refuse
>> until you have consented to die.

Therefore, see without looking, hear without
    listening, breathe without asking;
The Inevitable is what will seem to happen to you
    purely by chance;
The Real is what will strike you as really absurd;
Unless you are certain you are dreaming, it is
    certainly a dream of your own;
Unless you exclaim—"There must be some mistake"—
    you must be mistaken.

. . . . . . . . . . . . . . . . . . . . . . . . . . . . . . . . . . . . . . . . . . . . . . .

For the garden is the only place there is. . . .[72]

Just as revolutions are signs of transfiguration, so also there are signs that revolutions themselves are undergoing the miracle of transfiguration. At least four such signs may be discerned. They indicate that the dynamics of revolution have successfully resisted the conversion of violence from a risk into a policy and have subordinated the passion and expectation of revolutionary commitment to the logic and practice of a revolutionary vocation. The signs are:

1. A revolutionary movement on the move beyond the spurious distinction between a "hard" revolution and a "soft" revolution toward the patient persistence of revolutionary faithfulness;
2. A revolutionary movement on the move beyond ideology and utopia toward the ideological implementation of the truth that makes humanity free;
3. A revolutionary movement on the move beyond immediate and/or historical fulfillment toward an eschatological present whose presence is the power that liberates as it binds and binds as it liberates;
4. A revolutionary movement on the move beyond iconoclasm and idolatry toward the regenerative vocation of supplication.

Some comment is called for upon each of these signs in turn.

*1. Beyond "Hard" and "Soft" Revolution*

In the course of a discussion of the theme of *permanent revolution* at the concluding session of a Colloquium in commemoration of Karl Barth, two colleagues, who have meanwhile become competent and challenging interpreters of a "political theology," perceptively and sharply brought the argument of an essay that had just been read under the searching question whether I was proposing a Christian's ongoing involvement in a "hard" revolution or in a "soft" revolution. Frederick Herzog of Duke University asked, gently and circumspectly, "What would be the reason Professor Lehmann might see for a hard revolution to occur in the near future where a 'theology of revolution' might be applicable?"[73] To this question my colleague, James Cone, added a forceful and existential variant of his own. "Yes, Paul," he said, "I want to know on which side *do* you come down?"

At the time, these questions seemed to me to be at once timely and on target. One had, indeed, to consider whether they had not devastated the argument for a theology of permanent revolution, on the part of Karl Barth or anyone else, by exposing its abstract self-involution. If so, how much more precarious would these questions seem to be if, in the light of them, one should glance retrospectively over the course of the preceding pages? Nevertheless, I wish here to report to these collagues that the possibly devastating thrust of their interrogation has, owing to their prompting and the foregoing analysis, undergone a transfiguration of discernment. It now seems to me that the distinction between a "hard" revolution and a "soft" revolution is a spurious distinction. It is a spurious distinction because it is rooted in a false revolutionary consciousness that has insufficiently attended to the threshold of violence dividing a revolutionary future from a revolutionary fate. On this threshold, a "hard" revolution would seem to mean the readiness of revolutionary commitment and practice to convert the risk of violence into policy. By contrast, a "soft" revolution would mean the readiness of revolutionary commitment and practice to take the risk of violence, only to retreat from the dynamics of such a risk at the time and place for revolutionary action. There is, I submit, a third option beyond the distinction between "hard" revolution and "soft" revolution. This is the recognition of violence as indeed a risk of revolutionary passion, promise, logic, and practice. It is the recognition also that the risk of violence ever and again erupts in violent actions. But it is precisely these recognitions that render the distinction between "hard" and "soft" revolution problematical.

If a "hard" revolution does not mean the conversion of violence from risk into policy, it is difficult to know what it does mean. If a "soft" revolution does not mean a retreat from this conversion and thus a surrender of revolutionary seriousness at the moment of truth and point of no return, it is likewise difficult to know what it does mean. If Herzog's *temporal* question—whether a "hard" revolution to which a theology of revolution might apply is foreseeable in the near future?—is not transposable into the *violence* question, it is reducible to a truism of revolutionary experience, namely, that the integrity and validity of revolutionary commitment, logic, and practice are not established by the prospect of immediate or long-range realization, of a near or a more distant future. Similarly, if Cone's *loyalty* question—on which side *does* one come down?—is not transposable into the *violence* question, it also is reducible to a truism of revolutionary experience, namely, that revolutionary iconoclasm, either as rhetoric or in action, is a dubious criterion of revolutionary commitment or achievement. Indeed, it is precisely the pertinence and task of a theology of revolution to provide perspectives, language, and power for revolutionary commitment and expectation, especially as the dynamics of revolutionary activity reach the critical threshold of violence.

A theology of revolution has primary responsibility for the nurture of revolutionary faithfulness and for the guardianship of a revolutionary future against revolutionary fate. As and when revolutions convert violence from risk to policy, they exhibit a lost awareness of violence as an apocalyptic happening, and in this loss are on the way to the abandonment of the patient persistence of revolutionary faithfulness for an abortive implementation of revolutionary hopes. The loss of apocalyptic awareness also accelerates surrender to a calculus of revolutionary possibilities informed and formed rather by the *Realpolitik* of established collectivities than by the *political realism* of biblical politics. A political theology that draws its wisdom from such calculations has been insufficiently attentive to the coinherence of biblical and revolutionary politics as the human meaning of politics, and is gravely endangered by a transformation into ideology. The coinherence of biblical and revolutionary politics, however, discerns in revolutions a righteousness not their own and a destiny that makes sense of faithfulness to revolution as vocation.[74]

## 2. Beyond Ideology and Utopia

The close connection between ideology and revolution has been widely known and increasingly accepted since Karl Marx applied the term *ideology* to ideas operative in the political and economic struggle between the two principal social classes that emerged in consequence of the industrial revolution, viz., the bourgeoisie and the proletariat. *Ideology* meant the functional subordination of thought to the dominant power groups or group in a given historical and social situation. In short, *ideology* is the corruption of reason by interest in social interaction, particularly in social conflict. It is understandable that Marx should have thought of ideology as a particular corruption of the bourgeoisie, and to have contrasted with it an uncorrupted mode of the relation between thought and power on the part of the proletariat, that is, a *utopian* mode. *Utopia*, in this general sense, is the functional liberation of thought from domination by power; in short, the freedom of reason for social and historical fulfillment.

Against this general Marxian background, Karl Mannheim published his well-known and influential analysis of the relations between ideological and utopian mentalities.[75] Mannheim emphasizes that "to determine concretely . . . what in a given case is ideological and what is utopian is extremely difficult" (176). This is especially so at the "evaluative" in distinction from the "nonevaluative" level of thought in action. The latter level simply exhibits the fact that all ideas are influenced by the social character of existence and, in turn, influence that existence. Sociologically, " 'existence' (whatever the term may mean ontologically) is that which is 'concretely effective,' i.e. a functioning social order, which does not exist only in the imagination of certain individuals but according to which people really act" (174; parenthesis mine). At the evaluative level, a judgmental factor operates, so that "what in a given case appears as utopian, and what as ideological, is dependent, essentially, on the stage and degree of reality to which one applies this standard" (176). Thus representatives of a given order will experience as reality that structure of relationships of which they are the bearers, a perspective that those in opposition to this order will regard as ideological. Conversely, these same "representatives of a given order will label as utopian all conceptions of existence which *from their point of view* can in principle never be realized" (176–77; italics Mannheim's). By Mannheim's "criterion of realization," however, it becomes possible to make a significant relative, though not absolute, distinction between ideology and utopia. On the basis of "actualized realities of the past," ideas that function in such a way as "merely . . . to conceal reality" may be said to be ideological; whereas ideas that "were realized in the succeeding social order" but were actually transcendent to the situation in which they were first put forward, may be said to be utopian, that is, ideas that were "*bursting asunder the bonds of the existing order*" (184; italics mine). By this criterion also, revolutions are relatively utopian, whereas upholders of the given order are relatively ideological, as regards the ideas that they espouse and endeavor to put into practice.

It is important to recall Mannheim's analysis of the relations between ideology and utopia at this point because one hears it noised abroad with increasing frequency these days that the revolutionary struggle against colonialism, imperialism, and racism has entered a *postideological* phase. Just as the decade of the 1960s was characterized by the intensification of ideological passion, rhetoric, and proliferation, so the present decade is characterized by *the end of ideology*. Insofar as the phrase "the end of ideology" refers to the obvious ineffectiveness and loss of referentiality of the rhetoric and politics of the socialism of the Second and Third Internationals, to the uneasy truce between NATO and the nations under the Warsaw Pact, and above all to the nuclear détente and the technological rationality of a globalized industrial-military complex, there is a certain "end of ideology" in the current sociopolitical situation. But one suspects that there are other meanings hidden in the phrase, designed to suggest that just as we may be said to be living culturally in a post-Christian world, so we are also living socially and politically (and thus also culturally) in a post-Marxian world. The implication somehow is that Marxism no longer offers a context and key for understanding the sociopolitical actualities of these times and indeed that the revolutionary ardor of even half a decade ago has spent itself and has ended in the disillusionment foreseeable for "rebels without a cause."

The demise of ideology, so conceived and so arrived at, exhibits nothing so much as another ideology, concealing reality in the name of realism. How precariously and thinly the alleged post-Marxian, transideological, and revolutionarily enervated present veils an intensification of the struggle against colonialism, imperialism, and racism is almost daily apparent from the mounting hostility between the Union of Soviet Socialist Republics and the People's Republic of China; from the "peace with honor" that crudely masks a dishonorable armistice in Southeast Asia; from the seething restlessness of the "underdeveloped" peoples against the so-called "developed" nations, together with the deepening chasm dividing economic luxury and poverty within all nations; and from the paradigmatic conflict in the Middle East, not to mention the no longer concealable "energy crisis." The "end of ideology" seems indeed, like the prelude to an Orwellian phantasmagoria, long heralded by Marxist theoreticians and seers as the inevitable consequence of capitalist contradictions.

These scarcely veiled actualities, however, are more soberly and wisely understood as the accelerating tempo of the revolutionary dynamics of the struggle against colonialism, imperialism, and racism, steadily moving toward the apocalyptic threshold of violence. The imminence and urgency of confrontation politics seem indeed to have abated. But it would be a miscalculation to suppose that this imminence and urgency have been overtaken by events. In the light of the coinherence of biblical and revolutionary politics, the discernment grows in pertinence and plausibility that a politics of confrontation is giving place to a reassessment of the relations between violence and power. The Marxian matrix of the revolutionary ferment of our times still offers the profoundest clues to the terms, the possibilities, and the limits of such a reassessment. The critical point of no return is whether the humanistic vision, commitment, *and* ideology of Marxism will significantly check and thus alter the bureaucratic-technocratic violation of that vision, commitment, and ideology; or whether the practice of violence as policy will deprive the revolutionary promises of our still very Marxian world of their realization. To put it another way: The critical issue before a world in revolution is whether the revolutionary movements in the vanguard will move beyond ideology and utopia toward an ideological implementation of the truth that makes humanity free. The *power of an ideology*, we have said, is the power of a humanizing vision to shape values and of values to shape the organization of a social order in which time and space make room for the freedom that being human takes.[76]

All truth, not least the truth that sets people free for being human in the world, functions ideologically, i.e., it exerts its power in and through *ad hoc* critical alterations of established patterns and structures. These "situationally transcendent ideas . . . never succeed *de facto* in the realization of their projected contents" (175). But in the power of the truth that sets humanity free, a transfiguration of the relations between ideology and utopia happens through the availability of "the living principle which links the development of utopia with the development of an existing order" (179). The dialectical reality of existence is disclosed, according to which "the existing order gives birth to utopias which in turn break the bonds of the existing order, leaving it free to develop in the direction of the next order of existence" (179). Everything depends upon whether and in how far revolutionary passion and purpose are transfigured as liberation—liberation *from* oppression and *for* being human in the world, liberation of *all* that being human in the world requires. *When the transfiguration of which revolutions are a sign, happens to revolutions in the making, revolution is liberated from itself for itself.* The *via dolorosa* bypasses the *via guillotina* and enters the *via humana humanorum* directly.[77] The risk of violence has overtaken its conversion into policy. An ideology of power has been displaced by the power of the truth that makes humanity free.

### 3. Beyond Immediacy and Historical Fulfillment Toward Eschatology

The power of the truth that makes humanity free is the power of a presence that liberates as it binds and binds as it liberates. Biblical politics identify this power with the presence of Jesus of Nazareth in the human story. The life and death, the resurrection and ascension, of Jesus Messiah disclose the God-man structure of reality that is experienced whenever and wherever time gives shape to space, people to things, persons to processes, and providence to history. In the precise, poetic imagery of W. H. Auden:

> ... because of His visitation, we may no longer desire God as if
> He were lacking: our redemption is no longer a question of pursuit
> but of surrender to Him who is always and everywhere present.

Because of this visitation, the sociological experience of existence "as a functioning social order . . . according to which people really act" (Mannheim) is transfigured as an experience of:

> ... Living Love replacing phantasy,
> (Of) Joy of life revealed in Love's creation;
> Our mood of longing turns to indication:
> Space is the Whom our loves are needed by,
> Time is our choice of How to love and Why.[78]

With this transfiguration, the coinherence of biblical and revolutionary politics as the human meaning of politics undergoes its severest strain. A credibility gap widens almost beyond bridging. Particularly formative of this gap is the obvious fact that with few exceptions revolutionaries have not only not been Christians, they have not even been theists. They have been atheists. Why this is the case, and what the case means, call for an inquiry of its own, which lies beyond the scope of the present exploration. One may, however, derive some clues to the meaning of this fact from the sociology of knowledge that at least would show that Christianity was the prevailing institutional mode of religious faith against which Marxism directed its atheistic rejection. Marxist atheism was and is an almost inevitable, if not necessary, response to the antirevolutionary ideology of the Church. The anticlericalism of the French Revolution must also be recalled in this connection, as well as the general weakening of the Christian Creed under the ascending creed of rational religion since the Enlightenment. The question whether atheism is a tactical or a substantive article of revolutionary faith does not, however, nullify a profounder consideration. This is the critical question of the roots and range of Marxist humanism.

A compound of biblical, positivistic, and broadly ethical and philosophical humanistic perspectives and convictions, Marxist humanism is at once an ally and an enemy of Christian faith. As an ally, it shares with Christianity the biblical indictment of existing patterns and structures of power, owing to the dehumanizing consequences of their self-justifying self-absolutization. As an enemy, it confronts biblical politics with a stern interrogation of the integrity of their humanistic commitments and with the insistently searching question whether God is not, after all, expendable to "the proper study of mankind" (Pope), which is humanity. The present exploration of the pertinence of Jesus Christ to the question of revolution is an attempt, not to dispose of the Marxist question, but to juxtapose to it a question of like depth and force. On the agenda of an ongoing Christian-Marxist dialogue must be the question of the possibility and limits of humanism. Biblical politics find a primal sin (the Fall) and a vicarious redeemer (Christ) indispensable to the actual and responsible consideration of this question. Hence the focus upon the messianic story, which is the gospel that Jesus of Nazareth is the Christ, whose very human presence is at the center where being and staying human in the world make all the difference in the world. He it is who, in and through his presence, sets power free in binding power to his new beginning for the whole of mankind; and in that bondage, liberates power from the futility of its self-justifying self-absolutization.[79]

There is, however, another and more immediately pressing factor in the widening credibility gap between biblical and revolutionary politics. This is a profoundly different understanding of the relation between reality and time.[80] It is well known that both in Marxist theory and in revolutionary practice, the tension between immediate and historical fulfillment of revolutionary commitments and goals has been a critical one. This tension focuses upon what Barrington Moore has called "the dilemma of power."[81] Revolutionary movements have their full share of perplexity over the question whether to seize the time at hand or to wait for the historical moment of fulfillment that is to be seized. Within the parameters defined by a development from historical to dialectical materialism, from the class struggle to the historical destiny of the proletariat, there is a relatively determinable calculus of possibilities and logistics at the disposal of these movements. The intersection of an eschatological time-sense with the historical sense of time and of timing can only intensify, the always already mounting tension in revolutionary planning and action between impatience and expectation. A perspective and practice informed by a providential destiny, whose moment of fulfillment converges upon a problematical present out of a critical future, almost inevitably seems to revolutionaries like a Trojan horse within the camp just when the decisive battle is about to begin. Thus an eschatological present must be the diametrical opposite of the moment of revolutionary realization. It is the moment of revolutionary betrayal.

The coinherence of biblical and revolutionary politics does not exclude the emergence of such a critical instant. It is the time of decision for a revolutionary movement whether those who are formed and informed by biblical politics are to be rejected as laggards and traitors to the revolutionary cause and destiny, or whether they are the liberating (saving) vanguard of the revolution itself. Similarly, such a critical instant is the time of decision for those who are formed and informed by biblical politics whether or not a revolutionary movement must be rejected because the leadership and membership of that movement have turned aside from the vocation and destiny of revolution and have converted the power of its ideology into an ideology of power, the risk of violence into violence as policy, and the iconoclasm proper to revolutionary theory and practice into the idolatry of a self-justifying absolutization of revolution itself. In such a case, the human meaning of politics would have been abandoned to a politics of dehumanization. The storming of the Bastille would have been drowned in the blood of a new Reign of Terror. The Revolution would have missed the moment to found freedom and have become a new Directoire.

On the other hand, the coinherence of biblical and revolutionary politics is the critical safeguard against such a critical moment of decision. The dynamics of this coinherence define the office of revolution as the preservation of the perspective and practice of biblical politics from an ideological sanctification of established power, which means that apostasy masquerades as faithfulness; and from a pious utopianism that abandons political involvement under the vain illusion that there can be salvation without justice. Conversely, the dynamics of coinherence define the office of biblical politics as the preservation of the commitment and destiny of revolutionary politics from the ideological self-justification that leads to a confusion of power and truth. There is no intrinsic warrant either in biblical or in revolutionary politics that guarantees each against a default upon the office of each, and thus against the rupture of their coinherence. There is, however, an eschatological warrant for the expectation that the moment of critical decision is the moment of transfiguration. The transfiguration means that both biblical and revolutionary politics have been overshadowed— "and with a whiteness no bleacher on earth could equal" (Mark 9:3)—by the presence of Jesus of Nazareth in the human story, whose power liberates as it binds and binds as it liberates. Should this "moment to found freedom" (Robespierre) have been missed, biblical and revolutionary politics alike would have succumbed to the *rabies humanorum* that, *furens et credens*, reenacts the primal crime of fratricide in a fallen world, and would afresh "have crucified the Lord of glory" (I Cor. 2:8).

## 4. Beyond Iconoclasm and Idolatry

The iconoclasm proper to revolutionary theory and practice is the unmasking of the false consciousness that generates the ideological self-justification and the utopian illusions that nourish the absolutization of power by established collectivities. It was Marx who first identified "false consciousness" as the source and bulwark of "the bourgeois illusion" in its ideological as well as in its utopian expressions. This Marxian discernment made possible a more comprehensive understanding of the theory and practice of ideology in Marxist analysis itself and paved the way for the rise and development of the sociology of knowledge.[82] The prophetic roots of biblical politics indicate that what Marx had come to identify as "false consciousness" had been anticipated in the vocation of Israel's prophets to unmask the false in distinction from the true "covenant consciousness" of that particular segment of humankind that had been singled out by divine election and providence for a messianic destiny. Thus the unmasking of "false consciousness" that revolutionary politics had learned from Marx to undertake as a basic iconoclastic responsibility, biblical politics had learned from Moses and the prophets and Jesus to undertake as a basically iconoclastic protest against apostasy. The apostasy that for Moses and the prophets is a violation of the first and second commandments (Exod. 20:2–4), and for Jesus is a violation of the love commandment (Deut. 6:5; Lev. 19:18), is paralleled in Marxism by the experience of alienation and dehumanization that the class struggle shows to be the lot of the proletariat at the hands of the bourgeoisie. Iconoclastic criticism and action are the means by which the messianic destiny of the covenant people and the historical destiny of socially, politically, and economically disenfranchised people are furthered toward their appointed human fulfillment.

There is, however, a fateful flaw in the Marxist analysis of false consciousness that has been overtaken by subsequent sociological theory, as indeed it had been anticipated in the prophetic protest against apostasy. Marxism overlooked the fact that revolutionary politics are as vulnerable to false consciousness as are the politics of established power. As Max Weber vividly put it: "The materialistic conception of history is not to be compared to a cab that one can enter or alight from at will, for once they enter it, even the revolutionaries are not free to leave it."[83] The failure of Marxist revolutionary analysis to discern and to allow the possibility of the corruption of revolutionary consciousness by false consciousness intensifies the peril to revolutionary realization, particularly on the threshold of violence, on which the liberation of revolution from its fate and for a future takes shape or is lost. Biblical politics, knowing that the iconoclastic protest against apostasy is as "inner-directed" as it is "outer-directed,"[84] are less apt to be surprised by the absolutization of apostasy in idolatrous self-justification than are revolutionary politics, highly sophisticated and competent in "seeing the mote in the brother's eye" while being totally blind to "the beam in (its) own eye" (Matt. 7:3–5 AV; parenthesis mine). It is the presence of this humanistic and hermeneutical "suspicion"[85] endemic to biblical politics and its endemic absence from revolutionary politics that make the rupture of their coinherence so crucial for the human meaning of politics. Unless the contrapuntal companion of iconoclasm is recognized as idolatry, the radicality of the apostasy and false consciousness by which biblical and revolutionary politics are constantly imperiled will be overlooked. Consequently, the code words of revolutionary promise and realization will have obscured the possibility and power of transfiguration. And another revolution will have failed. *Submission* and *silence* will have been abandoned as the rhetoric of disobedient surrender rather than have been embraced as that obedient waiting that overshadows revolutionary anxieties in a rebirth of wonder.[86]

Waiting for a rebirth of wonder will, of course, seem to revolutionaries like nothing so much as the abandonment of a revolutionary future to revolutionary failure. The coinherence of biblical and revolutionary politics makes available for such a moment of truth and point of no return a sustaining insight, as far-reaching toward a revolutionary future as is the critical discernment of the radical tension between iconoclasm and idolatry. This insight has to do with the *regenerative vocation of supplication* to which revolutionaries are called because of the historical and providential ordination of revolution itself. We come here upon another coincidental—or is it providential?—facet of the revolutionary story and of the story by which revolutions are saved. The coincidence is the ironical circumstance that the coinherence of biblical and revolutionary politics, which has been nurtured so largely by the encounter between Jesus and Marx in the Western Christian and political tradition, undergoes a significant amplification and correction from the side of the Eastern Church that nourished the people and culture within which Marxism was first tried out.

Orthodox Christianity has formed and informed a piety of supplication that is compounded of mystical and monastic, cosmic and
liturgical, responses to the messianic story, and directed toward a
paradigmatic practice of social regeneration.

In a distinguished, as yet unpublished, doctoral dissertation,
Professor Paul Valliere of Columbia University has shown, through
a study of the nineteenth-century Russian theologian M. M. Tareev,
how the piety of "glory in humiliation" was applied to the practice
of love where the action is. Tareev tried to arrive at a theology
and ethics of responsible involvement in social change.[87] Tareev
called for a Christianity that would not be "a subjective dream but
an objective historical force . . . an organized force with which
historical agents have to reckon" (244). The Christian presence in
history would differ from that of temporal powers insofar as it
"would enter into history, would cut into social reality—solely by
its actual moral force" (244). Again and again, Tareev's concerns
return to the theme of humility, which Dostoevski called "a great
force, the most powerful force of all." Valliere notes that "the
charm of the idea lies in the paradoxical union of humility, which
connotes powerlessness and weakness, with power" (245).[88]
Clearly, humility in this sense is different from the forces of individual or collective self-assertion against which it is directed.
"But the implication of the idea is that the two sorts of power
actually compete and that in a test of strength humility may even
overcome the other sort of power" (245). The critically significant
proposal of Valliere is that "*humiliation in its social and political
aspect is supplication*" (245; italics mine).

The explication of this proposal constitutes a phenomenology of
revolution in transfiguration. Valliere writes:

> Supplication establishes a relationship between the weak and
> the strong: it is the appeal of the weak to the strong, of the poor
> to the rich, of the alien to the citizen, of the citizen to the State,
> of the slave to the free, of the unfortunate to the happy. *Inequality
> is the context of supplication.* The remarkable dynamic of the
> relationship of supplication, however, lies in the fact that the weak,
> in spite of their weakness, are actually the ones who have the
> active, initiating role in the relationship, while the strong, in spite

of their strength, in spite of their resources for action, find themselves for once cast in the role of recipients, as if on trial. *Supplication is a testing of the powerful by the powerless.* Still more, when genuine supplication occurs, it effects an ironic reversal in the power relations of weak and strong as a result of the transcendent frame of reference to which the suppliant appeals. The suppliant does not speak merely for himself, for "the ego and its own," for in these terms he amounts to little; the supplicated one is immeasurably greater. The suppliant appeals to a sovereign ideal of justice or humanity or to the judgment or grace of God. His word is prophetic. The supplicated one can only speak for himself, which is a great weakness in the presence of the suppliant, however glorious it might be in a purely secular context. . . . It is this prophetic power of supplication that establishes the dialectic of power and powerlessness, thus putting the whole question of power into a new perspective. . . . *Supplication is historical action which bears witness to social and political theonomy.* (246, 248-49; italics mine)[89]

Ultimately, as well as penultimately, a revolutionary movement exhibits its transfiguration in the movement beyond iconoclasm and idolatry toward the regenerative vocation of supplication. *The revolutionaries are the suppliants of history.* As such, they are not only bearers of a righteousness not their own but the saving remnant of humanity in the world. This is why revolutionaries are nearer to the heart of God than are existing authorities, "the law-and-order people," as the letter to the Romans has reminded us.[90] As suppliants, revolutionaries bear concretely in their bodies, where the action is, "the dying of Jesus, so that the life of Jesus may also be manifested . . . in (their) mortal flesh" (II Cor. 4:10-11 RSV; parenthesis mine). The unmasking of power by truth is the power of weakness that shows itself as strength and turns the flank of existing power whose strength is exhibited as weakness. There are, indeed, "lives the executives/Know nothing of." The suppliants are the emissaries of that "other world" that "is like a jagged stone/Flying toward (the supplicated) out of the darkness."[91] Paradigmatically, the silence of the suppliant before the supplicated, as the confrontation between Jesus and Pilate has underlined, is that moment of maximum radicalization in which the liberating Name has been hidden in the power of a Presence that liberates as it binds and binds as it liberates.[92]

The transfiguration of revolution is that faithfulness of revolutionaries to the regenerative vocation of supplication that makes revolutions a principal "hiding place" through which, "*quasi in latebris*, God mercifully preserved his church" (Calvin). In the transfiguration of revolution, the transfigured people of God become the vanguard of a new and fulfilling human order in the world. By standing firm, the suppliants will win true life for themselves and ultimately for all mankind because their liberation is near. Ultimately, the regenerative vocation of supplication means that the coinherence of biblical and revolutionary politics has achieved a testimonial integrity that assures the victory of revolutionary promise and possibility over revolutionary fate.[93]. In that integrity, revolutionary politics will have kept biblical politics concretely human, and biblical politics will have kept revolutionary politics steadfast in vocational faithfulness and hope.

E. REVOLUTION AND RESURRECTION

As the argument of these pages has unfolded, an instructive congruence has emerged between a biblical understanding of the nature and function of paradigms and that put forward by Thomas Kuhn in his brilliant account of *The Structure of Scientific Revolutions*.[94] Although Kuhn's analysis concerns itself with the history and theory of science, his discussion of the paradigmatic relation between the way scientists go about their work (method) and "their incommensurable ways of seeing the world and of practicing science in it" (4) parallels the discussion of the paradigmatic relation between biblical ways of seeing the world and the revolutionary and human meaning of politics. If, as Kuhn observes, "scientific revolutions . . . are the tradition-shattering complements to the tradition-bound activity of normal science" (6), political revolutions are in similar case as regards "the tradition-bound activity" that occasions the tension between conservatism and radical criticism in social theory and practice. This congruence does not mean that science and politics are identical in theory and practice, differentiated only by the distinctive spheres of human investigation and activity. It means rather that in both spheres, perspectives and commitments are as decisive as are data when it comes to seeing the world and acting toward and in it. Of scientific, as of political revolutions, it may be said that

> each of them necessitated the community's rejection of one time-honored scientific (political) theory in favor of another incompatible with it. . . . And each transformed the scientific (political) imagination in ways that we shall ultimately need to describe as a transformation of the world within which scientific (political) work was done. . . . That is why the unexpected discovery is not simply factual in its import and why the scientist's (political) world is qualitatively transformed as well as quantitatively enriched by fundamental novelties of either fact or theory. (6-7; parentheses mine)

Kuhn uses the term *paradigm* to denote achievements in the theory and practice of science that are "sufficiently unprecedented to attract an enduring group of adherents away from competing modes of scientific activity" and "simultaneously . . . sufficiently open-ended to leave all sorts of problems for the redefined group of practitioners to resolve" (10). Paradigms "include law, theory, application and instrumentation together" and function as "models from which spring particular coherent traditions of scientific research" (10). The word *paradigm* is perhaps older in the theory and practice of biblical exegesis. In exegesis, a paradigm expresses an achievement in the making as regards a way of looking at life and of living it, whereas in science, a paradigm presupposes an achievement already accomplished. Nevertheless, the formative significance of paradigms for identifying and affecting the shape of things to come is the same. Of paradigms in both senses, it may be affirmed that

> when paradigms change, the world itself changes with them. Led by a new paradigm, scientists adopt new instruments and look in new places. Even more important, during revolutions scientists see new and different things when looking with familiar instruments in places they have looked before. It is rather as if the professional

community had been suddenly transported to another planet where familiar objects are seen in a different light and are joined by un-familiar ones as well. Of course, nothing of quite that sort does occur. . . . Nevertheless, paradigm changes do cause scientists to see the world of their research-engagements differently. In so far as their only recourse to that world is through what they see and do, we may want to say that after a revolution scientists are responding to a different world. (110)

A transfiguration has occurred, in the light and wake of which transformations and transvaluations follow.[95] In science, as in politics, paradigms are the clue to what is going on.

What is going on in paradigmatic discernment and formation is a response to the length and breadth and height and depth of human experience within which there is intellectual and cultural as well as social and political warrant for revolutionaries and non-revolutionaries alike to be open to the theonomous perspectives, possibilities, and commitments intrinsic to biblical politics. According to the coinherence of biblical and revolutionary politics, there is a providential pressure of reality upon human affairs, making time and space make room for the freedom and fulfillment that being human takes. It is this reality that radically alters the Church's time-honored addiction and allegiance to the existing authority of established collectivities, and requires an identification of the people of God with the suppliants of history. It is this reality also that radically alters the time-honored addiction and allegiance of revolutions to that criticism of religion that is practiced in the rejection of biblical faith and politics and hope, and requires an openness to formation by "the fellowship of Christ's sufferings and the power of his resurrection" (Phil. 3:10 RSV). "For it is in Christ that the complete being of the Godhead dwells. . . . Every power and authority in the universe is subject to him as Head. . . . On that cross he discarded the cosmic powers and authorities and led them as captives in his triumphal procession" (Col. 2:9, 11, 15). As the Transfiguration of Jesus was the prelude to his death and resurrection to free and fulfilled human life at the right hand of God in a world born anew in the power and presence of God, so the transfiguration of revolution is the prelude to the general resurrection

of "the whole human running race" to life in freedom and fulfillment in a world of God's new beginning and *in secula seculorum.*

>                    A world of made
>        is not a world of born—
>        ........................................
>        how should contented fools of fact envision
>        the mystery of freedom?
>        ........................................
>                                  yet, among
>        their loud exactitudes of imprecision,
>        ........................................
>        seeming's enough for slaves of space and time
>        —ours is the now and here of freedom. Come.[96]

# NOTES AND REFERENCES

## PREFACE

1. See Richard A. Falk, Gabriel Kolko, and Robert Jay Lifton (eds.), *Crimes of War* (New York: Random House, 1971), p. 447. On the crisis at Columbia see *The Cox Commission Report* (New York: Random House, 1968).

2. As one faces the pulpit in Memorial Church, the wall on the right lists the names of Harvard students and alumni who died in the service of the armed forces of the United States during World War II.

3. William Butler Yeats, "The Second Coming," in *The Collected Poems of W. B. Yeats* (New York: The Macmillan Company, 1951), pp. 184–85.

4. Blaise Pascal, *Pensées*, Fr. 555 (New York: Everyman Library, E. P. Dutton, 1931).

5. Professor George Williams of Harvard Divinity School has noted that it was a theological quarrel that launched "a disastrous pattern in American education." Although Williams notes that at Harvard "medicine preceded divinity in becoming a separate school within the Uni-

versity," he goes on to say that "the generalization remains valid that it is the withdrawal of theology from the center to the margin of the academic community which most seriously weakens the constitution of the University, in so far as it wishes to preserve its sense of corporate continuity with the past, to safeguard the place of the humanities quite apart from any argument as to their social utility, and to secure the corporate liberties of the Republic of Letters from unwarranted assignments from the State." So George Huntston Williams (ed.), *The Harvard Divinity School* (Boston: Beacon Press, 1954), pp. 5–6. In the aftermath of the events of 1968 one may perhaps be allowed to wonder what would happen in Harvard University if the Memorial Church came to be identified as "the center for confrontation," confrontation, that is, between "the influence of Jesus as the way, the truth, and the life" and "the highest interests of humanity." A sporadic hint of such a possibility actually occurred during the tumult in Harvard Yard in the spring of 1970 when a mediating group of concerned faculty and students took their first initiatives from the steps of Memorial Church. *O tempora! O mores!*

6. Herbert Marcuse, *One-Dimensional Man* (Boston: Beacon Press, 1964).

7. Francis Greenwood Peabody was Plummer Professor of Christian Morals at Harvard University from 1886–1913, and Dean of the Divinity School from 1901–7. The first series of the William Belden Noble Lectures was given in 1898, and Peabody was one of six distinguished divines to address themselves to the purpose of the lectureship. The series as a whole was published under the title *The Message of Christ to Manhood* (Boston: Houghton Mifflin Company, 1899). Peabody's lecture bore the title "The Message of Christ to Human Society." A year later Peabody elaborated the theme of his Noble Lecture in a widely read book, *Jesus Christ and the Social Question* (New York: The Macmillan Company, 1900). The passage quoted appears in the course of the Noble Lecture. See *The Message of Christ to Manhood*, pp. 56–57. Peabody cites the *Contemporary Review* of March 1896 that contained an article by W. Walsh with the flamboyant title "Jesus the Demagogue." In the same year the 23rd edition of Ernest Renan's *La Vie de Jésus* appeared in an English translation by J. H. Allen. In our time, Renan's view of Jesus, as in part anarchist, has been heralded in a higher-critical documentary study that makes Jesus an all but activist member of the Zealot party of his day. See S. G. F. Brandon, *Jesus and the Zealots* (New York: Charles Scribner's Sons, 1967). It is scarcely merely coincidental that in the years immediately surrounding 1968, lapel buttons announced that "Jesus was the first hippie."

8. "The revolution devouring its own children" is the way Vergniaud, the great orator of the Gironde, put it. See Hannah Arendt, *On Revolution* (New York: Viking Press, 4th printing, March 1947), p. 42.

9. The remark of Robespierre occurs in a speech of 5 February 1794. See Arendt, op. cit., pp. 42, 292. Hamilton wrote in *The Federalist* 11: "It belongs to us to vindicate the honor of the human race" against "these arrogant pretensions of the European." See *The Federalist Papers*, with an Introduction by Clinton Rossiter (New York: Mentor Books, New American Library, 1961), p. 91.

PART ONE
REVOLUTION, HUMANIZATION, AND STORY

*Chapter 1*

1. "Humanization" is not Arendt's word. She speaks instead of "the human condition," of "human affairs," of "a complete change of society." We use the word *humanization* to include this variety under a term that seeks to express at once the goal, the dynamics, and the happenings of the radical social change for which *revolution* is the political word. The present discussion is in considerable measure dependent upon Arendt's brilliant analysis of a highly complex and semantically confused phenomenon. She has brought impressive penetration and clarification to a social phenomenon whose passion, diversity, and subtlety almost defy specificity.

2. "Postscript to an Election," in the *New York Times*, Thursday, 14 November 1968, p. 46.

3. See further Amos 5, Isa. 9, 11, Jer. 49, Ezek. 34 *inter alia*. See also Hannah Arendt, *On Revolution* (New York: Viking Press, 4th printing, March 1947), p. 122, and further p. 258, pp. 279 ff.

4. Arendt, op. cit., pp. 40–41.

5. Ibid., p. 30. This possibility is rooted not only in the appeal to Machiavelli by the "men of the French Revolution" but also in Machiavelli's admiration for ancient Rome and in his frank espousal of violence in politics. Arendt quotes Robespierre: "The plan of the French Revolution was written large in the books . . . of Machiavelli" (*Oeuvres*, ed. Laponneraye, 1840, vol. 3, p. 540). In Arendt's view the espousal of violence is traceable to Machiavelli but not to the paradigm of Rome. On this point Robespierre followed Machiavelli into error "since in the Roman republic it was authority, not violence, which ruled the conduct of the citizens." Ibid., p. 30. As regards Hegel, Marcuse thinks that "the rise of fascism calls for a re-interpretation of Hegel's philosophy"; and he seeks to show not only that "Hegel's basic concepts are

hostile to tendencies that have led into Fascist theory and practice" but also "to a *positive philosophy* which undertook to subordinate reason to the authority of established fact." See Herbert Marcuse, *Reason and Revolution* (Boston: Beacon Press, 1960), Preface, p. xv. The Preface to the Original Edition (1941) is included in the 1960 edition.

6. Arendt, op. cit., chap. 6, pt. 4; and Marcuse, *Reason and Revolution*, pp. ix, x; also *One-Dimensional Man* (Boston: Beacon Press, 1964), pp. 256–57. In similar vein, Ernst Bloch's dictum is worth noting here: "*Das Faktum ist eine geschichtsfremde Klotzmaterie*" ("A fact is a clod-material alien to history"). *Das Prinzip Hoffnung*, Bd. I, 1959, p. 242; translation mine.

7. The allusion is to I Cor. 1:28.

8. Arendt, op. cit., p. 103; italics Arendt's.

9. See especially chap. 2.

10. James Madison, in *The Federalist* 10. See *The Federalist Papers*, with an Introduction by Clinton Rossiter (New York: Mentor Book, New American Library, 1961), p. 81; and Marcuse, *One-Dimensional Man*, pp. 254–55.

11. Marcuse, *One-Dimensional Man*, pp. 247, 228. Marcuse quotes A. N. Whitehead, *The Function of Reason* (Boston: Beacon Press, 1959), p. 5.

12. Arendt, op. cit., p. 85. See also pp. 53–81, 100–105. It might be instructive also to consider whether the dynamics of sociopolitical consciousness, which shift their human identifications from *les citoyens* to *le peuple* and from *le peuple* to *le monde*, exhibit also an emerging "anonymity-syndrome."

13. Ps. 145:4, Acts 2:11; also Pss. 48, 107. As regards "the far off" and "the nigh," see Acts 2:39.

14. See Plato, *Laws*, Bk. XI, especially 893–900, and 966, as translated by Benjamin Jowett (New York: Random House, 1937), vol. II, pp. 407–703.

15. Charles Cochrane, *Christianity and Classical Culture* (New York: Oxford University Press, 1940). The Preface states the theme.

16. Arendt, op. cit., p. 35. Arendt notes as her source for the whole discussion of "The Meaning of Revolution" (chap. 1), and apparently for this point also, a work by the German historian Karl Griewank, *Der neuzeitliche Revolutionsbegriff* (1955). In her judgment, this book, together with an earlier article (1952–53), "supersede all other literature on the subject." Op. cit., p. 291, nn. 24 and 30.

17. Ibid., p. 37. "The men of the revolutions" is Arendt's phrase repeatedly applied to the leaders of the French and American Revolutions. As for the language of revolution, particularly instructive are her etymological reminders concerning *revolution* (p. 35), *authority*

(p. 202), *state* (p. 291), *republic* (p. 208); and her *excursus* upon the human functions of this language, e.g., *compassion* and *pity* (pp. 69 ff., 85); *hypocrisy* and *wickedness* (p. 77); *authority* and *order* (pp. 178, 298).

18. Ibid., p. 15.
19. *Ibid.,* p. 41; italics Arendt's.


*Chapter 2*

20. Ludwig Wittgenstein, *Phliosophical Investigations* (Oxford: Blackwell, 1958), par. 23.

21. Arendt, op. cit., especially chap. 5. Lincoln is not referred to. His words are, of course, in the Gettysburg Address.

22. Hermann Hesse (1877–1962) wrote his novel *Demian* in a few months in 1917. It was published in German in 1919 and in English, not until 1965, by Harper & Row, and in paperback by Bantam Books in 1966. Herman Melville (1818–91) wrote his last novel, *Billy Budd,* in the late 1880s. It was first published in 1924. See Arendt, op. cit., p. 83, and preceding.

23. Hesse, *Demian*, Bantam Books Edition, p. 25.

24. See Arendt's reading of the Socratic endeavor: "To be sure, the polis, and the whole political realm, was a man-made space of appearances where human deeds and words were exposed to the public that testified to their reality and judged their worthiness." Op. cit., p. 98.

25. *"Dum condoret urbem!"* Virgil, *Aenead,* I, 5.

26. Quoted by Arendt, op. cit., p. 315, from Boorstin's *The Americans* (New York: Random House, 1958), p. 19.

27. *"Romanae stirpis origo,"* Aenead, XII, 166. *Stirpis* conveys the image of a stock or plant with its roots. *"Ilium in Italiam portans victosque Penatis,"* *Aenead,* I, 68.

28. The phrase is Arendt's; op. cit., p. 206. The phrase has acquired dialectical importance in revolutionary theory through the widening attention to the work of Ernst Bloch, whom one might describe as the most distinguished philosopher of revolution since Hegel. Bloch, like Marcuse, lies regrettably outside the purview of Arendt's study. Nevertheless, it is intriguing to consider what might happen to the revolutionary spirit of our times, if its vanguard should become as fascinated by *das Prinzip Hoffnung* as by "repressive tolerance." If the dialectical rigor and excitement of *das Noch-nicht*, as a category of revolutionary thought and action, should begin to come alongside the rigorous consistency with which Marcuse has reduced political options to the "poetry of the Great Refusal," "one-dimensional man" might be overtaken by the "open-endedness" of history in which he is involved. Indeed, there

are already signs that Marcuse is being overtaken by Bloch as the formative revolutionary theoretician of the present time.

29. Arendt takes no note of the first case while making much of the second. Her argument thus lacks an additional support that it might otherwise have had. See especially op. cit., pp. 156 ff., 212 ff.

30. The phrase is in Virgil's *Fourth Eclogue*, (P. Virgili Maronis, *Opera Omnia* I [London: A. J. Valpy, A.M.], line 5), and reads: *"Magnus ab integro saeclorum nascitur ordo"* ("The great order of times is born anew'). Arendt, op. cit., pp. 212–13. Virgil's poem has been widely regarded as a Roman parallel to the messianic expectation of salvation central to Hebrew-Christian thought and piety. Whether or not Virgil's vision of a new beginning is a historical analogue of Hebrew-Christian messianism has been debated anew by scholars in the mid-twentieth century. But this debate does not diminish the significance of Virgil's celebration of the founding of Rome as an earthly prototype of the Eternal City toward which human aspirations for a new and fulfilling order of personal and social freedom have been perennially directed.

31. I.e., in the English civil war, the French Revolution, and the October Revolution. Arendt, op. cit., pp. 156 ff.

32. Ibid., p. 161.

33. Ibid., p. 166.

34. Quoted by Arendt, op. cit., p. 184; parenthesis mine.

35. Ibid., p. 185.

36. Quoted by Arendt, op. cit., p. 55.

37. Ibid., pp. 213–14.

38. Alexander Hamilton, in *The Federalist* 1, op. cit., p. 33.

39. Arendt, op. cit., p. 19.

40. Ibid., p. 20.

41. Ibid., pp. 212–15. See Augustine, *De civitate dei* (*The City of God*), Bks. XI:1–6; XII:20; XVIII; XIX.

42. Arendt, op. cit., p. 309.

43. Ibid., p. 309.

44. John Rawls, *A Theory of Justice* (Cambridge: Harvard University Press, 1971), especially chap. 3. See further, below, pt. Four, chap. 12, B.

45. Arendt, op. cit., pp. 309–10; also Ola Winslow, *Meeting-House Hill*, 1630–1783 (New York: The Macmillan Company, 1952); especially chap. 14.

46. Arendt, op. cit., p. 159.

47. Ibid., pp. 159, 186.

48. Ibid., pp. 76–77; parenthesis mine.

49. Ibid., p. 77.

50. Ibid., p. 77.

PART TWO
A POLITICS OF CONFRONTATION

*Chapter 3*

1. See further Paul Lehmann, *Ideology and Incarnation* (Geneva: John Knox Association, 1962), pp. 18–23.

2. See above, pt. One, chap. 2, at n. 34.

3. See above, pt. One, chap. 1.

4. Herbert Marcuse, *Reason and Revolution* (Boston: Beacon Press, 1960), p. 35. It is instructive to recall in this connection that Marcuse and Richard Kroner, two widely influential interpreters of Hegel, widely differ over Hegel's relation to Christianity. Marcuse thinks that Hegel gradually, intrinsically, and inevitably left Christianity behind. Kroner thinks that Hegel, in going beyond Christianity, falsified it. But both Marcuse and Kroner stress the formative influence of Christianity upon Hegel's developing mind. See also Richard Kroner, *Von Kant bis Hegel*, 2 Bd., 1921–24; 2 Aufl. (Tübingen: J. C. B. Mohr, 1961); *Between Faith and Doubt* (New York: Oxford University Press, 1966); and Emil Fackenheim, *The Religious Dimension in Hegel's Thought* (Bloomington: Indiana University Press, 1967).

5. Marcuse, *Reason and Revolution*, p. 35.

6. T. S. Eliot, *Four Quartets: Burnt Norton*. See *Collected Poems 1909–62* (New York: Harcourt Brace and World, 1963), p. 177.

*Chapter 4*

7. It is astonishing really that Arendt's analysis of revolution ignores the continuing importance of the Marxian analysis of power for the understanding of revolutionary promise and frustration. She acknowledges Marx as "still the greatest pupil Hegel ever had" (*On Revolution* [New York: Viking Press, 4th printing, March 1947], p. 47) and "the greatest theorist the revolutions ever had" (55), but she regards the Marxian account of power as, at best, in contradiction with itself (269), at worst, as overtaken by events (17–18, 271 ff.). Again, it is the American development that she thinks has refuted Marxist analysis. The February Revolution of 1917 in Russia, and the Hungarian Revolution of 1956, seem to her to have been occasioned by the spontaneous eruption of councils or soviets that, "jealous of their capacity to act and to form opinion, were bound to discover the divisibility of power as well as its most important consequence, the necessary separation of powers in government" (271). Thus the councils confirm the American experience and expose the contradiction between Lenin's proclamation

of the Soviet Republic with "all power to the *soviets*," as he said, and his support of the Bolshevik party in its attempt to seize power (269).

It may be that Arendt has correctly assessed the ultimately minor role of the Marxist view of revolutionary power in the history of revolutions. But she can scarcely claim that the American federal achievement has already refuted the Marxian analysis. If this *were* the case, the social question (i.e., the poor) should be less prominent in the revolutionary ferment of our present time of troubles than it is. We agree with Arendt that the issue between the Soviet Union and the West is not "the disparity between two economic systems" but "the conflict between freedom and tyranny, between the institutions of liberty, born of the triumphant victory of a revolution, and the various forms of domination . . . which came in the aftermath of revolutionary defeat" (220). But contrary to Arendt, we judge that, especially after 21 October 1967, a federal government that knows only how to respond to the cries of dissent and rage with barbed wire and bayonets shows a faltering confidence in the victory alleged by Arendt to have been won, and an ominous indifference to the technological one-dimensionality by which the governments of the "federalist republican democracy" and the "people's democratic republics" are increasingly convergent, the one upon the other. If "political freedom, generally speaking, means the right 'to be a participator in government,' or it means nothing" (221), neither the American nor the Marxian revolutionary theory and practice can be so neatly assigned to victory or to defeat. At least, not yet!

8. Karl Marx, *Die deutsche Ideologie* (Berlin: Dietz, 1957), p. 35; translation mine. The treatise was first published in 1845–46, with Engels.

9. Quoted by Friedrich Engels, *Anti-Dühring*, 3rd German edition, translated by Emile Burns (New York: International Publishers, 1935), p. 209.

10. N. Lenin, *The State and Revolution*, in *Essential Works of Marxism*, with an Introduction and Commentaries by Arthur P. Mendel (New York: Bantam Books, 1961), pp. 193–94; italics Lenin's.

11. Herbert Marcuse, *One-Dimensional Man* (Boston: Beacon Press, 1964), p. xvi.

12. Frederick Engels, Introduction to Karl Marx's *The Civil War in France*. See Karl Marx, *Selected Works*, vol. II (New York: International Publishers, 1939), pp. 459–60. Quoted by Lenin, op. cit., pp. 163–64.

13. Lenin, op. cit., p. 149.

14. Arendt, op. cit., p. 284.

15. Lenin, op. cit., p. 130; italics Lenin's.

16. In a letter to Kugelman, on 12 April 1871, at the time of the

Paris Commune. Marx's word is *zerbrechen*, and the italics are his. See Marx, *Selected Works,* vol. II, pp. 528–29. Quoted by Lenin, op. cit., chap. 3.

17. Lenin, op. cit., p. 129.

18. Marcuse, *One-Dimensional Man,* pp. xii, xvi; parenthesis Marcuse's. The italicization of the word *political* is Marcuse's; the other italics are mine.

19. See Marcuse's essay in the small volume in which he has joined with Robert Wolff and Barrington Moore, called *A Critique of Tolerance* (Boston: Beacon Press, 1967).

Wolff, Moore, and Marcuse concur in the judgment that tolerance is at once a *sign* and a *symptom* of the fundamental relation between rationality and society. As a *sign*, the place and development of tolerance in society exhibit the possibility and effectiveness of the rational criticism of social, economic, and political institutions in achieving a humane relation between social power and human freedom. As a *symptom*, the place and function of tolerance in society exhibit the widening gulf between rational criticism and the institutional instruments of social reality, with the result that reason is increasingly abstracted from social reality, and impotent in shaping the social change required by a humane relation between social power and human freedom.

Especially pertinent to the concerns of these pages with the relation between religion (Christianity), on the one hand, and reason, revolution, and social change, on the other, is the consensus of the three authors on the limitations inherent in the capitalist, pluralist, and technological society of the present time. These limitations focus upon the rational application of social power to the achievement of the freedom to be and to stay human in the body politic. Wolff, however, does not appear to take account of the *explosive* character of the tension between the dynamics of social reality and a "pluralism . . . fatally blind to the evils which afflict the entire body politic" and obstructive of "consideration of precisely the sort of thoroughgoing social revisions which may be needed to remedy those evils" (52). This tension underlies the role of *violence* in the precipitation of revolutionary social change, about which Wolff is curiously silent. Moore and Marcuse, in their turn, do not hesitate to let the skeleton out of the closet. They reject the notion that revolutions accomplish no constructive social change, and thus also the notion that violence is an unmitigated social evil. Although Moore's adherence to the scientific application of reason to evidence, in the discovery of the structure and meaning of social reality (60), shares Wolff's view of the primacy of rationality in the dynamics of social reality, he is able and willing to specify "some of the conditions under which the resort to violence is justified in the name of freedom" (75), and even to lift the problem of violence to the level of a calculus of human suffering and degradation (76). But this is as far as Moore's critical scientific method of social analysis takes him. Ultimately, he draws back from assuming "the burden of responsibility" that he thinks must be assumed by "anyone who chooses to step outside the current frame-work of peaceful debate to advocate an extreme course" (77).

It is exactly "this burden of responsibility" that Marcuse unhesitatingly accepts. For Marcuse, the dynamics of social reality are the determining matrix of rationality. Consistent with his Marxian view of history, and of the progress of civilizaton, Marcuse argues that "the distinction between true and false tolerance can be made rationally on empirical grounds" (105). He notes that "with all the qualifications of a hypothesis based on an 'open' historical record, it seems that the violence emanating from the rebellion of the oppressed classes broke the historical continuum of injustice, cruelty and silence for a brief moment, brief but explosive enough to achieve an increase in the scope of freedom and justice, and a better and more equitable distribution of misery and oppression in a new social system . . ." (107). Consequently, "democratic" or "liberating tolerance" (109) may be distinguished from "repressive tolerance." The former is in theory and practice a revolutionary reappropriation of the humanizing bond between social power and human freedom. The latter is the prevailing theory and practice of the false consciousness that arises from a miscalculation of the relations between rationality and social reality and sustains the present economic and political order. These matters will concern us again in the concluding section of this book.

20. Barrington Moore, *Soviet Politics—the Dilemma of Power* (Cambridge: Harvard University Press, 1950). See especially chap. 3.

21. The discussion of the Marxist-Leninist account of power has been adapted from a fuller discussion in an essay on "Christian Theology in a World in Revolution," in Thomas Ogletree, *Openings for Marxist-Christian Dialogue* (Nashville: Abingdon Press, 1968), pp. 98–139.

22. Sister Corita, *Footnotes and Headlines* (New York: Herder & Herder, 1967), p. 2.


*Chapter 5*

23. Martin Luther, *Lectures on Romans,* newly translated and edited by Wilhelm Pauck in The Library of Christian Classics, vol. XV (Philadelphia: Westminster Press, 1961), p. 359.

24. Ibid., p. 359.

25. Anders Nygren, *Commentary on Romans* (Philadelphia: Muhlenberg Press, 1949), p. 426.

26. I am indebted for this suggestion to an unpublished paper by Bishop Bertil Gaertner of Gothenburg, Sweden, formerly Professor of New Testament at Princeton Theological Seminary. The sentence in quotation marks, including the parenthsis, is Gaertner's.

27. John Calvin, *Commentaries on the Epistle of Paul the Apostle to the Romans*, translated and edited by the Reverend John Owen (Grand Rapids: Wm. B. Eerdmans Publishing Co., 1948), p. 479.

28. John Calvin, *Institutes of the Christian Religion*, edited with an Introduction by John T. McNeill and translated by Ford Lewis Battles, in The Library of Christian Classics, vols. XX and XXI (Philadelphia: Westminster Press, 1960), IV, 20, 1. See also III, 19, 15: *"Duplex in homine regimen"* ("There is a twofold government in man") are Calvin's original words. For the original see P. Barth and G. Niesel, *Ioannis Calvini Opera Selecta* (München: Chr. Kaiser, 1931), vols. IV and V.

29. Ibid., IV, 20, 2.

30. Ibid., IV, 20, 8.

31. Ibid.; see editor's note, no. 20, p. 1493. *Ut tutius sit ac magis tolerabile plures tenere gubernacula.* Commenting on this phrase, McNeill remarks: "Calvin sees safety in numbers and . . . the word *plures* throws the emphasis not on the fewness of the ruling body but on the fact that numbers share the responsibility."

32. Ibid., IV, 20, 8.

33. Ibid., IV, 20, 31; and the related nn. 53, 54, in which McNeill shows how much Calvin was a child of his time, yet how far he struggled to go in the matter of resistance to authority.

34. Calvin, *Commentaries on Romans*, p. 479. See also Introduction to McNeill edition of the text of *Institutes*, especially sec. XIV.

35. Calvin, *Institutes*, IV, 20, 32.

36. Calvin, *Commentaries on Romans*, pp. 480, 484.

37. Calvin, *Institutes*, IV, 20, 10. McNeill gives the source of the saying as Dio Cassius, *Nerva*, Epitome of Bk. lxviii, 3.

38. See above, pt. One, chap. 2.

39. See above, at n. 26.

40. Karl Barth, *Der Römerbrief*, fuenfter Abdruck der neuen Bearbeitung (München: Kaiser, 1929), p. 477; translation mine. Barth is commenting upon Rom. 13:1–8. We shall be following Barth in the new few paragraphs; where he is quoted directly, pagination will be indicated in parentheses, translation mine.

41. Ibid., pp. 476–77; italics and parentheses Barth's.

42. Ibid., p. 472. English parentheses contain words supplied by

translator to facilitate English rendering. Apropos of this point, and with its characteristic epigrammatic crispness, the first edition of the *Römerbrief* says: *"Lasst die in euch vorhandene Spannung nicht verpuffen in voreiligen Explosionen. . . . Der Geist klopft nicht an den harten Schalen der Politik herum"* ("Do not let the tension present within you blow up in premature explosions. . . . The Spirit does not knock idly against the hard shells of politics"; translation mine"). See edition by G. A. Baeschlin (Bern, 1919), p. 387.

43. Tom Wicker, "In the Nation: The Nightmare in Chicago," in the *New York Times,* Tuesday, 3 December 1968, p. 46.

44. See above, pt. One, chap. 2.

45. My New Testament colleague, J. Louis Martyn, has made an illuminating suggestion with regard to the word *submit* in the interpretation of this passage. The Greek text reads at v. 1: *"Pasa psyche exousiais uperchousais upotassestho"* ("Let everyone submit to the higher authorities"). Or, as the NEB puts it: "Everyone must submit to the supreme authorities."

Martyn derives from the verb *upotasso* and the grammatical construction of the text the striking nuance that would properly read: *order yourselves under* instead of *submit.* Two matters may be briefly mentioned as particularly pertinent to the point under discussion. (1) The aorist passive subjunctive: *upotassestho* underlines an indeterminate course of behavior in view of the concrete orderliness and variety of the givenness of daily existence as creation and as penultimate to a world that is coming to be and is, indeed, already breaking in. The hortatory subjunctive is a kind of gentle imperative reminding Christians that they are to act with due regard to the way things really are. (2) More significant perhaps is Paul's use in this place of *upotasso* instead of his more usual *upakouo.* The latter expresses the clear and unqualified obedience that the Christian owes to God. The displacement of *upakouo* by *upotasso* in this passage is not accidental. It deliberately underlines Paul's point that there is a significant difference between the obedience due to God and the obedience due to the state. The former is unexceptional: *upakoe* (the noun related to *upakouo*) means obedience due to God. *Upotage* (the noun related to *upotasso*), however, means that realistic regard for the daily *tagmata* (ordinances, arrangements, orderings) that simply are the context of humanness in the world. See further to this point Ernst Käsemann, "Grundsätzliches zur Interpretation von Römer 13," in *Exegetische Versuche und Besinnungen,* Bd. 2 (Göttingen: Vandenhoeck u. Ruprecht, 1964), especially, pp. 214-15.

*Upotassestho,* translated as *order yourself under* instead of *submit,* rescues *submit* and *submission* from their time-honored association with passivity and gives them a meaning at once more active and purposed. Thus revolutionaries, in *ordering themselves under,* are *not* passively submitting to established power. On the contrary, they are expressing the power intrinsic to their historical vocation and destiny: the power of the human reality of freedom in an unmasking action that exposes who the bearers of true freedom in the world are. Although I have followed the usual wording, the use of the word *submit* in this discussion really means: *order yourselves under.* Once again, I have been instructed and enriched by Martyn's work.

46. Lawrence Ferlinghetti, "I Am Waiting," in *Coney Island of the Mind* (New York: New Directions, paperback 1958; London: Hutchinson, 1959).

47. John 18:36–37.

48. Adolf Schlatter, *Der Evangelist Johannes* (Stuttgart: Calwer Vereinsbuchandlung, 1930); Rudolf Bultmann, *Das Evangelium des Johannes,* 13 Aufl. (Göttingen: Vandenhoeck u. Ruprecht, 1953).

49. Bultmann, op. cit., pp. 505 ff.

50. Indeed, the phrase runs through the Book of Judges almost as a refrain. See 17:6; 18:1; 19:1.

51. On the other hand, I Sam. 10, and related passages, are positive about the kingship. See G. von Rad, *Theologie des Alten Testamentes,* Bd. I (München: Chr. Kaiser, 1962), pt. I, C, pp. 48–82. A summary passage strikingly exhibits the crisis of kingship in Israel owing to the tension between historical and religious factors in the development of structures of power, and also to the tension between the operation of power and the authority of power. Von Rad writes:

". . . With the formation of the state, the Jahweh cult entered a crisis, in which, once again of course, the issue concerned its existence or non-existence. A structural change was under way which brought with it a wholly new center of gravity and new relations of the parts to the whole. It is unnecessary to add that faith in Jahweh entered in this way into wholly new dangers and temptations, against which it had to arm itself; indeed, which it first had to learn to recognize; for this also required a certain time. This crisis, occasioned by the formation of the state, was the more severe because accompanied by the still continuing crisis of the conquest. . . . Living together with the Canaanites was now intensified, and closer political contacts with neighboring peoples led to a stronger influence of foreign cults upon Israel." (P. 61; translation mine, punctuation altered for clarity.)

The role of Israel's experience in shaping American institutions makes this assessment of the ambiguity of kingship and the crisis of authority astonishingly contemporary. See Reinhold Niebuhr's timely and forceful article: "The King's Chapel and the King's Court," in *Christianity and Crisis,* vol. XXXIX, no. 14, 4 August 1969, pp. 211–12.

52. Von Rad, op. cit., p. 53; translation and parenthesis mine.

53. Compare Charles Cochrane, *Christianity and Classical Culture* (New York: Oxford University Press, 1957).

54. Bultmann, op. cit., p. 505; translation mine. Here a Lutheran doctrine of "the two kingdoms" seems to show through, which our own revised reading of Rom. 13 has tried to avoid.

55. "But because in this man," says Bultmann, " a claim other than human is encountered, the mythological *elelytha eis ton kosmon* is paradoxically tied together with the *gegennemai*. The origin—and also the reality *(Wesen)*—of this man is not of this world but he has 'come' into this world." Bultmann, op. cit., p. 507; parentheses mine.

56. Bultmann, op. cit., p. 507.

57. The phrase in parenthesis has been inserted, owing to an adaptation of the passage without altering the meaning of the original.

58. Bultmann, op. cit., p. 333; parentheses mine.

59. Ibid., p. 333; translation, italics, and parentheses mine. I have ventured both to appropriate and to interpolate Bultmann here. Literally, *Haltung* means both position and attitude, a stance and a style. Since the "position" and "attitude" are thought of as formative or shaping of a way of looking at life *and* of living it, *Haltung* has been translated *lifestyle*.

60. As regards the movement from the question of truth to the question of identity to the question of authority, John 18:33–37; 19:8–11 are particularly instructive.

61. So, in paraphrase, Eberhard Bethge, *Dietrich Bonhoeffer* (München: Chr. Kaiser, 1968), p. 759; Eng. p. 579; translation mine. The point is at least as old as the second-century Letter to Diognetus, the course of which may be paraphrased by saying that *Christians are those who uphold the fabric of the world*. It is scarcely possible to overlook the congruence of both remarks with the confrontation between Jesus and Pilate. For the Letter to Diognetus see *Early Christian Fathers,* The Library of Christian Classics, vol. I (Philadelphia: Westminster Press, 1953), pp. 205–24.

62. Compare Rom. 12:2 RSV.

63. James Reston, writing in the *New York Times* of Sunday, 16 August 1970, in a piece called "The Nixon Technique," strikingly, though scarcely intentionally, describes the operation of this skepticism as regards the relation of the question of truth to the question of power. He writes:

"The Nixon Administration has been around long enough now so that, if you don't mind getting in a fight, you can generalize about its personality. It is cautious, tidy, industrious, and monumentally dull. It is a flypaper for efficient, well-meaning bores. It is engaged in some of the most exciting conflicts in the history of the Republic, but it has somehow managed to reduce them all to the level of a mathematical equation. It has all the figures but very little poetry. . . . What is missing, I think, is the capacity of the President and his associates to convey to the people or even to themselves a deep feeling of conviction. . . . (The problems) are so difficult that they cannot be proved but have to rely upon goodwill and faith. . . . Still, the Nixon Administration has not established that sense of trust or affection necessary to carry the country through the terrible ambiguous issues that often have to be taken on the personal word of the President. It is trying to be both moral and slick at the same time . . ." (parenthesis mine).

What is truth? *Pilatus sic!*

64. Christopher Fry, *The Dark Is Light Enough* (New York: Oxford University Press, 1954). John 1:5.

65. Adolf Schlatter, op. cit., pp. 340–41; translation mine.

66. Sister Corita. See above, pt. Two, chap. 4, and n. 22.

67. Bultmann, op. cit., pp. 511, 513; translation, parentheses, and italics mine.

68. See above, Preface, at n. 9.

69. It is instructive to ponder over the translation variants. We follow here the JB, which has expressly maintained the parallelism: "Here/Here." The NEB, with perhaps greater philological precision, says; "Behold the Man!" (v. 5). But at v. 14, the NEB says: "Here is your king!" On the other hand, when Pilate initiates the climax of the paradigm in v. 4, the NEB says: "Here he is; I am bringing him out . . . ," whereas the RSV says: "Behold, I am bringing him out" etc. The variants could, of course, signal nothing more than what *The New Yorker* might report in a "Which Expletive Particle Is Which?" department. Or—and this is more likely—the variants may derive from the interchangeable nuances in the use of *idou* and *ide* in Semitic idiom (see Bultmann, op. cit., p. 66, n. 2; p. 510, n. 5). Our own venture is the suggestion that, whatever may be the linguistics of the matter, the sense of the passage is of a climactic happening that focuses upon the concrete presence of Jesus and upon the reality question that his presence raises as regards the state and its claim to authority and power. "Here he is!" "Here is the man!" "Here is your king!" is the language of direct and inescapable *indication*. "Behold" has the same idiomatic force, but sounds archaic in our ears. A threefold repetition of "Here!" would be an appropriate redundancy reinforcing the irony with which the radicality of the power confrontation is expressed.

70. In a Lenton sermon on John 18:38—19:5, and another on John 19:10–14. The first was preached on 27 February 1529; the second was preached two weeks later, on 13 March 1529. *"Sehet, welch ein Mensch! . . . Sehet, das ist euer König!"* About the first *indication* Luther remarks: "As though he (Pilate) wanted to say: may he have mercy on you! . . . It is an unexcellable witness of the truth on behalf of Jesus that Pilate declares not once, but two or three, yes, six times, that an injustice is being done to Jesus. . . . This is how the gospel is condemned. This is how we are condemned. We are reported to possess the sort of teaching about which even our enemies must admit: 'It is probably true but we do not wish to tolerate it because this one or that one teaches it and because it is preached in this place!' " About the second *indication* Luther remarks: "So you see how Pilate, the unbeliever (*der Heide*), identifies two reasons why they should be ashamed. He wants to say: If you were right, you would have to attack me with weapons and drive me and all those beholden to me out of town because I crucify your king. Instead, you drive ahead (*fahrt zu*) and pressure me to do away with him whom I should prefer to release. . . . The mouth of the unbeliever, Pilate, must cry throughout the whole world, that Christ was killed though he was innocent. . . . It is the same today. Those who should protect the gospel, persecute the gospel in persecuting those who are eager to hear it." See *D. Martin Luthers Evangelien-Auslegung*, edited by Edwin Muehlhaupt, pt. V (Göttingen: Vandenhoeck u. Ruprecht, 1950), 60–61; translation and parentheses mine.

71. See Matt. 27:29 f; Mark 15:19. Perhaps the author of the Fourth Gospel wants to underscore the contrast between the trappings of power without authority and the authority of power without the trappings of power. The description expresses with ultimate irony the power of weakness.

72. So Bultmann, op. cit., p. 510; translation mine.

73. According to the New Testament, Jesus is the herald in the "present age" of the "age to come." As for "the man for others," Eberhard Bethge has suggested that in Bonhoeffer's thought, the phrase is best understood as a christological title. See Eberhard Bethge, "Bonhoeffer's Christology and His 'Religionless Christianity,' " in *Union Seminary Quarterly Review*, vol. XXIII, no. 1, Fall 1967, p. 75. This essay was later published together with the other papers presented to a Bonhoeffer Colloquium at Union Theological Seminary, New York, in a small volume edited by Peter Vorkink, *Bonhoeffer in a World Come of Age* (Philadelphia: Fortress Press, 1969).

74. The phrases are those of Jean-Paul Sartre's play, *Huis Clos,* and of Charles Cochrane, op. cit., Preface. See above, pt. One, ch. 1, n. 15.

75. Harvey Cox, *The Secular City* (New York: The Macmillan Company, 1965, rev. ed. 1966), p. 132.

76. Bultmann, op. cit., p. 514; translation mine.

77. Friedrich Nietzsche, *Thus Spake Zarathustra,* Prologue, 3–6. See *The Philoshophy of Nietzsche* (New York: The Modern Library, Random House, n.d.).

78. Harvey Cox has imaginatively analyzed the contrast between the immolation of the future and the immolation of the past as twin responses to the freedom for celebration of the human offered by the Harlequin symbol of the Christ. The creative relation between festivity and piety (religion) is thus corrupted by fantasy and by fanaticism and celebration is turned into immolation. Although Cox's attention is directed toward the oncoming generation and its revolutionary passions and hopes, the distinction that he has drawn between the immolation of the future by the past and of the past by the future seems to us applicable also to the contrast between the revolutionary and the Establishment. Jesus as the Christ is the immolated victim all around. See Harvey Cox, *The Feast of Fools,* The William Belden Noble Lectures of 1967 (Cambridge: Harvard University Press, 1970), chaps. 2 and 10.

79. See I Pet. 2:24 AV; also Isa. 53, Lev. 16, Dan. 7. The problems involved in relating these various designations, except for Leviticus, to Jesus have been instructively sorted out and clarified by Reginald Fuller, in *The Foundations of New Testament Christology* (New York: Charles Scribner's Sons, 1965).

80. Schlatter, op. cit., p. 344; translation and parentheses mine. Schlatter's remark is noteworthy also as suggesting the limits as well as the sensitivity of humanism when a power confrontation has been radicalized by the arrival of its moment of truth.

81. See Plato, *Phaedo,* 63, d, e. See *The Collected Dialogues of Plato,* including the *Letters,* edited by Edith Hamilton and Huntington Cairns, Bollingen Series, LXXI (Princeton: Princeton University Press, 1961).

82. See Bultmann, op. cit., pp. 514–15.

83. See above, pt. One, chap. 1.

84. As, for example, in a radio news report on 14 September 1970, noting a remark of former Vice President Agnew in a speech at Las Vegas, Nevada, in which he warned that adults receptive to rock music were consciously or unconsciously supporting the music of the drug-culture, and thus that culture itself. The more subtle the lie, the more transparently the crucifixion of truth by power is under way. This is the truth made room for in the silence of Jesus.

85. Bultmann, op. cit., p. 515; translation and parenthesis mine. Saigon, Prague, Suez, Cambodia, Watts, Jackson, Kent State—*sic!*

86. Schlatter, op. cit., p. 345; translation and parenthesis mine.

87. Ibid., p. 241 (on John 10:24); translation and parentheses mine. See also Josh. 24:14 ff.; I Kings 18:21.

88. "The Sound of Silence," words and music by Paul Simon (New York: Charing Cross Music Co., 1964).

89. Dan. 1—5; and especially 5:24–31. *"Mene, mene, tekel u-pharsin,"* the graffiti said. And the meaning was: "God has numbered the days of your kingdom and brought it to an end; you have been weighed in the balance and found wanting; and your kingdom has been divided and given to the Medes and Persians."

90. So ex-President Richard M. Nixon in the course of a telecast to the American people announcing his order sending ground troops into Cambodia in a "military incursion." The address was given on Thursday, 30 April 1970, and reported in the *New York Times* on Friday, 1 May 1970. As reported in the *Times,* the President's address included the following sentence: "If when the chips are down, the world's most powerful nation—the United States of America—acts like a pitiful helpless giant, the forces of totalitarianism and anarchy will threaten free nations and free institutions throughout the world."

91. One of them indeed recently signaled in a preface, "To the Reader," the connection between identity and involvement, between prophetic messianism and the quest for authentic humanity:

"I am a part-time novelist who happens also to be a part-time Christian because part of the time seems to be the most I can manage to live out my faith: . . . but most of the time I am indistinguishable from the rest of the herd that jostles and snuffles at the great trough of life. Part-time novelist, Christian, pig.

"That is who I am. Who you are I do not know, and yet perhaps I know something. I know that like me you wake up each morning to a day that you must somehow live, to a self that you must somehow be, and to a mystery that you cannot fathom if only the mystery of your own life. . . . Think of these pages as *graffiti* maybe, and where I have scratched upon in a public place my longings and loves, my grievances and indecencies, be reminded of your own. In that way at least, we can hold a kind of converse. And there is always some comfort in knowing that Kilroy also was here." Frederick Buechner, *The Alphabet of Grace* (New York: Seabury Press, 1970), pp. vii, viii; italics Buechner's.

92. See the *New York Times,* Sunday, 10 May 1970, in a front-page report of President Nixon's impromptu early-morning visit and conversation with students demonstrating for peace in Vietnam on the steps of the Lincoln Memorial.

93. Reported by I. F. Stone in his *Bi-Weekly* of 18 May 1970.

94. I.e., the Constitution. As reported in the *New York Times*, Wednesday, 20 May 1970, p. 19.

95. As reported in the *New York Times*, Monday, 11 May 1970, pp. 1, 23.

96. W. H. Auden, *City Without Walls* (New York: Random House, 1966), p. 51.

97. Robert Bly, *The Light Around the Body* (New York: Harper & Row, 1967), p. 9.

98. "Descent into hell"—the phrase is from the *Symbolum Romanum* (Apostles' Creed), which in its second article tells in staccato fashion the story of Jesus as Son of God and Son of Man.

99. Gen. 37–50; especially chaps. 37 and 39 f.

100. Jürgen Moltmann, *Religion, Revolution, and the Future* (New York: Charles Scribner's Sons, 1969), pp. 146–47; parenthesis mine.

101. The aphorism of Che Guevara is cited by Moltmann and amended in accordance with a modification of a student in Tübingen University. The student said: "The duty of every revolution is to bring about love" (ibid., p. 147). In the context of the present discussion, we have ventured to appropriate with appreciation the student's formulation and to alter it slightly.

PART THREE
A POLITICS OF TRANSFIGURATION

*Chapter 6*

1. Reinhold Niebuhr, *Moral Man and Immoral Society* (New York: Charles Scribner's Sons, 1932), chaps. 9, 10; *An Interpretation of Christian Ethics* (New York: Harper & Brothers, 1935), chaps. 1, 8; *Beyond Tragedy* (New York: Charles Scribner's Sons, 1937), chap. 10; *Faith and History* (New York: Charles Scribner's Sons, 1949), chap. 8; among others. In these passages, the sense is plain, although the phrase is not used.

2. The case of the Catonsville Nine has to do with an act of civil disobedience, committed in Catonsville, Maryland (a suburb of Baltimore), on 17 May 1968 by seven men and two women, all Roman Catholics, including priests, among these the now widely known Berrigan brothers, Philip and Daniel. For a concise and informative account of the incident and the subsequent trial, see Francine du Plessix Gray, *Divine Disobedience* (New York: Random House, 1969).

3. Søren Kierkegaard, *Fear and Trembling*, with Introduction and Notes by Walter Lowrie (Princeton: Princeton University Press, 1952), Problem I.

4. On 24 September 1969 eight persons were brought to trial under a dubious federal law prohibiting interstate travel for the purpose of inciting to riot. The accused persons were alleged to have violated this statute at the time of the National Convention of the Democratic Party in Chicago in late August 1968. They were charged with organizing a mass demonstration against certain proceedings of the Convention, notably the question of the party's position on the war in Indo-China and the seating of the Democratic Freedom Party's delegation, an elected civil rights group from Mississippi. Furthermore, these eight persons were well known for their activities in the peace movement, in civil rights struggles, and, in the case of some of them, in the Black Panther Party. On 18 February 1970, the defendants were acquitted of the conspiracy charge after being held without bail for many months. The verdict of the jury finding six of them guilty of certain other charges was appealed and pending the disposition of the appeal, the defendants were at liberty on bail. For a full-length account of the trial, its background, process, and significance, see Jason Epstein, *The Great Conspiracy Trial* (New York: Random House, 1970).

Mr. Epstein's account is in the nature of the case incomplete. It may be supplemented by noting that on 21 November 1972, the Seventh Circuit Court of Appeals reversed the convictions and found in favor of the defendants. It must also be noted that according to *World Almanac 1974* (New York: Newspaper Enterprise Association), the trial concerned the *Chicago Seven*, of whom *five* were convicted of crossing state lines with the intent to incite to riot and subsequently won an appeal. The disparity between the *Almanac*'s record and this account is due to the circumstance that Judge Hoffman ordered the trial of Bobby Seale separated from that of the other seven. Hence the court record refers to the trial of the *Chicago Seven* and to the *five* who won their appeal. Two of the eight (or seven) were acquitted of the charges initially brought. The defendants themselves, however, continued to adhere to the sign of their comradeship in the struggle against incivility and injustice by referring to themselves as the Chicago Eight. The difference between the *Almanac* account (pp. 870, 981) and the account here, based upon press accounts at the time of the trial and Epstein's book, nicely confirms the point under discussion.

5. The address was delivered before a meeting of the American Law Institute, in Washington, D.C., on 18 May 1971. See the *New York Times*, Wednesday, 19 May 1971.

6. The allusion is to I Cor. 1:28–29 RSV.

7. Dietrich Bonhoeffer, *Letters and Papers from Prison* (London: SCM Press, rev. ed., 1967), p. 155.

8. The well-known definition of war by the Prussian General Karl von Clausewitz (1780–1831) in his book *Vom Kriege*. See Karl von

Clausewitz, *War, Politics and Power,* translated and edited with an Introduction by Edward M. Collins (Chicago: Henry Regnery Co., 3rd printing, 1967), p. 83.

9. See above, pt. Two, chap. 4, and n. 19.

10. Dan. 5:27–28. The whole chapter is an instructive, symbolic assessment of the perils and limits, the sources and responsibilities, of power in human affairs. It concerns the succession to Nebuchadnezzar's power of Belshazzar, his son. The time would have been toward the close of the third century B.C. Of Nebuchadnezzar we read that "the Most High God (had given him) a kingdom and power and glory and majesty; and because of this power which he gave him, all peoples and nations of every language trembled before him and were afraid. . . . But when he became haughty and presumptuous, he was deposed from his royal throne and his glory was taken from him. He was banished from the society of men . . ." (Dan. 5:18–21; parenthesis mine). Of Belshazzar we are told: "But you, his son Belshazzar, did not humble your heart, although you knew all this. You have set yourself up against the Lord of heaven. . . . and you have not given glory to God, in whose charge is your very breath and in whose hands are all your ways" (vv. 22–24). The handwriting on the palace wall is, accordingly, to be read as follows: "*Mene, mene, tekel up-pharsin.* Here is the interpretation: *mene:* God has numbered the days of your kingdom and brought it to an end; *tekel:* you have been weighed in the balance and found wanting; *u-pharsin:* and your kingdom has been divided and given to the Medes and the Persians" (vv. 25–29). The grim conclusion is: "That very night Belshazzar king of the Chaldeans was slain, and Darius the Mede took the kingdom, being then sixty-two years old" (vv. 30–31). The chapter calls to mind also the banquet hall in the palace of Macbeth (Act III, Scene 4). See also above, pt. Two, chap. 5, n. 89.

11. II Cor. 4:6. For a suggestive account of the relation between doxological language (glory-language) to ordinary language, and of both to the interpretation of historical events, see Dietrich Ritschl, *Memory and Hope* (New York: The Macmillan Company, 1967), chap. 4, and especially pp. 174–76.

12. See above, pt. One, chap. 2, n. 34; also pt. Two, chap. 3, n. 2.

*Chapter 7*

13. Matt. 17:1-7. The parallels are: Mark 9:2–8; Luke 9:28–36. The Fourth Gospel has no account of the Transfiguration. It is noteworthy, however, that in 12:27–33 there is a passage, in a context similar to the Synoptic contexts of the Transfiguration, that describes Jesus' agony of spirit on the verge of his suffering and glorification.

14. Gerhard Kittel (ed.), *Theologisches Wörterbuch zum Neuen Testament,* vol. IV (Stuttgart: W. Kohlhammer), p. 764.

15. Ibid., p. 765.

16. I am indebted to my colleague, Walter Wink, for instructive conversation on the dynamics and the difficulties of the Transfiguration pericope in itself and in its bearing upon the present discussion. Wink has also drawn my attention to an unpublished paper by Martin H. Scharlemann prepared for a seminar under the direction of Professor W. D. Davies. The paper deals with the Transfiguration in Synoptic Criticism and in particular with the interpretation of it in Heinrich Baltensweiler's *Die Verklärung Jesu* (Zürich: Zwingli Verlag, 1959). In addition, Wink has made available to me a reprint of an article by Margaret E. Thrall on "Elijah and Moses in Mark's Account of the Transfiguration," in *New Testament Studies* 16, no. 4, July 1970 (London: Cambridge University Press), pp. 305–17, together with an excerpt from his own book on John the Baptist, dealing with the suffering of Elijah in Mark 9:9–13, *John the Baptist in the Gospel Tradition* (London: Cambridge University Press, 1968). These discussions —together with Adolf Schlatter, *Das Evangelium nach Matthaeus* (Stuttgart: Calwer, 1953); Rudolf Bultmann, *Geschichte der Synoptischen Tradition* (Göttingen: Vandenhoeck u. Ruprecht, 1957); Martin Luther, *Evangelien-Auslegung, zweiter Teil, das Matthaeus —Evangelium* (herausgegeben von Lic. Erwin Muelhaupt [Göttingen: Vandenhoeck u. Ruprecht, 1939]); John Calvin, *Harmony of the Evangelists,* vol. II (Grand Rapids: Wm. B. Eerdmans Publishing Co., 1949); and the remarkable exegetical and dogmatic discussion of the Transfiguration by Karl Barth, *Kirchliche Dogmatik,* III/2 (Zürich-Zollikon: Evangelischer Verlag, 1948), par. 47, 1, pp. 574–82—underlie the paradigmatic interpretation of the Transfiguration ventured in these pages.

To return to the objectivity of what is going on, it may be noted that *horama* may and often does mean a vision, for instance, of the kind described in Isa. 6. Likewise, *ophthe* seems to be a special word for the appearance of a vision. But when in Acts 7:26 Moses is said to have *appeared* ("come up, on," NEB) to two of his fellow Israelites in a fight; or again, in I Kings 3:16, when two women are said to have been *presented* ("came into the king's presence," NEB) to Solomon, *ophthen ophthesan* is used. Similarly, in Acts 7:31, in a reference to Moses' seeing the burning bush, *horama* stands alone as in the Transfiguration account, and denotes a perception of an object. *Eidon* is a second aorist form of *orao,* the force of which is: "I have surely seen." Of these usages, Scharlemann has made me aware.

17. Also called in the Eastern Church the "Feast of Taborion" because of the widely held notion, at least since Cyril of Jerusalem

(Cathechesis XII ,16 Migne, P.L., 33, 745), that the "high mountain" referred to in the pericope was Mt. Tabor. Luther still allowed the identification, on the poetic basis of Ps. 89:13 (op. cit., p. 574), although Calvin does not trouble to mention it. That Mt. Tabor was actually the Mount of Transfiguration is highly improbable, and no longer maintained in our time. The Roman and Protestant Churches, however, concur with the Eastern Church in according to the Transfiguration a place in the liturgical calendar. The Feast falls between Trinity and Advent, on August 6.

18. Origen seems to be the first in the literature of the later Church to give attention to the Transfiguration. See *In Matthaeum*, XII, 31 (Migne, PG, 13, 1052); and in the earlier *Contra Celsum*, II, 64, IV, 16 (Migne, PG, XI, 896 f., 1048).

19. So Scharlemann. For Bultmann, see his article in *Religion in Geschichte und Gegenwart* (RGG), 2nd ed., vol. II (1928), 418–22; also *Geschichte der Synoptischen Tradition*, pp. 280 f.

20. The principal variations are: (1) as to time: Mark and Matthew say six days, Luke says eight days; (2) as to the disciples: Matthew identifies John as "the brother of James," Mark and Luke do not; (3) as to Moses and Elijah: Mark names Elijah first, Luke follows the order of Matthew; (4) Luke omits the command to silence after the event; (5) there is some difference in the account of the experience of awe, as well as in the whiteness of the Transfiguration. Except for the variation regarding Moses and Elijah, these variations need not concern us here, since we are not mainly engaged in a text-critical discussion.

21. *Prodromal*, from the Greek *prodromos* (n.), *prodromeuo* (v.): running forward with headlong speed. On *prodromal* see Crane Brinton, *The Anatomy of Revolution* (New York: Random House, 1952), pp. 17–18:

> "In the society during the generation or so before the outbreak of revolution, in the old regime, there will be found signs of the coming disturbance. Rigorously, these signs are not quite symptoms, since when the symptoms are fully enough developed the disease is already present. They are perhaps better described as *prodromal* signs, indications to the very keen diagnostician that a disease is on its way, but not yet sufficiently developed to be the disease. Then comes a time when the full symptoms disclose themselves, and when we can say the fever of revolution has begun." Italics Brinton's.

22. In view of the consensus among the Synoptic authors, one could make the paradigmatic point with reference to the text of any one of them. We have chosen the Matthean account partly because Matthew follows Mark, the earliest account, more closely than does Luke; and

partly because the cadences are more resonant with the drama of the messianic focus and setting of the Transfiguration paradigm.

23. Martin Luther, op. cit., pp. 575–76; translation and italics mine, English parentheses Luther's. German words in parentheses are Luther's and suggest a variant rendering, i.e., *Heil:* salvation; *Dreieinigkeit:* the tri-unity of the whole Godhead; *Einfloessen:* literally, "streaming in," thus, perhaps, indwelling. The renderings chosen are intended to suggest the dynamics and concreteness of what is going on.

24. Dietrich Bonhoeffer, *Nachfolge* (München: Chr. Kaiser, 1964), p. 35; translation mine. In a subsequent chapter Bonhoeffer goes on to say:

> "The concrete call of Jesus and single-minded obedience have their irrevocable meaning. In this way, Jesus calls into the concrete situation in which he can be believed; he calls concretely and wishes to be understood in this way because he knows that only in concrete obedience will man be free to believe." Ibid., p. 57; translation mine.

25. Quoted by the *Christian Century* in its eulogy after Niebuhr's death on 2 June 1971. Vol. LXXXVIII, no. 24, 16 June 1971, p. 735.

26. Reinhold Niebuhr, *Moral Man and Immoral Society* (New York: Charles Scribner's Sons, 1934), p. 4.

27. Aristotle, *Nichomachean Ethics,* Loeb Classical Library (New York: G. P. Putnam's Sons, 1926), Bk. I, i, ii; also *Politics*, Bk. I, 2, Bk. II, 1. For a fuller discussion of the point see Paul Lehmann, *Ethics in a Christian Context* (New York: Harper & Row, 1963), pp. 82–86.

28. See above, pt. Three, chap. 7, n. 6.

29. See Mark 9:9, 11–13. "On their way down the mountain, . . . they put a question to him: 'Why do our teachers say that Elijah must come first?' He replied, 'Yes, Elijah does come first to set everything right. . . . However, I tell you, Elijah has already come and they have worked their will upon him, as the scriptures say of him.' " See also Walter Wink, op. cit., pp. 13–17.

30. So Wink, op. cit., p. 15.

31. So Thrall, "Elijah and Moses in Mark's Account of the Transfiguration" (above, n. 16), the time with which the narratives begin, i.e., "six days later," in Mark 9:2 and 16:1; Jesus' garments become shining white (9:3) and the messenger has a white robe (16:5); the prominence of Peter in both narratives; and others.

32. Ibid., p. 311; parenthesis mine.

33. Ibid., p. 314.

34. Wink, op. cit., p. 16.

35. Calvin, op. cit., pp. 310, 308–9.

36. Wink, op. cit., p. 15.

37. Gerhard von Rad, *Theologie des Alten Testamentes* (München:

Chr. Kaiser, Bd. I, 1962), p. 382; translation and parentheses mine.

38. Ibid., pp. 382–84. The citation is on pp. 383–84; translation mine. The phrase "Here, too, reciprocity is called for: "is my attempt to express von Rad's words, which are: *"Auch hier gilt das gleiche:".* The phrase "demonstrations of salvation" is my way of expressing von Rad's *"Heilserweisungen." Heil* is a word often connoting *salvation.* But in English the precise force of the German, which is closer to the Latin *salus,* is lost. In a fundamental sense, *salvation* means *wholeness* or *health.* So *Heil* means literally *healing.* Thus the somewhat colorless English term *salvation*—colorless, at least, in these days—really means, in the context of the Old Testament, the experience of human wholeness in and through all the various relationships in which people are involved with one another. This experience is the gift of Jahweh, and what Jahweh is chiefly up to in the world.

39. See Ludwig Koehler, *Old Testament Theology,* translated by A. S. Todd (Philadelphia: Westminster Press, 1957), pp. 30–35.

40. See above, pt. Two, chap. 5, A: the discussion of Rom. 13.

41. James Russell Lowell's romantic lines ("The Vision of Sir Launfal," Prelude to pt. I, st. 5) are themselves at best a transfiguration of the messianic age in foretaste. If at its worst, romanticism is a too eager foreshortening of the time; at its best, it prefigures the deep longings for immediacy, transquility, and joy that also belong to human wholeness and fulfillment. On this mountain the inauguration of this wholeness and fulfillment had begun, but the travail had not yet been overcome. The transfiguration "here" belonged meanwhile to the proleptic conjunction of Jesus and John the Baptist in the comradeship of suffering and death. Compare Matt. 17:5, 6 with Matt. 3:9–10, 16–17.

42. Heinrich Baltensweiler, "Die Verklärung Jesu," in *Abhandlungen zur Theologie des Alten und Neuen Testamentes,* no. 33, Zürich: Zwingli-Verlag, 1959), pp. 69–82. See Thrall, op. cit., p. 307.

43. Baltensweiler, op. cit., pp. 50, 51.

44. Scharlemann has noted in his unpublished paper (p. 22) that the Sukkoth seventh-day ritual was taken so literally by the members of the Qumran community that they withdrew to the desert of Judah to await, and thereby even to hasten, the coming of the end. I am indebted to my Old Testament colleague, George Landes, for drawing my attention to 1QS VIII, 12–16, in which the Hebrew version of Isa. 40:3 is cited as a paradigm of withdrawal for the members of the Qumran community. The Isaiah passage reads:

"There is a voice that cries:
Prepare a road for the Lord through the wilderness,
clear a highway across the desert for our God."

See 1 QS VIII, 12–16, published in *The Dead Sea Scrolls of St. Mark's Monastery*, vol. II, Fascicle 2; edited by Millar Burrows (New Haven: American Schools of Oriental Research, 1951).

45. The question of the Zealots has recently been raised with persuasive (if not finally convincing) and provocative (not easily dismissable) freshness by S. G. F. Brandon, *Jesus and the Zealots* (Manchester, England: Manchester University Press, 1967). Although not expressly a reply to Brandon's vigorous attempt to bring Jesus into touch with the revolutionary movements of our day by a historical reappraisal of his relations with the revolutionary movements of his own day, Oscar Cullmann has addressed himself to this very attempt in a succinct and instructive treatment of *Jesus and the Revolutionaries*, translated from the German by Gareth Putnam (New York: Harper & Row, 1970). Brandon goes very far toward connecting Jesus with the Zealots, who were the revolutionary fanatics of his day, without, however, asserting that Jesus was actually a member of the party (pp. 245 ff.). Cullmann, on the other hand, tries very hard to show that Jesus was by no means either apolitical or politically conservative, without, however, being able to avoid the conclusion that Jesus' ultimate expectation of radical social change through God's act, not man's, led him, penultimately, to work for social reforms through individual conversion (pp. 56–57). "Should not our reform-minded age," Cullmann asks, "exactly in the interest of reforms take entirely seriously Jesus' exhortation to a conversion of the heart, which also includes nonviolence?" (56). Our own suggestion is that a consideration of the paradigmatic political significance of the Transfiguration points to a third possibility—not between, but beyond political fanaticism and political amelioration.

46. It is probable that Judas, surnamed Iscariot, was so named because he was a Sicarius, i.e., a carrier of *sicae* (daggers), which especially marked the presence and practice of the Zealots.

47. So Cullmann, op. cit., p. 58.

48. See above, pt. Three, chap. 7, A, n. 16.

49. Just as there is a difference between *humanistic messianism* and *messianic humanism*. Indeed, *humansitic messianism* is a secularized version, chiefly Marxist, of the religiously inspired political messianism of the Zealots. For a fuller discussion of this distinction and its relation to Marxism, see Paul Lehmann, *Ideology and Incarnation,* op. cit., pp. 18 ff.; also Rubem Alves, *A Theology of Human Hope* (Washington: Corpus Publications, 1969), especially pt. 3, "The Historicity of Freedom," pp. 85–101.

50. Cullmann, op. cit., p. 12.

51. Ibid., p. 45; italics Cullmann's, parenthesis mine.

52. Ibid., pp. 58–59; parenthesis mine.

53. Ibid., p. 55. The translation seems to be in error here, an oversight that I have ventured to correct. Cullmann could scarcely have written: "It is certain that for centuries Jesus did not reckon with the continuation of the world." The proposed emendation seems more consonant with the context and course of Cullmann's argument.

54. Calvin, op. cit., p. 307; italics Calvin's. The comment refers to Matt. 16:28, which concludes a conversation of Jesus with his disciples about the coming of the kingdom and the sufferings attendant upon it.

## Chapter 8

55. Lewis Carroll, *The Annotated Alice,* with an Introduction and Notes by Martin Gardner (New York: Bramhall House, 1960), *Through the Looking-Glass,* pp. 209–10; italics Carroll's. About this passage Gardner notes that it "has probably been quoted more often (usually in reference to rapidly changing political situations) than any other passage in the *Alice* books" (p. 210).

56. Crane Brinton, *The Anatomy of Revolution* (New York: Random House, 1952), p. 36; italics Brinton's. The reference in the passage is to G. S. Pettee, *The Process of Revolution* (New York: Harper & Brothers, 1938).

57. See above, pt. One, chap. 1; and pt. Two, chap. 3. This assertion does not contradict the view expressed by Che Guevara in *La Guerra de Guerrillas* (*Guerrilla Warfare* [New York: Random House, 1965]) and Régis Debray in "The Theory of the Foco" (in Régis Debray, *Revolution in the Revolution?* [New York: Grove Press, 1967], p. 22n.) that "one need not always wait for all conditions favorable to revolution to be present; the insurrection itself can create them" (Che). When Robin Blackburn declares with reference to the *foco theory* that "Modern revolutions do not happen; they are made; . . . ", he goes too far. (See his Introduction to Régis Debray, *Strategy for Revolution* [London: Jonathan Cape, 1970], p. 11; italics Blackburn's.) He goes too far, it seems to me, because Che himself has noted that *some,* though not *all* conditions for revolutionary action must be present before initiatives can fruitfully be taken. The question of "making a revolution" is the question of strategy; and the question of strategy presupposes that a revolutionary situation has *happened.* Indeed, all revolutionary movements have been haunted by the dilemma between waiting too long and failing to wait long enough. Thus, to return to Blackburn's point, the difference between "modern revolutions" and their predecessors is not the difference between revolutions that *happen* and revolutions that are made but rather that modern revolutions, i.e.,

from Lenin onward, have steadily emphasized and refined the strategies by which revolutionary conditions already present may be effectively made the most of.

Rosenstock-Huessy has instructively suggested that at the core of the dynamics of revolution a paradoxical relation between *happen* and *made* may be discerned. He reminds us of Danton's remark: "We have not made the revolution, the revolution has made us"; and in the same context, he notes the convergence of revolutionary upheaval and revolutionary consciousness, of "heaven and earth" (Hegel), of "objective event" and "subjective idea" intrinsic to the "rhythm of revolution" as "total revolution." See Eugen Rosenstock-Huessy, *Die europaeischen Revolutionen* (Jena: Eugen Diederichs, 1931), chaps. 1 and 2, but especially pp. 13–15; translation mine.

58. See Brinton, op. cit., Introduction, especially at pp. 13, 17.

59. Dürrenmatt, "Kafka in the News," in the *New York Times,* Sunday, 11 July 1971, sec. 4, p. 11.

60. *The Pentagon Papers,* as published by the *New York Times,* collated by Neil Sheehan, Hedrick Smith, E. W. Kenworthy, and Fox Butterfield (New York: Bantam Books, July 1971).

61. I. F. Stone, *Bi-Weekly,* 28 June 1971; parenthesis mine.

62. "The war of all against all," Thomas Hobbes, *Elementa philos. de cive, Praefatio ad lectores* (Amsterdam 1668), pp. 12–13. Compare also Plato, *Laws,* Bk. I, 625, e, 626, a.

63. "Whom God wishes to destroy, he first makes mad." See the Scholia to Sophocles' *Antigone,* V, 620. The Latin has abbreviated in paraphrase the Greek original from an unknown Greek tragedian. A brief account of the story of this widely known and oft-cited epigram is in Georg Büchmann, *Geflügelte Worte,* 31 Aufl. (Berlin: Hande u. Spenorsche Verlagsbuchhandlung, 1964), pp. 475–76. "A new order of times." See Arendt. op. cit., chap. 5.

64. Ralph L. Stavins, "Kennedy's War," in the *New York Review of Books,* vol. XVII, no. 1, 22 July 1971, p. 23. MAAG is the Military Assistance Advisory Group that had been in South Vietnam since the mid-fifties. General Maxwell Taylor, Chairman, Joint Chiefs of Staff, 1962–64, and Professor Walt W. Rostow, Presidential Assistant for National Security, 1961, on leave from MIT, were special advisers to the President at the White House. Their mission to examine the feasibility of dispatching U.S. troops to Vietnam was authorized by President Kennedy on 11 October 1961.

*Chapter 9*

65. See Bibliographical Appendix below.

66. The quoted phrase is Rosenstock-Huessy's. So also are its im-

plications, except that in my view, Marxism presupposes as well as *"needs* a broader framework," which it is both able and unable to supply. See Eugen Rosenstock-Huessy, *Out of Revolution* (New York: W. Morrow & Co., 1938, repr. Norwich, Vt.: Argo Books, 1969), pp. 107–8; italics mine.

67. See above, pt. Two, chaps. 3 and 4.

68. See above, pt. One, chap. 2.

69. Rosenstock-Huessy, op. cit., especially chaps. 1 and 15–17; Jean-François Revel, *Ni Marx ni Jésus* (Paris: Editions Robert Laffont, 1970), especially pp. 89 ff. Revel has written an extended précis of the argument of his book, soon to be published in English translation, in *Saturday Review*, vol. LIV, no. 30, 24 July 1971, pp. 14–31. The English translation is by J. F. Bernard, with an Afterword by Mary McCarthy. See Jean-François Revel, *Without Marx or Jesus: The New American Revolution Has Begun* (New York: Doubleday, 1971).

70. Rosenstock notes that a century after Molière's *Le bourgeois gentilhomme* (1688), Beaumarchais wrote *The Marriage of Figaro* (1778), in which the concluding chorus apostrophizes Voltaire. It was the very year of Voltaire's death. The chorus runs:

> *"Par le sort de la naissance*
> *L'un est roi l'autre berger,*
> *Le hazard fit leur distance:*
> *L'esprit seul peut tout changer.*
> *De vingt rois que l'on encense*
> *Le trépas brise l'autel,*
> *Et Voltaire est immortel!"*

> ("In the end, it is by birth
> That one is king, the other shepherd,
> Chance creates the distance:
> Only the spirit can change all this.
> Twenty kings whom one has incensed
> Are robbed by death of the smoke from the altar,
> And Voltaire is immortal!")

See Rosenstock, op. cit., p. 309; translation mine. *"Revolution denkt also auf eine Art Geschichtsökonomie . . ."* (p. 3).

71. Revel, op. cit., p. 89: *"De la première à la deuxième Révolution mondiale."*

72. Ibid., p. 92; translation and parentheses mine.

73. Ibid., p. 93; translation mine.

74. Rosenstock-Huessy, op. cit., p. 5; translation and parenthesis mine.

75. Revel, op. cit., pp. 18–19. The passage is a close paraphrase, not

a direct quotation. Revel's enthusiastic conviction that these character-istics mark the United States as the center and the pioneer of "the new world revolution" (*la nouvelle révolution mondiale*) is reminiscent of Hannah Arendt's view of the American Revolution as the only suc-cessful revolution, referred to in pt. One, chap. 2, above. Whether Revel's case is as plausible as it is enthusiastic need not concern us directly at this point. To foreclose it would be a kind of prejudgment of a historical future. We simply note the corroboration of Arendt's positive estimate of the first American Revolution by Revel's account of the conditions of the second American Revolution. We regard both assessments, especially in their convergence, as competent and instruc-tive analyses of revolutionary experience and possibility. They pose an option that no responsible account of revolution could wish to ignore. Whether Arendt's celebration of Madison's discovery of "the federal principle . . . whose principle was neither expansion nor conquest but the further combination of powers" (op. cit., p. 167), and Revel's celebration of "the capacity of innovation," of the correlation of legality and protest, even violent protest in the United States (op. cit., pp. 137, 250), are consonant with their own acknowledgments of the ambiguity of power and with the dynamics of American power today, must be left open also.

The present exploration of the question of revolution is rather more sanguine than celebrant of the revolutionary promise of American power. It is scarcely merely coincidental that ex-President Nixon's an-nouncement of 14 July 1971 that he planned to visit Peking stirred remembrances of the Stalin-Hitler pact of August 1939. (See the *New York Times* of Thursday, 15 July 1971, and the article on "The Chi-nese Strategy" by Harry Schwartz, in the *Times* of Monday, 19 July 1971.) *Newsweek* of 26 July 1971 includes in its extensive discussion of the Nixon China visit a favorable assessment by John King Fair-bank of Harvard. But then, this is not the first time Fairbank has been available as a "court prophet" on call. My view is that the dy-namics of American society and the exercise of American power, far from being in the forefront of "the new global revolution," on the contrary are in the forefront of counterrevolutionary Establishment politics, under judgment and rejection by the dynamics of messianic politics. Of this judgment and rejection, current revolutionary experi-ence is a vanguard sign. Revel's anticlericalism, like ex-President Nix-on's Grahamesque pietism, ill equip them for the sensibilities and subtleties of a politics of transfiguration. Revel, at all events, should be read together with *Crimes of War*, edited by Richard Falk, Gabriel Kolko, and Robert Jay Lifton (New York: Random House, 1971), and a book by Joyce and Gabriel Kolko, *The Limits of Power: The*

*World and United States Foreign Policy, 1945–1954* (New York: Harper & Row, 1972).

76. Brinton, op. cit. chap. 9.

77. I am not unaware of the primary referentiality of the original, which is to the people who belong to the covenant tradition, heirs of Abraham, in the "old Israel" and in the "new Israel." But just as these people came into this heritage by adoption rather than by descent, so they are called to be the vanguard in the world of the destiny and promises of God's covenant with all mankind. The "chosen race," the "royal priesthood," and "dedicated nation," are marked by steadfast adherence to the Word and signs of Promise in face of utmost suffering and oppression; and in this steadfastness they are "called in revolution" for the vindication and liberation of all peoples whose human wholeness and fulfillment are being denied to them. See Bruce Morgan, *Called in Revolution* (New York: The Student Volunteer Movement for Christian Missions, 1956), especially chaps. 3 and 6, the discussion of the church "as a demonstration of the way God works *in the world* when he sets about to reconcile *the world* to himself" (pp. 98 ff.). See also Barth, *Kirchliche Dogmatik,* II/2, pp. 473–75, on the relations between election, church, and all mankind in the light of I Pet. 2:9.

78. Revel, op. cit., p. 255; translation mine. Somewhere in the course of Rosenstock-Huessy's account of the European revolutions there is a deprecation of Confucius in similar vein. This, too, is regrettable as a continuation of Western bias especially in a book about "total upheaval." On the other hand, it illustrates the difference between French and German forms of hauteur. If the former is biting, the latter is vain; which may be the difference between Voltaire and Goethe. In both cases, the condescension is arrogant and shows that a total upheaval in Western mentality is long overdue.

79. Mao Tze-tung, *On the New Stage: The Sinification of Marxism;* and *Reform in Learning: The Party and Literature*; in Stuart R. Schram, *The Political Thought of Mao Tse-tung* (New York: Frederick A. Praeger, 1963), pp. 113, 116.

80. "I thank thee, Father, that thou hast hidden these things from the wise and understanding and revealed them unto babes" (Matt. 11:25 RSV). Or: "He also said to the people: 'When you see cloud banking up in the west, you say at once, "It is going to rain," and rain it does. And when the wind is from the south, you say, "There will be a heat-wave," and there is. What hypocrites you are! You know how to interpret the appearance of earth and sky; how is it you cannot interpret this fateful hour?'" (Luke 12:54–56).

81. "So they took him (i.e., Paul the Apostle) and brought him to Mars' Hill and said, 'May we know what this new doctrine is that

you propound? You are introducing ideas that sound strange to us, and we should like to know what they mean.' (Now the Athenians in general and the foreigners there had no time for anything but talking or hearing about the latest novelty.) . . . When they heard about the raising of the dead, some scoffed; and others said, 'We will hear you on this subject some other time' " (Acts 17:19–20, 32–33; first parenthesis mine).

Or: "Scripture says, 'I will destroy the wisdom of the wise, and bring to nothing the cleverness of the clever.' Where is your wise man now, your man of learning, or your subtle debater—limited, all of them, to this passing age?" (I Cor. 1:20).

82. See Robert Payne, *Portrait of a Revolutionary: Mao Tse-tung* (New York: Abelard-Schuman, 1950), p. 261 *et seq.*

In an annotated bibliography concerning Mao Tse-tung, which Stuart R. Schram has appended to his authoritative selections from Mao's writings on political thought (see Bibliographical Appendix below), attention has been called to the sympathetic and competent but less than careful interpretation of Mao offered by Payne's *Portrait*. According to Schram, Payne's "instinctive understanding of the personality of Mao, whom he has met," is marred by "many errors of detail" (p. 311). My indebtedness to Payne's *Portrait*, however, is occasioned by the *human* reality of Mao that this "instinctive understanding" paints. I have tried to keep "the detail" to a minimum, and to include only matters that, in assisting the human purpose of their use, are not substantively contradicted either by the brief but authoritative introduction to *The Political Thought of Mao Tse-tung*, or by the subsequently published full-length biography that Schram has written. See Stuart R. Schram, *Mao Tse-tung* (Baltimore: Penguin Books, 1966. Meanwhile, a revised edition of *The Political Thought of Mao Tse-tung* has been published by Frederick A. Praeger in New York, 1970.

83. Payne, op. cit., p. 272. *Tso Chuan* refers to *The Traditions of the Tso*, a widely known Chinese classic of the sixth century B.C., and attributed to Confucius. It gives an account of persons and events of a slightly earlier period in the form of history. See further to the matter, Edwin O. Reischauer and John Fairbank, *East Asia: The Great Tradition* (Boston: Houghton Mifflin Co., 1958), pp. 67, 68. *All Men Are Brothers* is an ancient Chinese novel, read by Mao at the age of ten, and particularly influential upon him.

84. Quoted by Payne, op. cit., p. 294.

85. Ibid., p. 153.

86. Ibid., p. 147.

87. Ibid., p. 37.

88. Ibid., pp. 40 ff.

89. According to Bartlett, this bit of Americana was written by one

David Everett (1770–1813) for a school declamation for Ephraim H. Farrar, aged seven, of Ipswich, New Hampshire (1791). See *Book of Quotations* (Boston: Little, Brown, 14th edition, 1968), p. 507a.

90. Compare Oswald Spengler, *The Decline of the West* (New York: A. A. Knopf, 1932); and further, Lewis Mumford, *Technics and Human Development: The Myth of the Machine,* vol. I (New York: Harcourt Brace and World, 1967), p. 294; also *The Pentagon of Power: The Myth of the Machine,* vol. II (New York: Harcourt Brace and World, 1970), especially chap. 2.

91. Mao Tse-tung, *The Chinese Revolution and the Communist Party,* published in Chinese 15 November 1939; translated into English 22 March 1949. The passage is quoted from a pamphlet in mimeographed form, available in the Missionary Research Library of Union Theological Seminary, New York. The pages are: 7, 8, 6, 9, 18, 1; parentheses mine. The parenthesis (x) follows a sentence from Mao's speech of 1 February 1942, already cited. The passage comes from a section entitled "What is a Marxist Theoretician?" See Schram, *Mao Tse-tung,* p. 120.

92. In 1939, Mao's estimate was that 80 percent of China's 450 million people were peasants. So the pamphlet just cited, at pp. 1, 13.

93. So Alan Levy, "On Audenstrasse—In the Autumn of the Age of Anxiety," in the *New York Times Magazine,* Sunday, 8 August 1971, p. 42.

94. For the first text see Schram, *The Political Thought of Mao Tse-tung,* II, E, *On Contradiction,* 1937; III, E, *The Relation Between External and Internal Contradictions,* 1930; VII, A, 1–3, *Nonantagonistic Contradictions,* 1937; *Contradictions under Socialism,* 1956; and the extract from the well-known speech of 27 February 1957, *On the Correct Handling of Contradictions Among the People.* The text *On Guerrilla Warfare* is available in a translation with Introduction by Brigadier General Samuel B. Griffith, USMC (Ret.) (New York: Frederick A. Praeger, 1961). Specific use of these texts will be indicated in parentheses following. A separate edition of *On Contradiction* is also available (New York: International Publishers, 1953).

95. Schram, *The Political Thought of Mao Tse-tung,* pp. 44 and 3.

96. Marx's words are: *"die Waffe der Kritik kann allerdings die Kritik der Waffen nicht ersetzen. . . ."* See Karl Marx, *Zur Kritik der Hegelschen Rechtsphilosophie (Towards the Criticism of Hegel's Philosophy of Right),* in *Historisch kritische Gesamtausgabe.* Werke, Schriften, Briefe, herausgegeben von D. Rjanov (Frankfurt a.M: Marx-Engels Archiv, 1927), Erste Abt., Bd. 1, Erster Halb., s. 614; translation mine.

97. Marcuse, *A Critique of Tolerance,* with Robert Paul Wolff and

Barrington Moore, Jr., p. 83. See also above, pt. Two, chap. 4, and n. 19.

98. Ibid., pp. 81, 84, 85; italics and parentheses Marcuse's.

99. See Schram, *The Political Thought of Mao Tse-tung*, V, H, p. 209. A more popular version of the same runs: "Power comes out of the barrel of a gun."

100. ". . . In the largest sense, the Cultural Revolution was a spirited attempt to rectify the thinking of the entire nation through an all-out assault on 'revisionism,' capitalism, and undesirable strands of tradition, and a campaign to foster a proletarian culture." See James Chieh Hsiung, *Ideology and Practice* (New York: Praeger Publishers, 1970), p. 217. Hsiung has given a clear and succinct account of the Cultural Revolution in chap. 12 of his book. The account shows the connection between Mao's epigram about the "hundred flowers" and the ensuing struggle between Mao's passion for the ideological formation by means of Marxist-Leninist orthodoxy, of a revolutionary consciousness among the masses of the Chinese people, and the revisionist elements in his own government, and to an uncertain extent in the army. The two principal years of the Cultural Revolution (1965–66, 1966–67) are a particularly vivid instance of the tension between the power of an ideology and an ideology of power in a revolution, and of the crisis in which a revolutionary seizure of power sooner or later finds itself, a crisis marked by a fateful turn in the road, either toward the consummation of revolutionary goals or toward the conservation of revolutionary gains. The displacement of the "weapon of criticism" by the "criticism of weapons" seems to threaten a revolution with its own undoing at the very moment of its achievement of power.

101. See above, n. 95, for the text upon which this summary is based, and for reference identification. Sun Tzu, to whom Mao refers, is also known as Sun Wu or Sun Wu-tzu, an eminent Chinese expert in military science and strategy in the fifth century B.C.

102. Mao quotes Lenin in *People and Revolution* and in *On Guerrilla Warfare*. But the latter is more probably Lenin's essay translated under the title *Partisan* Warfare. So Griffith, op. cit., pp. 41, 46.

103. So Payne, op. cit., p. 148.

104. See Schram, *The Political Thought of Mao Tse-tung*, p. 279.

105. Louis Barcata, *China in the Throes of Cultural Revolution* (New York: Hart Publishing Co., 1968), p. 279.

106. Ibid., p. 279.

107. Arendt, op. cit., pp. 54–55.

108. See above, pt. One, chap. 2, n. 36.

109. In an instructive discussion of ideology and power in the People's Republic of China, James Chieh Hsiung, Chairman of the

East Asian Studies Program at New York University's Washington Square College, has called attention to the difference in the meaning of ideology in Mao's usage, as compared with its Western meaning and usage (op. cit. above, n. 100). In the West, as Karl Mannheim has pointed out, ideology is a sociopolitical type of thinking characteristic of ruling groups and reflecting the bondage of those groups to their own interests and a corresponding blindness to facts that undermine their domination (*Ideology and Utopia* [New York: Harcourt Brace, 1936; paperback by Harcourt Brace Jovanovich, 1970], p. 36). This also is the principal Marxist-Leninist understanding of ideology (as, for example, in *Poverty of Philosophy* and in *State and Revolution*). Mao's usage, however, is much broader and has to do with the altering of behavior in relation to a radically altered consciousness. According to Hsiung, "the word 'ideology' is coterminous with 'culture,' as the latter is understood by most Chinese, and has anthropological connotations." Referring to Yehudi A. Cohen's anthropological definition of culture (*Man in Adaptation* [Chicago: Aldine Publishing Company, 1968], p. 1), Hsiung continues: "In Communist China, ideology has a comparable wide range of application, in the sense that it seeks to establish a new culture, a new way of life, through purposeful, collective means. It is all-inclusive. It offers society an apocalyptic vision, a spiritual force, a philosophy of life, a goal structure, a value system, a body of concepts and vocabulary for communication, and a methodology" (James Chieh Hsiung, op. cit., p. 7). In this sense, it is possible, and even appropriate, to speak of faith as an ideology; at least of Christian faith as a transfigurational *modus operandi* in the world. Hsiung's account lends support to the usefulness of the distinction between the *power of an ideology* and the *ideology of power* in the interpretation of revolutionary theory and practice. The distinction also points to what we have elsewhere described as "the human substance of Marxism." See *Ideology and Incarnation*, pp. 18, 22–23; also above, pt. Two, ch. 3, n. 1.

110. Schram, *The Political Thought of Mao Tse-tung,* pp. 82–84.

111. James Reston, "Letters from China: II," in the *New York Times,* Friday, 30 July 1971, p. 31.

112. Notably in *The Greening of America* (New York: Random House, 1970); more recently, in an illuminating article analyzing—in the light of the shocking May Day 1971 mass arrests in Washington, D.C., at the insistence of the government—the revolution in legal mentality and practice indispensable to the survival of Western democracy under conditions of technological power. See the *New Yorker,* 19 June 1971, pp. 52–57.

113. Bernard B. Fall, *Ho Chi Minh On Revolution: Selected Writ-*

*ings, 1920–66, edited* and with an Introduction (New York: Frederick
A. Praeger, 1967), p. vi; italics Fall's. References to Ho's writings
will be given in parentheses to indicate the pages in Fall's edition.

114. From Ho's "Speech Opening the First Theoretical Course of
Nguyen Ai Quoc School," 7 September 1957; and from an article
written for the fortieth anniversary of the October Revolution, entitled
"The October Revolution and the Liberation of the Peoples of the
East," 6 November 1957).

115. Roland E. Bonachea and Nelson P. Valdes, *Che: Selected
Works of Ernesto Guevara* (Cambridge: The MIT Press, 1969), p. 368.
Hereinafter, references to Che's speeches and writings, unless other-
wise indicated, will be given in parentheses following the citation, as
(Ch, and the page or pages).

116. Régis Debray, *Strategy for Revolution,* edited and with an
Introduction by Robin Blackburn (London: Jonathan Cape, 1970),
pp. 81, 75. Hereinafter, references to these writings will be indicated
in parentheses following, as (D, and the page or pages).

117. So Leo Huberman and Paul M. Sweezy, *Cuba: Anatomy of a
Revolution* (New York: Monthly Review Press, 1960); italics theirs.
Quoted by James O'Connor, *The Origins of Socialism in Cuba* (Ithaca:
Cornell University Press, 1970), p. 9. Hereinafter, this study will be
referred to in parentheses following citations, as (0, and the page or
pages).

118. See above, pt. Two, chap. 5, B, at n. 101.

119. In the autumn of 1953, Che had been persuaded to go to
Guatemala and participate in the revolution going on there. The revolution collapsed with the fall of Arbenz in 1954, when the North American Army trained, equipped, and organized the mercenary troops of
Castillo Armas (So Che, 6; and D, 146).

120. The leaving of Fidel refers to the departure from Mexico on
the *Granma* in command of the eightytwo men on 25 November 1956.

121. "Dear Hildita, Aleidita, Camilo, Celia, and Ernesto," the
letter continued after the salutation "To my children." It was published
in October 1968, a year after Che's death.

122. Zeitlin has coauthored a book with Robert Scheer, *Cuba: An
American Tragedy* (Harmondsworth, Middlesex, England: Penguin
Books, 1964), in which this interview appears.

123. The Cuban Revolution thus confirms the significance attached
to Lenin's book on *The State and Revolution* in pt. Two, chap. 4 above.

124. A more extended account of the political context of this process
is given in the essay on "Problems of Revolutionary Strategy," in
Debray, op. cit., pp. 111–52.

125. See Bibliographical Appendix below for the identification of
the source. Hereinafter, references to it will be indicated in parentheses

following, as (Z, and the page or pages). The reference to *Thursday* and *Friday* clearly recalls Maundy Thursday and Good Friday. Death came to Nestor Paz Zamora, from inanition and starvation, on 9 October 1970, almost three years to the day after the assassination of Che Guevara. Some confusion appears in the Zamora story over whether he died on 8 or 9 October (2, 5). I have accepted the later date.

A brief account of Zamora has reached me through the courtesy of James E. Goff, Apartado Postal 1024, Cuernavaca, Morelos, Mexico. The material is drawn from *Néstor Paz Zamora, el Mistico Cristiano de la Guerrilla* (Lima: Noticias Aliadas, NADOC, no. 184, 13 January 1971), pp. 1–7. Secs. I and II translated by James E. Goff; sec. III translated by Jordan Bishop and James E. Goff; sec. IV translated by James E. Goff from *"Carta de Néstor Paz," Volvimos a las. Moñtanas* (n.p.: Estado Mayor del E.L.N., Julio 1970, mimeographed), pp. 35–38. This material is now catalogued as a *Pamphlet* in the Missionary Research Library of Union Theological Seminary, New York.

126. Alves, op. cit., pp. 17, 98, 99. The sequence of subject and predicate in the first sentence, and of the sentences in the remainder of the citation, have been altered from Alves' usage, but without altering Alves' meaning. Their original arrangement can be readily identified in the text.

127. The references to Torres' writings and work will be indicated in parentheses following. They are taken from the edition edited by John Gerassi, *Revolutionary Priest: The Complete Writings and Messages of Camilo Torres* (New York: Random House, 1971). Regrettably, the book lacks an index.

128. On the influence of Torres, and indeed, the Latin American guerrillas, on Daniel Berrigan, see Francine du Plessix Gray, *Divine Disobedience* (New York: Random House, 1971), p. 105. For Ivan Ilich's sharp repudiation of the Torres and Berrigan position, see further ibid., pp. 284 ff.

129. Cardinal Concha, after an interview that shows how far apart the institutional church and the revolutionary church can be, ordered the laicization of Torres on 26 June 1965 (T, 28). Two years later a declaration of Bishops of the Roman Church in Latin America, written under the direction of Dom Helder Camara (15 August 1967), shows how revolutionary the institutional church had meanwhile become. It would be difficult indeed for any candid reading of that declaration to fail in discerning the life and death of Camilo Torres between the lines (T, 430–41).

130. I have altered the order of the text somewhat by combining two sentences into one, without, however, altering Torres' meaning.

131. See Francine Gray, op. cit., pp. 286, 284. *CIDOC,* it may be

noted, identifies the Center for Intercultural Documentation established by Ilich as a kind of combined New York's New School and California's Center for the Study of Democratic Institutions.

132. Torres has a long and searching essay on the question of "Social Change and Rural Violence in Colombia" (T, 188–244). He endeavors to focus upon the sociological reality of violence in order the better to assess the moral aspects of violence, and thus to lift the whole question above the level of ethical cliché and self-justifying trivialization. The analysis is heavily dependent upon a thorough sociological analysis of the phenomenon of *La Violencia* by Monsignor Germán Guzmán (T, 192) that seems to offer a striking parallel on the sociological level to the analysis offered on the psychological level by Frantz Fanon in *The Wretched of the Earth*. In Colombia, at any rate, the phenomenon of *la violencia* "can be defined as a kind of social conflict that manifests itself through armed action of groups, especially in peasant neighborhoods, a situation geographically general in Colombia —and endemic, inasmuch as it has continued for several years without solution." From a jointly authored monograph cited by John Gerassi, T, 192. The text referred to is *La Violencia en Colombia*, by Germán Guzmán, Eduardo Umaña Luna, and Orlando Fals Borda, of the Facultad de Sociología in the Universidad Nacional de Colombia, 1962. The quoted passage is on p. 368.

133. The stubbornness, as well as the diminishing future of *apartheid* in South Africa, together with a quickening boldness and resistance of the Christian churches to the policies of the government in that country, has recently been documented in a United Nations monograph. See Kenneth N. Carstens, *Church and Race in South Africa*, Unit on Apartheid, Department of Political and Security Council Affairs, no. 23/71, May 1971.

134. Frantz Fanon, *The Wretched of the Earth* (New York: Grove Press, 1963), p. 40. Hereinafter references to this book will be indicated in parentheses following, as (F, and the page or pages).

135. The parenthetical references, LB, 20, etc., are to the recently published biography of Martin Luther King, Jr., by David L. Lewis, *King: A Critical Biography* (Baltimore: Penguin Books, 1970). Citations from this source hereinafter in this section will be so indicated.

136. Eldridge Cleaver, *Soul on Ice* (New York: Dell Publishing Co., 1970), p. 24. Hereinafter, references to this book will be indicated in parentheses following, as (CSI, 24). Cleaver's *Post-Prison Writings and Speeches*, edited with an Introduction by Robert Scheer (New York: Random House, 1969) will be referred to, when cited, as (CPP, and the page or pages).

137. Subsequently, the Panthers have abandoned all titles. See below, par. 4 and n. 185.

138. Robert Scheer has remarked that "without the Panthers, Cleaver would undoubtedly have developed a much more personal, career-oriented, literary way of life. With the Panthers, he became a political revolutionary as well as literary polemicist, although there was hardly any time for writing" (CPP, xiii). The "Oakland shoot-out" occurred on 6 April 1968, two days after the assassination of Martin Luther King, Jr. The affair was one of the uglier instances of harassment of the Panthers by the Oakland police. Seventeen-year-old Bobby Sutton died in the gun battle, shot in the back. Cleaver's parole was revoked and for two months he sat at Vacaville Prison. The Oakland incident lends grim confirmation to Huey Newton's allusion to Mao Tse-tung's epigram about political power and gun power in the treatise *On Guerrilla Warfare*. See above, pt. Three, chap. 9, A, n. 99.

139. In the text of the Ephesian letter, the pronoun "It," with which the passage cited begins, refers to "the privilege of proclaiming to the Gentiles (i.e., to all peoples of the earth) the good news of the unfathomable riches of Christ, and of bringing to light how this hidden purpose was to be put into effect" (3:8; parenthesis mine). We have endeavored to explore the implications of these riches and this hidden purpose for our revolutionary times through an exegesis of certain New Testament paradigms. (See above, pt. Two, chap. 5, and pt. Three, chap. 7.)

140. James H. Cone, *A Black Theology of Liberation* (New York: J. B. Lippincott, 1970), pp. 232, 233.

141. Franz Fanon, *Black Skins, White Masks* (New York: Grove Press, 1967).

142. See above, pt. Two, chap. 5, at n. 65.
What the Countess said was:

> "In our plain defects
> We already know the brotherhood of man.
> Who said that?"
>                    "You, Countess."
>                                      "How interesting.
> I thought it was a quotation."

Christopher Fry, *The Dark Is Light Enough* (New York: Oxford University Press, 1954), p. 21.
With due regard for the distance between Sheridan and Fry, and between the satirization of aristocratic manners and mores and the ironic characterization of the sophistries of a culture whose values and certainties have been overtaken by events that have not yet evoked "a shock of recognition," the Countess seems somehow an echo of Mrs. Malaprop. The gulf between manners and meanings, and *pari*

*passu* between politics and reality, is steadily widening, and at an accelerating pace. Fanon's indirect citation of the New Testament is drawn from the conclusion of Matthew's account of the parable of the wedding feast in chap. 22:1–14.

143. In February and May 1972, ex-President Richard M. Nixon made state visits to Peking and to Moscow. Results to date: for the immediate future of peace, the greater the odds, the more tenaciously do the embattled North Vietnamese continue the struggle for their own liberation and that of Indo-China; for the long-range future of peace, an arms limitation agreement is arrived at that includes an "escape clause" in the form of a distinction, at once too subtle and too obvious, between a *quantitative* limit and a *qualitative* buildup of strategic weapons. The "Diary of Little Tanya" is on public view in Leningrad. Meanwhile, the "peace with honor" in Southeast Asia has scarcely put an end to the fighting.

144. See above, pt. Two, chap. 9, A, n. 84; and Fanon, *The Wretched of the Earth,* pp. 106, 235. It will be recalled that Fanon writes out of the struggle of Algerian liberation from French colonialist imperialism. But as Jean-Paul Sartre's stinging Preface makes plain, the thrust of Fanon's analysis is against the Western mentality of domination and exploitation that permeates the mentality and exercise of American power as well.

145. Aimé Fernand Césaire, b. 25 June 1913, in Fort-de-France, Martinique, and educated in his native city and in Paris, has been since 1946 a member of the French National Assembly, as Deputy for Martinique.

146. See above, pt. Three, chap. 9, B, 4, n. 132.

147. See above, pt. Three, chap. 7, A, n. 22; chap. 9, A, 2.

148. See above, pt. Three, chap. 8, n. 56.

149. See below, pt. Four, chap. 11, C.

150. Paris, 1968 *sic!* Meanwhile, colonialism has been "radicalized," and in the protracted negotiations, which opened on 13 May 1968, in the Majestic Hotel in Paris between the United States and the North Vietnamese and Vietcong, has not hesitated to convert the "green baize table" into a device for shedding more and more blood. As the self-righteous arrogance of American technological power drives toward the boundary set at Nuremberg between civility and criminality in warfare, the apocalyptic reality of the Indo-Chinese conflict becomes a concomitant boundary between political messianism and messianic politics. "Therefore the deeper guilt lies with the man who handed me over to you" (John 19:11). See further Telford Taylor, *Nuremberg and Vietnam: An American Tragedy* (Chicago: Quadrangle Books, 1970).

151. See further:

"Racial feeling, as opposed to racial prejudice, and that determination to fight for one's life which characterizes the native's reply to oppression are obviously good enough reasons for joining the fight. But . . . the leader realizes day in and day out that hatred alone cannot draw up a program. (F, 139)

"The task of bringing the people to maturity will be made easier by the thoroughness of the organization and by the high intellectual level of its leaders. . . . The rebellion gives proof of its rational basis and expresses its maturity each time that it uses a particular case to advance the people's awareness. In defiance of those inside the movement who tend to think that shades of meaning constitute dangers and drive wedges into the solid bloc of popular opinion, the leaders stand firm upon those principles that have been sifted out in the national struggle, and in the worldwide struggle of mankind for his freedom. (F, 146–47)

"The awakening of the whole people will not come about all at once; the people's work in the building of the nation will not immediately take on its full dimensions: first because the means of communication and transmission are only beginning to be developed; secondly, because the yardstick of time must no longer be that of the moment or up till the next harvest, but must become that of the rest of the world; and lastly because the spirit of discouragement which has been deeply rooted in people's minds by colonial domination is still very near the surface. (F, 193–94)

"A bourgeoisie that provides nationalism alone as food for the masses fails in its mission and gets caught up in a whole series of mishaps. But if nationalism is not explicit, if it is not enriched and deepened by a very rapid transformation into a consciousness of social and political needs, in other words into humanism, it leads up a blind alley. . . . The living expression of the nation is the moving consciousness of the whole people; it is the coherent, enlightened action of men and women. The collective building up of a destiny is the assumption of responsibility on the historical scale. Otherwise there is anarchy, repression, and the resurgence of tribal parties and federalism." (F, 204–5)

152. See above, pt. Three, chap. 9, C, n. 135.

153. See above, Preface, n. 8.

154. On 1 December 1955, Mrs. Rosa Parks violated the Montgomery City Bus Lines' seating regulations; and on 12 March 1968, Memphis Local 1733 of the American Federation of State, County and Municipal Employees voted a strike of the Sanitation workers for

redress of wage discrimination and job safety provisions that had reached a point of no return on 1 February when two black Memphis garbage collectors were crushed to death by the automatic compressor of their truck, which had been accidentally triggered (LB, 378).

155. The quoted phrases are the aptly chosen titles of chaps. 9 and 12 of David Lewis' critical biography. The "killers" inferentially identified in chap. 12 are: the white backlash, certain Supreme Court decisions in 1966 and 1967, the inevitable convergence of the civil rights struggle with the war in Vietnam, and of course, the Memphis strike and the assassin himself. "It has been suggested that a man of lesser stature than Martin King would have 'written Memphis off' " (LB, 383). The Warren Court had been "the mainstay of civil rights." But in November 1966, Justice Byron White broke with the usual majority of the Court and voted to uphold a lower court conviction of civil rights demonstrators in Tallahassee, Florida. In June 1967, the Justices upheld Martin's conviction by a Birmingham court for demonstrating without a permit (LB, 367).

156. The Civil Rights Act of 1964 and the Voting Rights Bill, signed into law on 6 August 1965, marked, according to Coretta King's account, "a major advance in the legal protection of Negro rights." See Coretta King, *My Life with Martin Luther King, Jr.* (New York: Holt, Rinehart and Winston, 1969), p. 270. Subsequent references to this volume will be indicated in the text in parentheses, as (CK, and the page or pages).

157. Gettysburg looked out upon a battlefield and back over four years of civil war. The "Dream Speech" looked out upon the rising hopes of "black and white together" in a mass petition of civil grievance and redress, and upon the expectations of a new dawn of justice and reconciliation for all the exploited and oppressed, the poor and deprived, in the land. It looked back upon the terror and torment, the fury and destruction, of life and property in the struggle for the desegregation of Birmingham, Alabama, in the spring of 1963. See LB, chap. 7.

158. *Gustave le Bon* (1841–1931) was a French physician and social psychologist. His important work was *La psychologie des foules* (Paris: F. Alcan, 1895; nouv. ed., Paris: Presses Universitaire de France, 1947), translated as *The Crowd*, 1922. See Gustav le Bon, *The Crowd: A Study of the Popular Mind* (New York: The Macmillan Company, 19th printing, 1947; also London: E. Benn, 20th printing, 1952). Mention may also be made in this connection of *La révolution française et la psychologie des révolutions* (Paris: E. Flammarion, 1912, 1925). There is an English translation by Bernard Miall, *The Psychology of Revolutions* (New York: G. P. Putnam's Sons, 1913).

159. Martin Luther King, Jr., *Where Do We Go from Here: Chaos*

*or Community?* (New York: Harper & Row, 1967; Bantam Books paperback, 1967), p. 52 (Bantam ed.) Hereinafter this last and summary book will be referred to in the text, and in parentheses following, as (CC, and the page or pages).

160. The disasters of 1967 alluded to by Martin Luther King, Jr., were a series of riots erupting volcanolike from the seething unrest among black people owing to intolerable conditions of living and of employment, and spreading across the eastern third of the United States from Boston to Tampa, from Cincinnati to Detroit to Buffalo and Newark, New Jersey. The worst explosions occurred in Newark in mid-June and in Detroit during the last week of July. It is not accidental that the summer of 1967 has been referred to as "the long hot summer." There had been forewarnings through similar outbreaks in Harlem in July 1964, and in Watts, near Los Angeles, in August. 1965. I wish here to thank John Kinney, a doctoral student at Union Theological Seminary, New York, for drawing my attention to a brief and instructive account of these happenings in Benjamin Muse, *The American Negro Revolution: From Nonviolence to Black Power, 1963–1967* (Bloomington: Indiana University Press, 1968).

161. There is a slight discrepancy in the account of "the birth of the Black Power slogan in the civil rights movement" (CC, 29), between King's own account and that of his biographer, David Lewis. King dates the use of the slogan as occurring first in Greenwood, Miss., during the first fortnight of June 1966, in connection with the march in support of James Meredith. Lewis notes its use on that occasion "for one of the first times" (LB, 324). Since King also recognizes that the slogan "had been used long before by Richard Wright and others . . ." (CC, 34), the point at issue concerns the adoption of the slogan by the Civil Rights Movement. King identifies the time and place of first use. Lewis is more indefinite and leaves the question open.

162. See above, pt. Two, chap. 5, A.

163. Coretta King so reports it (CK, 278). But her husband and David Lewis seem to agree instead that the conversation was part of the ideological confrontation and debate in the Catholic parish house at Yazoo, Miss. See CC, pp. 36–37; and LB, 325.

164. *The Autobiography of Malcolm X,* with the assistance of Alex Haley. Introduction by M. S. Handler. Epilogue by Alex Haley (New York: Grove Press, 1964. First paperback edition, 1966), p. 399; parenthesis Haley's. Citations from this work are from the paperback edition, and hereinafter will be in parentheses, as (A–, and the page or pages).

165. See above, pt. Three, chap. 8, n. 56.

166. Rubem Alves, *Tomorrow's Child* (New York: Harper & Row, 1972). See especially "Part 1: Rationalization, or The Logic of the

Dinosaur." Whether there is a "child" tomorrow depends upon whether there is "tomorrow"; and whether there is "tommorw" depends upon "Friday's Child," as W. H. Auden has put it "in commemoration of the martyrdom of Dietrich Bonhoeffer at Flossenbürg, April 9th, 1945." At all events, that is what the Black Revolution is all about, as the double assassination of its providential leadership seems to underline. And that is what our argument is really also all about. See W. H. Auden, *Homage to Clio* (New York: Random House, 1955–60), pp. 77–78.

167. Compare the footnote in *The Wretched of the Earth,* in which Fanon discusses "torture by brainwashing" as carried on in Algeria. In this connection, he refers to "a particular school of psycho-sociology," and goes on to explain that "in the United States of America a trend toward psycho-sociology has developed. Supporters of this school think that the tragedy of the contemporary individual is contained in the fact that he has no longer any part to play, and that present-day social conditions force him to exist only as a cog in the machine. From this comes the proposal of a therapeutic which will allow a man to take various roles in a veritable game of activity. Anyone can play any role; it even happens that in a single day a person's role may be changed; symbolically you may put yourself in the place of anyone you please. The factory psychiatrists in the United States are, it seems, making huge strides in group psychotherapy among workers" (F, 286). We have already noted Fanon's grimly ironic allusion to Matt. 22:14. (See above, pt. Three, chap. 9, C, 1 [F, 42]). But Fanon does not even hint at another passage in the gospels, namely, Mark 5:1–10. "In the country of the Gerasenes," Jesus encountered a demented man who lived "among the tombs." Commanding the unclean spirit to come out of the man, Jesus asked the spirit, " 'What is your name?' 'My name is Legion,' he said, 'there are so many of us' " (v. 9).

168. As reported in the *New York Times,* Sunday, 21 January 1973, sec. One, p. 40.

169. The correlation is even more striking when one considers that two of ex-President Nixon's most trusted spiritual advisers darken counsel with false prophecy, saying "Peace, peace," when there is no peace. In *The Jerusalem Bible,* the oracle that came to Jeremiah said:

> "Yahweh Sabaoth says this:
> Do not listen to what those prophets say:
>
> . . . . . . . . . . .
>
> they retail visions of their own,
>
> . . . . . . . . . . .
>
> to those who reject the word of Yahweh they say,

'Peace will be yours,'
and to those who follow the dictates of a hardened heart,
'No misfortune will touch you.' "

(Jer. 23:16–17)

It would seem that successors of Hananiah, the court prophet in the days of Zedekiah, king of Judah, against whom the Lord of earth and heaven, and of history, vindicated Jeremiah, have turned up in the White House itself. (See Jer. 28.)

170. See above, pt. Two, chap. 5, A.

171. Augustine, *Confessions,* The Library of Christian Classics, vol. VII, edited by Albert C. Outler (Philadelphia: Westminster Press, 1954), Bk, V, chaps. 6–7. The journey took him, as is well known, from Manicheism via Neoplatonism to Christianity.

172. My colleague, James H. Cone, has made this point with instructive clarity and force, particularly in *A Black Theology of Liberation* (New York: J. B. Lippincott, 1970), and in *The Spirituals and the Blues* (New York: Seabury Press, 1972). Although Cone's theological interpretation of black experience is being sharply challenged from within the black community, particularly his interpretation of the spirituals, the debate itself shows both the extent to which the black community has been nurtured by the messianic story and the extent to which the dynamics of the Black Revolution seem to involve the rejection of that story.

173. See C. Eric Lincoln, *The Black Muslims in America* (Boston: Beacon Press, 1961), especially pp. 199–209, where Lincoln discusses the Fruit of Islam, the "Secret Army" of the Black Muslims, and the question of violence. Although Lincoln does not touch the question of responsibility for Malcolm's death, one can scarcely escape the inference that the consequences of Malcolm's break with Elijah Muhammad were closing in upon him. A similar implication of a connection may be inferred from the Epilogue to the *Autobiography* (AX, pp. 422 ff.).

174. Lincoln, op. cit., pp. 229, 245–46; italics Lincoln's. The decade to which he refers is that between 1950 and 1960. Meanwhile, another decade has passed. Looking back on it, Lincoln's words seem like a prophecy, which he did not intend, but which events have confirmed. The confirmation attests his integrity and discernment, not his clairvoyance; unless *clairvoyance* be but another word for the integrity and discernment with which happenings in history are interpreted. Of the same genre must have been Jeremiah's conviction of the fall of Jerusalem (586 B.C.) and Jesus' lament over Jerusalem (Matt. 23:37–38; Luke 19:41–44).

175. So Bobby Seale, *Seize the Time* (New York: Random House,

1968), p. 59. In *The Black Panther Speaks*, edited by Philip S. Foner (New York: J. B. Lippincott Company, 1970), the date is given more generally as "the fall of 1966" (p. xv). But then we are told that *The Black Panther*, the Party's weekly, published its first issue on 25 April 1967, "a year after the Party was organized in Oakland, California" (xxviii). Precision on this matter is not important. Indeed, the imprecision underscores the revolutionary urgency and misson that saturate the Party's beginning and its development. Its meteoric rise and activity are commensurate with its founding, almost "on the run" as it were, and with its precarious future. It is well known that Seale is Chairman of the Black Panther Party. Foner is Professor of History at Lincoln University, Pa., and a member of the Board of Editors of the *Journal of Negro History*. These two books offer a basic and reliable account of the Panthers and are the principal documentation underlying the present discussion. They will be referred to in the text in parentheses following citations or paraphrases as (S, and the page or pages) in the case of Seale's account, and (F, and the page or pages) in the case of Foner's "documentary record." I wish here to thank the Reverend Katherine Shindel of Edwardsville, Ill., a former student at Union Theological Seminary, New York, for clarifying conversations and for drawing my attention to this literature.

176. An anti-imperialist poem by Henry Blake Fuller, published in the *New Flag*, in 1899, depicted American imperialism as a "hog," which in its expansionist greed consumed everything even remotely edible. (See F, xx.)

177. See Lee Lockwood, *Conversation with Eldridge Cleaver* (New York: Dell Publishing Co., a Delta Book, 1970), for a summary account of the "shoot-out" and of Cleaver's odyssey. When cited below, Lockwood's report will be referred to in parentheses, as (LCC, and the page or pages). See also Seale, op. cit., pp. 228–37.

178. See Lockwood, op. cit., pp. 86–91.

179. In a world in which the politics of God and the politics of people are strangely intermixed, historical futility and historical fulfillment are precariously juxtaposed. This is why Rom. 13 concludes with the admonition to "remember how critical the moment is. It is time for you to wake out of sleep, for deliverance is nearer to us now than when first we believed. It is far on in the night; day is near" (v. 11). This is why we are bidden to "be most careful then how you conduct yourselves: like sensible men, not like simpletons. Use the present opportunity to the full, for these are evil days" (Eph. 5:15–16). "For our fight is not against human foes, but against cosmic powers, against the authorities and potentates of this dark world, against the superhuman forces of evil in the heavens" (Eph. 6:12). This is what the dynamics and direction of a politics of transfiguration are all about.

180. See Appendices on "The Persecution of the Black Panther Party," in Foner, *The Black Panther Speaks*, pp. 257–66.

181. See above, pt. Three, chap. 6.

182. See Lockwood, op. cit., pp. 27–29.

183. See Frontispiece to *The Politics of Escalation in Vietnam* by Franz Schurmann, Peter Dale Scott, and Reginald Zelnik (Boston: Beacon Press, 1966).

184. See above, pt. One, chap. 1.

185. Lee Lockwood, whose account of Eldridge Cleaver has been referred to above, was assigned by *Playboy* to interview Huey P. Newton after his release from prison in August 1970, when the California State Court of Appeals overturned his conviction and two hung juries led finally to the dropping of all charges against him by the State of California in October 1971. Lockwood's important report was published in *Playboy*, March 1973. It brings Newton's present thoughts and concerns clearly into view and has been prefaced by a succinct biographical résumé of Huey's rise to preeminence as the Party's theoretician and tactician as well. The *Playboy* article, together with the publication in the same year of *In Search of Common Ground: Conversations with Erik H. Erikson and Huey P. Newton*, Introduced by Kai T. Erikson (New York: W. W. Norton, 1973), make available a dispassionate and reliable assessment of the latest phase of the Black Revolution. I have relied upon this assessment in bringing the present account of the Black Panthers to a close. References to these sources will be indicated in parentheses as (P) for the article in *Playboy*, and (E) for the discussion between Newton and Erikson.

186. See above, pt. Three, chap. 9, C, 4, n. 174.

PART FOUR
THE TRANSFIGURATION OF POLITICS

*Chapter 10*

1. William Stringfellow, *An Ethic for Christians and Other Aliens in a Strange Land* (Waco: World Books, 1973), chap. 2.

2. Ludwig Feuerbach, *Das Wesen des Christentums* (Leipzig: Alfred Kröner Verlag, 1923; published in English as *The Essence of Christianity* [New York: Harper Torchbooks, 1957]), chaps. 1 and 2.

3. John Calvin, *Institutes of the Christian Religion*, edited with an Introduction by John T. McNeill and translated by Ford Lewis Battles, in The Library of Christian Classics, vol. XX, Bk. I, 1, 1.

4. Ibid., Bk. IV, 1, 2. It might be noted also that the line from Calvin to Feuerbach includes Pascal and Kierkegaard and goes on to Jean-Paul Sartre, Maurice Merleau-Ponty, and the French Structuralists, in an impressive overtaking of the Cartesian split between

thought and experience, as well as the dubious distinction upon which Idealism *in extremis* came to rest, i.e., the distinction between the *ratio essendi* and the *ratio cognoscendi*. The hermeneutical impasse between literalism and higher criticism, between symbolization and experiential immediacy at which the interpretation of Scripture has arrived in these days, is haunted, if not occasioned by, the same distinction.

5. So Funk and Wagnalls, *The New "Standard" Dictionary of the English Language* (New York, 1961). See also Origen, *First Principles*, Bk. IV, "The Ante-Nicene Fathers" (Buffalo: The Christian Literature Publishing Company, 1885), vol. IV; also Augustine, *On Christian Doctrine,* translated by J. F. Shaw (Edinburgh: T. & T. Clark, 1892), especially Bk. III, chaps. 1 and 29); *Expositions in the Psalms,* edited by A. Cleveland Coxe, in "The Nicene and Post-Nicene Fathers" (Grand Rapids: B. Eerdmans, 1956, vol. VII.

6. So Jesus, according to Luke 12:56 RSV. The NEB translates: "How is it you cannot interpret this fateful hour?"

7. Stringfellow, op. cit., pp. 41–42.

8. Or, in a robust phrase of Calvin's, "God's eternal decree by which he determined with himself what he willed to become of each Man." *Institutes,* III, 21, 5. Or, more movingly, perhaps, "the hidden sanctuary of God's plan." III, 23, 9.

9. Dietrich Bonhoeffer, *Ethics,* translated by Neville Horton Smith from the 6th German edition, 1963 (New York: Macmillan paperback edition, 1965), pp. 144–145.

10. Or, as Professor John Rawls of Harvard University has exhaustively and brilliantly shown, with perhaps insufficient attention to the theological resonance of the phrase: "Justice as fairness." See John Rawls, *The Theory of Justice* (Cambridge: Harvard University Press, 1972), p. 11. One thinks again of Augustine's stricture against Cicero who, being unable to establish a creative reciprocity between the "order of times" and the "order of causes," "in order to make men free, made them sacrilegious," *The City of God,* Bks. IV, V especially Bk. V, chap. 9.

11. This is an attempt to put in terms of biblical politics what Augustine formulated in the quieter mood of a biblical philosophy of history tinged with Platonism. The similarities and dissimilarities between these two contexts need not concern us further here. For the present purpose, it is instructive to recall that the providential view of history described in Bk. IV of *The City of God* is the matrix of the illuminating definition of social stability and social order in Bk. XIX, chap. 13: "The peace of all things is the tranquility of order. Order is the distribution which allots things equal and unequal, each to its own place." See above, pt. One, chap. 2, n. 41.

12. Horace Bushnell, *Preliminary Dissertation on the Nature of*

*Theological Language;* see H. Shelton Smith, *Horace Bushnell,* The Library of Protestant Thought (New York: Oxford University Press, 1965), p. 76. Bushnell is concerned with *metaphorical* not *metaphysical* relations. So also is the present analysis.

13. Paul Tillich, *The Interpretation of History* (New York: Charles Scribner's Sons, 1936), pt. Two, chap. 2, "Kairos and Logos."

14. With the possible exception of the American Revolution, as Arendt has noted. See above, pt. One, chap. 1. It may be that the tragedy of the Watergate is a current instance in support of Arendt's exception, and counter to the reservation expressed above about her assessment of the founding of this Republic. Whatever may be the outcome of the efforts of the Senate Select Committee or of the Special Proescutor, the nation's narrow escape from a calculated subversion of its constitutional foundations and its governmental structures too ominously parallels those that overtook the Weimar Republic in 1933. At the moment, a reprieve, if not an ultimate release, from the fate of revolutions seems to be in the making. The quickening reassertion of the checks and balances among executive, legislative, and judicial powers suggests a resiliency of revolutionary passion, insight, and commitment that could transform the nation's Bicentennial from a celebration of the past into a revolutionary breakthrough extending the lifetime of the American Revolution.

If such a prospect should be realized, it could be that, in the long future, the conscience of Daniel Ellsberg will prove to have been the prophetic eruption of a Puritan strain, widely scorned in the body politic, yet too deep within the bones and sinews of the nation to be discounted or ignored. At stake is indeed the survival of the American Revolution as the historic exception to revolutionary fate. Meanwhile, ex-President Nixon's Watergate Address to the nation on 16 August 1973 documents the distance still to be traversed by the people of the United States. Accepting full responsibility for everything while specifying nothing, intoned with the humility of arrogance, and totally devoid of contrition, the ex-President resorted to a thinly veiled indictment of those movements of conscience in the body politic in behalf of civil rights and against the brutality and dubious legality of American power in Southeast Asia. By way of an almost puerile resort to an *ad hominem* argument over law and order, the address was not only tedious in its self-righteous cant, but at once irreverent and insensitive to the bond between piety and politics that informed the founding of this Republic. The ex-President's insistence upon his personal uninvolvement in the Watergate cover-up—even were one able to accept it— scarcely softens the shocking awareness that the address as a whole came through as a calculated cover-up of the truth that an expectant nation longed to hear, and that could have greatly healed and set the nation free. A virtual "replay" occurred on Monday, 29 April 1974, when the ex-President announced that he was releasing the transcripts of his Oval Office conversations between September 1972 and April 1973. Pointedly *not* the actual tapes. *Sic!* The principal new factor is the depth of moral deterioration at the highest level of government.

15. So—the biblical meaning of politics is the human meaning of politics and the human meaning of politics is the biblical meaning of politics. Let those who find in this assessment of revolutionary reality an inadmissible tautology pause over the question whether their own attempts to avoid tautology convey them either into a flight from politics for the sake of logical tidiness, or into another kind of world altogether than the world in which revolutions happen because the struggle for human freedom and fulfillment goes on. The conjunction of revolution and humanization is intrinsic to human destiny in a world of unfreedom and insecurity; a fallen world in which the life for which death is no problem has been exchanged for the life over which death holds sovereign sway. On this point, William Stringfellow's chapter on "The Morality of Death" is singularly concrete, contemporary, and illuminating. Op. cit., chap. 3.

16. See above, pt. One, chap. 2, and at n. 38.

## Chapter 11

17. See above, pt. Two, chap. 5, A.

18. One thinks of Pss. 2, 9, 46, for example; and of the imprecatory Psalms in general (see Robert H. Pfeiffer, *Introduction to the Old Testament* [New York: Harper & Brothers, 1941, 1948], pp. 638–40; and of Jesus' strictures against "the lawyers and Pharisees" in Matt. 23, and Luke 11:37–54.

19. It will be recalled—and should not be forgotten—that in his successful campaign for election as Vice President of the United States, in 1968, Spiro T. Agnew launched a strident ideological attack upon the universities and the media, upon students and other dissenting youth, upon those in the party of the opposition, in the name of law and order as the presupposition and the condition of freedom and of the security of the nation. The former Vice President's 1968 exhibition of unholy malice was followed by a muted repetition in the campaign of 1972, and a return to office. The press and the telecasters courageously stood firm, as did a number of university presidents, notably at Yale, Dartmouth, and Amherst. Notwithstanding, a climate of unease began to be discernible across the country, the totalitarian direction and consequences of which have been, at least temporarily, interrupted by the Watergate disclosures.

20. The sense in which the relation between freedom and truth is

decisive in the saving story, and is the critical divide between the ful-fillment and the demonization of human destiny, is strikingly expressed in a forceful passage of the eighth chapter of the Fourth Gospel:

"Turning to the Jews who had believed him, Jesus said, 'If you dwell within the revelation I have brought, you are indeed my disciples; you shall know the truth, and the truth will set you free.' They replied, 'We are Abraham's descendants; we have never been in slavery to any man. What do you mean by saying, "You will become free men"?' 'In very truth I tell you,' said Jesus, 'that every one who commits sin is a slave. The slave has no permanent standing in the household, but the son belongs to it for ever. If then the Son sets you free, you will indeed be free.

. . . " 'If you were Abraham's children . . . you would do as Abraham did. As it is, you are bent on killing me, a man who told you the truth, as I heard it from God. That is not how Abraham acted. You are doing your own father's work. . . .

" 'Your father is the devil, and you choose to carry out your father's desires. He is a murderer from the beginning, and is not rooted in the truth; there is no truth in him. When he tells a lie he is speaking his own language, for he is a liar and the father of lies. . . . He who has God for his father listens to the words of God. You are not God's children; that is why you do not listen.' " (vv. 31–47)

See further to the passage and the point, Raymond E. Brown, *The Gospel According to John* ("The Anchor Bible," vol. 29, chaps. 1–12, and vol. 29a, chaps. 13–21 [Garden City, N.Y.: Doubleday, 1960–70]), vol. 29, pp. 355–58.

21. Georg Simmel, *The Sociology of Georg Simmel,* quoted by Peter M. Blau, *Exchange and Power* (New York: John Wiley and Sons, 1964), p. 1; italics mine; parenthesis Simmel's. Professor Blau is past president of the American Sociological Association. He is a recognized authority on the theory of social organization and on *The Dynamics of Bureaucracy,* which was the title of an earlier book. In the present volume, Blau undertakes to bring the theoretical work of Weber, Simmel, Parsons, Homans, and others to bear upon the fundamental sociological phenomenon of social interaction and to illuminate this phenomenon in an original analysis of his own. Further references to this work will be noted in parentheses, following the citation.

22. See especially Reinhold Niebuhr, *Moral Man and Immoral Society* (New York: Charles Scribner's Sons, 1934), and *The Nature and Destiny of Man* (New York: Charles Scribner's Sons, vol. II, 1943), especially chap. 9, where a distinction is drawn between "the

organization and the balance of power" in the "struggle for justice."

23. Augustine, *Confessions*, as translated by Edward B. Pusey, in the Modern Library Edition (New York: Random House, 1949), Bk. I, chap. 7.

24. See above, pt. Three, chap. 8, n. 56.

25. Karl Mannheim, *Freedom, Power and Democratic Planning* (New York: Oxford University Press, 1950), p. 275; parenthesis mine. The chapter contains a brief but instructive bibliography on social and political freedom as human freedom. Subsequent references to Mannheim's book will be indicated in parentheses following.

26. Karl Barth, *Kirchliche Dogmatik*, II/2 (Zürich-Zollikon: 1942), p. 569. The same point is made by John Rawls, *A Theory of Justice* (Cambridge: Harvard University Press, 1971), chap. 8. Whenever Rawls' work is referred to in what follows, the pages will be indicated in parentheses following the reference.

27. Paul Lehmann, "A Christian Alternative to Natural Law," in *die moderne Demokratie und Ihr Recht*, Festschrift fuer Gerhard Leibholz, herausgegeben von Karl Dieter Bracher, *et alia* (Tübingen: J. C. B. Mohr [Paul Siebeck], 1966), Bd. I, p. 526. The argument here concerns the tension between sovereignty and law as a crucial instance of the tension between stability and change, or between sanctions and society, that has overtaken contemporary ethics and politics. Owing to the crisis of the Natural Law tradition, these tensions have virtually reached a point of polarization in face of the pressures of secularism and religious and political pluralism upon the absolutism of divine law, divine right, and a divinely illumined reason upon which the natural law was based. In retrospect, this essay seems a kind of first try at an indication of the correspondence between the biblical and the human meaning of politics.

28. So Arendt. op. cit., pp. 186 ff., and quoting Francis M. Cornford, *From Religion to Philosophy: A Study in the Origins of Western Speculation* (Harper Torchbooks, 1957), chap. 1, p. 30. In pt. Four, as in pt. One, hereinafter, references to Arendt's book will be given in parentheses following.

29. The phrase is a recurrent theme in Rawls' discussion of the relations between liberty and justice, law and order. The phrase is, of course, reminiscent of Plato's *The Laws*, and of the *Nichomachean Ethics* and the *Politics* of Aristotle, as also of Bks. V and XIX of *The City of God*. Since Rawls contents himself, according to the Index at least, with two references to Plato (and these in footnotes), it is less puzzling than it would otherwise be that he ignores Augustine altogether. Plato and Augustine exhibit a livelier sense of the limits of "the rule of reason" (Aristotle) and *pari passu* of "what is reasonable for rational men to choose to do in a hypothetical choice situation"

(11–12). The limits are given in the transcendental derivation of the virtues and in the precariousness of the human condition, particularly the ambiguity of choice. Although Rawls acknowledges that a commentary on Kant's moral theory would be desirable, such a commentary is missing and "perhaps . . . impossible to write" (251), especially in relation to a theory of justice. It would seem, nevertheless, that Kant's doctrine of radical evil would bring him closer to Plato and to Augustine than to Rousseau and to Rawls. The doctrine significantly calls into question the attempt "to present a natural procedural rendering of Kant's conception . . . detached from its metaphysical surroundings" (264). In fairness to Rawls, it must be noted that he admits departing from Kant "in several respects," particularly in relation to Rousseau's doctrine of the general will (256). The critical question, however, remains. This is the question whether a humanistic theory of justice deprived of transcendental referentiality can provide either hypothetically or practically (in Kant's sense of those terms) what a well-ordered society requires if it is to be a humane society and invulnerable to revolutionary challenges.

30. *"Saturni gentem haud vinclo nec legibus aequam, sponte sua veterisque dei se more tenentem." Aenead*, Bk. VII, 11, 203–4.

31. Cicero, *De legibus*, I, 6, 18.

32. See *De finibus*, V, 23, 65: *"iustitia est animi affectio suum cuique tribuens"* ("justice is the disposition of the soul paying tribute to each according to his own"). The medieval *corpus juris* contains the more elaborate formulation: *"iustitia est perpetua et constans voluntas suum cuique tribuendi"* ("justice is the perpetual and constant willingness to give to each according to his due"), *Digesta*, I, 1, 10, cited by Emil Brunner, *Justice and the Social Order* (New York: Harper & Brothers, 1945), p. 17. See further F. Flueckiger, *Geschichte des Naturrechts*, Bd. I, Zürich-Zollikon: Evangelischer Verlag, 1954), Siebentes Kapitel.

33. See above, pt. One, chap. 2, at n. 34.

34. The phrases "the Laws of Nature" and "of Nature's God" are, of course, from the Declaration of Independence. The explication of self-evident truths is in Jefferson's draft preamble to the *Virginia Bill for Establishing Religious Freedom*. Cited by Arendt, op. cit., pp. 193, 314; parenthesis Arendt's. If one detaches Jefferson's attempt to explicate the relations between sovereignty and justice from its Newtonian physics and Lockean and even Kantian "metaphysical surroundings," and transposes it to another context of physics and metaphysics, the "Truths we hold to be self-evident" is very close to Rawls' "original position." See Rawls, op. cit., par. 4.

35. See G. Leibholz, *Politics and Law* (Leyden: A. W. Sythoff, 1965), p. 46. The quoted phrase is Leibholz'. He writes: "Thus, ac-

cording to Hobbes, law derives its validity from the fact that 'it is authority, not wisdom, makes the law.' " The chapter on "Politics and Natural Law," in which this dictum is formulated, was originally presented as a paper for discussion by a Symposium on Natural Law in London, 1946. One may readily identify its matrix in Hobbes' *Leviathan*, pt. II, especially chaps. 26 and 27. Leibholz further remarks that "the idea that 'authority not wisdom makes the law' has gained much ground in modern times. It has been the motto of the prevailing legal positivism."

36. So Crane Brinton. See above, pt. Three, chap. 8, n. 56; pt. Four, chap. 11, n. 24. Perhaps this is why the observational genius of Aristotle could lead him to remark, in the course of a discussion of conflicting interpretations of justice which give rise to revolutions, that "In all states revolutions are occasioned by trifles." See Aristotle, *Politics,* edited by W. D. Ross (1921), Bk. V, chaps. 1–8. The quoted remark is V, 7, 1307 a, 1.40.

37. The anticipation, even fear, of this erosion is the burden of *The Federalist Papers*. The Papers are a succinct and masterful attempt to arrest this erosion through the vision and experience of revolutionary ferment and achievement, and thus to free the story of the polis, and the story of revolution as well, from the nemesis of futility. Recall the Hamiltonian *tertium quid* noted above: pt. One, chap. 2, at n. 38.

38. See above, pt. Four, chap. 11, A, just before 11, B; also pt. Two, chap. 3, at n. 19. Unless, of course, one indulges oneself in the *reductio ad absurdum* of a psychoanalytic interpretation of the crisis of sovereignty in the contemporary world. Then the reciprocity between the responsible life and human life dissolves in the emotional depths of the unconscious where "the Kennedy assassination and the Nixon impeachment are nothing more than paraphrases of each other. The phenomenon at the heart of each is parricide, the murder of the father by the son." According to Freud, we are told, parricide was "the primal crime of humanity." According to the primal story by which revolutions have been nourished, it is fratricide. (See above, pt. One, chap. 2.) Nothwithstanding, we are to know that "the assassination of President Kennedy was a parricide, an enactment in the political arena of the ancient drama." In the case of ex-President Nixon, "the rifle and the bullet are missing, but the feelings underneath are the same: the primal wish to kill the father, guilt and horror over this and, at last, a desire to protect him, to keep him in his place after all." So the place for revolutionaries is the couch, not the barricades! "Authority, not wisdom, makes the law," *ad infinitum*. Judgment would seem indeed to have fled to brutish beasts, and men (and in this instance, women too) to have lost their reason. By what *lapsus mentis* the *New York Times* seems to have joined the flight is left to conjecture. But among

the recollections on the tenth anniversary of the assassination of President John F. Kennedy that occupied the Op-ed page of the *Times* of Thursday, 22 November 1973, was a piece by Priscilla McMillan called "That Time We Huddled Together in Disbelief." The *Times* noted that McMillan was writing a book on the Kennedy assassination.

39. *Republic,* I, 331, e (edited by Edith Hamilton; see above, pt. Two, n. 81).

40. So Aristotle, *Nichomachean Ethics,* Bk. V, 1, 1129–1130; and the *Rhetoric,* Bk. I, 13, 1373b, lines 1–18. W. D. Ross (ed.), *The Works of Aristotle* (Oxford: The Clarendon Press, vol. IX, 1944; vol. XI, 1946).

41. Brunner, op. cit., p. 45.

42. See Otto Gierke, *Natural Law in the Theory of Society* (New York: Cambridge University Press, 1950; Boston: Beacon Press, 1957); also the instructive article by John T. McNeill on "Natural Law in the Teaching of the Reformers," in the *Journal of Religion,* vol. XXVI, no. 3, July 1946.

43. Gerhard von Rad, *Theologie des Alten Testamentes* (München: Chr. Kaiser, Bd. I, 1962; Bd. II, 1965). Bd. I, pp. 205 ff., especially pp. 382–95; Bd. II, pp. 156 ff., 274 ff., 377. See also above, pt. Three, chap. 7, B, at n. 38.

44. Ludwig Koehler, *Old Testament Theology,* translated by A. S. Todd (from the 3rd rev. ed.; Philadelphia: Westminster Press, 1953). The work originally appeared as *Theologie des Alten Testamentes* (Tübingen: J. C. B. Mohr [Paul Siebeck], 1935). See especially the English translation, pp. 32 ff.

45. Von Rad, op. cit., Bd. II, pp. 433–36.

46. See above, pt. Three, chap. 6, nn. 2 and 4.

47. See above, pt. Three, chap. 8; also pt. Four, chap. 10, D.

48. See above, pt. Three, chap. 9, B, 4.

49. See above, pt. Three, chap. 9, C, 1, at (F, 58).

50. See above, pt. Three, chap. 9, A, 2.

51. See above, pt. Two, chap. 4 at n. 10; parenthesis mine.

52. See above, pt. Two, chap. 4, at nn. 11 and 19.

53. See above, pt. Three, chap. 9, B, 4.

54. See above, pt. Three, chap. 9, C, 2 and 3.

55. See above, pt. Four, chap. 10, D, and at n. 15. The phrase "the moral reality named death" is Stringfellow's; op. cit., chap. 3. The second quoted phrase is familiar from Shakespeare's *Macbeth,* Act V, Scene 5.

56. Stringfellow, op. cit., p. 123.

57. Ibid., p. 151.

58. Ibid., chap. 5; also, above, pt. Four, chap. 11, before A.

59. See above, pt. Three, chap. 8; and chap. 9, C, 1, at n. 149.

60. See above, pt. Three, chap. 7, A.

61. Dietrich Bonhoeffer, *Ethik* (München: Chr. Kaiser, 1949), pp. 247 and 85; translation mine. See also *Ethics*, Smith translation, op. cit., pp. 233 and 80. In a different context, the interpretation of violence that follows was attempted in an exploratory way in a paper delivered at the Dietrich Bonhoeffer Colloquium at Düsseldorff-Kaiserswerth, Germany, 6–8 October 1971; also as the concluding James A. Gray Lecture at the Divinity School, Duke University, 27 October 1971. The Bonhoeffer essay was subsequently published in a German translation under the title "Politik der Nachfolge," in *Evangelische Theologie* (München: Chr. Kaiser, 32 Jahrgang, November–Dezember 1972), no. 6, pp. 560–79.

62. James H. Cone, *Black Theology and Black Power* (New York: Seabury Press, 1969; Jacques Ellul, *Violence* (New York: Seabury Press, 1969). References to these discussions will be indicated in the text in parentheses following.

63. Bonhoeffer, *Ethics,* Smith translation, pt. One, chap. 4, especially pp. 120–133.

64. Rubem Alves, *A Theology of Human Hope* (Cleveland: Corpus Books, 1969), p. 125, parentheses mine.

65. Bonhoeffer, *Ethics,* p. 297, *inter alia*; *The Cost of Discipleship,* translated by Reginald H. Fuller (New York: The Macmillan Company, 2nd edition, unabridged and revised, 1959), p. 49.

66. See above, Preface, and pt. Two, chap. 3.

67. J. Glenn Gray, *The Warriors: Reflections on Men in Battle* (Harper Torchbooks, 1967). One agrees cordially with Hannah Arendt's judgment in the Foreword of this work that it is a "singularly earnest and beautiful book" (p. ix).

68. Stringfellow, op. cit., chap. 6.

69. I hope Father Berrigan will find this response to his post-imprisonment concerns and direction as a grateful and respectful effort to understand him and to express to him a deep admiration of the incandescent integrity of his own witness to what has been finely called his "humanism of the Incarnation." See Daniel Berrigan, *Encounters* (New York: World Publishing Company, 1960). It may be assumed that the phrase is the publisher's, since it appears on the jacket. These poems, together with our too infrequent association as colleagues at Union Theological Seminary and Woodstock College (where Berrigan was giving a course on "The Politics of God and the Politics of Jacques Ellul"), have amplified and kept before me an intense and searching luncheon conversation in April 1972, about the meaning and the limits of violence. The conversation has haunted me ever since, not least because of the tantalizing sense of kinship yet distance between a

poetic and a paradigmatic reading of the Bible and its implications for political responsibility.

70. See above, pt. Two, chap. 3, and chap. 5, B, 3.

71. See above, pt. Four, chap. 10, D.

72. W. H. Auden, "For the Time Being: a Christmas Oratorio," in *The Collected Poetry of W. H. Auden* (New York: Random House, 1945), p. 412.

73. See Paul Lehmann, "Karl Barth: Theologian of Permanent Revolution," and Frederick Herzog, "A Response," in the *Union Seminary Quarterly Review*, vol. XXVIII, no. 1, Fall 1972, pp. 67–81, 83–85. James Cone both presided over the session and participated in the discussion. I trust that these colleagues will receive this return to their interrogation as a sign of the seriousness with which I have continued to be vexed by their questions, and of my indebtedness to them for having occasioned a discernment that I might otherwise have missed.

74. See above, pt. Two, chap. 5, B, 4, and n. 101.

75. Karl Mannheim, *Ideology and Utopia* (New York: Harcourt Brace, 1936). We have already referred to this volume in the course of the discussion of the Chinese Revolution. See above, pt. Three, chap. 9, A, 4, and n. 109. Returning briefly here to Mannheim's discussion, citations will be indicated in parentheses following.

76. See above, pt. Three, chap. 9, A, 4.

77. See above, pt. Three, chap. 9, A, 2, after n. 98.

78. Auden, op. cit., pp. 454, 447; parenthesis mine.

79. See above, pt. Two, chap. 3. That Marxist humanists are not indifferent to this question and a Christian perspective upon it, is evident from the searching and painstaking study of the gospels by Milan Machovec, Professor of Philosophy in the Charles University at Prague before his deposition in the wake of the fall of the Dubček government in the fall of 1968. Machovec was a leading Marxist theoretician. He still is. See Milan Machovec, *Jesus für Atheisten* (Stuttgart: Kreuz Verlag, 2 Aufl. 1973).

80. I am indebted to my colleague, Ileana Marculescu, herself a Marxian humanist, and formerly Professor of Philosophy in the University of Bucharest, for an incisive and instructive conversation that has drawn my attention to the importance of both these questions, not only to ongoing Christian-Marxist discussion but to the argument of this book. These remarks are a tentative and admittedly inadequate response to her careful consideration of what is here under discussion, and an incommensurate token of my respect and gratitude.

81. See above, pt. Two, chap. 4, at n. 20.

82. See Mannheim, op. cit., pp. 62–67.

83. Quoted by Mannheim, op. cit., p. 67; from Max Weber, "Politik als Beruf," in *Gesammelte politische Schriften* (München: Drei Masken Verlag, 1921), p. 446.

84. To adapt the distinction made widely current by David Riesman in *The Lonely Crowd* (New Haven: Yale University Press, 1950; rev. ed. 1969).

85. The phrase "hermeneutical suspicion," or "surmise," is an allusion to Professor Paul Ricoeur's profound and instructive account of illusion as a cultural category, owing chiefly to the work of Nietzsche, Marx, and Freud. A hermeneutical suspicion or surmise (*la Soupçon*) is the beginning of remythologization following the demystification of false consciousness by these analysts of the will to power, of alienation, and of the unconscious as formative factors in contemporary culture. See Paul Ricoeur, "La critique de la religion et le language de la foi," in *Bulletin du Centre Protestant d'Etudes* (Geneva), June 1964. A translation of this essay by Bradford de Ford is available in the *Union Seminary Quarterly Review*, vol. XXVIII (1972/73), pp. 203–24.

86. See above. pt. Two, chap. 5, A, at n. 46.

87. Paul R. Valliere, "M. M. Tareev: A Study in Russian Ethics and Mysticism." A dissertation submitted in partial fulfillment of the requirements for the degree of Doctor of Philosophy in the Faculty of Philosophy of Columbia University, 1973. Valliere's illuminating study, after noting the sources and significance of Tareev's interpretation of the theme of "glory in humiliation"—and his "failure to find a meaningful role for the piety of 'glory in humiliation' in modern social and political culture," undertakes to correct and extend Tareev's theology and ethics in "his own theory of the constructive power of humility in social and political life" (Abstract, p. 2). Valliere seeks to show that and how *supplication* is the link between a piety of glory in *humiliation* and *revolution* in Russian spirituality, politics, and society. Valliere's central question, "What has humility to do with humanity?" parallels the central question of this book, "What has transfiguration to do with the humanization of human life?" or "What has Jesus Christ to do with the question of revolution?" The coincidence that by widely different routes we have converged upon a virtually identical question, recalls the steady observance of the Feast of Transfiguration in the liturgy and piety of the Eastern Church in almost total disregard of its political perspectives and implications. (See above, pt. Two, chap. 7, A, nn. 18, 19.) In any event, Valliere's exploration of the category of *supplication* bears so directly upon the transfiguration of revolution that we readily acknowledge no small indebtedness to him in bringing to a close these reflections upon the coinherence of biblical and revolutionary politics. Quotations or allusions to Valliere's work

refer to the pagination of his dissertation and are indicated in parentheses following.

88. See above, pt. Two, chap. 4.

89. Valliere adduces, in further explication of this phenomenology of supplication, an account of Charles Péguy's essay *Les suppliants parallèles* (1905). In that essay, the French poet and activist reflects upon the happening known as "Bloody Sunday," 22 January 1905. The Russian workers demonstrating before the Imperial Winter Palace in Petrograd, to present a petition for redress of grievances to the Tsar, were fired upon instead by Tsarist troops and dispersed with heavy casualties. Péguy is led by this event to think of King Oedipus in Sophocles' play *Oedipus the King*. "It is not the supplicated one," writes Péguy, "it is on the contrary the suppliant who has the upper hand in the dialogue in the last analysis" (247–48).

90. See above, pt. Two, chap. 5, A.

91. See above, pt. Two, chap. 5, B, n. 97; parenthesis mine.

92. See above, pt. Two, chap. 5, B, especially the concluding three paragraphs.

93. See above, pt. Four, chap. 11, C.

94. Thomas Kuhn, *The Structure of Scientific Revolutions* (Chicago: University of Chicago Press, 1962; 6th impression, 1968, paperback). References will be identified in the text in parentheses following. My colleague David Lotz has drawn my attention to a most instructive discussion of the phenomenon of revolution in recent scholarship by Isaac Kramnick of the Department of Government in Cornell University. See Isaac Kramnick, "Reflections on Revolution: Definition and Explanation in Recent Scholarship," in *History and Theory,* 11, 1972, pp. 26–63. In addition to his illuminating survey of the difficult question of the semantics of revolution and of the cognate question, "What makes revolutions happen?", I find in Professor Kramnick's appropriation of the parallelism between Kuhn's account of scientific revolutions and other modes of revolution (political, social, psychological) some confirmation of the parallelism suggested in this volume between Kuhn's analysis of the function and significance of paradigm and the significance and function of paradigm in biblical politics.

95. Compare the thesis of the Hegelian, T. G. Droysen: "That out of the already given conditions, new thoughts arise and out of the thoughts new conditions—this is the work of men." Quoted by Mannheim, op. cit., p. 180; from T. G. Droysen's *Outline of the Principles of History* (Boston: Ginn and Co., 1893), pp. 45–46. "The work of men!" or, is it more accurately what the experience of transfiguration is about?

96. e. e. cummings, *XAIRE: seventy-one poems* (New York: Oxford

University Press, 1950), no. 61; *1 x 1* (New York: Henry Holt and Company, 1944), no. XIV; *95 Poems* (New York: Harcourt Brace Jovanovich, 1950–58), n. 73.

# A BIBLIOGRAPHY

# OF SELECTED LITERATURE

# OF AND ABOUT REVOLUTION

## A BIBLIOGRAPHICAL APPENDIX TO PART THREE, CHAPTER 9

### A TYPOLOGY OF CURRENT REVOLUTIONS

The literature of revolution is virtually inexhaustible. The writings of revolutionaries, together with those of historians, social scientists, philosophers, and theologians offer materials in such abundance and diversity as to exclude an authoritative mastery of the phenomenon of revolution, or of its interpretation. Not least among the merits of Crane Brinton's masterful analysis of revolution as a sociohistorical phenomenon is the extensive, annotated bibliography that accompanies it. This work, together with that of Hannah Arendt, already drawn upon in the early chapters of the present discussion, provide a basic literary foundation for a study of revolution in its modern political sense, i.e., since the formative event of the French Revolution. To these discussions may be added the brilliant, learned, and imaginative cultural-historical interpretation of revolution by Eugen Rosenstock-Huessy. Rosenstock brings the formidable resources of German scholarship together with flashes of insight that are sometimes luminous, sometimes contrived, but always tantalizing, in a massive panorama of the revolutionary terrain.

Against the background of these general studies, the following list of specific accounts of revolutionary theory and practice underlies the present attempt at a typological interpretation of current revolutions.

Obviously the list is partial, random, and not in every instance expressly drawn upon. It is suggested, however, simply as one attempt to be open to the impact and data of a cumulative reading and thinking about what current revolutionary experience, some of it firsthand, has to tell us about "who's who and what's what"—in short, about "where it's at" —in the world today. The general titles are noted first.

## A. GENERAL INTERPRETATIONS

ARENDT, HANNAH. *On Revolution.* New York: Viking Press, 1947; Paperback, 1965.

BRINTON, CRANE. *The Anatomy of Revolution.* New York: W. W. Norton, 1938, revised edition, 1952. Paperback edition, New York: Random House, 1952.

ROSENSTOCK-HUESSY, EUGEN. *die europaeischen Revolutionen: Volkscharaktere und Staatenbildung.* Jena: Eugen Diedrichs, 1931.

————. *Out of Revolution: Autobiography of Western Man.* New York: William Morrow and Company, 1938.

## B. SPECIFIC DOCUMENTS AND ESSAYS

### 1. *From Marx to Mao and Ho Chi Minh*

BARCATA, LOUIS. *China in the Throes of Cultural Revolution,* An Eyewitness Report. New York: Hart Publishing Company, 1967.

HO CHI MINH. *On Revolution: Selected Writings, 1920–66,* edited and with an Introduction by Bernard B. Fall. New York: Frederick A. Praeger, 1967.

HSIUNG, JAMES CHIEH. *Ideology and Practice.* New York: Praeger Publishers, 1970.

LENIN, V. I. *The State and Revolution.* Written in 1917; English translation first published in London: Allen and Unwin, 1919.

MAO TSE-TUNG. *The Chinese Revolution and the Chinese Comunist Party.* Pamphlet, published in Chinese, 15 November 1939; translated into English, 22 March 1949.

————. *On Guerrilla Warfare.* Translated and with an Introduction by Brigadier General Samuel B. Griffith, USMC (Ret.). New York: Frederick A. Praeger, 1961.

MARX AND ENGELS. *Basic Writings on Politics and Philosophy,* edited by Lewis S. Feuer. New York: Doubleday Anchor, 1959.

MARX, ENGELS, LENIN. *The Essential Left: Four Classic Texts on the Principles of Socialism.* New York: Barnes and Noble, 1955, 1961. Paperback.

PAYNE, ROBERT. *Portrait of a Revolutionary: Mao Tse-tung.* New York: Abelard-Schuman, 1950.

SCHRAM, STUART R. *Mao Tse-tung.* Baltimore: Penguin Books, 1966.
———. *The Political Thought of Mao Tse-tung.* New York: Frederick
A. Praeger, 1963; revised edition, 1970.

2. *From Fidel and Che Guevara to Camilo Torres and Néstor Paz*
*Zamora*

*Che, Selected Works of Ernesto Guevara,* edited and with an Introduc-
tion by Rolando E. Bonachea and Nelson P. Valdes. Cambridge,
Mass.: The MIT Press, 1969. The volume includes a full bibliog-
raphy of Che's speeches and writings.
DEBRAY, RÉGIS. *Revolution in the Revolution?* New York: Grove
Press, 1967. Paperback.
———. *Strategy for Revolution,* edited and with an Introduction by
Robin Blackburn. London: Jonathan Cape, 1970.
FRERE, PAULO. *Pedagogy of the Oppressed,* translated by Myra Berg-
man Ramos, with a Foreword by Richard Shaull. New York:
Herder & Herder, 1970.
GERASSI, JOHN. *Revolutionary Priest: The Complete Writings and Mes-*
*sages of Camilo Torres,* edited and with an Introduction by John
Gerassi. New York: Random House, 1971.
O'CONNOR, JAMES. *The Origins of Socialism in Cuba.* Ithaca: Cornell
University Press, 1970.
TORRES, CAMILO. *Revolutionary Writings.* New York: Herder & Her-
der, 1969.
ZAMORA, NÉSTOR PAZ. *The Mystic Christian Guerrilla,* pts. I, II, and
IV translated by James E. Goff; pt. III translated by Jordan
Bishop and James E. Goff. Text in mimeograph, 1971. The origi-
nal is available under the Spanish title: *Néstor Paz Zamora, el*
*Mistico Cristiano de la Guerrilla.* Lima: Noticias Aliadas,
NADOC, no. 184, 13 January 1971; and *Carta de Néstor Paz,*
Volvimos a las Montañas, Estado Mayor, del E. L. N., Julio 1970.

3. *From Frantz Fanon to Martin Luther King, Jr., Malcolm X*
*and the Black Panther Party*

CLEAVER, ELDRIDGE. *Post-Prison Writings and Speeches,* edited with an
Introduction by Robert Scheer. New York: Random House, 1969.
———. *Soul on Ice.* New York: Dell Publishing Co., 1970.
CONE, JAMES H. *Black Theology and Black Power.* New York: Seabury
Press, 1969.
ERIKSON, KAI T. (ed.). *In Search of Common Ground: Conversations*
*with Erik H. Erikson and Huey P. Newton.* New York: W. W.
Norton, 1973.

FANON, FRANTZ. *The Wretched of the Earth.* New York: Grove Press, 1963.

JACKSON, GEORGE. *Soledad Brother,* with an Introduction by Jean Genet. New York: Bantam Books, 1970.

KING, MARTIN LUTHER, JR. *Where Do We Go from Here: Chaos or Community?* New York: Harper & Row, 1967; Bantam Books paperback, 1968.

LEWIS, DAVID L. *King: A Critical Biography.* Baltimore: Penguin Books, 1970.

LINCOLN, C. ERIC. *The Black Muslims in America.* Boston: Beacon Press, 1961. Unfortunately out of print.

LOCKWOOD, LEE. "Interview with Huey P. Newton." *Playboy,* March 1973.

WILLIAMS, DANIEL T. Supervisor, Departmental Libraries and Archives, Tuskegee Institute, Alabama, has prepared an extensive bibliography of writings by and about Martin Luther King, Jr. A portion of this bibliography was reproduced with Dr. Williams' permission in October 1969 by the Martin Luther King, Jr. Memorial Center, 671 Beckwith St., S. W., Atlanta, Ga. 30314. Copies of the more extensive bibliography may be obtained from the Kraus Reprint Co., 16 E. 46th St., New York, N.Y. 10017.

X, MALCOLM. *The Autobiography of Malcolm X,* with the assistance of Alex Haley. Introduction by M. S. Handler. Epilogue by Alex Haley. New York: Grove Press, 1964. First paperback edition, 1966.

## 4. *Perspectives and Reflections*

ALVES, RUBEM. *A Theology of Human Hope.* Cleveland: Corpus Books, 1969.

BETHGE, EBERHARD. *Ohnmacht und Mündigkeit: Beitraege zur Zeitgeschichte und Theologie.* München: Chr. Kaiser, 1969.

BIGO, PIERRE. *Marxisme et Humanisme: Introduction a L'Oeuvre Economique de Karl Marx.* Paris: Presses Universitaires de France, 1953.

CASALIS, GEORGE. *Prédication acte politique.* Paris: Les Editions du Cerf, 1970

CONE, JAMES H. *A Black Theology of Liberation.* New York: J. B. Lippincott, 1970.

COX, HARVEY (ed.). *The Church Amid Revolution.* New York: Association Press, 1967. Paper.

GRAY, FRANCINE DU PLESSIX. *Divine Disobedience.* New York: Random House, 1971.

# A Bibliography of Selected Literature     355

LOCHMAN, JAN MILIC. *The Church in a Marxist Society*. New York: Harper & Row, 1970.

LÖWY, A. G. *Die Weltgeschichte ist das Weltgericht: Bucharin*. Visi Wien: Europa Verlag, 1969.

MARCUSE, HERBERT. *Eros and Civilization*. Boston: Beacon Press, 1955.

―――. *One-Dimensional Man*. Boston: Beacon Press, 1964.

MOLTMANN, JÜRGEN. *Religion, Revolution and the Future*. New York: Charles Scribner's Sons, 1969.

MOORE, BARRINGTON, JR. *Soviet Politics—The Dilemma of Power*. Cambridge: Harvard University Press, 1950.

OGLESBY, CARL AND SHAULL, RICHARD. *Containment and Change*. New York: The Macmillan Company, 1967.

REVEL, JEAN-FRANÇOIS. *Ni Marx ni Jésus: la nouvelle révolution mondiale est commencée aux Etats-Unis*. Paris: Editions Robert Laffont, 1970. English translation by J. F. Bernard, with an Afterword by Mary McCarthy. Garden City, N.Y.: Doubleday, 1971.

SHAULL, RICHARD. *Befreiung durch Veränderung*. München: Chr. Kaiser, 1970.

TÖDT-RENDTORFF, H. *Theologie der Revolution*. Frankfurt a. M.: Edition Suhrkamp, 1968.

WIELENGA, BASTIAAN. *Lenins Weg Zur Revolution: eine Konfrontation mit Serge Bulgakov und Peter Stiuve im Interresse einer Theologischen Besinnung*. München: Chr. Kaiser, 1971.

# INDEXES*

## 1. BIBLICAL REFERENCES

* David Garth, a candidate for the degree of Doctor of Theology in the Union Theological Seminary in Virginia, has greatly assisted in the preparation of the Indexes.

357

## 3. SUBJECT